Attitudes and Persuasion: Classic and Contemporary Approaches

Attitudes and Persuasion: Classic and Contemporary Approaches

Richard E. Petty
University of Missouri

John T. Cacioppo
University of Iowa

ωcb
Wm. C. Brown Company Publishers
Dubuque, Iowa

wcb group

Wm. C. Brown
Chairman of the Board

Mark C. Falb
Corporate Vice President/Operations

wcb

Wm. C. Brown Company Publishers, College Division

Lawrence E. Cremer
President

Raymond C. Deveaux
Vice President, Product Development

David Wm. Smith
Assistant Vice President/National Sales Manager

David A. Corona
Director of Production Development and Design

Matthew T. Coghlan
National Marketing Manager

Janis Machala
Director of Marketing Research

William A. Moss
Production Editorial Manager

Marilyn A. Phelps
Manager of Design

Mary M. Heller
Visual Research Manager

Book Team

Susan Soley
Editor

Marian B. Warner
Production Editor

Anthony L. Saizon
Designer

Mavis Oeth
Permissions Editor

Mary M. Heller
Visual Research Editor

Reviewers

Icek Ajzen
University of Massachusetts

David R. Shaffer
University of Georgia

Harold Sigall
University of Maryland

Mark P. Zanna
University of Waterloo

Dedicated to our families:
The Pettys
(Edmund, Jo Ann, Arlene, Jane, Tom, and Lynn)
and
The Cacioppos
(Cyrus, Mary Katherine, Susan, Nick, Bob, and Barbara)

Contents

Foreword xiii
Preface xv
Acknowledgments xvii

1 Introduction to Attitudes and Persuasion 3

6 What Is an Attitude?
7 Why Do People Have Attitudes?
9 How Are Attitudes Measured?
9 Direct Procedures
16 Indirect Procedures
22 Direct versus Indirect Assessment of Attitudes
22 Do Attitudes Predict Behaviors?
23 What Kinds of Attitudes Predict Behaviors?
28 What Other Variables Enhance Behavioral Prediction?
29 How Is Attitude Change Studied Experimentally?
30 Conceptual and Operational Levels of Research
31 The Validity of the Attitude Change Experiment
34 Evaluating a Theory
35 The Approaches to Persuasion
36 Retrospective

2 Conditioning and Modeling Approaches   39

40   **Classical Conditioning**
40   Classical Conditioning of Attitudes
43   Demand Characteristics and Contingency Awareness
47   **Operant Conditioning**
47   Operant Conditioning of Attitudes
49   Two-factor Theory of Verbal Conditioning
51   **Observational Learning**
54   **Vicarious Classical Conditioning**
56   **Evaluation**
56   **Retrospective**

3 The Message-learning Approach   59

59   **Skills Learning as a Model for Persuasion**
60   **Determinants of Attitude Change in Persuasive Communications**
61   Source Factors
69   Message Factors
80   Recipient Factors
85   Channel Factors
87   The Persistence of Attitude Change
93   **Retrospective**

4 Judgmental Approaches   95

95   **Adaptation Level Approach**
99   **The Social Judgment—Involvement Approach**
105   Communication Discrepancy
107   Ego Involvement
109   Evaluation of Social Judgment Theory
110   **The Variable Perspective Approach**
115   Indirect Influence

	117	Unresolved Issues in Perspective Theory
	120	Comparisons of Approaches: Perception versus Description
	122	**Retrospective**
5 Motivational Approaches	**125**	
	125	**Cognitive Elements and Systems**
	126	**The Motive to Maintain Cognitive Consistency**
	127	**Balance Theory**
	127	Terminology
	128	Determining Imbalance in a Cognitive System
	128	Consequences of Imbalance
	129	Empirical Research
	133	**Congruity Theory**
	134	The Domain of Congruity Theory
	134	Determining and Resolving Disequilibrium (Incongruity)
	135	The Mathematics of Congruity Theory
	135	Empirical Research
	137	**Cognitive Dissonance Theory**
	138	Effects of Cognitive Dissonance
	139	Effect of Disconfirming an Important Belief
	140	Dissonance and the Decision Process
	142	Insufficient Justification
	145	Necessary Conditions for Dissonance Arousal
	148	Temporal Characteristics of Dissonance Reduction
	148	The Nature of Cognitive Dissonance
	152	**Impression Management Theory**
	155	**Psychological Reactance Theory**
	156	What Does It Take to Arouse Reactance?
	157	Consequences of the Arousal of Reactance
	160	**Retrospective**

6 Attributional Approaches   **163**

165   **Self-perception Theory**
167   The Foot-in-the-door Effect
169   Overjustification Effects
170   **Effects of Internal Sensations on Self-perception and Attitudes: Dissonance versus Self-perception**
174   **Effects of Ambiguous Internal Cues on Attitudes**
174   Emotional Plasticity
175   Effects of Bogus Physiological Feedback
177   **Recipients' Attribution Regarding the Cause of a Communicator's Behavior**
180   **Retrospective**

7 Combinatory Approaches   **183**

184   **Probabilogical Approaches to Belief Change**
193   **The Theory of Reasoned Action**
194   Attitude
196   Subjective Norm
197   Behavioral Intention
198   Behavior
200   Summary of the Theory
200   Changing Beliefs, Attitudes, Norms, Intentions, and Behaviors
204   **Information Integration Theory (Cognitive Algebra)**
211   **Retrospective**

8 Self-persuasion Approaches   **213**

213   **The Role-playing Approach: Active Participation versus Passive Exposure**
216   The Persistence of Attitude Changes Produced by Role Playing

216 Why Is Role Playing So
Effective?

219 Can Dissonance Theory Account
for Role-playing Effects?

220 **Mere Thought as a Determinant
of Attitude Polarization**

221 Empirical Research on Mere
Thought

223 Other Determinants of Mere
Thought

225 **The Cognitive Response
Approach to Persuasion**

226 Premessage Inductions That
Produce Resistance to
Persuasion

232 Premessage Inductions That
Affect the Motivation to Process
a Message

238 Effects of Message, Context, and
Recipient Inductions

248 The Postmessage Persistence of
Persuasion

251 **Evaluation of Self-persuasion
Approaches**

252 **Retrospective**

9 **Epilog: A General
Framework for
Understanding
Attitude Change
Processes** 255

255 **Central versus Peripheral Routes
to Attitude Change**

257 Anticipatory Attitude Changes

258 The Relative Importance of
Source and Message Factors in
Persuasion

260 The Relative Importance of
Recipient and Message Factors
in Persuasion

262 **The Elaboration Likelihood
Model**

263 Motivation and Ability to Process
the Message

265 Motivation and Ability to Think about the Issue

266 The Central Route: A Difficult Way to Change Attitudes

267 The Peripheral Route: Attitude Change without Issue-relevant Thinking

268 **Retrospective**

References **271**
Author Index **301**
Subject Index **309**

Foreword

The present book provides a needed survey of a truly remarkable number of different theoretical approaches to the related phenomena of attitude and belief change. Aside from the obvious advantage of summarizing the relevant literature within one source, the book also serves the function of calling our attention to neglected theories, such as variable perspective theory, which are far more deserving of attention than the present level of research activity, or inactivity, would indicate. This is a competent and important book; a book deserving of attention by both beginning and advanced students of attitude and belief change.

In view of Richard Petty and John Cacioppo's impressive and important research within the framework of the cognitive-responses approach to persuasion it is perhaps not surprising that they would write a discerning book. In view of the recent paucity of interest in attitude change, however, what is perhaps more surprising is that there appears to be an increasing receptivity to research and theory in this general area. Interest in attitude change appears to be resurgent. Why is this? Without any claim to certainty, it is possible to point to a number of possible causes. First, as Petty and Cacioppo point out, past skepticism regarding the effect of attitude on behavior has been replaced by the realization that, under some circumstances, at least, attitudes *do* affect behavior. Second, it may well be that renewed interest in attitude change is fostered to some extent by a more general interest in cognitive processes both within social psychology and other subfields or disciplines. Third, skepticism regarding the external validity of laboratory studies of attitude change has been mitigated by the realization that the large number of "field" studies done with subjects who do not know that they are subjects has not greatly altered our conclusions. It is increasingly recognized that while the demand-characteristics problem, for example, may arise in some circumstances and certainly does need to be guarded against, the problem has been vastly overestimated. Generalized cynicism regarding laboratory findings simply is not justified. Fourth and finally, attitude change as a field may be benefitting from the decline of "anti-establishment" attitudes. During the sixties the field of attitude change clearly was part of the establishment in social psychology, and also, because of its association with commercial advertising, had an obvious relation with the business establishment.

For those of us who have persisted in maintaining a positive attitude toward the field of attitude change, the current renewal of interest is understandably welcome. In my judgment the present book will make an important contribution to that renewal.

Chester A. Insko
University of North Carolina

Preface

The study of attitudes and persuasion cuts across many academic disciplines and is of interest also because of its relevance to and pervasiveness in our daily lives. Our goal was to write a book that would not only provide students with an up-to-date background in the psychological theory and research on attitude change processes, but one that would also give an appreciation for how basic research can yield useful insights into the types of social influence situations that occur frequently in our day-to-day living.

Over the last forty years, a large number of theories have developed to explain how and why peoples' attitudes change. We have grouped these theories into seven major approaches, and each approach is presented and evaluated in a separate chapter in this text. We believe that each of the approaches contributes in an important way to a complete understanding of the persuasion process. Our subtitle characterizing the seven approaches as "classic and contemporary" is not meant to imply that some approaches are classic whereas others are contemporary, but that all of the approaches we discuss are classic *and* contemporary. The approaches are all contemporary in that all have their current advocates. They are classic in that we believe that they all have made—and will continue to make—a vital contribution to explaining certain attitudinal phenomena. None of the approaches, however, is capable of accounting for the full range of attitudinal phenomena that exists. In the concluding chapter of this book, we present an integrative framework for thinking about the persuasion process that synthesizes the various approaches into two distinct routes to persuasion. This framework provides a method for organizing and understanding the basic commonalities and differences among the seven approaches.

We have attempted to write this book at a level that will be understandable to undergraduates who have had an introductory psychology course and perhaps a course in social psychology, but the book contains material that should be informative to graduate students as well. Any material that would be of interest primarily to graduate students, however, has been placed in footnotes. Courses for which the book would be most appropriate are taught in psychology, sociology, and communication departments, usually under the titles Attitude Change, Attitude Theory, Persuasive Communication, and so forth. In addition, some instructors might find the book to be a useful supplement in such courses as the

Psychology of Advertising, Marketing Research, Consumer Behavior, and Public Opinion, which are usually taught in journalism, marketing, and political science departments.

On a more personal level, we note that writing this book led to more of just about everything than we initially expected—more time, more disagreements, but also more rewards, more fun, more dining out, and a greater appreciation for the advances made in understanding the complex process by which one person comes to influence another.

R. E. Petty
J. T. Cacioppo

Acknowledgments

There are many people to thank in preparing this text. First, we would like to thank John Harvey, a friend and colleague at Vanderbilt University who first suggested to us the idea of writing this book. Four other colleagues (Hal Sigall, University of Maryland; Icek Ajzen, University of Massachusetts; David R. Shaffer, University of Georgia; and Mark P. Zanna, University of Waterloo) provided detailed comments on the first draft of the text that were thoughtfully prepared and most helpful. Chet Insko (University of North Carolina) graciously consented to our request to write the foreword. We also acknowledge a debt to the earlier works on attitude change from which we learned so much (especially Hovland, Janis, & Kelley, 1953; Insko, 1967; Kiesler, Collins, & Miller, 1969; and McGuire, 1969b). We are grateful to our advisors in graduate school, Tim Brock and Tony Greenwald of Ohio State University, whose enthusiasm about scientific inquiry was contagious and who gave us the freedom and guidance to pursue those research topics that we found most appealing. Our editors at the Wm. C. Brown Co. (Susan Soley and Marian Warner), our colleagues at the universities at which we served (Missouri, Iowa, and Notre Dame), our students (especially Martin Heesacker and Charlotte Lowell), and our secretaries (Lenore Hizer and Sue Staub) also made valuable contributions to the text. Much of our own research reported in this text was supported by grants from the National Science Foundation (BNS 7818667, 7913753, 8023589), the National Institute of Mental Health (31798–01, BRSG–G603), and our universities (Research Council summer grants, Old Gold Fellowship, Faculty Scholar Award No. A240). Finally, and most importantly, we are grateful for Lynn and Barbara who fill our lives with joy and love.

Attitudes and Persuasion: Classic and Contemporary Approaches

Introduction to Attitudes and Persuasion

The process of persuasion is such an ever-present aspect of our daily lives that we often fail to even notice its occurrence. From the moment you are awakened in the morning by the friendly voices on the clockradio (who are likely telling you how to smell good, get rid of your dandruff, have whiter teeth) until you go to bed at night, you may have been exposed to over a hundred influence attempts. As you eat your breakfast (while reading the back of the cereal box or glancing at a newspaper ad for a presidential candidate), walk or ride the bus to school or work (and see various billboards along the way), go shopping (where the sales clerk tells you how wonderful the sweater looks that you are trying on), talk to a friend (who tells you how good a new record album is), or go to a movie (where there will be previews of future movies), somebody is attempting to get you to change your mind about something. Even Sunday is not a day of rest from persuasion: on this day, thousands of ministers deliver persuasive messages in an attempt to inculcate certain values.

Of course, it is not only individuals who try to persuade each other—the dissemination of propaganda is often part of corporate or government policy. For example, *Time* magazine (10 July 1978, p. 68) reports that in one typical month in 1969 at the height of the American involvement in the Vietnam war, the United States dropped 713 million propaganda leaflets over that country. Although most American citizens were aware of the war being fought with bombs and bullets, few were aware of the extensive war of persuasion being conducted as well. Persuasion attempts have always been an integral part of psychological warfare. Box 1.1 presents an example of a propaganda leaflet employed by Nazi Germany in an attempt to destroy the morale of U.S. troops during World War II.

The goal of *propaganda* is to change other people's views in order to further one's own cause or damage an opposing one. Propaganda is sometimes viewed as a biased form of *education* (Zimbardo, Ebbesen, & Maslach, 1977). The goal of education is to teach a person certain factual information (e.g., Washington, D.C., is the capital of the United States) and to teach a person how to think logically so that the person will be capable of making up his or her own mind. The goal of propaganda is to teach nonfactual information or to make opinion appear as fact (e.g, Washington, D.C., is the loveliest capital city in the world).

Box 1.1

Psychological Warfare

U.S. plane dropping propaganda leaflets, mostly safe-conduct passes for potential Viet Cong defectors, January 1966 (photograph by Don North)

The propaganda leaflet has been a staple of modern warfare. The Nazi leaflet on the right attempts to reduce the morale of the American troops by getting them to think about the good old days at home. Presumably, the more the soldiers think about the good old days and how wonderful they were, the less satisfied they will be with their present situation. This is called a *contrast effect* (discussed in chapter 4). Notice, however, that the leaflet is designed to appear as a morale booster! This presumably disguises its persuasive intent and makes it less likely to be ignored or thrown away. The manner in which persuasive intent modifies the effectiveness of propaganda is discussed further in chapters 3 and 5.

A communication presenting propaganda is designed so that one conclusion appears more reasonable than another, and thus it may sometimes involve withholding material favorable to the opposing side. Viewed in this way, much of what we call persuasion—advertising copy, presidential campaign speeches, the defense attorney's appeal to a jury, parents' lectures on acceptable morality—comes closer to qualifying as propaganda than education. In this text, however, we use the term *persuasion* to refer to any instance in which an active attempt is made to change a person's mind because the word is relatively neutral and because one person's propaganda may be another person's education.

Maneuvers the Easy Way

The psychiatrists were right when they said life is what you make it.

Take this maneuver. It can be rough and miserable, or it can be a soft touch for any guy with an imagination.

For example, when you're standing around in the chow line waiting for cold salmon and beans, why make matters worse by griping about it.

GIVE YOURSELF A BREAK AND
THINK ABOUT THE GOOD OLD DAYS

Our discussion of persuasion focuses on various approaches that have developed in experimental social psychology. Social psychologists have conducted thousands of experiments on the topic, and the body of accumulated knowledge is now quite large. Interest in developing some general principles of persuasion is certainly not new, of course. For example, in the fourth century B.C., Aristotle identified three kinds of persuasion:

Of the modes of persuasion furnished by the spoken word there are three kinds. The first kind depends on the personal character of the *speaker*; the second on putting the *audience* into a certain frame of mind; the third on the proof, or apparent proof, provided by the *words* of the speech itself. Persuasion is achieved by the speaker's personal character when the speech is so spoken as to make us think him credible. . . . Secondly, persuasion may come through the hearers when a speech stirs their emotions. . . . Thirdly, persuasion is effected through the speech itself when we have proved a truth or an apparent truth by means of the persuasive arguments suitable to the case in question. [*Rhetoric,* 1941 edition, pp. 1329–1330; italics added.]

So some 2,400 years ago three aspects of the persuasion situation—the source, the audience, and the message content—were clearly identified. Surprisingly perhaps, it was not until quite recently (only forty years ago) that these features of the persuasion setting were given any systematic research attention. To some extent, the modern experimental study of persuasion began with Carl Hovland, a Yale psychologist who took a leave of absence during World War II to become chief psychologist and director of experimental studies for the War Department. During the war, Hovland and his colleagues investigated the social-psychological variables responsible for military morale and, in the process, completed a number of studies that documented the importance of different factors in persuading people (Hovland, Lumsdaine, & Sheffield, 1949). Hovland continued this research on communication and persuasion when he returned to Yale after the war. This research program produced a number of highly influential volumes (e.g., Hovland, Janis, & Kelley, 1953; Hovland et al., 1957). Hovland was a student of a prominent learning theorist, Clark Hull, and so it is not surprising that Hovland emphasized the role of learning processes in persuasion. We will discuss the Hovland approach in depth in chapter 3, but before beginning our discussion of this and other approaches to persuasion, some important background questions should be addressed. We will take up the following questions in turn:

1. What is an attitude?
2. Why do people have attitudes?
3. How are attitudes measured?
4. Do attitudes predict behaviors?
5. How is attitude change studied experimentally?

What Is an Attitude?

We have already noted that persuasion represents an attempt to change a person's mind. But what specifically is it that a persuasion attempt seeks to influence? Researchers in the field have usually distinguished among the following possibilities: attitudes, beliefs, and behaviors.

There is now widespread agreement among social psychologists that the term *attitude* should be used to refer to a general and enduring positive or negative feeling about some person, object, or issue (Bem, 1970; Insko & Schopler, 1972; Oskamp, 1977). "I like Chevrolets," "I hate Chuck," and "Capital punishment is horrible!" would all be considered attitudes because they express a general positive or negative feeling toward something. "Chevrolets are economical," "Chuck is prejudiced," and "Capital punishment is legal in my home state," are all examples of beliefs. The term *belief* is reserved for the information that a person has about other people, objects, and issues. The information may be factual or it may be only one person's opinion. Furthermore, the information may have positive, negative, or no evaluative implications for the target of the information. The following represent the *behavioral* or overt action category: purchasing a Chevrolet, throwing a pie in Chuck's face, and campaigning against capital punishment. Behaviors may also have positive, negative, or no evaluative implications for the target of the behavior.[1]

Gordon Allport called *attitude* "the most distinctive and indispensable concept in contemporary social psychology" in his chapter in the original *Handbook of Social Psychology* (1935); and since then, the study of *attitude change* has been the primary focus of persuasion researchers. "Attitude" became the preeminent concept because of the important psychological functions that attitudes were thought to serve and because of the presumed ability of attitudes to direct (and thus allow prediction of) behaviors. Beliefs were thought to be related to behaviors only because they contributed to the formation of attitudes. Thus, an advertiser might want to convince you that a certain kind of car got good gas mileage (belief change), so that your liking for the car would increase (attitude change) and that you would become more likely to buy the car the next time you needed one (behavior change). Our discussion of the various approaches to persuasion in this text focuses on attitude change; but because of the interrelationships among beliefs, attitudes, and behaviors hypothesized by some theorists, our discussion also necessarily deals with belief change and behavior change when appropriate. Furthermore, the principles that are involved in persuading someone to change an attitude are the same as those that are involved in persuading someone to change a belief or a behavior.

Why Do People Have Attitudes?

As you and a friend walk out of a movie that you have just seen, one of the first things that one of you asks the other is "What did you think of it?" When you are introduced to your brother's new girlfriend, he asks you after the meeting "How does she seem to you?" In response to these questions, you are not initially likely to give your beliefs about the movie (e.g., "the direction was weak"), or about the girl (e.g., "she has blonde hair"). The response that you assume the other person wants, and the response that you are most likely to give, is a general attitude: I liked it (or her). Only further probing is likely to elicit your more specific thoughts. Your attitude serves as a convenient summary of a wide variety of beliefs about the movie or the girl. People are usually eager to hear our attitudes, and we are often eager to give them. Why are attitudes such an important part of social interaction?

In addition to the fact that attitudes serve as convenient summaries of our beliefs, they are important to other people for another reason—they help others to know what to expect from us. Knowing our attitudes presumably helps others predict the kinds of behaviors we are likely to engage in more accurately than almost anything else we can tell them. If you tell a person that "movies are rated G, PG, R, and X," and that "American movies usually emphasize entertainment rather than a message," that person wouldn't know whether or not to invite you to a movie. However, if you say to this person, "Movies today are sleazy, disgusting, and make me want to vomit," all doubt and uncertainty would be removed! Knowledge of others' attitudes, then, makes the world seem like a more predictable place. Of course, if a person's attitude was neutral (neither positive nor negative), it would not be as informative as if it was very polarized (extreme).

Attitudes may also express some important aspects of an individual's personality (Smith, Bruner, & White, 1956). For example, Katz (1960) has described four functions that attitudes might serve for a person. According to Katz, some attitudes serve an *ego-defensive function*. These are attitudes that are held because they help people protect themselves from unflattering truths about themselves or about others who are important to them. By despising homosexuals, for example, some men are able to enhance their own feelings of masculinity and self-worth. This negative attitude about homosexuals serves an ego-defensive function. Attitudes may also serve a *value-expressive function*, which occurs when holding a certain attitude allows the person to express an important value. For example, the person who likes solar hot water heaters because their use demonstrates an important concern about energy conservation has an attitude that serves a value-expressive function. A third purpose served by attitudes is a *knowledge function*. Such attitudes allow people to better understand events and people around them. If your dislike of former President Richard Nixon helps you to understand his participation in the Watergate coverup (dislikable people do dislikable things), the attitude serves a knowledge function. Finally, attitudes may serve a *utilitarian function*. These attitudes help people to gain rewards and avoid punishments. When an employee adopts the attitudes of the boss prior to asking for an increase in salary, it is clear that the new attitudes are serving a utilitarian function. According to Katz's functional view of attitudes, different people may hold the same attitudes, but the attitudes may serve very different purposes for them. Thus, Mr. Smith may like the Republican candidate for president because he perceives that he stands for morality in America (value-expressive function), whereas Mr. Jones likes the Republican candidate because he perceives that the candidate's election would be good for his business (utilitarian function).

How Are Attitudes Measured?

Now that it is clear that attitudes can serve a number of useful functions, it is important to know how psychologists measure a person's attitudes. Without techniques for measuring attitudes, research on the determinants of attitude change would be impossible. The procedures for measuring attitudes can generally be divided into two major categories—direct and indirect. With *direct* procedures, a person is asked to provide a self-report of his or her attitude. With *indirect* procedures, an attempt is made to measure a person's attitude without the person knowing it. In some cases, the person may think that something other than an attitude is being measured, and in other cases the measurement may be completely unobtrusive.

Direct Procedures

Thurstone Scale

One of the earliest direct procedures was developed by Louis Thurstone, who in 1928 published a paper boldly titled "Attitudes Can Be Measured." Thurstone had been working on scaling human perceptions of such sensory stimuli as light and sound, and he reasoned that similar techniques might be employed to develop scales for more emotionally involving stimuli. Just as people can rank-order noises in terms of their loudness, Thurstone realized that people could also rank opinion statements in terms of their favorableness toward some object or issue. If a scale of opinion statements relative to an issue could be constructed, then an indication of people's attitudes could be obtained by finding out what statements they personally favored.

Construction of a Thurstone scale begins with obtaining a list of about one hundred opinion statements relevant to some issue. These may be self-generated by the investigator or taken from newspapers, books, and magazines. The statements should represent the full range of favorableness toward the issue about which attitudes are being measured. Any statements that are confusing or open to multiple interpretations should be eliminated. The investigator then asks about one hundred people to serve as judges to rank-order the statements in terms of how favorable they are to the issue. Specifically, the judges are asked to sort the statements into eleven categories, where category one indicates that the statement is as opposed to the issue as it could possibly be and eleven indicates that the statement is as favorable toward the issue as it could possibly be. The judges would try to categorize the statements on an *equal interval basis* so that the difference in favorableness between any two positions on the scale would be equal. After the judges rate each statement, the investigator assigns a "scale value" to each statement corresponding to the median (middle) category to which the judges have assigned it. Thus each statement is assigned a scale value such that

Box 1.2

Different Direct Scales for Assessing Attitudes toward the Church

1. Thurstone Scale (Adapted from Thurstone & Chave, 1929)

Check the statements with which you agree:

_____ 1. I enjoy the church because there is a spirit of friendliness there. (3.3)

_____ 2. I respect any church members' beliefs, but I think it is all "bunk." (8.8)

_____ 3. I think the organized church is an enemy of science and truth. (10.7)

_____ 4. I believe in what the church teaches but with mental reservations. (4.5)

_____ 5. I feel that church services give me inspiration and help me to live up to my best during the following week. (1.7)

_____ 6. I feel the need for religion but do not find what I want in any one church. (6.1)

2. Likert Scale

For each statement, check the extent to which you agree.

1.   I believe that the church is the greatest institution in America today.

(+2) _____ strongly agree

(+1) _____ moderately agree

(0) _____ neutral

(−1) _____ moderately disagree

(−2) _____ strongly disagree

it is rated higher than this value by half the judges and lower than this value by the other half. In the final step in scale construction, the investigator selects from the one hundred statements about twenty that have a high degree of agreement among the judges on their appropriate category and that represent every position on the underlying one to eleven scale. An abbreviated Thurstone scale appears in box 1.2. When using the scale, the statements would appear in a random order without the accompanying scale values. To measure an attitude, the investigator asks each person to check all items with which he or she personally agrees. The attitude score is the median of the scale values of the statements that the person endorses.

2. The church represents shallowness, hypocrisy, and prejudice.

(−2) _____ strongly agree
(−1) _____ moderately agree
(0) _____ neutral
(+1) _____ moderately disagree
(+2) _____ strongly disagree

3. Semantic Differential Scale

Rate how you feel about the church on each of the scales below.

good	_____	_____	_____	_____	_____	bad
	(+2)	(+1)	0	(−1)	(−2)	
unfavorable	_____	_____	_____	_____	_____	favorable
	(−2)	(−1)	0	(+1)	(+2)	
pleasant	_____	_____	_____	_____	_____	unpleasant
	(+2)	(+1)	0	(−1)	(−2)	
negative	_____	_____	_____	_____	_____	positive
	(−2)	(−1)	0	(+1)	(+2)	

4. One-item Rating Scale

How much do you like the church?

not at all	—	—	—	—	—	—	—	very much
	1	2	3	4	5	6	7	

Likert Scale

Although the Thurstone scale is rather difficult to construct, it does allow a fairly precise estimate of where a person stands on the underlying attitudinal dimension. In many instances, however, this precision is not necessary. Often it is sufficient merely to know how people can be ranked relative to each other (without the equal interval assumption). In 1932, Rensis Likert published a paper, with the relatively restrained title, "A Technique for the Measurement of Attitudes," that described such a scale. The first step in constructing a Likert scale is similar to the Thurstone procedure—a large number of opinion statements relevant to the attitude issue are collected. Each statement should clearly express either a positive or negative feeling about the issue under consideration.

In the next step, a large sample of people express the extent of their own agreement with each of the statements on a five-point scale (see box 1.2). Since the scale assumes that each of the items measures the same underlying attitude, any items that do not correlate highly with the total test score (obtained by summing the responses to the individual items) are eliminated from the scale. Thus, the person's attitude score is obtained by summing the responses to the items that remain. Unlike the Thurstone procedure, scale construction and administration can be accomplished with the same set of people. Because the Likert scale is easier to construct than the Thurstone scale, and because both scales have equivalent reliabilities (McNemar, 1946; Poppleton & Pilkington, 1964) and typically correlate highly with each other (Edwards & Kenney, 1946), the Likert procedure is more popular.[2] One unwieldy aspect of both the Thurstone and the Likert procedures, however, is that a different scale (with new items) must be constructed each time an attitude toward another issue is to be measured.

The Semantic Differential

In an attempt to understand the dimensions of meaning of words, Osgood, Suci, and Tannenbaum (1957) developed a convenient way to assess attitudes toward a wide variety of people, objects, and issues. These researchers discovered that three factors accounted for most of the meaning that we assign to different words: *evaluation* (how good or bad, valuable or worthless something is), *potency* (how strong or weak, heavy or light something is), and *activity* (how fast or slow, excitable or calm something is). The first factor corresponds to what we consider an attitude. Osgood (1965; Osgood et al., 1957) suggested that attitudes could be measured by having subjects rate the attitude object on bipolar adjective pairs that represented the evaluative dimension of meaning. An example of how such a scale might look is presented in box 1.2. The person's attitude score would be the sum of the numbers corresponding to the positions checked on the four subscales. The semantic differential technique is comparable in *reliability* to the Thurstone and Likert procedures (Robinson & Shaver, 1969).

The One-item Rating Scale

One way to assess attitudes that is popular in much attitude research but is not as reliable as the Thurstone, Likert, and semantic differential scales is the one-item rating scale. For this procedure, the investigator selects *one* question that he or she feels would most directly assess a particular attitude of interest. For many research and survey purposes, this very simple procedure is sufficient.[3] An example of this type of scale is presented in box 1.2.

The Validity of Direct Measurement Procedures

All of the scales that we have just discussed make the assumption that people are perfectly willing and able to tell you about their attitudes. Sometimes this assumption is unwarranted. For example, at different points in history people have been afraid to respond to attitude surveys for political reasons. A more common problem is that people may be so concerned about making a good impression on the investigator that only desirable attitudes are reported correctly, and attitudes that may be socially undesirable are concealed or misrepresented. These and other problems that may lead to attitude misrepresentation (Cook & Selltiz, 1964) have caused psychologists to search for a way to ensure that the self-report attitude scales really reflect a person's true feelings (see box 1.3).

One interesting procedure for assessing a person's true feelings is called the *bogus pipeline* (Jones and Sigall, 1971), in which the investigator convinces the subject that the sophisticated equipment being used allows a determination of the subject's true attitudes. For example, the subject might be asked to hold onto a steering wheel connected to a pointer; turning the wheel allows the pointer to move in either a positive or negative direction on some attitude scale. The subject is told that electrodes will be attached to his or her wrist so that electromyographic (EMG) recordings can be made. The EMG, which measures minute muscle movements, presumably provides a measurement of the subject's initial tendency to move the wheel in either a positive or negative direction. The intensity of the EMG response allows a determination of how far the wheel would be turned. A few "practice" trials are then conducted in which the investigator asks the subject to respond to some inocuous questions (for which the subject's true responses are already known), and the EMG is shown to "predict" the subject's true answers. Once the subject is convinced that the EMG can read minds, the experimenter can ask the real questions of interest. The subject is told to give the responses, and the experimenter will check to see how well the subject knows his or her own true feelings by comparing the verbal responses to the true responses given by the EMG. The logic of the bogus pipeline procedure is that a subject prefers to tell the experimenter his or her true feelings rather than be proven a liar by the EMG.

Several pieces of evidence suggest that the bogus pipeline procedure produces more truthful statements on the part of subjects. For example, in one study (Quigley-Fernandez & Tedeschi, 1978) subjects were first wrongly informed about how to perform well on an experimental test. They were then given a chance to "cheat" on the test and were later asked if they possessed any prior information about the test. Subjects questioned under the bogus pipeline condition "confessed" more often than those who were not. In a study more directly related to attitudes (Sigall & Page, 1971), white subjects attributed more negative characteristics to blacks with the bogus pipeline procedure than with the regular self-report rating scales. These studies indicate that the bogus pipeline procedure may be effective in getting people to reveal socially undesirable information about themselves, thus providing a more valid measure of attitudes.

Box 1.3

The White House Report Card

OFFICE:_____
Name of Rater:_____

STAFF EVALUATION

Please answer each of the following questions about this person.

Name:_____
Salary:_____
Position:_____Duties:_____

Work Habits

1) On the average when does this person:
   arrive at work_____
   leave work_____
2) Pace of Work:

1	2	3	4	5	6
slow					fast

3) Level of Effort:

1	2	3	4	5	6
below capacity					full capacity

4) Quality of Work

1	2	3	4	5	6
poor					good

5) What is he/she best at? (rank 1-5)
   __Conceptualizing
   __Planning
   __Implementing
   __Attending to detail
   __Controlling quality
6) Does this person have the skills to do the job he/she was hired to do?
   yes__
   no__
   ?__
7) Would the slot filled by this person be better filled by someone else?
   yes__
   no__
   ?__

Personal Characteristics:

8) How confident is this person? (circle one)

1	2	3	4	5	6
self doubting		confident		cocky	

9) How confident are you of this person's judgment:

1	2	3	4	5	6
not confident					very confident

10) How mature is this person?

1	2	3	4	5	6
immature					mature

11) How flexible is this person?

1	2	3	4	5	6
rigid					flexible

12) How stable is this person?

1	2	3	4	5	6
erratic					steady

13) How frequently does this person come up with new ideas?

1	2	3	4	5	6
closed					open

15) How bright is this person?

1	2	3	4	5	6
average					very bright

16) What are this person's special talents?

   1)_____
   _____
   2)_____
   _____
   3)_____
   _____

17) What is this person's range of information?

1	2	3	4	5	6
narrow					broad

Interpersonal Relations:

18) How would you characterize this person's impact on other people? (for example, hostile, smooth, aggressive, charming, etc.)

   1)_____
   _____
   2)_____
   _____
   3)_____
   _____

This is a reproduction of a questionnaire distributed by White House Chief of Staff Hamilton Jordan during the administration of President Jimmy Carter. The questionnaire was to be used to grade top aides in the Carter administration. It consists of some open-ended questions and some rating scales from the semantic differential. Since the questionnaire is not to be completed anonymously, how honest do you think the raters were likely to be?

Reprinted from the *St. Louis Post-Dispatch.* Used with permission.

19) How well does this person get along with

Superiors	1	2	3	4	5	6
Peers	1	2	3	4	5	6
Subordinates	1	2	3	4	5	6
Outsiders	1	2	3	4	5	6

            not well   very well

20) In a public setting, how comfortable would you be having this person represent:

you or your office	1	2	3	4	5	6
The President	1	2	3	4	5	6

           uncomfortable   comfortable

21) Rate this person's political skills.

        1   2   3   4   5   6
     naive   savvy

Supervision and Direction

22) To what extent is this person focused on accomplishing the

Administration's goals_____%

personal goals_____%

_____

100%

23) How capable is this person at working toward implementing a decision with which he/she may not agree?

    1   2   3   4   5   6
 reluctant   eager

24) How well does this person take direction?

    1   2   3   4   5   6
          resists   readily

25) How much supervision does this person need?

    1   2   3   4   5   6
 a lot   little

26) How readily does this person offer to help out by doing that which is not a part of his/her "job"?

    1   2   3   4   5   6
 seldom   often

Summary:

27) Can this person assume more responsibility?

yes__

no__

?__

28) List this person's 3 major strengths and 3 major weaknesses.

29) List this person's 3 major accomplishments.

30) List 3 things this person that have disappointed you.

Indirect Procedures

The bogus pipeline method improves the validity of a direct attitude measure when an investigator fears that, for some reason, people are unwilling to provide accurate information about their attitudes. Another approach is to employ an indirect attitude measure. With an indirect attitude measure, the subjects are unaware that attitudes are being measured, thus minimizing their concerns about giving an "appropriate" or a "desirable" response. In this section, we will discuss some disguised self-report techniques, some behavioral measures, and some physiological indicators of attitudes.

Disguised Self-reports

With a disguised self-report, people provide verbal reports about themselves, but they are unaware that the purpose of the self-report is to measure their attitudes. For example, if you want to measure a person's attitudes toward the church, you might show the person a picture of a minister standing at the pulpit and ask the person to make up a story about the picture. The idea of this *projective technique* (Proshansky, 1943) is that people will project their own personal feelings into their stories. To the extent that a group of judges can agree on the themes expressed in a person's story (pro- or antichurch), an inference about the person's attitude can be made.

A technique called the *information error test* (Hammond, 1948), involves giving people what appears to be an objective multiple-choice test. The test is unique, however, in that none of the answers are correct! To measure attitudes toward the church using this technique, the subject is presented with a series of questions like this:

What has happened to church attendance in the United States in the past ten years?
a. It has decreased 15%.
b. It has decreased 10%.
c. It has stayed the same.
d. It has increased 5%.

If church attendance has actually declined by five percent, two of the responses overestimate the decline and two of the responses underestimate the decline. The person is thus forced to select a position that is relatively favorable or relatively unfavorable to the church. This technique assumes that, over a series of items, the person's own attitude toward the church will consistently influence the direction of the bias (either pro- or antichurch).

Hendrick and Seyfried (1974) introduced a clever technique for obtaining a disguised measure of peoples' attitudes based on the well-documented finding that people generally like those who have attitudes similar to theirs and generally dislike people whose attitudes are dissimilar (Byrne, 1969). To determine, then, if subjects are generally favorable or unfavorable toward the church, the investigator could show them some attitude scales that were presumably filled out by various other people. The subjects would be asked to indicate whether or not they would like the people whose attitudinal responses they saw. Presumably, if the subjects said that they would like another person who expressed antichurch attitudes and dislike one who expressed prochurch attitudes, the inference could be drawn that the subjects themselves had unfavorable attitudes toward the church.

Behavioral Indicators of Attitudes

A number of behavioral measures have been used to obtain an indication of attitude toward people, objects, and issues. For example, Wells and Petty (1980) secretly videotaped peoples' head movements as they listened to a proattitudinal or a counterattitudinal message. People listening to a message that supported their own positions engaged in more vertical and fewer horizontal head movements than people listening to a message that contradicted their own attitudes. Researchers interested in interpersonal attraction have used the following measures of attitude toward other people: the amount of eye contact (Argyle, 1967; Rubin, 1970), one's body position (Mehrabian, 1968), and the physical distance that two people stand from each other (Byrne, Ervin, & Lamberth, 1970). The more eye contact, the more people lean toward each other; and the closer they stand to one another, the greater the liking that has been reported.

Virtually any positive act toward a person might be viewed as indicating a positive attitude toward that person, and any negative act might be viewed as indicating a negative attitude. We presumably do not often do positive things for people that we dislike, nor do we often do negative things to people we like. Milgram, Mann, and Harter (1965) reasoned that people would be willing to mail a lost letter addressed to a group that they liked (e.g., UNICEF) but would be less willing to mail a lost letter to a group that they disliked (e.g., the Communist party). In a test of this *lost letter* technique for measuring attitudes, these researchers scattered a number of letters addressed to various positive and negative groups around several different cities. The people who found the letters mailed significantly more of them that were addressed to the positive groups than to the negative groups. Presumably, this technique could be used to predict the outcome of a political election in a city. Letters addressed to the various candidates would be "lost" in each target city and the return rates monitored. This technique is expensive, since a stamp is required for each "lost letter," but in some cases the technique may be cheaper than hiring interviewers to poll the electorate (although not as accurate). The technique may be particularly useful in assessing political attitudes in a country where people may be afraid to give their true opinions to interviewers (Milgram, 1977).

Webb, Campbell, Schwartz, and Sechrest (1966) have described a number of unobtrusive measures for assessing attitudes that might be useful in particular contexts. For example, to determine which paintings the visitors to a museum like without asking them to fill out a questionnaire, an investigator could monitor the amount of wear on the tiles underneath the various paintings (Melton, 1933, 1936). If people stand longer under paintings that they like, then the tiles would have to be replaced more often under the more popular paintings. Unfortunately, a number of factors other than popularity undoubtedly contribute to tile wear. For example, people probably drag their feet more at the end of the museum, making the paintings in this area appear to be more popular than they actually are.

Physiological Indicators of Attitudes

The indirect techniques that we have discussed so far all rely on various inferences about how attitudinal biases might influence certain things—the stories people tell about pictures, the answers people select to multiple-choice tests, or the behaviors they perform that *appear* relevant to the attitude object or issue. If the assumptions about how certain behaviors relate to the underlying attitude are incorrect, or if the behavior observed is not representative of the behaviors that the person typically engages in, the measure of attitude will contain error.

The ideal attitude measure would be one that avoids the major problems of the direct self-report techniques (e.g., that people are sometimes unwilling or unable to report their attitudes correctly) and the problems of the indirect techniques already discussed (e.g., that the assumptions on which the measures are based may be faulty or that unrepresentative behaviors may be observed). Some researchers have sought such a "perfect" measure in the human body's natural physiological responses to attitudinal stimuli (see review by Cacioppo & Sandman, 1981). In this section we discuss three physiological measures that have been employed to assess attitudes.

One of the first measures used was the *galvanic skin reflex* (GSR). The GSR measures the electrical resistance of the skin, or how well the skin conducts an electric current that is passed between two electrodes that are usually placed on the surface of the hand. When the hand is sweaty, it conducts electricity better than when it is dry, and the GSR measures this change in the activity of the sweat gland. Because people perspire more when emotionally aroused, it was thought that the GSR could be used to assess a person's emotional response to a stimulus. Early investigators reported that the GSR predicted such things as the intensity of racial prejudice (Westie & DeFleur, 1959) and the effectiveness of an advertisement for pancake flour (Ekstrand & Gilliland, 1948).

In a representative early study, Dysinger (1931; reported in McCurdy, 1950) monitored the GSR of subjects as they were presented with words that varied in their pleasantness. For example, if the following words were rated on a scale of -3 (very unpleasant) to $+3$ (very pleasant), *love* would be a very pleasant word, *rape* would be a very unpleasant word, and *chair* would fall somewhere in between. Dysinger found that the closer the word was rated to either extreme, the greater the GSR that the word elicited. The GSR did not, however, predict whether the subjects' responses to the words were positive or negative. Because the GSR correlates with the intensity of an emotion but not the direction, its use for assessing attitudes is rather limited. A more important drawback of the GSR measure, however, is that it also correlates with other features of stimuli. The more strange, the more novel, and the more unexpected a stimulus is, the greater the GSR that is elicited (Sokolov, 1963). Thus, until a study is conducted in which all of these features of the stimuli are controlled, it is not even clear that the GSR can provide a unique measure of the intensity of attitudes.

Hess (1965) reported that the *pupillary response* might be used to assess the direction of an attitude toward a stimulus. The pupil of the eye is capable of both expanding, as when the lighting becomes dim, and constricting, as when the lighting becomes bright. Hess suggested that pupillary expansion would accompany the repeated presentations of stimuli that the person liked, whereas pupillary constriction would accompany the repeated presentations of stimuli that the person disliked.

To test the validity of the pupillary response measure, Atwood and Howell (1971) monitored the pupillary responses of ten pedophiliac prisoners (convicted of child molestation) and ten control prisoners (convicted of nonsexual crimes) while they viewed nude or partially nude pictures of adult females and young girls. Table 1.1 presents the average change in the prisoners' pupils when viewing the experimental pictures as opposed to blurred slides. Note that all but one of the pedophiliacs' pupils dilated more when viewing the pictures of the children than the pictures of adult females; and all but one of the control prisoners' pupils dilated more to the pictures of the adults than to the pictures of the children.

Although other demonstrations (e.g., Barlow, 1969) suggest that the pupillary response measures subjects' attitudes, there are far more studies that fail to find support for the pupils' response as an indicator of attitudes (see review by Wood-mansee, 1970). There appear to be several problems with the pupillary measure. First, it is clear that the pupils respond to various features of a stimulus. Besides the obvious feature of the amount of light in a picture, the pupillary response also correlates with the interest or attention value of a stimulus and the amount of cognitive effort devoted to thinking about a stimulus (Kahneman, 1973; Libby, Lacey, & Lacey, 1973). Second, some studies have shown that the pupils dilate to both pleasant and unpleasant stimuli rather than distinguishing these two states, and there is presently no evidence that the pupils are successful in predicting attitudes for nonvisual stimuli (Goldwater, 1972). The initial promise, then, of the pupillary measure has yet to be documented.

Table 1.1

Mean Pupil Changes of Pedophiliac and Control Prisoners to Pictures of Adult Females and Young Girls

	Picture Type	
	Adult Females	**Young Girls**
Pedophiliac Prisoners		
1	+ 15	+38
2	− 2	+22
3	− 7	+17
4	− 6	+ 6
5	− 5	+31
6	−11	+24
7	− 2	−10
8	−10	+25
9	− 4	+28
10	+ 6	+29
Mean	− 2.6	+21.0
Control Prisoners		
1	+28	+25
2	+18	+ 5
3	+29	− 8
4	+21	+14
5	+25	+ 5
6	+21	− 7
7	+22	− 6
8	+35	+ 3
9	−26	0
10	+16	− 8
Mean	+18.9	+ 2.3
(*p < .01)	t = 4.51*	t = 3.43*

Data from Atwood & Howell (1971). Copyright by the Psychonomic Society. Used with permission.

NOTE: The data, presented in millimeters, do not refer to actual changes in the size of the pupil but instead to changes on a 24-inch television screen on which the pupil was projected.

The final physiological procedure we address is *facial EMG,* a measure of the contractions of the major facial muscles (see fig. 1.1). Over one hundred years ago, Charles Darwin (1872) argued that different facial expressions were biologically tied to different emotions. In fact, Darwin used the term *attitude* to refer to a facial expression of emotion. More recently, Ekman (1971) concluded that at least six distinct emotions could be linked to unique facial expressions across a wide variety of cultures: happiness, sadness, anger, fear, surprise, and disgust.

Figure 1.1

Major facial muscles and recording sites for electrode placement.

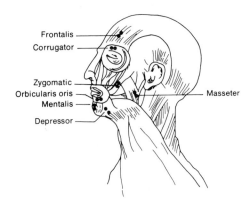

NOTE: Pleasant in contrast to unpleasant affective reactions are associated with relatively increased EMG activity over depressor and zygomatic muscles, but relatively diminished output over the corrugator and frontalis muscles. (From Cacioppo & Petty, 1981b).

In a series of studies, Schwartz and his colleagues (e.g., Schwartz, Fair, Salt, Mandel, & Klerman, 1976) demonstrated the usefulness of the facial EMG procedure for assessing positive and negative affective states. Specifically, they have shown that people who are asked to imagine positive events or "think happy thoughts" generally show more electrical activity in the depressor and zygomatic muscles, but less electrical activity in the corrugator and frontalis muscles, than subjects who are asked to "think sad thoughts."

Cacioppo and Petty (1979a) reasoned that measures of facial EMG might distinguish positive from negative reactions to a persuasive communication. To test this hypothesis, they asked college students to listen to either an involving proattitudinal message (e.g., advocating more lenient visitation hours in dormitory rooms) or an involving counterattitudinal message (e.g., advocating more strict visitation hours in dormitory rooms) while their facial muscle activity was monitored. Subjects hearing a proattitudinal message displayed the facial muscle pattern of happiness, whereas those hearing a counterattitudinal message displayed the facial muscle pattern of sadness. These subtle facial muscle patterns, as in the Schwartz research, were not detectable by observers—the patterns were only distinguishable in the highly sensitive electromyographic recordings. It appears that the facial EMG measure may be sensitive to gross differences in the direction of one's feelings, but it is not yet clear whether the measure will be useful in determining the intensity of feelings as well.

Direct versus Indirect Assessment of Attitudes

We have reviewed a potpourri of procedures developed by psychologists to assess the degree to which people feel positively or negatively about other people, objects, and issues. Without question, the great majority of attitude change studies reviewed in the remaining chapters of this book (and the vast majority of persuasion studies conducted) rely almost exclusively on direct self-report measures of attitude. There is a good reason for this. When reliability and validity checks are made on the various direct and indirect procedures, the indirect procedures are often found to be inferior to the direct attitude scales (Lemon, 1973). Researchers therefore prefer the direct techniques. Another advantage of the direct techniques is their greater *precision* or *sensitivity*—that is, they are better than the indirect techniques at pinpointing relatively small differences in attitudes that may exist between subjects. In contrast, the indirect techniques have been most useful in detecting relatively large differences in affect between people. The primary disadvantages of the direct techniques—that people may be unwilling to give their attitudes or may be deliberately misleading about their attitudes—have not really proven problematic in research. This is probably because most attitude research does not deal with highly sensitive issues, and in many studies the subjects' attitudinal responses are kept anonymous. If the issues are relatively uninvolving and anonymity is assured, there is little reason to misrepresent one's attitude. Nevertheless, social psychologists have developed a wide variety of indirect assessment procedures that are highly useful in those few (but important) situations in which it is reasonable to question the validity of a direct attitude measure.

Do Attitudes Predict Behaviors?

Before we discuss how psychologists study attitude change experimentally, there is one more important question to be addressed: do attitudes predict behaviors? Recall that psychologists have focused on the concept of attitude because of the assumed relationship between attitudes and behaviors. Defense attorneys want you to like their clients so that you will vote to acquit them; manufacturers want you to like their products so that you will buy them; and other people want us to like them so that we will do favors for them or protect them or marry them.

Soon after the first attitude scales were developed, questions arose about the usefulness of attitudes in predicting behaviors. In perhaps the most widely cited early study on the attitude-behavior "problem" (as it came to be known), LaPiere (1934) investigated whether or not he could predict peoples' prejudiced behaviors from their self-reports of prejudice. In the early 1930s, LaPiere, traveling with a Chinese couple, stopped at sixty-six hotels and 184 restaurants across the

United States. The Chinese couple was refused service at only one of the establishments. Six months later, LaPiere wrote to all of the places at which they stopped, asking them if they would give service to Chinese guests. Of the 128 places that responded, ninety-two percent stated that they *would not* serve Chinese guests. On the surface, at least, there appears to be an extreme discrepancy between the verbal reports and the actual behavior toward Chinese. On closer examination, however, it is clear that there are several problems with this study. One major problem is that there is no way to be certain that the people who admitted the Chinese couple to the hotels and restaurants were the same people who completed the questionnaire when it arrived six months later! In fact, it is highly unlikely that the two measures were obtained on the same people.

If this were the only study failing to find a relationship between verbal reports and behaviors, the attitude-behavior "problem" would never have arisen. However, there were numerous other more carefully conducted studies that also failed to find significant relationships. Corey (1937), for instance, measured his students' attitudes toward cheating and then attempted to predict cheating on the tests that he gave during the semester. He was able to determine whether or not the students cheated by grading their true-false tests before giving them back, but allowing the students to believe that they were going to grade the tests themselves (students beware!). The difference between the score the students assigned to themselves and their actual scores, as determined by Corey's initial grading, served as the index of cheating. Corey found that the correlation between the students' attitudes toward cheating and the extent to which they actually cheated on five tests was close to zero. Students with positive attitudes toward cheating were no more or less likely to cheat than students with negative attitudes toward cheating. Moreover, in this study, there was no problem in ensuring that the same people who completed the attitude measures also completed the behavioral ones.

What Kinds of Attitudes Predict Behaviors?

These and other studies that seem to show an inability of attitudes to predict behaviors led one relatively recent reviewer to conclude that "taken as a whole, these studies suggest that it is considerably more likely that attitudes will be unrelated or only slightly related to overt behaviors than that attitudes will be closely related to actions" (Wicker, 1969, p. 65), and that "it may be desirable to abandon the attitude concept" (Wicker, 1971, p. 29). Wicker was not alone in his disillusionment with the attitude concept, and by the mid-1970s the study of attitudes by social psychologists declined dramatically (Lambert, 1980). The fact that you are now reading a current book on attitudes and persuasion suggests that this pessimism did not last very long. In the past decade, enough careful research has been conducted by a number of scholars, most notably Fishbein and

Ajzen (1974, 1975; Ajzen & Fishbein, 1977, 1980), to conclude confidently that attitudes *are* related to behaviors. Furthermore, the recent research outlines the conditions under which the relationship is likely to be strong rather than weak.

Attitudes and Behaviors That Are Measured Appropriately

Ajzen and Fishbein (1977) noted that a behavior can be viewed as consisting of four elements. The first element is the *action* performed: is the behavior one of cooking, smoking, or driving? The second element is the *target* at which the action is directed: is the action directed at a cake, a cigarette, or a bus? The third element is the *context* in which the action is performed: is the action performed in the kitchen, in front of the minister, or on the interstate highway? Finally, every behavior has a *time* component: is the action performed on New Year's Eve, in the morning, or at noon? By putting these components together, the complete behavior is specified: the person is cooking a cake in the kitchen in the morning, or the person is smoking a cigarette on the interstate highway on New Year's Eve.

In order to predict one of these specific behaviors, Ajzen and Fishbein argue that the attitude measure employed should correspond to the behavior on the action, target, context, and time categories. If there is no correspondence, a significant relationship between attitudes and behaviors will usually not be obtained. Given this analysis, it is understandable why Corey was unable to predict cheating behavior from attitudes toward cheating. The problem was that he employed a general measure of attitude toward cheating (assessing attitudes toward the action component) but tried to predict a very specific behavior (whether the students would cheat on a particular kind of test, in a particular course).

A study by Davidson and Jaccard (1979) illustrates the enhanced prediction that can be obtained by measuring attitudes and behaviors at corresponding levels of specificity. In this study, they attempted to predict whether women would actually use birth control pills during a particular two-year period. Table 1.2 shows how well different attitude measures predicted the women's use of the pills. The attitude toward birth control pills (target component only) does not predict behavior very well. After all, the women may think that the pills themselves are wonderful (they are small, round, colorful, and should be available to women who want them), but they may not have positive feelings about *using* the pills. By adding this action component to the attitude measure, prediction is increased. Finally, by adding the time component, prediction is increased even further. This is because a woman might have favorable feelings about using birth control pills generally but does not have favorable feelings about using them in the next two years because she wants to have a baby then.

Table 1.2

Correlations of Attitude Measures Varying in Specificity with Behavior (Use of Birth Control Pills during a Two-year Period)

Attitude Measure	Correlation with Behavior
1. Attitude toward birth control	.083
2. Attitude toward birth control pills	.323
3. Attitude toward using birth control pills	.525
4. Attitude toward using birth control pills during the next 2 years	.572

Data from Davidson & Jaccard (1979). Copyright by the American Psychological Association. Used with permission.

NOTE: Based on a sample of 244 women.

In the example on birth control pills, the investigators were able to predict a specific behavior by employing a specific attitude measure. According to Ajzen and Fishbein's analysis, however, a general attitude measure should be able to predict a general behavioral criterion. In other words, a general attitude measure on cheating might not be able to predict one specific instance of cheating, but it should predict general cheating behavior across a wide enough variety of targets (e.g., cheating on tests, income taxes, when playing monopoly), contexts, and times. In order to test this notion, Weigel and Newman (1976) administered a general attitude measure (Likert scale) about the environment to forty-four residents of a New England town that were randomly selected from a telephone directory. Three months after giving the attitude measure, the first behavioral measure was administered. Someone came to the homes of the subjects and asked them if they would be willing to sign any one of three petitions relevant to environmental concerns (e.g., opposing oil drilling off the New England coast). On the behavioral measure, subjects were given one point for each petition they signed and one additional point if they agreed to keep some petitions and actually mailed them back with at least one new signature. Six weeks after the petition-signing opportunity, the subjects were contacted by a different person and asked if they would agree to join a roadside litter cleanup. They were given a choice of three different times during which they could participate. Subjects were given one point for actually showing up for the cleanup and were given an additional point if they brought along another person as requested. Eight weeks later, the subjects were again contacted by a different person and were told about a recycling program for bottles, cans, and newspapers that was to take place in their community over an eight-week period. The subjects were awarded one point for

Table 1.3

Predicting Specific and General Behavioral Criteria from a General Attitude Measure

Correlations between Subjects' Environmental Attitudes and Behavioral Criteria

Single Behaviors	r^a	Categories of Behavior	r^b	Behavioral Index	r^b
Offshore oil	.41**	Petitioning behavior scale (0–4)	50**		
Nuclear power	.36*				
Auto exhaust	.39**				
Circulate petitions	.27				
Individual participation	.34*	Litter pick-up scale (0–2)	.36*		
Recruit friend	.22			Comprehensive behavioral index	.62***
Week 1	.34*	Recycling behavior scale (0–8)	.39**		
Week 2	.57***				
Week 3	.34*				
Week 4	.33*				
Week 5	.12				
Week 6	.20				
Week 7	.20				
Week 8	.34*				

Data from Weigel & Newman (1976). Copyright by the American Psychological Association. Used with permission.

NOTE: $N = 44$.
[a] Point-biserial correlations are reported in this column.
[b] Pearson product-moment correlations are reported in this column.
*$p < .05$.
**$p < .01$.
***$p < .001$.

each week that they brought some materials in to the recycling station. Table 1.3 shows how well the general attitude measure predicted the subjects' various behaviors. Notice that although the general attitude measure did not predict any one specific behavior very well, it predicted the subjects' general pattern of behaviors toward the environment quite well.

In their extensive review of attitude-behavior studies, Ajzen and Fishbein (1977) found that, in those studies in which the attitude and behavior measures did not correspond, the correlation between attitudes and behaviors was usually not significant. In the twenty-six studies in which appropriate measures were obtained, all twenty-six showed significant attitude-behavior correlations.

Besides ensuring correspondence between the measures of attitude and behavior, two other measurement issues have been shown to affect the ability to predict behaviors from attitudes. The first is the amount of time that elapses between the attitude and the behavioral measurement. The more time that elapses between the two measures, the lower the correlation that is usually observed between attitudes and behaviors (Davidson & Jaccard, 1979; Schwartz, 1978). This is because the more time between the two measures, the more likely it is that a person's attitude will change in the interval. If attitude change occurs, the behavior prediction will be based on the wrong attitude.

The second measurement factor that has been shown to make a difference is the extent to which the subjects' attention is focused on their "inner states" when either the attitude or the behavior measure is taken. For example, when subjects are asked to complete either the attitude or the behavior measure while facing a mirror, the attitude-behavior correlations are enhanced over nonmirror conditions (Gibbons, 1978; Pryor, Gibbons, Wicklund, Fazio, & Hood, 1977). The presence of the mirror presumably makes subjects more "self-aware," and this increases attitude-behavior consistency. In other words, when subjects' thoughts are focused on their true internal feelings (Scheier & Carver, 1980), they are more likely to act in a manner consistent with those feelings than when their thoughts are not internally focused (Carver & Scheier, 1978; Snyder & Swann, 1976).

Attitudes That Are Based on Direct Experience

Two people may have identical attitudes toward some person, object, or issue, but these attitudes may have been formed in different ways. In fact, the remaining chapters in this book discuss the many different ways in which an attitude may be formed. Fazio and Zanna (1981), focusing on attitudes formed as a result of direct experience with the attitude object, have proposed that these attitudes should predict behaviors better than attitudes that are not based on direct experience. In a test of this hypothesis, Regan and Fazio (1977) tried to predict the proportion of time that people would spend playing with different types of puzzles from their attitudes toward the puzzles. In this experiment, they gave subjects in the *direct-experience* condition an opportunity to play with some sample puzzles before their attitudes were measured. For subjects in the *indirect-experience* condition, the experimenters only described the various types of puzzles to them before their attitudes were measured. Subjects in both conditions expressed the same attitudes about the puzzles on the attitude scales, but the method by which their attitudes were formed was different. Later, all subjects were given an opportunity to play with the different puzzles, and the experimenters recorded the order in which the different types of puzzles were attempted and the proportion of available puzzles of each type with which the subjects played. The average correlation between the attitude and the behavior measures for direct experience subjects was .53, whereas for indirect experience subjects, the correlation was only .21.

In a subsequent study, Fazio and Zanna (1978) tried to predict students' willingness to participate in psychological research projects on the basis of their attitudes toward psychology experiments. They divided students into three groups based on how many experiments they had already participated in. Those with the most experience with psychology experiments showed the highest attitude-behavior correlation ($r = .42$), those with a moderate amount of experience showed the next highest correlation ($r = .36$), and those with the least direct experience showed no correlation ($r = -.03$).

Fazio and Zanna (1981) suggest that attitudes based on direct experience predict behaviors better than attitudes not formed in this manner, because direct experience makes more information about the attitude object available to the person. The more information a person has about the attitude object, or the more an attitude is based on salient beliefs about the object, the more confident the person might be in acting on that information (see also Norman, 1975). Fazio and Zanna also suggest that attitudes based on direct experience are more memorable than other attitudes: the more accessible an attitude is in memory, the more likely it is that it can influence the person.

What Other Variables Enhance Behavioral Prediction?

Although it is now clear that attitudes can be used to predict behavior with considerable success under the appropriate conditions, some investigators argue that by considering some variables in addition to attitudes, prediction of behavior can be substantially improved. Snyder (1979), for example, has argued that people low in the personality trait of *self-monitoring* typically show greater attitude-behavior consistency than people who are high in the trait. Low self-monitors tend to guide their behavioral choices on the basis of salient information about their internal states (e.g., they eat when they are hungry), whereas high self-monitors tend to guide their behavior more on the basis of situational information (e.g., they eat when it is dinnertime). Attitudes, which are internal predispositions, will therefore generally be a better predictors of behaviors for low than high self-monitors (Snyder & Monson, 1975; Snyder & Tanke, 1976; Zanna, Olson, & Fazio, 1980).

Fishbein and Ajzen (1975) have argued that *norms*, or what other people think about the behavior, are also important considerations for predicting an individual's behavior. They have formulated and tested a model of behavioral prediction based on attitudes and norms that they call "the theory of reasoned action." This theory, discussed in depth in chapter 7, has generated a considerable amount of research.

In addition to attitudes, norms, and personality, Triandis (1980) argues that, of the several other factors to consider in attempting to predict behavior, the most important is *habit*. Habits are behaviors that have become automatic in certain situations. These behaviors occur without much, if any, thought. Triandis suggests that the first few times a person performs a particular behavior, cognitive factors such as attitudes and norms play a significant role in determining the nature of the behavior; but as the person engages more and more in the behavior, there is a shift away from these cognitive factors, and habit plays a more important role (see also Triandis, 1977). In fact, some social psychologists have characterized much of a person's day-to-day behavior as "mindless" (Langer, Blank, & Chanowitz, 1978). For these highly routine, relatively unimportant daily behaviors, attitudes will likely be poor predictors. Furthermore, even though the person may have a great deal of direct experience with a particular attitude object, if the person engages in the behavior so often that it becomes automatic, attitudes may change, but the behavior may persist due to habit.

Nevertheless, even behaviors that have become almost completely automatic, in that they occur without much thought, may again come under the control of attitudes if the person once more becomes motivated to think about the behavior. For example, Smith (1977) found that, on a typical work day, the attitudes of the employees of a large corporation toward their jobs could not be used to predict who would show up for work. On the day after an unusually severe blizzard, however, attitudes toward work did predict employee attendance. On a typical work or school day, for example, most people go without much thought. When a blizzard leaves ten-foot high snowdrifts outside, however, people have to make a conscious decision about whether or not they want to leave the comfort of their homes. On such "thoughtful" days, attitudes will have an important influence on their behaviors—the more they like their jobs, the more they are likely to brave the weather and attempt to get to work.

How Is Attitude Change Studied Experimentally?

We now know that attitudes can serve important functions for people, that they can be measured with high reliability and validity, and that they can be useful in predicting behaviors. We are now ready to focus on persuasion, or the process of changing attitudes. First of all, it is important to note that virtually all of the research on persuasion conducted by social psychologists is guided by some theory. A *theory of attitude change* specifies the variables that are important in producing persuasion, and it further specifies the processes by which these variables induce attitude change.

Despite many differences in variables and processes that persuasion theorists claim are responsible for inducing attitude changes, investigators from all theoretical approaches have relied on the experimental method for testing their theories. So before we begin our descriptions of the major theoretical approaches to persuasion, it is necessary to discuss the attitude change experiment.

Conceptual and Operational Levels of Research

In a simple research effort, diagrammed in figure 1.2, the *conceptual level* represents what the theory of attitude change states should occur and why. The theory in figure 1.2 says that an expert source should increase attitude change by increasing the number of message arguments that a person will learn from the advocacy. The *operational level* represents how the researcher translates the conceptual (theoretical) variables into variables that can actually be manipulated and measured.

Two types of experimental designs are most often used to study attitude change (Campbell & Stanley, 1963). The first design—*the pretest-posttest control group design*—is diagrammed below.

Experimental Group	R	O_1	X	O_2
Control Group	R	O_3		O_4

In this design, subjects are randomly assigned (R) to one of the two groups, so that any given subject has an equal chance of being assigned to either the experimental or the control group. The pretest attitudes of the experimental group (O_1) and the control group (O_3) are measured using any of the attitude measurement techniques described earlier in this chapter. Some treatment or manipulation (called the independent variable X) is then presented to the experimental group only, followed by a posttest measurement of the attitudes of both the experimental (O_2) and control (O_4) groups. For example, to test the hypothesis that an expert source increases attitude change, two groups might hear a speech advocating that wage and price controls be instituted. For one group, the source of the speech would be a Nobel prize-winning economist (experimental group); for the other group, the source would remain unidentified (control group). Attitudes about wage and price controls (on semantic differential scales) would be taken both before and after the speech for both groups. If the experimental group shows more change in the direction of favoring wage and price controls as a result of hearing the speech ($O_2 - O_1$) than does the control group ($O_4 - O_3$), then the hypothesis is supported.

An alternative experimental design for testing the same hypothesis is the *posttest-only control group design.* In this design (see diagram below), subjects are again randomly assigned to experimental and control groups, but only one measure of attitudes is taken—the posttest. Because of random assignment to conditions, subjects in the experimental and control groups can be assumed to have

Experimental Group	R	X	O_1
Control Group	R		O_2

Figure 1.2

The conceptual and operational levels of a simple research effort on source expertise.

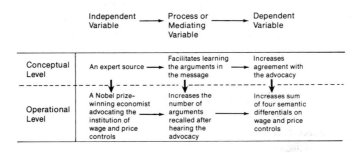

the same *initial* attitudes. Attitude change, then, can be defined as the difference between the posttest attitudes of the experimental group and control group. Since the subjects are randomly assigned to the two groups, and the two groups are treated identically except for the independent variable (X), nothing should contribute to the differences between the attitude measures (O_1 and O_2) except the effects of the manipulation. The posttest-only design is sometimes preferred over the pretest-posttest design because (1) completing a pretest may commit subjects to an initial attitude, and when they are confronted with the same attitude scales at the time of the posttest, they may simply report their pretest attitudes again; and (2) completing an initial attitude measure may sensitize subjects that attitude change is being studied, and they may not show change to avoid the appearance of indecisiveness.[4] Of course, the two basic experimental designs that we have discussed are often extended to include more than one experimental and control group.

The Validity of the Attitude Change Experiment

Cook and Campbell (1976) have argued that there are four kinds of validity of concern to an investigator when evaluating the outcome of any experiment. As an example of these four kinds of validity, let's examine our hypothetical experiment on source expertise. Recall that we found that the subjects in the experimental group, who were exposed to the Nobel prize-winning source, showed more agreement with the institution of wage and price controls than did subjects in the control group, for whom the source remained anonymous. The question of *statistical conclusion validity* asks whether the difference observed between the experimental and control groups may have been due to a chance fluctuation, or whether the observed difference is reliable (likely to be obtained again if the experiment is repeated). A statistical test allows determination of the likelihood that the observed difference represents a chance occurrence (Kirk, 1968; Winer, 1971). If the probability that the difference is due to chance is 5% or less ($p < .05$), as revealed by the statistical test, then the result is considered to be statistically *significant* (or reliable).

A second concern in evaluating an experiment is *internal validity*. If the experiment passes the conclusion validity test, something other than chance is responsible for the observed difference, but the statistical test does not assure that the manipulation (source expertise) is responsible for the observed difference. It is assured that the attitude change effect is not due to some variable other than the manipulation if there is an appropriate control group and if subjects have been randomly assigned to conditions. Since an appropriate control group is treated identically to the experimental group except for the manipulation, if the two groups are found to differ, then this difference must either be attributed to the manipulation or to the fact that the two groups have different kinds of subjects. By randomly assigning subjects to conditions, the latter possibility can be eliminated and it may be concluded that the manipulation was necessary to produce the observed effect.

A third kind of validity, *external validity*, is concerned with how well the observed effect generalizes to other possible subject populations, other locations, and different experimental materials. When only one experiment is conducted, the investigator can never be sure that the observed effect has any general applicability. Perhaps expert sources produce more attitude change only for economic topics but not for others. The only way to check on the external validity of a finding is to conceptually *replicate* (repeat) the experiment. In other words, in the second and third experiments, the same conceptual hypotheses will be tested, but the specific procedures will be different. An experimenter will use different subjects, in different locations, with different experimental materials. To the extent that the findings can be replicated with a wide variety of different procedures, the findings have external validity.

Finally, in evaluating an experiment, the investigator must be concerned with *construct validity*. This is the question of whether or not what was meant to be manipulated was actually manipulated and what was meant to be measured was actually measured. We have already discussed some of the problems encountered in assessing the construct validity of attitude measures (e.g., sometimes people may attempt to mislead us as to their true attitudes). It is equally important to be sure that the manipulation is valid. In our example, the expert source is a Nobel prize winner. Is the increased persuasion observed in the experimental group due to the source's expertise, or is it due to some irrelevant aspect of the manipulation? Maybe subjects were persuaded because our source had won a prize, and any source that had won a prize—whether it was an Academy Award, the Miss America Pageant, or the South County Hog-Calling Championship— would have been liked more by subjects, and this liking would have produced more agreement. In our example, "winning a prize" was *confounded* (covaried) with the expertise of the source. A certain degree of confounding is probably inevitable in most research, because experimental treatments are complex and are unlikely to manipulate only one thing. Researchers typically deal with this problem in one or both of the following ways. First, a *manipulation check* measure can be taken, which is designed to see if subjects in the experimental group felt that the source had greater expertise on the issue than did the subjects in the control group. If this occurred, and furthermore if experimental subjects did not report *liking* the source more than did the control subjects, confidence in the construct validity of the manipulation is increased. A second way to deal with this problem is to employ *multiple operations* of the treatment. Ideally, the experiment should use several different manipulations of source expertise (expert sources who had won prizes, expert sources who hadn't, male expert sources, female expert sources). If all of these expert sources have the same effect, then one can more confidently attribute their effect to that which they have in common, namely, expertise.

In addition to specific confounds that may be present in any one study, social psychologists have identified three general biasing factors that may be confounded with an experimental manipulation:

1. *Demand characteristics* (Orne, 1962). This occurs when the experimental treatment gives the subject a hint about the "correct" response or the response that the experimenter would like the subject to make.
2. *Evaluation apprehension* (Rosenberg, 1969). This occurs when the experimental treatment makes the subjects concerned about being evaluated by the experimenter. This makes subjects more likely to engage in a socially desirable response, a response that makes them look good (but not necessarily a response that would confirm the experimenter's hypothesis).
3. *Experimenter bias* (Rosenthal, 1966). This occurs when the experimenter's behavior, rather than the experimental manipulation, influences the subjects' responses. For example, if the experimenter were to nod his head in agreement when subjects listened to the expert source but not when they listened to the anonymous source, this could produce the observed difference between conditions.

Because these biasing factors can creep into the experimental situation quite unintentionally, the experimenter must be aware of them in conducting research. In most persuasion research, these biasing factors are minimized by the use of one or more of the following procedures:

a. giving subjects a *cover story*—a false rationale that presumably explains to subjects why they are participating in the study;
b. removing the attitude measure from the experimental setting;
c. testing nonobvious hypotheses that are unlikely to be guessed by subjects;
d. minimizing the status difference between the experimenter and the subjects;

e. automating experimental procedures and keeping the experimenters blind to the experimental condition that subjects are in. (See Carlsmith, Ellsworth, & Aronson, 1976; Crano & Brewer, 1973; Petty & Brock, 1981; and Rosenthal & Rosnow, 1969, for more details on the experimental method.)

Evaluating a Theory

If the experiment passes all four of the validity tests, you can conclude that source expertise increases persuasion. You may not conclude, however, that your theory of *why* source expertise increases persuasion is correct. The experiment has provided evidence for an empirical statement of the nature "X produces Y." The process by which this occurs has not been demonstrated. If you refer to the initial conceptual diagram for the example on source expertise (fig. 1.2), you will note that the theory states that source expertise enhances persuasion *by facilitating the learning of the message arguments*. This suggests that, in addition to measuring attitude change, the investigator should also obtain some measure of the number of arguments that subjects in the experimental and control groups have learned. If experimental subjects show more attitude change than control subjects and also show more learning of the message arguments, support is obtained for the investigator's theory of why source expertise works.

On the other hand, just because a researcher measures the hypothesized *mediating or process variable* (message learning in this case) and finds the expected result, this does not *prove* that the theory is correct. It might be that an expert source affects both learning and persuasion but that message learning is not what produces the persuasion. For example, an alternative theory might say that the reason an expert source sometimes produces more attitude change is that people do less thinking about messages from highly credible sources. So, if the audience would normally be counterarguing (thinking up arguments against) the position advocated, an expert source would inhibit them from doing this, and more persuasion would result than if no source were specified. Furthermore, if an investigator wanted to provide support for this hypothesis, the number of counterarguments that experimental and control subjects think of could be measured. If experimental subjects generate fewer counterarguments than control subjects, evidence for this alternative theory is obtained.

It is actually quite common for different theorists who are trying to explain the same effect to obtain data that appears to support two or more different theories. When this occurs, it is desirable to perform a *crucial experiment* (Stinchcombe, 1968)—one which attempts to set up a situation in which two plausible competing theories make different predictions about how the data should come out. For example, a crucial experiment to allow a choice between the message learning and thought inhibition explanations for the effects of source expertise might go as follows. Instead of using a message for which subjects would normally be generating many negative thoughts, a message would be used for which subjects would normally be generating many positive thoughts. According to the message-learning theory, switching the messages should make no difference. Learning should still be greater for the expert than for the anonymous source, and the expert should produce more persuasion than the anonymous source. On the other hand, according to the thought inhibition explanation, if subjects do less thinking when a message is presented by an expert, they should generate fewer thoughts than they normally do. If they normally would have generated many favorable thoughts to the message, and the expert source inhibits these favorable thoughts, the expert source might actually produce less persuasion than an anonymous source. Since the two theories make different predictions in this situation, the outcome of this simple experiment would allow a choice between them.

The Approaches to Persuasion

We have grouped the various theories of attitude change that have developed over the last forty years into seven major approaches, and these are discussed in chapters 2 through 8. Each of the approaches focuses on a different basic process to explain how and why peoples' attitudes change. The approaches are presented roughly in the order in which they captured the imagination of the discipline. All of the approaches, however, continue to retain their adherents, and all of the approaches continue to generate a great deal of research.

Our discussion of the approaches to persuasion begins in chapter 2 with theories that emphasize some rudimentary learning principles like conditioning and modeling. These approaches focus on the direct administration of rewards and punishments to the target of influence or on the effects of the target observing others being rewarded or punished for expressing certain attitudes. In chapter 3, we discuss the message-learning approach developed by Hovland and his colleagues at Yale. These researchers examined how different variables affected a person's attention to, comprehension of, yielding to, and retention of the arguments in a persuasive message. Chapter 4 presents perceptual-judgmental theories of persuasion, which focus on how a person perceives the message and how attitude judgments are made in the context of a person's past experiences. These past experiences can lead a person to distort the position of a persuasive message. Next, in chapter 5, we discuss different human motives as they relate to attitude change; we will see that certain motives, like the desire to maintain consistency between beliefs and between attitudes and behaviors, have implications for the manner in which an attitude is changed. In chapter 6 we begin our discussion of the "information processing" approaches to persuasion. The theories in this chapter examine how the inferences that a person makes about a communicator's behavior (why is he saying that?) or the person's own behavior (why am I doing this?) can have implications for a person's attitudes. The theories in chapter 7 present some precise mathematical models of how the information that a person receives in a persuasive message is evaluated and integrated to form an overall attitude about a person, object, or issue. The theories in chapter 8 emphasize the information that people generate themselves, either in response to a persuasive message or in the absence of a persuasive message.

These seven different approaches to persuasion emphasize different variables and different processes, but all of them have something to contribute to a complete understanding of how and why people's attitudes change. In the last chapter in this book, we note that, although the various theoretical approaches to persuasion differ in many ways, they really seem to indicate that there are only two fundamentally different "routes" to changing a person's attitudes. One route, which we call the *central route*, emphasizes the information that a person has about the person, object, or issue under consideration; and the other route, which we call the *peripheral route,* emphasizes just about anything else (e.g., information about the communicator or about the immediate consequences of adopting a certain attitude). As we will see later, the route responsible for persuasion appears to be an important determinant of how enduring the attitude change will be. Changes induced via the central route tend to be more permanent than changes induced via the peripheral route. We will postpone discussion of these two routes until the final chapter, but as you proceed through the different theories presented in chapters 2 through 8, you might consider whether the theory appears to emphasize a central or a peripheral route to persuasion.

Retrospective

In this chapter we have introduced the study of attitudes and persuasion. We made an important distinction between education (conveying objective facts or teaching how to think) and propaganda (making opinion appear as fact or providing a biased sample of fact to further one's own ends); it was noted that most persuasion attempts qualified as propaganda. We also distinguished between attitudes (how we feel about something), beliefs (what we know about something), and behaviors (how we act toward something); it was noted that persuasion attempts could be aimed at each of these targets. We argued that attitudes served a number of important functions for people and that attitudes could be measured both with direct self-reports and with more indirect, unobtrusive procedures. The last half of the chapter documented the conditions under which attitudes allowed prediction of behaviors and also discussed how an attitude change experiment should be conducted. With these preliminary questions behind us, we turn in the remaining chapters to the different theoretical approaches that have developed for understanding the basis of attitudes and persuasion.

Notes

[1]Verbal statements concerning one's future behavior (e.g., "The next pie I see, I will throw in Chuck's face") are called *behavioral intentions,* and they can be distinguished from the actual overt behaviors that a person performs (Fishbein & Ajzen, 1975, 1981). Although we will discuss some general factors that affect the relationship between attitudes and behaviors in this chapter, a detailed discussion of the relationships among attitudes, beliefs, intentions, and behaviors is postponed until chapter 7.

[2]When an attitude scale is called *reliable,* this means that the scale measures something consistently. Thus, the score obtained on one half of the scale should correlate highly with the other half of the scale (split-half reliability), and if there has been no real attitude change, a person should receive the same score on the scale on repeated testings (test-retest reliability).

[3]One important implication of using an attitude scale with low reliability, however, is that it will be more difficult to detect a statistically significant difference between two groups whose true attitudes are different.

[4]These problems can be overcome by separating the pretest from the posttest by a long interval or by embedding the crucial attitude measure in a series of other measures; but the longer the delay between pretest and posttest, the more likely that the subjects' attitudes will change from the pretest measure (thus invalidating it); and the longer the list of irrelevant attitude items in which the key item is embedded, the more likely extraneous factors (e.g., fatigue) are to influence the measure.

Conditioning and Modeling Approaches

2

Julie was 23 years old, from an affluent family, and had completed two years of college. Friends of Julie say that she had been dating a senior for several months. Julie was sure they would be married after he graduated, but several weeks ago they quarreled and broke up. Last weekend, she attended a retreat sponsored by a religious cult and became a member. She no longer speaks with her old friends, and she avoids many of what previously had been her favorite foods and places.

What might account for such a rapid and apparently complete change in attitudes and behavior? As in the case of Julie, a rapid conversion often follows an emotionally traumatic event in a person's life, as the past rewards associated with the person's attitudes and behaviors are suddenly removed or reversed. For instance, Julie may have enjoyed a particular restaurant with her boyfriend, but now the restaurant stirs unpleasant memories and shattered expectations. Many cults carefully foster this feeling of alienation, loneliness, and disorientation by interrupting sleep frequently, changing eating hours continually, and disallowing potential converts to see or speak with old acquaintances. These steps effectively exaggerate the dissociation between a person's attitudes and the rewards with which they were associated. In addition, steps are taken to introduce and reward attitudes that are incompatible with the person's former attitudes but consistent with the ideology of the cult (Ellul, 1965; Frank, 1961; Hunter, 1951; Oman, 1972; Schien, Schenier, & Barker, 1961).

The conversion techniques of cults provide a dramatic example of persuasion by learning principles. In this chapter, we will examine a few of the basic notions of conditioning and their counterparts in attitude theory. It will become apparent that many of our feelings and reactions to issues, objects, and events in our everyday lives are based, at least in part, upon previously conditioned responses. It should also become apparent that the techniques so effectively employed by cults are widely practiced in society today. Many of these methods are evident, though to a lesser degree, in advertisements, church sermons and propaganda, political and social campaigns, classroom discourses, and family interactions.

Learning can be described as a relatively stable change in behavior that results from prior experiences. Since no one would argue that we are born with our attitudes, there is little disagreement with the proposition that attitudes are learned. Disputes do arise, however, regarding exactly *how* attitudes are learned. In this chapter, we discuss some of the most basic explanations of how attitudes might be learned. In the next chapter we focus on verbal learning processes, and in the remaining chapters we see how a wide variety of prior experiences can affect one's attitudes.

Classical Conditioning

The most basic form of learning, termed associative learning, occurs when a connection is drawn between two events in the environment. One form, *classical conditioning,* occurs when an initially neutral stimulus (the conditioned stimulus, or CS) is associated with another stimulus (the unconditioned stimulus, or UCS) that is connected inherently or by prior conditioning to some response (the unconditioned response, or UCR). For instance, whenever you give a hungry dog a piece of meat (UCS), the dog salivates (UCR). The meat is the unconditioned stimulus, and salivating is the unconditioned response, because the meat by its very nature leads to a salivatory response in the hungry dog. Now, if you ring a bell (CS) whenever you give the dog the meat, you create a CS-UCS pairing (pairing of bell with delivery of meat). The bell doesn't inherently cause the dog to salivate, so it is called a conditioned stimulus. By pairing the bell repeatedly with the delivery of meat to the dog, however, you create a situation in which ringing the bell alone causes the dog to salivate. This salivatory response is now termed the conditioned response (CR), since it is the result of conditioning rather than of an inherent link between the stimulus and response. The process of classical conditioning and a straightforward analogy to attitude formation are illustrated in figure 2.1. The pairing of the CS and UCS, which is followed by the UCR, leads to the formation of a new association between the CS and the UCR. Soon the presentation of the CS alone elicits the response, which is then termed the conditioned response, or CR.

Classical Conditioning of Attitudes

How might this apply to attitude formation? Staats and Staats (1958) suggested that if an object or recommendation is paired repeatedly with anything that elicits either a favorable or unfavorable response, the object or recommendation will come to elicit the same type of favorable or unfavorable response. That is, an attitude will form regarding the object or recommendation.

Figure 2.1

Top panel: Illustration of the classical conditioning of salivation to a bell. *Bottom panel:* Illustration of the classical conditioning of a positive attitudinal response toward a cult. After repeated pairings of the CS and UCS, the CS alone elicits in the recruit a positive evaluative response to the cult.

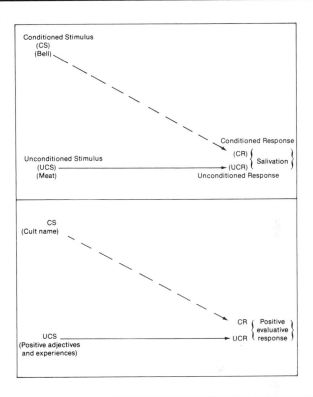

Several studies have been conducted that illustrate how attitudes might be acquired by classical conditioning; one of the first was by Razran (1940). He presented a variety of slogans (CS) to his subjects, such as "Workers of the world, unite." Subjects expressed how much they approved of each of the slogans. Later, Razran repeatedly presented these slogans to his subjects while they were either enjoying a free lunch, inhaling unpleasant odors, or sitting in a neutral setting (each served as the UCS in separate conditions of his study). Following these "conditioning trials," subjects again judged each slogan. Razran found that the slogans paired with the free lunch were approved of more than before, slogans paired with the unpleasant odors were evaluated less favorably than before, and slogans paired with the neutral environment were unaffected. He also reported that his subjects were unable to report which of the slogans were associated with the lunch, odors, and neutral conditions.

Staats, Staats, and Crawford (1962) similarly illustrated the formation of negative attitudes by pairing words with stimuli (electric shocks or loud, harsh sounds) that inherently elicited an unpleasant emotional response. Following repeated pairings with the unpleasant stimuli, the words alone were shown to subjects. When each was presented, subjects expressed their attitude, and electrodermal activity (the galvanic skin response) was monitored. Staats and his colleagues found that the words paired with the unpleasant stimuli were evaluated more negatively than control words. In addition, the words paired with unpleasant stimuli evoked increased electrodermal activity; and the more disliked the word, the larger the increase in electrodermal activity. These results were interpreted as indicating that the more successful the conditioning procedure was (as measured by the size of the electrodermal response), the more negative the attitude toward the initially neutral word became (cf. Cacioppo & Sandman, 1981; Maltzman, 1968).

Although neutral stimuli are sometimes associated with an *inherently* pleasant or unpleasant event (see fig. 2.2), neutral stimuli are often associated with words or events about which we *already have been conditioned* to feel something. Staats and Staats (1957, 1958) have proposed that *higher-order* classical conditioning accounts for the acquisition of attitudes in these instances. In higher-order conditioning, a stimulus (e.g., a word, a person) that was once neutral, but which has since attained the power to elicit an emotional response, is used as the UCS. For instance, the word *good* has no inherent qualities about it that would elicit a favorable emotional response. Past associations of the word *good* with a UCS that *did* inherently elicit favorable responses (e.g., "Drink your soda; it's good", as the child drinks) have empowered *good* with the capacity to evoke positive responses, too. The Staats asserted that pairing a neutral stimulus with stimuli about which we have learned to feel positively or negatively (such as the words *good* and *bad*) can produce a positive or negative feeling about the neutral stimulus.

This hypothesis was tested in a study disguised as an experiment on verbal learning (Staats & Staats, 1957). Subjects were instructed to learn the stimuli that were presented visually and to repeat aloud the word announced by the experimenter following each presentation. Subjects *saw* neutral nonsense syllables (e.g., laj, wuh), but *heard* words that elicited either a favorable (sweet, gift, beauty), unfavorable (ugly, sad, sour), or neutral (chair) reaction. As expected, Staats and Staats found that the subjects' attitudes toward the nonsense syllables were influenced by the type of word associated with each.

Demand Characteristics and Contingency Awareness

The studies we have reviewed so far have provided data consistent with the view that attitudes may be classically conditioned. Staats and Staats (1957) asserted that attitudes could be conditioned *without awareness*—that subjects would not know that their attitudes were being altered by the pairing of the attitude object or recommendation with an evaluatively positive or negative stimulus (such as the word *good*).

Opposing views have been proposed, however. Page (1969, 1974), for instance, argued that attitudes were not classically conditioned in the Staats's experiments, but rather that subjects guessed the experimenter's hypothesis and simply complied with his presumed wish (e.g., expressing more liking for words that are paired with positively evaluated stimuli). That is, Page argued that the results of the Staats's experiments were attributable to *demand characteristics* (recall our discussion of this problem in chapter 1).

Page (1969) replicated the Staats and Staats (1958) study and found that the only subjects who showed the conditioning effect were those who were aware of the CS–UCS *contingency* (i.e., aware that certain nonsense syllables were consistently paired with positive stimuli while others were consistently paired with negative stimuli) *and* were aware of the experimenter's hypothesis (i.e., aware of the fact that the experimenter wanted them to rate positively paired nonsense syllables favorably and negatively paired nonsense syllables unfavorably). Since then, Page and his colleagues have demonstrated that subjects who are aware, who can be made aware, or who are especially likely to become aware of the CS–UCS contingency may account for the conditioning effect observed in the Staats's studies (Kahle & Page, 1976; Page & Kahle, 1976).

To determine which subjects are "aware" and which are not, Page uses what he calls a "funnel interview." Briefly, Page interviews each subject following their participation in the conditioning experiment. He begins by asking them general questions about the experiment, but as the interview progresses, he asks more and more specific questions about what they thought the experimental hypothesis might be. Any subject who, during this increasingly leading interview, states the contingency, is deemed "contingency aware." Any subject who states the correct hypothesis is deemed "demand aware." Staats has criticized Page's use of the funnel interview, noting that the subjects' attitudes may have been conditioned without awareness, but that the leading questions asked of them following their participation in the study may have suggested to them the nature of the contingency and the experimenter's hypothesis (Staats, Minke, Martin, & Higa, 1972). Subjects who are conditioned without awareness therefore may become aware not during the course of the conditioning, as Page argues, but during the postexperimental interview.

Figure 2.2

What we like may depend on classical conditioning. When something neutral (like alien beings in the cartoon or Jordache jeans in the advertisement) is paired with something that elicits a positive affective reaction (like food or sexy models), the neutral stimulus may come to evoke a positive evaluative response.

Reprinted by permission. © 1980 by Warner Bros., Inc.

Experimental demands are especially problematic when the subjects know that their attitudes are being measured. If subjects' attitudes were assessed in what they believed was a separate experiment, then there would be few, if any, experimental demands with which the subjects might comply, and a better test of the classical conditioning of attitudes could be obtained. This line of reasoning was developed by Berkowitz and Knurek (1969); they demonstrated that attitudes formed by classical conditioning in one study could influence a person's interpersonal behavior in an "unrelated" second study. Specifically, they presented a long list of names to each subject. Using the procedure employed by Staats and Staats (1957), Berkowitz and Knurek developed a negative attitude in half of their subjects toward the name *George* and a negative attitude in the other half of their subjects toward the name *Ed*. Following the conditioning trials, each subject was taken to a second laboratory for what was presumably a different experiment. The subject was asked to engage in a discussion with two other subjects (who were actually the experimenter's confederates) named Ed and George.[1] The confederates were unaware of whether the subject had been conditioned to dislike the name *Ed* or *George*. Nevertheless, the confederate who bore the name that the subject had been trained to dislike reported that the subject was less friendly toward him than the confederate who bore the neutral name. These results suggest that demand characteristics are not necessary for the classical conditioning of attitudes.

Zanna, Kiesler, and Pilkonis (1970) also used what subjects believed were separate experiments to demonstrate the classical conditioning of attitudes. In the "first" study, subjects were told that they would receive a series of electric shocks while their physiological activity was recorded. The ostensible goal of the study was to develop a more sensitive measure of physiological responses. Subjects were told that it was important to relax between the shocks to get "a baseline measure of physiological responding" (p. 324). A spoken word signaled the onset of the shock; a second spoken word signaled its offset. For half the subjects, the word *light* signaled onset and the word *dark* signaled offset of the shock; for the other half of the subjects, these signal words were reversed. Since shock onset was unpleasant and shock offset was (relatively) pleasant, Zanna et al. predicted that favorable and unfavorable attitudes, respectively, would be conditioned to these signal words.

Afterwards, subjects' attitudes toward the words *light* and *dark* (and related words, i.e., *black, white*) were measured in what appeared to be an unrelated experiment. This "second" study was conducted by a different experimenter who was unaware of the conditioning contingencies. These precautions were taken to reduce the demand characteristics inherent in most of the studies we discussed above. Their hypotheses were confirmed: words that signaled the onset of shock were evaluated more negatively, and words that signaled the offset of the shock were evaluated more positively than control (nonconditioned) words. Interestingly, the conditioning effect also appeared on the related words.

Together, these studies suggest that attitudes can be influenced by classical conditioning processes. The work of Page and his colleagues makes it clear that subjects are not passive participants in studies of attitude change, but the existing data suggest that demand characteristics are not necessary for the classical conditioning of attitudes. It is important to note that once the demand awareness problem can be ruled out, contingency awareness *per se* does not rule out a classical conditioning explanation of attitude change. For example, Gormezano and his colleagues have argued that whether or not people are aware of the contingencies in a classical conditioning procedure should be considered a moot question (Coleman & Gormezano, 1979; Gormezano & Kehoe, 1975; Moore & Gormezano, 1977). That is, people may be able to express the contingency but nevertheless have their attitudes altered by the association of the attitude object with the unconditioned stimulus. Indeed, although being able to state the contingency may not be necessary for the conditioning of attitudes, it may be related in these studies because it discriminates between subjects who paid attention to the experimental tasks and those who did not.

In sum, the Staats and Staats (1957) assertion that the conditioning of attitudes occurs "mindlessly" may be an overstatement, but attitudes do appear to be susceptible to the influence of classical conditioning processes. People tend to like objects and recommendations that previously have been paired with unconditioned stimuli that elicit positive affective responses (e.g., pleasant scenery) and to dislike objects and recommendations that previously have been paired with unconditioned stimuli that elicit negative affective responses (e.g., unpleasant odors).

Operant Conditioning

Operant conditioning is a second type of associative learning that occurs when some response becomes more (or less) likely because of its positive (or negative) consequences. The process of operant conditioning and an application to attitudes are presented in figure 2.3. Operant conditioning is based upon the supposition that people act to maximize the positive and minimize the negative consequences of their behavior (Skinner, 1938).

Operant Conditioning of Attitudes

We may come to adhere strongly to attitudes that yield rewards and to reject attitudes that result in punishments. For instance, "winners" in a debate are rewarded for taking a particular stand on an issue, whereas "losers" suffer "the agony of defeat." Scott (1957) showed that "winners" changed their attitudes in the direction of their advocacy; "losers," on the other hand, changed their attitudes away from the position they advocated.[2] In another study, Bostrom, Vlandis, and Rosenbaum (1961) induced students to write a counterattitudinal essay. The experimenters then randomly awarded the essays the grade of *A* or *D*. They found that students who received an *A* changed their attitude toward the position they advocated significantly more than students who received a *D*. You may have noticed that you get the best grades typically in courses you like most. An implication of the operant conditioning of attitudes is that your liking for the course is, at least in part, due to the rewards that you receive in the course.

Theoretical interest in the operant conditioning approach followed an experiment by Greenspoon (1955), in which he used verbal rewards to change what people would say. Greenspoon was able to increase the frequency with which a person used a plural noun simply by saying "mm-hmmm" each time the subject used one. Hildum and Brown (1956) hypothesized that attitude statements could be conditioned in the same way. They telephoned students at Harvard and questioned them about their attitudes toward Harvard's educational system. For half of the students, the experimenter said "good" or "mm-hmmm" every time a student praised the Harvard system; for the other half of the subjects, the experimenter said "good" or "mm-hmmm" every time a student criticized the educational system. Hildum and Brown found that the students who were rewarded for praising the system made more positive comments about it than students who were rewarded for criticizing the system.

Does this type of conditioning actually influence a person's attitude? After all, the students may have increased the frequency of their positive or negative comments about the Harvard educational system simply to maintain a civil telephone conversation. A series of studies on the verbal conditioning of attitudes suggests that people actually *do* change their attitudes as a result of rewards and

Figure 2.3

Repeated rewards for a response increase the likelihood of that response. This principle is illustrated in the panels. *Top panel:* Illustration of the operant conditioning paradigm (adapted from Staats, 1975). *Bottom panel:* Illustration of the operant conditioning of a positive attitudinal response toward a cult.

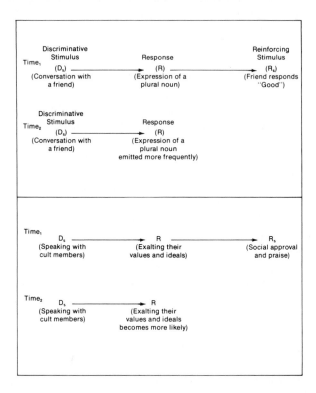

that these attitudes persist. In one study, conducted by Insko (1965) at the University of Hawaii, students were telephoned and interviewed about their attitudes toward establishing a Springtime Aloha Week Festival. Students heard fourteen statements about the issue and responded to each by indicating the extent to which they agreed or disagreed with it. Half of the students were rewarded with the word *good* every time they endorsed a statement favoring a Springtime Aloha Week Festival, and half were rewarded with the word *good* every time they endorsed a statement unfavorable toward the festival.

One week later, Insko asked the students in his classes to complete a multi-item attitude questionnaire. Among the students were those who had been interviewed (and conditioned) on the telephone the previous week, and among the issues toward which the students expressed their attitudes was a Springtime Aloha Week Festival. Insko found that students who had been rewarded for making favorable statements about the festival expressed a more positive attitude toward the festival on this posttest than students who had been rewarded for making unfavorable statements. These differences in attitude were obtained even though the measurement of the students' attitudes occurred a week after conditioning and in a very different setting.

Dulany (1962) raised the issue of demand characteristics in verbal conditioning. He noted that the subjects who evidenced a "conditioning effect" were also aware of the contingencies (e.g., whenever I say a plural noun, the experimenter says, "good") and thus may have been aware of the experimenter's hypothesis. Several other studies, however, suggest that demand characteristics need not operate to condition attitudes. For instance, in Insko's (1965) study, the telephone interview avoided the experimental demands associated with laboratory studies; and the measurement of the subjects' attitudes occurred in a different context and in a manner that eliminated suspicion on the part of the subjects (see also Insko, 1967). Furthermore, if experimental demands contribute to the verbal conditioning of attitudes in the laboratory, then dramatic differences should be observed when the conditioning procedures are applied in an experiment versus in a telephone interview, where subjects do not know they are in an experiment. Insko and Melson (1969) conducted such a study and found approximately the same pattern of results in the two settings.

Two-factor Theory of Verbal Conditioning

Though demand characteristics do not seem to be operating, social pressures to conform may contribute to the effectiveness of operant conditioning. Insko and Cialdini (1969; Cialdini & Insko, 1969) proposed that a verbal reward (e.g., "good") does two things: "First, it provides information as to the interviewer's attitude. Second, it tells the subject that the interviewer approves of or likes the agree-disagree responses and thus by implication approves of or likes the subject himself" (Insko & Cialdini, 1969, p. 334). The rapport created by the second process provides the subject with further incentive to emit the rewarded response, which obtains positive consequences for the subject (i.e., implicit approval by another person).

To test their two-factor theory of attitudinal verbal conditioning, Insko and Cialdini (1969) contacted 175 students by telephone and asked them the extent to which they agreed with twelve attitude statements regarding pay TV. Approximately half of the subjects were conditioned for statements favoring pay

Table 2.1

Factors That Influence the Verbal Conditioning of Attitudes

| | | Psychological Variable | |
		Information	Rapport
Verbal Responses by the Experimenter	"Good"	Moderate	High
	"Good" and "Humph"	High	Moderate
	"Humph"	Moderate	Low

*Entries in the box designate the extent to which the psychological variables underlying the verbal conditioning of attitudes (information and rapport) exist as a function of the experimenter's verbal responses. See the text for a complete discussion.

TV and the other half for statements disfavoring it. The experimenter said "good" after the subject's appropriate attitudinal responses (what was "appropriate" depended upon the condition the subject was in); some heard the experimenter say "humph" in a disapproving manner following inappropriate responses; and some heard both "good" following appropriate responses and "humph" following inappropriate responses. Insko and Cialdini reasoned that hearing "good" rather than "humph" would produce better conditioning, even though their informational value was equal, since the "good" leads to greater rapport (i.e., it implies that the experimenter likes the subject). Hearing both "good" and "humph" provides more information about the interviewer's attitudes but decreases slightly the rapport developed when only "good" is used (see table 2.1). Insko and Cialdini therefore reasoned that conditioning should be equally as effective for subjects who heard both "good" *and* "humph" as for subjects who heard only "good"; and that both these conditions should produce better conditioning than "humph" alone.[3] Insko and Cialdini obtained these results and found conditioning whether or not subjects were aware of the reward contingency.

Attitudinal responses, then, are affected by their consequences. When the expression of an attitude leads to positive consequences, the attitude is strengthened (Kerpelman & Himmelfarb, 1971). Accordingly, the more a person is rewarded for advocating a counterattitudinal position, the more a person's attitude may move toward that position (Elms & Janis, 1965). We will discuss this further in chapter 8, and we will discuss some important exceptions to this in chapter 5. In box 2.1 we note that not only can rewards influence attitudes, but that attitudes can serve as rewards.

Attitudes as Rewards

As we have shown thus far, the consequences of holding a particular attitude can alter the strength with which the attitude is held. For instance, if a friend praises your position on a particular issue, you likely will hold the position more strongly, since your attitude yielded positive consequences for you. Interestingly, research by Byrne and his colleagues suggests that your attitudes, and attitudes similar to your own, can serve as reinforcers for you and influence whom you consider to be your friend (e.g., Arenson & Morisano, 1977; Byrne, Young, & Griffitt, 1966; Clore & Byrne, 1974). Byrne has shown that people tend to be attracted to others who hold attitudes similar to their own. This means that if a friend of yours criticized you for your attitudes on a number of different issues, this would not only weaken the strength with which you held these attitudes (since they led to negative consequences), but you also would begin to like your friend less (since he or she has been paired repeatedly, as a conditioned stimulus, with dissimilar attitudinal positions—negative unconditioned stimuli). Note that the weakening of your attitudes can be explained in terms of *operant* conditioning, whereas the budding dislike for your friend can be explained in terms of *classical* conditioning.

Observational Learning

Often people learn which responses are rewarded and which are not by *observing* (rather than directly experiencing) the consequences of the behaviors of other people. Consider the television advertisement that depicts a young woman student alone in her room. Her roommate enters and suggests that she use a certain brand of toothpaste. Shortly thereafter, both women are seen with attractive dates and in apparent bliss. This advertisement is meant to change viewers' attitudes and behaviors by showing a rewarding sequence of events (the toothpaste leading to dates). To the extent that this is effective, *observational learning* has occurred (see fig. 2.4).

In the example of the toothpaste ad, the actions and outcomes of another person, who is called the *model*, were designed to influence the viewers attitudes and purchases. That is, the model's behavior was intentionally designed to influence attitudes and behavior. Even more common, particularly among children, are unintentional effects of modeling. For instance, imagine a father who preaches to his children that prejudice is wrong but who practices discrimination. The children's attitudes and behaviors may be more affected by their father's actions than by his words, especially when his *actions* are rewarded (Miller & Dollard, 1941; Rosenbaum & Tucker, 1962).

Figure 2.4

Top panel: Illustration of the observational learning of smoking after dinner. *Bottom panel:* Illustration of observational learning of a positive attitudinal response toward a cult. Repeated observations of rewards following a model's response increase the likelihood of the observer emitting the response.

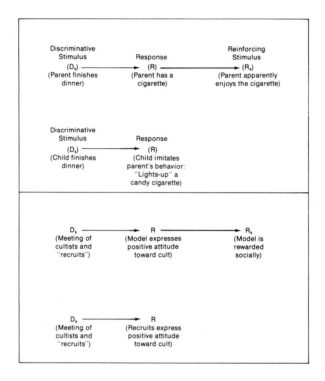

In a series of studies on compliance (e.g., Bryan, Redfield, & Mader, 1971; Bryan & Walbek, 1970), children were exposed to an adult model who either preached charity or greed and who practiced either charity or greed when asked for a donation. They found that what the model did influenced the children's donation to the charity more than what the model said. Rushton (1975) generally found the same result, even when the model's comments were directed at the children's behavior rather than couched in general terms (e.g., "You should be unselfish" rather than "People should be unselfish"). When Rushton assessed the children's charitable behavior two months later, he again found that the model's behavior was more influential than preaching.

Figure 2.5

A model's use of a product is shown to cause a positive outcome. This sequence is designed so that, by observational learning, the advertiser's product will come to evoke a positive evaluative response.

Most of the research on observational learning has focused on children, but it has been shown in adults as well (Gewirtz & Stingle, 1968). Indeed, millions of dollars each year are spent on commercials for adults in which the use of a product is shown to benefit a model (see fig. 2.5). But Bandura (1965) has drawn an important distinction between the *acquisition* and the *performance* of a response by observational learning. Viewers of a commercial may *know* the advertiser's message (e.g., using a certain mouthwash makes one a more desirable date) but choose *not* to use the product. Bandura has stressed that incentive or motivational factors are also important. Briefly, he asserts that people must believe that the rewards associated with the model's actions hold for them as well as the model *and* that these outcomes are worth the relative costs of performing the response (e.g., driving to the store and buying that particular product). Unless *both* of these conditions are met, observational learning may not lead to performance of the modeled behavior.

Vicarious Classical Conditioning

Vicarious classical conditioning represents a combination of classical conditioning and observational learning principles. What distinguishes vicarious classical conditioning from classical conditioning is that, in the former, the UCS is a strong emotional reaction on the part of a social model. Specifically, vicarious classical conditioning operates when a neutral stimulus (CS), initially incapable of eliciting a strong emotional reaction from observers, gradually acquires that ability when paired with signs of strong emotional reactions on the part of another person (i.e., the model). In other words, the emotional response on the part of one person acts as a UCS and is capable of eliciting a UCR in the form of a similar emotional response in an observer (see fig. 2.6).

The first experimental demonstration of vicarious classical conditioning was reported by Berger (1962). Subjects ("observers") watched a confederate (the model) receive what they thought were electric shocks. (In fact, no shocks were administered.) Each supposed shock was preceded by a buzzer (the CS) and was accompanied by a dimming light and an arm jerk by the model, which presumably signified a strong pain reaction. Three control groups were also included. In one, subjects saw a model receive shocks, but there was no arm movement (and thus no modeled pain). A second group of subjects saw the model display an arm movement when the light dimmed, but there was no mention of electric shock and thus the arm movement did not indicate a strong emotional reaction. In the third group, subjects heard a buzzer, but it was followed by neither an electric shock nor an arm movement by the model. Berger found that the greatest increases in emotional responses by observers (as indicated by changes in electrodermal, or sweating, activity) occurred following the buzzer when the arm movements were presumably reflecting a strong emotional reaction (pain) to an electric shock.

Vaughan and Lanzetta (1980), reporting similar results, found that observers' facial expressions could be vicariously conditioned to a stimulus that was initially neutral (the CS). In their study, subjects watched a person exhibit a painful facial expression (rather than an arm jerk) following a tone (the CS) and an electric shock. After a number of pairings of the tone and painful expression on the part of the model in response to the shock, subjects too began to show subtle painlike facial expressions when the tone was sounded (see also Venn & Short, 1973).

This research suggests that an initially neutral stimulus (such as a tone or a light) can become capable of eliciting a strong positive or negative attitude from people simply because they repeatedly observe others responding positively or negatively to it. Though this possibility has received little empirical attention, it suggests how people might acquire positive or negative attitudes, for example, toward a minority group, even though they know very little about or have never been directly exposed to the attitude object (e.g., the minority group). For instance, consider the case of Tom, a very young boy whose parents hold a strong prejudice against Eskimos. Tom has never heard his parents talk about Eskimos,

Figure 2.6

Top panel: Illustration of the vicarious classical conditioning of emotional arousal (based on data from Berger, 1962). *Bottom panel:* Illustration of the vicarious classical conditioning of a negative attitudinal response toward persons who are not supportive of the cult. After repeated pairing of the CS and UCS, the CS alone elicits in the observer a negative emotional reaction toward the nonsupportive person (e.g., a parent or old friend).

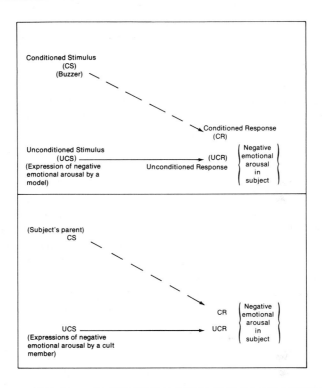

and he knows very little about them except that they are hard-working people who live in the Arctic. But on several occasions, Tom and his parents were watching television when a news story about Eskimos was reported. Tom was never able to hear the news story because, the moment the word *Eskimo* was mentioned, his father and mother would become enraged. Their faces would contort; their tone of voice would become more harsh; and their language, though incomprehensible to Tom, would sound extremely unpleasant. After several such episodes, the mere mention of the word Eskimo, or an encounter with a person whom Tom identified as an Eskimo, came to elicit strong negative affective responses in Tom as well.

Evaluation

We began our discussion of learning theories with an example of someone changing his or her attitudes toward people and places. In this chapter, we have surveyed several means by which some of these changes might have occurred. Several conclusions from our brief review seem warranted. First, there seems to be no single way in which attitudes are learned. Attitudes are complex mental structures that can serve one or more of a variety of functions (see chap. 1), and they can be acquired in a variety of ways.

Second, people can develop and change their attitudes even though they are not purposely trying to do so. People seldom set out to change their attitudes, but rather they usually are exposed to situations and information that cause them to think and feel differently about some object or issue. Attitudes are developed and changed in the process.

Third, most support for conditioning models of attitudes comes from research that has used unfamiliar and/or neutral stimuli as attitude objects. This means that most of this research pertains to the formation of new attitudes rather than the changing of old ones. People sometimes do display very little thought when altering their feelings about a stimulus (Zajonc, 1968, 1980), but this normally occurs when people are unfamiliar with or unknowledgeable about the stimulus (Grush, 1979). As people learn more about a stimulus (e.g., a minority group), their thoughts about it become increasingly more important determinants of their attitude toward it. Thus, although the same basic principles of learning may operate when forming new attitudes and changing old attitudes, the simple learning principles outlined in the present chapter will be a more potent influence on new rather than on well-established attitudes.[4]

Retrospective

The first major approach to attitudes and persuasion that we have presented has focused on relatively simple principles of learning, including classical and operant conditioning and observational learning (modeling). This rudimentary learning approach has emphasized ways to change a person's attitude by associating the attitude object with other stimuli like food or electric shock that already produce positive or negative responses (classical conditioning), by directly rewarding or punishing a person for expressing certain attitudes (instrumental conditioning), or by exposing the person to another person who is rewarded or punished for expressing certain attitudes (observational learning). In the next chapter, we discuss the message learning model that was proposed by Carl Hovland and his colleagues to explain attitude change. This approach assumes that learning the verbal content of a message is a primary determinant of attitude change, but the notion of rewards is also fundamental to Hovland's analysis. In Hovland's model, however, the rewards are often viewed as residing within the persuasive message, rather than being extraneous to it.

Notes

[1]Few subjects became suspicious about the confederates' names being the same as those the subjects previously saw. Berkowitz and Knurek suggest that this possibly is because such a large number of names were used in the conditioning phase of the study.

[2]Alternatively, debaters often may agree more with the position advocated by the "winner" because the reasons he or she gave during the debate for holding that position were convincing to both. We discuss this process of attitude change in chapter 8.

[3]We should note that Insko and Cialdini's analysis assumes that the reinforcers "good" and "humph" are equal with respect to their informational values and balanced with respect to their rapport value. Thus, each is presumed to contribute equally, though in opposing directions, to the development of rapport. In addition, it is assumed that the information value gained by saying "humph" equals the rapport value lost by saying it.

[4]Weiss's (1962, 1968) learning theory of persuasion and Wolpe's (1958) work on systematic desensitization might be invoked to explain some forms of attitude change; but these positions are not discussed here since neither has received widespread application in social psychology.

The Message-learning Approach

3

The president awakens one morning to headlines announcing that research using laboratory animals has proven that a popular food additive causes cancer. Realizing that he will be questioned about the issue, the president quickly calls a breakfast meeting of his cabinet. At breakfast, he admits that he personally enjoys many of the foods that contain the additive and that, due to habit, his initial reaction is to support the continued use of the additive in foods.

The secretary of the Department of Health and Human Services immediately suggests that the president reconsider his position. The secretary argues that the food additive be banned immediately for reasons of public safety. Citing statistics from the study reported in the newspaper, the secretary offers many reasons for this recommendation. The secretary ends by stating that the president would do best politically and morally to ban the additive.

The president *attends* carefully to the secretary's presentation, trying to *comprehend* and *remember* the secretary's advocacy and arguments. From the president's expression, the secretary's appeal about the political benefits of the recommendation is weighing heavily in his decision. The president pauses, thinks of the issue, his old attitude toward it, and the new attitude and arguments that have been offered. As the president rehearses and learns the new attitude and arguments, the issue becomes more powerfully linked to them than to his old attitude. The president has been persuaded. The food additive is banned.

Skills Learning as a Model for Persuasion

This scenario of communication and attitude change exemplifies the message-learning approach championed by Carl Hovland and his colleagues at Yale University in the 1950s (Hovland, Janis, & Kelley, 1953). In this chapter, we discuss the influence of the Yale Communication and Attitude Change Program and their message-learning approach to the study of attitudes and persuasion.

The Yale group never proposed a formal "theory" of attitude change, but rather they were guided by "working assumptions." These assumptions were loosely translated from principles of how people learn verbal and motor skills.

They suggested that a persuasive communication must gain a person's attention and must be comprehended. The person then must mentally rehearse the message arguments and conclusion, thereby establishing a link between the issue and these implicit responses. This rehearsal presumably established a memory trace for the arguments and conclusion, which was important because, for the Yale researchers, a communication had to be remembered to be persuasive.

Attending, comprehending, and remembering the message conclusion and arguments were only part of the story, however. Imagine for a moment that you are listening to a concert pianist teach a novice to play the piano. The pianist is playing at a very elementary level, displaying little of the skill that has gained her acclaim. She knows how to play the piano beautifully, but incentives in the present situation elicit none of her virtuosity. *Incentives*, which are promised or expected rewards, are also important in the Yale group's analysis of attitude change. Let's again consider our beginning example. The president may understand his secretary's advocacy and arguments but remain unconvinced until someone points out the political benefits of (or incentives for) adopting the advocated position. Hence, retention of the message arguments is important because it indicates that the person has attended, comprehended, and learned the persuasive communication. But Hovland and his colleagues believed that attitude change would occur only if the incentive for the new attitudinal position outweighed those associated with the initial attitude. Thus, attention, comprehension, and retention are necessary but not sufficient preconditions for attitude change.

Determinants of Attitude Change in Persuasive Communications

Hovland and his colleagues organized their studies of communication and attitude change around the question, "Who says what to whom with what effect?" (Smith, Lasswell, & Casey, 1946). They examined the effects on attitudes of the *source* (who said it), *message* (what was said), and *recipient* (to whom it was said). The effects of the *channel* (medium) of the communication and the *persistence* (durability) of message retention and attitude change were also studied. The interrelationships among these factors and the fundamental processes of attention, comprehension, yielding, and retention are illustrated in figure 3.1.

In sum, according to the message-learning approach, persuasive contexts (e.g., sources, messages) question a recipient's initial attitude, recommend the adoption of a new attitude, and provide incentives (e.g., promises to reduce an unpleasant drive-state such as fear) for attending to, understanding, yielding to, and retaining the new rather than the initial attitude.

Figure 3.1

According to the message-learning approach, the fundamental processes in attitude change are attention, comprehension, yielding, and retention. These processes are affected by source, message, recipient, and channel factors.

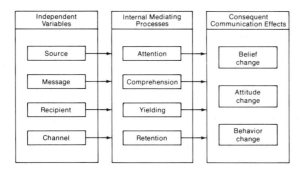

Source Factors

The originator or *source* of a persuasive communication may be a person (e.g., the president of the United States), a group (e.g., your family), an institution (e.g., Stanford University), and so forth. Identification of the source provides the audience with information above and beyond the arguments presented in the message. The typical method of studying source effects is as follows: everyone receives the same communication, but different subsets of people are given different sources to which to attribute the message. For example, 20 students may be asked to read a newspaper editorial, but half of the students are told that the university president authored it, whereas the other half are told that a cook from a dining hall authored it. After reading the editorial, students are asked their attitude about the position advocated in the editorial. Any differences in attitude change between the two groups of students would be attributable to source factors, since all other features of the study are the same for both groups.

Components of the Source Variable

Why might attitude change be different among groups of people if only the purported source of the message, and not the message itself, differed? According to the message-learning approach, incentives, which are one of the final links in the chain of events leading to attitude change, are affected by source factors. Hovland, Janis, and Kelley (1953) speculated about three source factors that would influence incentives and thereby influence attitude change. First, Hovland et al. noted that holding a "correct" attitude was associated with rewards in the past. They hypothesized that since experts are supposed to be more knowledgeable (and more often right) than nonexperts, advocacies by experts, all else equal, should be more readily accepted than advocacies by nonexperts. Second, Hovland et al. reasoned that being influenced by someone who was *untrustworthy* or who had manipulative intent has led to negative consequences for individuals in the past. Hence, recipients who thought the communication was untrustworthy, or who had suspicions about a source's *persuasive intent*, should show less attitude change than recipients who were not suspicious. Third, Hovland et al. noted that social approval was rewarding. They suggested that when adoption of a new attitude would gain the approval of others, attitude change would occur. Furthermore, *similar* communicators should be more persuasive than dissimilar communicators, since people seek the approval of similar people more than of dissimilar people.

In the following sections, we examine the evidence for these hypotheses. In the early studies, expertise and trustworthiness were manipulated together under the heading of "communicator credibility." We begin our review with these studies.

Communicator Credibility

The attitudinal effects of communicator credibility, or overall believability of the source, have been extensively studied. Most of the early research showed that a high credibility source was more persuasive than a low credibility source if attitudes were measured immediately after the message. For instance, Lorge (1936) found that people agreed more with statements attributed to respected and trusted sources, such as Abraham Lincoln, than with the same statements when they were attributed to nonrespected, nontrusted sources, such as Vladmir Lenin.[1]

Hovland and his colleagues suggested that a low credibility source cues the recipients that the conclusion of the message is not to be believed. The Yale group examined this notion using a variety of communications and communicators. For example, Hovland and Weiss (1951) presented a message about the practicality of building an atomic-powered submarine. Half of the subjects were told that the message was from U.S. physicist Robert Oppenheimer (high credibility), whereas half were told that the message was from the Russian newspaper *Pravda* (low credibility). In a different study (Kelman and Hovland, 1953), subjects listened to a message in which more lenient treatment of juvenile delinquents was advocated either by a prestigious juvenile court judge (high credibility) or by a man who had recently been arrested for peddling dope (low credibility). Generally, these studies found that a high-credibility source was more persuasive immediately following the message than a moderate- or low-credibility source.

Contrary to the message-learning approach, however, later research has shown that high-credibility sources are not always more persuasive than moderate or low-credibility sources. For instance, if you are approached by and freely choose to listen to a person advocate that nuclear power plants ought to be banned entirely, you might be more persuaded if the person is unattractive or moderate in credibility than if the person is attractive or high in credibility. We shall postpone discussion of these more complicated processes until chapters 5 and 8.

To summarize briefly, people sometimes accept or reject an advocacy immediately following its presentation on the basis of source cues rather than on the basis of the content of the message. This is especially likely to occur when (a) the source clearly possesses either high or low credibility so that the recipient need not carefully attend to know how to react to the advocacy (Husek, 1965); and (b) the communication pertains to an issue that is not personally relevant or significant to the recipient so that there is little reason to devote much attention to the message (Petty & Cacioppo, 1981; Sigall & Helmreich, 1969). We should note that most of the research issues employed by the Hovland group were specifically selected to be of a low-involving nature. When the messages are on personally involving topics, the credibility effect is less pronounced (see chapter 8).

Aspects of Communicator Credibility

Initially, researchers didn't distinguish among the attitudinal effects of the various characteristics that contribute to a communicator's credibility. For instance, in Kelman and Hovland's (1953) study, a juvenile court judge (high credibility) and a person who had recently been arrested for drug peddling (low credibility) served as the sources of a message about the treatment of juvenile delinquents. The judge and drug peddler might differ in terms of credibility for a number of reasons (Liska, 1978). The judge differs from the drug-peddler in terms of knowledge on the topic of treating delinquents (expertise), motive to speak honestly about the topic (trustworthiness), and so forth.

Could expertise alone account for the facilitating effects of communicator credibility? This question was addressed by Bochner and Insko (1966). They presented a written communication to subjects under the guise of a reading comprehension test. The message concerned the number of hours of sleep per night that people actually needed and was attributed to either a Nobel prize-winning physiologist (high expertise) or a YMCA director (low expertise). Although the arguments contained in the message were identical in all instances, some subjects read that people needed eight hours of sleep per night, others that people needed seven hours, some six hours, and so on down to zero hours of sleep per night. Note that the Nobel prize–winning physiologist and the YMCA director both are trustworthy sources. Neither has any apparent motives for misleading subjects. Nevertheless, Bochner and Insko found that the more extreme the advocacy by the highly expert source (at least until he argued for zero hours of sleep), the more attitude change that was produced. Similarly, when a low expert source moved from advocating positions that differed slightly to moderately from the recipients' (people need only five hours of sleep), more attitude change was produced; but as the less expert source advocated more and more extreme positions (two hours of sleep per night), less and less attitude change was produced. Expertise was therefore important in inducing attitude change especially when the advocated position was quite different from the recipients' initial attitude. In the next chapter, we will see how another theory—social judgment theory—can account for the interaction of credibility and discrepancy. The data from the Bochner and Insko study are graphed in figure 4.3 in the next chapter (p. 105).

What are the effects of *trustworthiness*? Hovland and his colleagues initially believed that greater trustworthiness produces greater attitude change. To test this notion, Hovland and Mandell (1952) manipulated trustworthiness while keeping the expertise of the sources approximately equal. Subjects heard a communication attributed to either an academic economist (high trustworthiness–high expertise) or the head of an import firm (moderate trustworthiness–high expertise) that advocated devaluing U.S. currency. (Devaluation would increase the profits of the import firm, so the head of the firm had something to gain by recommending that the U.S. devalue the dollar.) Hovland and Mandell found no differences in the attitude change produced by these two sources.

This study suggests that communicators arguing for their vested interests can sometimes be just as persuasive as those who have nothing to gain or lose by the advocacy. In most instances, however, whether or not a source is arguing for personal gain *does* make a difference. First, as the topic becomes more personally involving to the recipients, the source's trustworthiness becomes a more important determinant of attitude change (e.g., Choo, 1964; Craig & McCann, 1978). Second, Andreoli and Worchel (1978) have suggested that trustworthy sources (e.g., newscasters) are particularly persuasive compared to untrustworthy sources (e.g., candidates) when they deliver their message through a medium that highlights source characteristics, such as when they deliver the message on television rather than in printed form. This effect may be related to the increased attention and thought given to source characteristics that result when the communicator is visible throughout the message (which is more common in the audiovisual than the print medium). Third, sources arguing *against* their vested interests are more persuasive than ones arguing *for* their vested interests, especially when the sources initially appeared untrustworthy rather than moderately or highly trustworthy (Walster, Aronson, & Abrahams, 1966). In other words, the source who violates our expectations by being trustworthy when we expected untrustworthiness is especially effective. (We discuss this effect further in chapter 6.)

Intent to Persuade

Trustworthiness has also been examined by varying whether or not recipients were told that the source wants to persuade them. A source who has persuasive intent is presumed to be less trustworthy than one who simply wants to communicate some message to the audience. What are the attitudinal effects of persuasive intent? The initial studies of this question produced what appeared to be a flurry of conflicting results. Several studies indicated that persuasive intent reduced attitude change (e.g., Hass & Grady, 1975; Kiesler & Kiesler, 1964), whereas other investigations found no effects for persuasive intent (e.g., McGuire & Papageorgis, 1962). Papageorgis (1968) noted in an early review that the attitudinal effects of persuasive intent appeared to depend upon the involvement or personal importance of the issue to the recipient. Experiments that used involving issues demonstrated that foreknowledge of persuasive intent reduced the effectiveness of the message, whereas studies that used issues of low personal involvement indicated that a source's intent had no effect—the same pattern of findings that is observed for sources who argue for their own vested interests.

Petty and Cacioppo (1979a) tested the notion that issue involvement altered the attitudinal effects of persuasive intent. Students were told that they would evaluate radio editorials. Half were told that "the tape was designed specifically to try to persuade you and other college students of the desirability of changing certain college regulations," whereas others were instructed that "the tape was prepared as part of a journalism class project on radio recordings," which served to disguise the persuasive intent of the communicator. After these instructions, all subjects heard a three-minute message advocating that university seniors be required to pass a comprehensive exam in their major prior to graduation.

Involvement was manipulated by changing the introductory paragraph of the communication. Some subjects were told that these exams might be instituted at their institution by the end of the year, thereby making it likely that the proposal would affect the subjects. Other subjects were told that these exams might be instituted elsewhere by the end of the year; and still other subjects were told that the exams might be instituted at their institution but not until ten years later. The subjects would not be affected *personally* by the proposal in these latter two cases.

Two aspects of Petty and Cacioppo's findings are important here. First, the results confirmed the notion that a forewarning of persuasive intent inhibited attitude change more when the issue was personally important rather than unimportant. Second, persuasive intent had no effect on the number of message arguments that subjects could recall. This result suggests that there were no differences among the various groups in attending, comprehending, and learning the arguments contained in the message (see also Watts & Holt, 1979). We will see in chapter 5 that a forewarning of persuasive intent appears to reduce persuasion by motivating the recipient to counterargue the message while listening to it.

Figure 3.2

Source attractiveness can be an important determinant of attitudes. (Copyright 1979 by Field Enterprises, Inc. Used with permission.)

DUNAGIN'S PEOPLE

"I DON'T LIKE HIS FOREIGN OR DOMESTIC POLICY, HIS ENERGY PROGRAM OR HIS ECONOMIC PLAN... BUT I LOVE THE WAY HE PARTS HIS HAIR!"

Communicator Attractiveness

Two communicators may be trusted experts on some issue, but one may be more liked or more physically attractive than the other. What is their relative power to influence people?

Consider the televised debates between Richard Nixon and John Kennedy during the 1960 presidential campaign. Both men were articulate, experienced debaters; both were very knowledgeable about the issues in the campaign; and both had logical arguments to support their respective positions. John Kennedy, however, was considered by many to be a more likable communicator than Richard Nixon, in part because of his physical appearance, style of speaking, and mannerisms. For instance, Kennedy squarely faced the camera when he spoke and gazed directly into the lens, giving the appearance of looking the American public directly in the eye, which enhanced his credibility (Hemsley & Doob, 1978). Nixon, on the other hand, shifted his eyes as he spoke and seldom gazed directly into the camera. Kennedy won a close election partially because of Kennedy's superior appearance during the television debates (McGinniss, 1968; see fig. 3.2).

Chaiken (1979) conducted a naturalistic field study on communicator attractiveness in which students delivered a standard persuasive communication to other undergraduates on campus. The undergraduates were then asked to complete an opinion questionnaire and to sign a petition. Chaiken had previously collected information about the student communicator's physical attractiveness, Scholastic Aptitude Test (SAT) performance, communication skills, self-evaluation, and so forth. Chaiken found that physically attractive student communicators were more persuasive than unattractive communicators, as revealed both by the verbal and by the behavioral measure. In addition, Chaiken found that there were consistent differences between attractive and unattractive student communicators on a number of dimensions that may have contributed to their differential persuasiveness (e.g., physically attractive sources had higher grade point averages and SATs, more positive self-concepts, and better communication skills than physically unattractive communicators). These other factors apparently contributed to the greater persuasiveness of the attractive sources.

Communicator Similarity

A source may be liked by an audience for various reasons. For instance, similarity (Byrne, 1971; Rokeach, 1960), physical appearance (Berscheid & Walster, 1974), and familiarity (Sherif & Sherif, 1953; Zajonc, 1968) increase a person's likability and persuasiveness.

Brock (1965), in an interesting study on the role of similarity in persuasion, trained part-time paint salesmen to deliver one of two persuasive communications to customers who had decided to purchase paint. A salesman approached the customers as they headed toward the checkout counter and suggested that they buy a different brand of paint (which was either more or less expensive than the paint already chosen). To support this recommendation, the salesman told half the customers that he had personally tried both types of paint and that the alternative brand of paint was much better—that is, the salesman appeared *similar* to the customers on a dimension relevant to the issue (amount of paint previously used). The salesman told the other half of the customers that he had recently bought twenty times the amount of paint the customers had chosen and found the alternative brand of paint to be much better—that is, the salesperson appeared *dissimilar* to (though more expert than) the customers. Brock (1965) found that more customers bought the advocated brand of paint when the salesman seemed similar rather than dissimilar to the customer.

Similar communicators don't always have more impact on people than dissimilar communicators, however. Goethals and Nelson (1973) reasoned that, for issues dealing primarily with values or opinions where there is no verifiable "correct" answer, similar sources that agree with a subject engender more confidence in the subject's opinion than dissimilar sources. For example, people differ in their opinions about what makes a person physically attractive. If you hold the opinion that being slender is an attribute of a physically attractive person, you might be even more confident of that opinion if someone that you considered similar to you, such as your best friend, agreed with you than if someone agreed with you whom you considered dissimilar (such as a foreign exchange student).

Goethals and Nelson went on to argue, however, that when the issue concerns verifiable facts, agreement from dissimilar sources engenders more confidence in the truthfulness of the facts that agreement from similiar sources. For instance, if you believe that the Queen of England is 5'5" tall, you might become even more confident of that belief if someone dissimilar to you verified this (such as the foreign exchange student) than if someone similar verified it. This is probably because, on factual matters, verification is more meaningful if it comes from a person who has different sources of information than you do.

Communicator Power

The power of the communicator refers to the extent to which the source can administer rewards or punishments. A parent, for instance, has power over a child; a drill instructor has power over recruits. How does power work in persuasion? Kelman (1958) suggested that people express more *public* agreement (i.e., compliance) to a powerful communicator than to a powerless communicator, at least in the presence of the powerful source. This attitude change is not internalized, however, which means that the people don't *really* privately agree more with the powerful source than with the powerless source. Kelman argued that people simply report more agreement with the powerful source to maximize their rewards and minimize their punishments. For example, Kelman demonstrated that college students on scholarships expressed agreement with their financial aid officer when he was monitoring their attitudes, but they expressed no such agreement on a private measure of opinion.

What does it take to be a "powerful" communicator? First, the recipients of the communication must believe that the source can indeed administer rewards or punishments to them. Second, the recipients must decide that the source will use these rewards or punishments to bring about their compliance. And third, the recipients must believe that the source will find out whether or not they comply. All three of these conditions must be met for communicator power to produce and maintain the compliance (McGuire, 1969).[2]

In sum, according to the message-learning approach, source factors influence the incentives people have for attending to, comprehending, yielding to, and retaining the recommendations made in a persuasive message. In the next section, we examine factors pertaining to the *message* that influence persuasion. As shall become clear shortly, although Hovland and his colleagues viewed message content as important in persuasion, they tended to ignore what is perhaps the most obvious of all message factors—the quality or cogency of the arguments presented in the communication. Most of their research focused instead on factors *associated with* the message content (such as whether the arguments used fear appeals or not). The lack of attention to the quality of the arguments in a message sometimes led to situations in which, in one study, the high-fear message may have had more cogent arguments than the low-fear message, but in other studies the reverse may have occurred. As a result, conflicting findings were sometimes obtained.

Message Factors

Plato, in his *Dialogues*, regarded persuasion as the key to power and the *message* as the key to persuasion:

> What is there greater than the word which persuades the judges in the courts, or the senators in the council, or the citizens in the assembly, or at any other political meeting?—If you have the power of uttering this word, you will have the physician your slave, and the trainer your slave, and the money-maker of whom you talk will be found to gather treasures, not for himself, but for you who are able to speak and to persuade the multitude. [Cited in Jowett, 1937, p. 511.]

Plato's view might first appear outdated for our hurried, information-filled twentieth-century way of life. But reflections on Hitler's massive rallies and rise to power in the 1930s, or of the Ayatullah Khomeini's influence over Shi'ite Muslims in Iran a half century later, serve as startling reminders of the power of persuasive messages. Since Hovland and his colleagues began their study of persuasion during World War II, perhaps it should be expected that much of their research concerned the attitudinal effects of source *and* message factors.

The following discussion of message content looks at the attitudinal effects of comprehensibility, number of arguments, emotional tone, recognition of one or both sides of an issue, and type of conclusion. Factors that have been investigated concerning the *structure* or way of organizing the message include the timing for announcing the source, the ordering of conflicting messages, and message repetition. We end our discussion of message factors with a short section on the *style* of message presentation. Effective messages, according to the message-learning approach, provide incentives for learning and accepting the advocated attitudinal position. This notion guided much of the research on message factors that we discuss below.

Message Comprehensibility

Consider for a moment a couple trying to watch a presidential speech on the nation's economy. They are watching the speech in the midst of a department store and, because of the extraneous sights and sounds, they are having trouble hearing what the president is saying. They are able to understand the president say that people should save their money to help the economy, but the distractions of the department store drown out the rest of the message. A second couple is also watching the president's speech in the department store, but they are standing much closer to the television. They hear not only the advocacy but also all of the reasons that the president gives for saving money. Which of these couples is most likely to spend their money in the department store, rather than save it as advocated by the president?

According to Hovland and his associates, for a message to be persuasive it must first be attended to and comprehended. In the example above, the first couple did not comprehend the message, whereas the second couple did. If the couples are alike in all other respects and if the president gives some cogent reasons for saving, then the second couple is more likely to be persuaded by the president's plea to save their money than is the first. The research on this point supports this conclusion (Gardner, 1966).

A study by Eagly (1974) highlights the importance of message comprehensibility. In this study, all subjects heard a message advocating that people need much less sleep per night than they typically get. One group of subjects heard a reasoned sequence of arguments for sleeping less (good comprehensibility condition). A second group of subjects heard the same arguments, but the sentences were cut in half and put back together in a random order so that the sentences "appeared" to make sense, but really did not (medium comprehensibility condition). A third group of subjects heard the same *words*, but the sentences made no sense because the words of the sentences were completely randomized (poor comprehensibility condition). Not surprisingly, Eagly found that subjects in the good comprehensibility condition were the most persuaded and recalled the most message arguments, whereas subjects in the poor comprehensibility condition were the least persuaded and recalled the fewest arguments (see fig. 3.3).

Number of Arguments

If understanding message arguments increases the likelihood of changing a person's attitude, does it follow that adding arguments increases the effectiveness of the message? The answer appears to be yes—sometimes. For instance, Calder, Insko, and Yandell (1974) conducted a study in which subjects served as "jurors" in a simulated bigamy trial. The subjects heard either one or seven arguments favoring the defense and either one or seven arguments favoring the prosecution. Afterwards, subjects expressed their certainty of the innocence or guilt of the defendant. Calder and his colleagues found that the side having the most arguments for its case was the most persuasive.

Interestingly, more arguments are not always better. Norman (1976) had subjects read a statement made by either an expert or a smiling, physically attractive source. The source advocated that people sleep less than the usual eight hours. Half of the subjects read only this statement, whereas the other half

Figure 3.3

This ad, which is eye-catching, will be ineffective unless people bother to turn the magazine upside down to read it. Attention *and* comprehension together are important in attitude change. (Courtesy of Level IV Products Inc.)

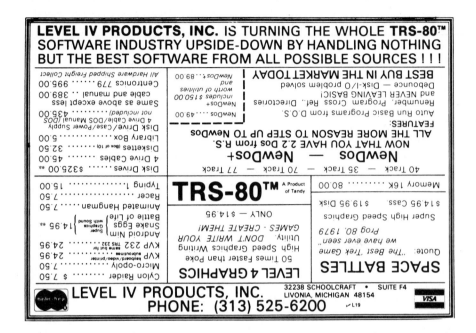

also read a three and one-half page message containing six arguments for sleeping less. Provision of supporting arguments increased the persuasive impact of the message when the statement was attributed to an expert, but subjects agreed with the advocacy when it was attributed to an attractive source whether or not supporting arguments were provided. These results suggest that an expert source is more persuasive than a physically attractive source because he or she causes the recipients to attend to and think about the reasons provided for adopting a recommendation.

Since including message arguments did not *diminish* the persuasiveness of the message, one still might have the impression that persuasive messages should contain as many supporting arguments as possible to maximize their effectiveness. There are several reasons though, to suspect this strategy. First, people may stop attending to a message if it goes on and on. If they are made to listen to a message, they may become bored with it or irritated by it after awhile, particularly if the arguments are highly repetitive (Cacioppo & Petty, 1979b). Second, people can think about and remember only a limited amount of information during a given time interval. This means that the more arguments presented within a given time span, the less time people have to think about or rehearse each one of the arguments (Calder, 1978). Hence, recipients are likely to remember a smaller proportion of the total number of arguments when many, rather than a few, are mentioned in a given time span (Eagly, 1974). Finally, some arguments are going to be stronger, more convincing, and more influential than others, and providing a person with a few very convincing arguments may promote more attitude change than providing these arguments along with a number of much weaker arguments (Anderson, 1974).

Rewards within the Message

As we noted previously, message arguments are presumed to motivate attitude change by the incentives they provide or because they serve as rewards within the message. The finding that more message arguments can lead to more attitude change is consistent with this notion. We noted also that rewards are more powerful when they are administered immediately, rather than after a delay (see chap. 2). Similarly, a persuasive message is more effective when the message arguments are separated from the conclusion by little, rather than a lot, of neutral material (Weiss, Buchanan, & Pasamanick, 1965).

The Arousal and Reduction of Fear

The promise of relief from a negative event may also provide an incentive to accept an advocacy. The notion that avoiding misfortune is rewarding led Janis and Feshbach (1953) to conduct their now classic study of fear-arousing messages and attitude change:

> Implicit in the use of fear appeals is the assumption that when emotional tension is aroused, the audience will become more highly motivated to accept the reassuring beliefs or recommendations advocated by the communicator. [P. 78.]

To test this hypothesis, Janis and Feshbach prepared three forms of a communication recommending good dental hygiene. Each message contained the same basic information about the causes of tooth decay and the same recommendations concerning oral hygiene practices. The three messages differed, however, in the amount of fear-arousing material that was included. A high-fear message was constructed including discussions of diseased gums, painful toothaches, and spreading infections that can "cause secondary infections which may lead to diseases such as arthritic paralysis, kidney damage, or total blindness." A moderate-fear message was constructed describing these dangers in a more detached factual fashion. Finally, a low-fear message was constructed that contained primarily neutral information about the growth and function of teeth.

Janis and Feshbach found that the low-fear message was the most effective in inducing students to practice good oral hygiene (an effect that was only marginally significant, $p < .10$). They argued that the high-fear message was so upsetting to the students that they engaged in defensive avoidance, that is, the students became so frightened by the high-fear message that they avoided thinking about the issue.

Leventhal (1970), however, found that high-fear appeals were usually more effective than moderate- or low-fear appeals, which led him to suggest an alternative explanation of Janis and Feshbach's observations. He argued that the high-fear-arousing message made the students feel uncomfortable about their oral hygiene habits, but the supporting arguments were not very reassuring. Subjects were left feeling vulnerable with no effective means of protecting themselves. Adopting the recommendations served little purpose, so few subjects did.

Let's look more closely at how fear-arousing messages are constituted. These messages describe: (a) the *unfavorableness* of the consequences that will occur if the recommended actions are not adopted; (b) the *likelihood* that these consequences will occur if the recommended actions are not adopted; and (c) the likelihood that these consequences will *not* occur if the recommended actions *are* adopted (Hass, Bagley, & Rogers, 1975; Rogers, 1975; Rogers & Mewborn, 1976). In other words, the message arouses fear in a person by questioning the adaptiveness of the current state of affairs (Mewborn & Rogers, 1979). In addition, the message arguments motivate a person to accept the recommendations by outlining explicit undesirable consequences of doing otherwise. That is, the message arguments explain the high likelihood that a set of dire consequences will occur if the recommendations are ignored, consequences whose seriousness and unpleasantness are graphically depicted. The better understood and the more reassuring the message arguments, the more attitude change toward the recommended action that should occur. One implication of this research is that the message arguments used by Janis and Feshbach (1953) were not sufficiently reassuring to reduce the unpleasant drivelike state created by the fear-arousing material.

In sum, fear-arousing messages are effective in inducing attitude change particularly when the following three conditions are met: (a) the message provides strong arguments for the possibility of the recipient suffering some extremely negative consequence; (b) the arguments explain that these negative consequences are very likely if the recommendations are not accepted; and (c) it provides strong assurances that adoption of the recommendations effectively eliminates these negative consequences. Defensive avoidance may occur (thereby reducing attitude change) when the message leaves a person feeling inevitably vulnerable regardless of the actions taken to deal with the danger.

One-sided versus Two-sided Messages

The Yale group also explored the relative attitudinal effects of "presenting only those arguments favoring the recommended conclusion (a one-sided message) and discussing also arguments opposed to the position advocated" (and then refuting them—a two-sided message) (Hovland et al., 1953, p. 105). Hovland, Lumsdaine, and Sheffield (1949) first faced this question during World War II. The War Department wanted to find the most effective means of convincing American soldiers that the war in the Pacific might continue for some time. Hovland and his colleagues conducted a study using a large number of soldiers to determine whether it was best to present only a one-sided message (which stressed Japan's advantages and resources) or to present a two-sided message (which contained all of the one-sided arguments but also mentioned and refuted arguments about Japan's weaknesses). They found no overall difference in effectiveness between these two types of communications. They did, however, find that the two-sided message was more effective for soldiers who were more knowledgeable about the issue and who were initially opposed to the advocacy. One-sided communications were more effective for soldiers who either knew very little about the issue or who initially agreed that the Pacific war would be drawn out.

Several years later, Lumsdaine and Janis (1953) conducted an important followup to this study. Their study was conducted several months before President Truman announced that the USSR had produced its first atomic bomb. Some subjects, serving as a control group, were simply asked how long it would take the USSR to produce large numbers of atomic bombs. Other subjects heard a message advocating that it would take at least five years for the USSR to develop an atomic arsenal. Half of these subjects heard a one-sided message that contained only arguments supporting this conclusion; and half heard a two-sided message that contained the same arguments and the same conclusion, but that also included some arguments and refutations for the opposite side of the question. As found previously by Hovland et al. (1949), Lumsdaine and Janis (1953) found that people who initially agreed with the advocacy tended to be more persuaded by the one- than the two-sided message, whereas people who initially disagreed with the advocacy showed the opposite effect.

The new and interesting aspect of this study was that, one week later, some of the subjects were exposed to a "counterpropaganda" message arguing that the USSR would develop an atomic arsenal fairly soon. Afterwards, the subjects completed a questionnaire in which they expressed how long they believed it would take Russia to produce large numbers of atomic bombs. The remaining subjects simply completed this questionnaire without hearing the counterpropaganda. They found that people who had first been exposed to the one-sided message were more persuaded by the subsequent counterpropaganda than people who had initially been exposed to the two-sided message. The increased resistance to the counterpropaganda shown by subjects who heard the two-sided message

Figure 3.4

Volkswagen advertisements have long been among the most appealing in the automotive industry. Here VW uses a variation of the two-sided persuasive appeal. The ad claims that the disadvantage of owning a car is that it uses expensive gasoline. The advantage of the VW is that it uses very little fuel—in fact, it uses diesel fuel, which is even cheaper than gasoline. (Courtesy of Volkswagen of America.)

is called an "inoculation effect." A detailed discussion of why this occurs is found in chapter 8. For now, it is sufficient to note that the initial exposure to the two-sided message appears to make people better able to argue against the later counterpropaganda message.

The implications of this research for marketing and advertising may be somewhat surprising. Most advertisements list the benefits derived from the use of a product and ignore the costs involved in its use or the benefits of competitive brands. In other words, most advertisements are one-sided communications. This strategy is probably most effective when the product is well liked, widely consumed, has few competitors, and enjoys loyal customers. However, if the audience is well informed about a product and its alternatives, the product is not widely preferred, *or* the audience is likely to be exposed to advertisements for competitive products (which is the case for most products), then two-sided rather than one-sided advertisements may be more effective (Faison, 1961; see fig. 3.4).

Conclusion-drawing

Once a message has been constructed and presented, what is the most effective way to end it? Should the message end by stating the conclusion explicitly, or should the conclusion be left for the audience to draw? Hovland and his colleagues reasoned that drawing a conclusion would increase the likelihood that recipients comprehend and retain the message arguments; but if recipients *could* draw the correct conclusion themselves, then retention and yielding would be enhanced. An example may clarify their reasoning. Consider the case of a professional racquetball player instructing a novice. As she explains the general dynamics of hitting a racquetball, she focuses on the proper position of the ball to the body, the trajectory of the arm, and the desired placement of the ball on the front wall. One purpose of her instruction is to convince the novice that she must snap her wrist when striking the ball. Is the novice more likely to change her swing and snap her wrist if the conclusion is stated explicitly ("Thus, you must snap your wrist . . .") or if she is left to "discover" this conclusion on her own?

The answer is that it depends. If the novice is either unmotivated or unable to discover that conclusion, then she can accept it only if the pro ends the instructions by stating the conclusion for her. But if the novice is able to "discover" the conclusion, either during the course of the message or shortly thereafter, then she will be more persuaded than if the conclusion is drawn for her. Observations such as these are the basis for the adages "Experience is the best teacher" and "I told you so."

Conclusion-drawing in persuasive communications appears to operate similarly. A conclusion is usually helpful or necessary for the audience to understand and remember fully the message arguments and advocacy (Hovland & Mandell, 1952; Thistlethwaite, de Haan, & Kamenetzky, 1955). Occasionally, however, an issue is sufficiently involving and a message is sufficiently understandable that people themselves are able and motivated to correctly surmise the contents and conclusion of a message. When these conditions are met, people are more persuaded (or maintain their attitudes longer) when left to draw their own conclusion (Linder & Worchel, 1970; Stotland, Katz, & Patchen, 1959; Thistlethwaite & Kamenetzky, 1959). In chapter 8 we will see further examples of circumstances in which self-generated information is more persuasive than information that originates externally. McGuire's (1969) statement regarding the attitudinal effects of conclusion drawing puts it aptly:

It may well be that if the person draws the conclusion for himself he is more persuaded than if the source draws it for him; the problem is that in the usual communication situation the subject is either insufficiently intelligent or insufficiently motivated to draw the conclusion for himself, and therefore misses the point of the message to a serious extent unless the source draws the moral for him. In communication, it appears, it is not sufficient to lead the horse to the water; one must also push his head underneath to get him to drink. [P. 209.]

Thus far, we have considered factors associated with the message content, and we have seen that findings have sometimes conflicted because of a lack of attention to how cogent or reassuring the message arguments were (e.g., fear appeals). In the next several sections, we shall consider investigations inspired by the message-learning approach that look at the effects of message factors even further removed from the message content. These message factors include the style in which the source presents the message, the structure of the message, and the number of repetitions of the message. For example, should the source be identified at the beginning or end of the message? If competing with another recommendation, is it best to present the arguments first or last? Repeating message arguments should facilitate people's retention of them—does this mean that they will be more likely to accept the recommendation they support as well? These issues are discussed next.

Identifying the Source First or Last

Consider an advertising agency that is producing commercials for a credit card company. The agency has obtained expert (financial and banking executives) and attractive people (movie stars) to serve as the communicators for their endorsements. The issue to be decided is: Should the communicator be identified at the beginning or at the end of the message? One advertising executive mentions that, by identifying the source at the outset of the message, the credibility of the message arguments might be increased so that they would attract more attention and encourage learning of them. A second executive notes, however, that knowing the source might prevent the audience from focusing on the message per se, thereby reducing its impact. Which would be better for the advertising agency to do?

Several studies bear upon this issue. Mills and Harvey (1972), for instance, asked subjects to read a message that argued in favor of broader education for college students. The message was attributed either to an expert or to an attractive source. Some subjects learned the identity of the source at the beginning, others at the end of the message. They found that subjects were more persuaded when the *expert* was identified at the outset of the message rather than at the end but that subjects were equally persuaded whether the *attractive source* was identified at the beginning or at the end of the message (Husek, 1965; Norman, 1976). These results suggest that a manipulation of source expertise may affect how a person thinks about the message but that a manipulation of source attractiveness does not. This is further discussed in chapters 8 and 9.

Ordering of Message Presentations

Next, consider the scheduling problems of a presidential candidate. The candidate knows that his adversary is speaking on Wednesday. Assuming that the candidate can arrange to speak to the same audience either before or after his opponent, which order of presentation would be most effective? The answer to

Figure 3.5

The effects of the order of presentation depend upon the time delay between the two messages and the time delay between the last message and attitude measurement. (Adapted from Miller & Campbell, 1959.)

Condition		Which message is favored by these conditions?
	Time Delay	
(1) Message A, Message B ⟶ Attitude Measurement		A (Primacy effect)
	Time Delay	
(2) Message A, ⟶ Message B, Attitude Measurement		B (Recency effect)
(3) Message A, Message B, Attitude Measurement		Neither
	Time Delay Time Delay	
(4) Message A, ⟶ Message B, ⟶ Attitude Measurement		Neither

this question depends upon (a) the length of time that separates the two presentations and (b) the length of time before attitudes are measured (in this case, on election day).

The classic study in this area was conducted by Miller and Campbell (1959), the design and results of which are presented in figure 3.5. They found that the position presented first is generally more effective, particularly when a considerable length of time separates the two presentations from the measurement of attitudes. Hence, if the candidate has a chance to speak immediately before or after the adversary, and if election day is several days away, the candidate would do best to speak first. That is, all else being equal, information with "prior entry" is more persuasive when some period of time passes before attitudes are measured (a "primacy" effect).

Miller and Campbell (1959) went on to argue that, as time passes, recipients forget fairly quickly what they learn in messages, though not quite so much if the information had prior entry. This suggests that speaking second would be more effective than speaking first *if* measurement occurred after the first message was forgotten but while the second was still fresh in memory. To test this, Miller and Campbell presented one position and, following a time delay, presented an opposing message. Immediately after the second message, Miller and Campbell measured the subjects' attitudes, and under these conditions, the second message was more effective than the first (a "recency" effect).

Finally, Miller and Campbell reasoned that if the messages were presented one after the other and measurement followed immediately, *no* forgetting would occur and therefore the order of presentation would not matter greatly. Similarly, if the messages were separated in time and both were followed by a long time delay before measurement, *both* messages would be forgotten. In this case, too, the order of presentation would not matter (see fig. 3.5).

These results make the scheduling for our fictional candidate easier. When speaking back-to-back, the candidate would do best by speaking first, unless voting was scheduled immediately following the speeches, in which case it would not matter whether he spoke first or second. Perhaps more importantly, these results suggest that a last-minute media blitz may be highly effective, especially when some time has lapsed since the opposing candidate has presented his or her views.

Message Repetition

Of course, campaigns, advertisements, public service announcements, promotions, and so forth are expensive to produce and present. If the same message is used over and over again, production costs can be minimized. But if repeating the message decreases its effectiveness, then the promotional costs are wasted. What might we expect from repeating messages? According to the message-learning approach, repetition should enhance the total attention to, comprehension of, and retention of a message. That is, just as reading a passage in a text several times may aid the student in understanding and accepting its point, repeating a message may aid an audience in following and accepting an advocacy.

Consistent with these suggestions, Wilson and Miller (1968) demonstrated that three presentations of jury trial excerpts led to better learning and retention of the arguments than one presentation. Subjects also agreed more with an attorney's recommendation when they were exposed to the arguments three times rather than one time. Less compatible with the message-learning model are the findings that continued presentations of persuasive messages may maintain retention at high levels but can decrease attitude change (Cacioppo & Petty, 1979b, 1980a; Gorn & Goldberg, 1980; Miller, 1976). We will return to this issue in chapter 8 and explain the conditions under which repetition decreases a message's persuasive impact.

Style of Presentation

The last category of message factors that we discuss here is the style in which the speaker presents the message. For example, is a humorous style (telling jokes to warm the audience up) more effective than a nonhumorous style? Unfortunately, the existing data about the use of humor and other style variables is not very consistent, perhaps because the probable effectiveness of a certain kind of style depends on so many other factors. Thus, a humorous message might work well for certain topics (getting you to try a new shampoo), but might be disasterous for other topics (getting you to favor capital punishment).

Despite this problem, a number of style variables have been investigated with some success. For example, Hemsley and Doob (1978) found that speakers who look at their audience are judged more credible and are more persuasive than speakers who gaze away as they speak. The rate and fluency of speech have also been shown to affect people's judgments of the speaker's credibility and their susceptibility to persuasion. Thus, Lind and O'Barr (1979) report that speakers who use a powerful style of speaking (characterized by the infrequent use of hesitations and hedges such as "well," "kinda," and "I guess") are more persuasive than people who use a powerless style; and Miller et al. (1976) report that people are more susceptible to persuasion when a speaker delivers a message at a rapid rate, rather than at a normal rate of speech. Speakers who use powerful speech and rapid speech are perceived to be more knowledgeable about the topic and hence more credible. Finally, Hall (1980) has indicated that the nonverbal voice cues that a speaker can use, such as the tone of voice, can also affect the susceptibility of a recipient to persuasion.

Recipient Factors

Proponents of the message-learning approach (e.g., Hovland & Janis, 1959; Janis & Field, 1956) were among the first to recognize the importance of recipient factors, and to examine their effects in persuasion.[3] The Yale group searched for differences in persuasibility among people that could generally be found regardless of the topic of the message. It is to this area of research that we turn next.

Intelligence

During World War II, Hovland et al. (1949) focused for a time on the persuasive impact of a series of indoctrination films called *Why We Fight*. The investigators were interested in what made the films effective and for whom they were the most effective. They found that the more years of schooling a soldier had, the more likely he was to agree with the film's indoctrinations. Hovland and his associates reasoned that the more educated soldiers paid more attention to, understood, and remembered more of the arguments in the films than the uneducated, less intelligent soldiers (see also Janis & Rife, 1959).

Other studies of recipient factors and persuasibility produced a more complex picture. For instance, a child is increasingly persuasible until around the age of eight, after which time the child becomes less persuasible each year until some stable level of persuasibility is reached. Studies of intelligence and persuasibility in young adults have sometimes indicated that the two go together; but more often they indicate that people with high intelligence are less persuasible than those with normal to low intelligence (see review by McGuire, 1969). What are we to make of these findings?

Figure 3.6

The relationship between recipient factors and persuasibility as outlined by McGuire (1968). As a recipient factor (such as intelligence) increases, the recipient is predicted to be more likely to comprehend (receive) the arguments contained in the message but less likely to yield to the arguments. Since *acceptance* of the arguments depends on both reception *and* yielding, the lower bound of the reception and yielding curves sets the upper bound for acceptance (or ability to be influenced).

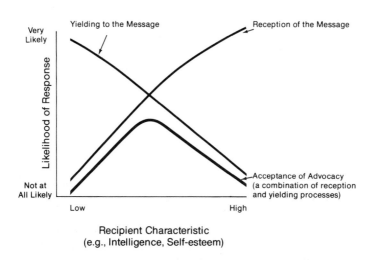

Extending the framework outlined by Hovland et al. (1953), McGuire (1968) proposed a model of personality and persuasibility that clarified much of the research in this area. According to McGuire's model (displayed in fig. 3.6) attitude change is determined by (a) the reception of the message arguments and advocacy, which includes the processes of attention, comprehension, and retention; and (b) yielding to influence. McGuire argues that recipient factors often have opposite effects on these two components. For example, the more intelligent members of an audience may comprehend and remember a communication better than the less intelligent audience members. This fact should enhance the attitude change in the more intelligent audience members. But intelligence may also make recipients less likely to yield to influence because they are more confident in their critical abilities and, therefore are more sure of their initial attitude; this attenuates attitude change. The result is a complex though understandable relationship between personality traits and persuasibility (see fig. 3.6).

Eagly and Warren (1976) examined the relative effects of these components on attitude change. Measures of intelligence (verbal ability) were obtained from subjects, who were later exposed to either a complex or a simple message. Eagly and Warren reasoned that intelligence should increase acceptance of the complex message, because if the message is complex, acceptance should be determined mostly by the reception curve in figure 3.6. The yielding curve is not very important for a complex message, because it is assumed that everyone would yield to a complex (cogent) argument if they could only understand it. On the other hand, intelligence should decrease acceptance of the simple message, because if the message is simple, acceptance should be determined mostly by the yielding curve in figure 3.6. The reception curve is not very important for a simple message, because it is assumed that virtually everyone can understand it. Consistent with this hypothesis, they found that higher intelligence was associated with better comprehension and slightly more agreement with the complex message but with equal comprehension and less attitude change to the simple message.

Self-esteem

McGuire's (1968) model of personality and persuasibility has also been applied to the relationship between self-esteem and attitude change. Self-esteem refers to the value, worth, or regard one places on oneself. People with low self-esteem are less confident, view themselves as less capable, and are less happy than people with high self-esteem. Hence, as McGuire has noted, people who lack self-esteem are more likely to yield to influence. On the other hand, self-esteem is positively related to intelligence, interest in events outside oneself, and so forth. This suggests that persons with low self-esteem are less likely to attend to, learn the contents of, and thereby be susceptible to persuasive communications. Overall susceptibility to influence as a function of self-esteem, therefore, may be described by McGuire's model, with self-esteem being positively related to reception but negatively related to yielding (see fig. 3.6).

Support for this line of thought was obtained in several studies (e.g., Gergen & Bauer, 1967; Nisbett & Gordon, 1967; Zellner, 1970). For instance, Nisbett and Gordon (1967) measured the self-esteem of 152 male and female undergraduates. A week later, subjects read a number of statements about health, which were attributed to the state health department. In some instances, these "health facts" were simple, unsubstantiated statements about health. In other instances, the "health facts" were followed by extensive documentation. The unsubstantiated message was easily comprehended but provided little reason to yield, whereas the substantiated message contained evidence that was compelling, though difficult to comprehend.

Nisbett and Gordon found that the relationship between self-esteem (low, moderate, and high) and attitude change depended upon how compelling and difficult to understand the message was. When the message was simple, people with moderate self-esteem showed the most attitude change (as indicated by their agreement with the "health facts"). But when the message was complex, people with high self-esteem displayed the most attitude change.

Significant gaps were found, however, between what was expected from McGuire's model and what was observed. The subjects in the Nisbett and Gordon (1967) study were university students, and presumably even those classified as possessing relatively low self-esteem actually possessed moderate self-esteem when compared to the average population. Nisbett and Gordon's unsubstantiated message was sufficiently simple that everyone, regardless of their level of self-esteem, should have comprehended the message. Since comprehension was high for all subjects, and self-esteem is associated with low yielding, one might have expected a *negative* relationship between self-esteem and attitude change. This effect was not found, however—people with moderate levels of self-esteem were the most persuaded by the simple message (rather than people with low self-esteem).

Several other lines of evidence also suggest that alternative processes contribute to the observed attitude change in these studies. For instance, Skolnick and Heslin (1971b) noted that self-esteem was sometimes positively, sometimes negatively, and sometimes curvilinearly related (in an inverted U-shaped fashion) to attitude change. They went back to the various studies reporting these data and collected the messages that were used in each. Then, they gave these messages to a group of subjects who rated each in terms of its quality (persuasiveness, validity, and logicalness) and comprehensibility (complexity, difficulty). Contrary to the message-learning approach, message comprehensibility did not distinguish the attitudinal effects of the messages in a meaningful way.

Sex Differences

A number of the early studies on persuasion that analyzed for sex differences reported that women appeared to be more persuasible than men (see reviews by Cooper, 1979, and Eagly, 1978). What accounts for these early findings? Eagly (1978) considered a message-learning account, which holds that women, having greater verbal abilities than men, would be better able to comprehend the arguments contained in the message and would thereby show more persuasion. Eagly argues against this account, however, because studies measuring comprehension differences between men and women have failed to support it (Eagly, 1974; Chaiken & Eagly, 1976).

There are currently two explanations for the observed sex difference that are given the most credence. First, the sex difference may be due to the social roles that men and women have learned. In other words, women have been socialized to be cooperative and to maintain social harmony, which would facilitate agreement (Eagly, 1978), whereas men have been socialized to be assertive and independent, which would facilitate resistance to influence (Eagly, Wood, & Fishbaugh, in press). Second, the sex difference may occur because the persuasive message in many influence studies are ones that men are more interested in and knowledgeable about than women. In fact, Eagly and Carli (in press) asked men and women to rate the topics used in a large number of persuasion studies and found that the more masculine topics (issues that men were more interested in than women) tended to be associated with greater female susceptibility to influence. Thus, the sex difference may simply represent the fact that it is easier to persuade someone who has very little interest in and/or knowledge about the issue under discussion.

Experimental tests of the sex difference effect have tended to support the interest or knowledge hypothesis. For example, Sistrunk and McDavid (1971) selected 45 statements about a variety of everyday opinions and matters of fact. Some of the items were prejudged to be masculine in nature, some were prejudged to be feminine, and the rest were prejudged to be neutral. These 45 statements were intermixed with 20 additional statements (filler items) to prepare a test booklet labeled "Inventory of General Information." Next to each statement in the booklet there was a "majority response," and subjects were asked to indicate the extent to which they agreed or disagreed with the "majority." Sistrunk and McDavid found that men agreed with the majority more on feminine items, but women displayed more agreement on masculine items.

Summary

We have seen that Hovland and his associates searched for general differences among people in their susceptibility to influence. Individual differences in message comprehension were thought to be especially important in this regard. However, Insko and his colleagues (Calder, Insko, & Yandell, 1974; Insko, Lind, & LaTour, 1976) found that fairly large differences in comprehension are needed for detectable differences in attitude change to result. Thus, the line labeled "reception" in figure 3.6 probably has much less influence on attitude change than depicted. In most studies, the large differences in comprehension that are needed to alter attitudes are absent: "Learning and recall of factual information from mass communications does occur. However, recall and retention measures seem, at best, irrelevant to the ultimate effects desired, the changing of attitudes and behavior" (Haskins, 1966). Subtle idiosyncratic effects of personality traits on understanding and memorizing a message may therefore be less important in persuasion than the effects of recipient factors on the thoughts and associations stimulated by the message. For instance, men appear to be more persuasible than women on "feminine" topics and vice versa, at least in part because as one's knowledge and interest in a topic increases, one is more motivated and able to think about and react, in both a positive and negative manner, to the recommendations made (Cacioppo & Petty, 1980b). We shall return to this matter in chapter 9.

Channel Factors

The early work of Hovland and his colleagues clearly demonstrates that mass communications could educate and influence the people exposed to them. In this section, we address the attitudinal effects of the various media through which communications can be transmitted, such as the *print media* of newspapers, magazines, and books; the *audio media* of radio, telephones, and recordings; and the *audio visual media* of television, movies, and videorecordings. Together, these channels constitute the mass media, the effects of which can be contrasted with face-to-face communications.

Face-to-face vs. Mass Media Appeals

In 1949, Cartwright reported on the U.S. government's drive to sell savings bonds. He compared the relative effectiveness of personal solicitations with media appeals to buy bonds and found that personal solicitations were more effective. The greater impact of the face-to-face channel has been found repeatedly since then (Berelson, Lazarsfeld, & McPhee, 1954; Katz & Lazarsfeld, 1955). These early studies should remind us also that persuasive arguments that produce attitude change do not have to come from some type of formal written or verbal communication. Burnstein and Vinokur (1975, 1977), for instance, have extensively analyzed attitude changes that result from *group* discussion. Their numerous investigations have shown that the arguments generated by people in a group are learned by and can change the attitudes of the other people in the group. Because people are often persuaded by the arguments that others in a group discussion generate, an interesting phenomenon may occur as a result of a face-to-face discussion—*group polarization.* That is, people's attitudes after group discussion are often more extreme than the attitudes held prior to discussion. The group polarization effect is most likely to occur when most group members are on the same side of the issue, and group members have *different* reasons for favoring that side of the issue. Thus, during discussion most group members will hear arguments on their own side of the issue that they had not considered previously (Burnstein & Sentis, 1981).

Even though face-to-face communications generally have more impact than media communications, tens of billions of dollars are spent each year on persuasive communications delivered through the mass media (McGuire, 1978). These channels are used as an "organized means of reaching large numbers of diverse kinds of people quickly and efficiently" (Weiss, 1969, p. 70). The mass media channels are popular because of the large number of people that can be reached. The politician's walk across the state or a president's speech to the nation would be relatively ineffective in changing public attitudes if these acts were not communicated to the mass public by newspapers, radio, and television. Even the campaigner who successfully convinced each of the 1,000 people with whom he or she spoke would be woefully behind the campaigner who convinced one percent of a prime-time television audience (Bauer, 1964). Though accomplishing the latter feat is by no means simple, the potential impact of an effective mass media campaign is unquestionably substantial.

Channel Attributes

Persuasive communications are most effective when tailored to suit the special attributes of the channel through which they are to travel (Klapper, 1960). Print media provide a fairly permanent record that people can consume at their own pace and re-expose themselves to should they desire. The audio and audiovisual media reach a larger, more diverse audience than the print media, and communications traveling along audio or audiovisual channels "go to" the recipient, whereas printed communications must lay in waiting (Weiss, 1969). Further, audiovisual media are especially potent channels of communication that people both see and hear (Bradac, Konsky, & Davies, 1976; Frandsen, 1963), and people tend to be more critical of and perceive as less valid the material that is written as opposed to the material presented on audio or videotape (Carver, 1935; Maier & Thurber, 1968). On the other hand, the nonverbal cues (and attendant distraction from reception of the message content) are more evident in audiovisual than audio communications and in audio than in printed messages (Wright, 1980).

The unique advantages and limitations associated with each channel suggest that no one form of transmission is "best," but rather that the most effective channel depends upon a variety of factors. These include the audience one wishes to reach; the interest value, comprehensibility, and personal relevance of the message; and the characteristics of the source. For instance, it is indicated that (a) complex messages are comprehended better in print than in audio or audiovisual form, and (b) yielding to what *is* comprehended is most likely in audiovisual communications and least likely in printed messages (Chaiken & Eagly, 1976). It follows then that an easily comprehended message should engender the most attitude change when it is videotaped and the least attitude change when it is printed. However, printed media may be the most effective when the message is complex, because substantially more of the message can be comprehended when presented in print rather than audio or audiovisual form. Furthermore, the relatively incomprehensible audio or audiovisual presentations can be more frustrating and unpleasant to follow than the more successfully comprehended printed presentation.

Chaiken and Eagly (1976) tested these notions using students at the University of Massachusetts. The subjects were told that the psychology department was helping the New England Law School evaluate its new training program for students, which would involve law students serving in community legal clinics. Subjects read background information about the "Victoria Company case," a fictional company-union dispute. Next, the subjects either read, listened to, or viewed a videotape of a law student's discussion of the case (the persuasive message). Half of these subjects heard a simply worded discussion (the easy message) and half heard essentially the same information stated in more difficult vocabulary and embedded in complex sentences (the difficult message). Subjects then expressed their judgment regarding the case and completed a "case evaluation" questionnaire.

Chaiken and Eagly found that when the law student's message was simple, subjects were most persuaded by the audiovisual presentation and least persuaded by the printed presentation. When the message was difficult, however, subjects were more persuaded by the printed than by audio or audiovisual presentations. Second, as expected, subjects found the audio and audiovisual presentations of the difficult message to be less understandable and more unpleasant than the printed presentation. These findings underscore the need to tailor messages to the channel through which they are transmitted.

The Persistence of Attitude Change

So far we have focused primarily on the *immediate* attitudinal effects of persuasive communications. Yet there would be little reason to study these phenomena if we had no basis for believing that changes in attitudes would be retained and would affect people's subsequent thoughts and actions. In this section, we address the message-learning perspective on the persistence of attitude change.

Message Retention

The durability of attitude change was not addressed by Hovland et al. (1949) until their work for the War Department during World War II was nearly ended. Until then, they had assumed that the effects of communications would be greatest immediately following their presentation.

Remember that Hovland and his colleagues proposed that learning the message arguments (i.e., "factual knowledge") potentiates, or sets the upper bounds on, attitude change. If attitude change was observed immediately following a communication, it was thought to be the result of attention, comprehension, and acceptance of the arguments and advocacy (see fig. 3.1). Accordingly, attitude change was thought to *persist* to the extent that the message could be remembered. If people forget most of the message arguments, then they would be expected to return nearly to their initial attitudes (see fig. 3.7). This model of persistence is stringent in that it assumes an intimate relationship between the retention of specific information in the message and attitude change. A less

Figure 3.7

The message-learning approach specifies the upper bounds of persisting attitude as a function of the retention of either the specific message arguments or the "substance" of the advocacy.

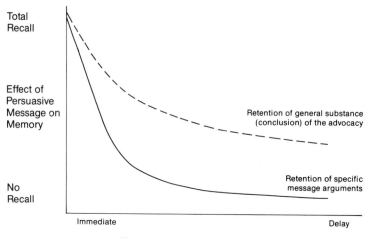

Time since Measurement Was Presented

stringent model of persistence was also suggested by Hovland et al. (1949). They noted that people sometimes remember the substance of a message even though the specific arguments are forgotten. If remembering the substance rather than the specific content of the message is important, then attitude change might outlast the retention of the message arguments (see fig. 3.7).

These formulations are based on the notion of a "forgetting curve", which proved useful at first in explaining why attitude change tends to decrease over time. For instance, Watts and McGuire (1964) obtained the initial attitudes of undergraduates on such issues as: The state sales tax should be abolished; The Secretary of State should be elected by the people, not appointed by the president; Courts should deal more leniently with juvenile delinquents; and Puerto Rico should be admitted to the Union as the fifty-first state. Over the following six weeks, subjects read four communications (though at various times), each advocating one of the above positions. Attitude change and retention of the messages were assessed at the end of the six-week period. Watts and McGuire found that attitude change and retention of the message content were maximal immediately after reading a persuasive communication. With the passage of time, attitude change and the retention of message arguments decreased.

Surprisingly, however, decrease in attitude change and decay of message retention did not follow the same time course. Attitude change and retention of arguments were correlated initially (i.e., the more one remembers, the more attitude change evidenced), but this association was broken, and actually tended to reverse, over time. Other studies have failed to substantiate even the initial learning-persuasion correlation (Cacioppo & Petty, 1979b; Insko, Lind, & LaTour, 1976; Petty & Cacioppo, 1979b). This latter finding suggests that attitudes persist because people remember the substance of the conclusion of the message, or perhaps their own thoughts about the message, rather than the specific arguments that are contained in the message (Greenwald, 1968; Petty, 1977). In the remaining portions of this chapter, we survey research and theory on persistance that emerged from the germinal work by Hovland and his associates. We will return in chapters 8 and 9 to the question of attitudinal persistence with a view that highlights the importance of people's thoughts about a message rather than the externally provided arguments constituting the message.

The "Sleeper Effect"

In 1933, Peterson and Thurstone conducted one of the earliest investigations of the persistence of attitude change. Silent motion picture indoctrination films about different ethnic groups were shown to children in secondary schools, and the immediate and delayed attitude effects of these "communications" were obtained. Peterson and Thurstone concluded that attitude change "persists for a considerable period of time" (p. 62). But surprisingly, one of the films, *Four Sons,* had a *delayed action effect:* the attitude change it created appeared to be *greater* six months later than immediately after its showing.

Hovland, Lumsdaine, and Sheffield (1949) found a similar effect in their study of the persistence of attitude change. One of the movies in the Why We Fight series, entitled the *Battle of Britain*, was designed to induce positive regard in American soldiers for their British allies. The film was quite effective in this task, at least as indicated by immediate attitude change. Hovland, et al. expected a sharp decline across time in attitude change and in the retention of the factual knowledge about the message. They too found slightly greater attitude change nine weeks after the message than existed after one week. (Message retention did decrease, though.) Hovland et al. called this delayed action effect on attitude change the "sleeper effect" (p. 188).[4]

The Dissociative-cue Hypothesis

These and subsequent studies of sleeper effects led to the formulation and refinement of *cue hypotheses* about the persistence of attitude change (e.g., Kelman & Hovland, 1953). According to this formulation, an attitude at any point in time is the result of: (a) associating the *message arguments* with a conclusion (we have discussed this process extensively already), and (b) associating *cues* with a conclusion. Two types of cues were postulated. A *discounting cue* is something (besides message arguments) that causes a person to reject an advocacy. For instance, an untrustworthy communicator may cause a person to "discount" the attitude change a message may otherwise have produced. Conversely, an *augmenting cue* is something (other than message arguments) that causes the person to accept a conclusion (e.g., an attractive source). It was thought that the cues and the message arguments have separate (noninteracting) effects on attitude change—that is, that cues did not affect the reception, retention, or yielding induced by the message arguments and that the arguments did not alter the effects of the cues. Thus, attitude change could be determined at any point simply by adding the *separate* effects of the cue(s) and the message arguments.

According to the message-learning approach, the pairing of the message arguments and the message conclusion is remembered longer than the pairing of a cue and the conclusion. This notion is dubbed the *dissociative-cue hypothesis.* This view holds that a sleeper effect occurs because a discounting cue is dissociated from the message conclusion by the passage of time, while the remaining (more slowly decaying) association between message arguments and message conclusion produces what appears to be an "awakening" of attitude change. Thus, in theory, the increase in attitude change is not due to the message content actually increasing its effectiveness, but rather is due to the removal (dissociation) of the counteracting influence of a discounting cue.

Recall the Kelman and Hovland (1953) study mentioned earlier in which a message about juvenile delinquency was attributed to either a highly credible and trustworthy source (a distinguished judge) or a totally noncredible and untrustworthy source (a man arrested recently for a drug offense). On the immediate postcommunication attitude measure, the high-trustworthy source produced more attitude change than the low-trustworthy source. Three weeks later, subjects' attitudes were again assessed. Half of the subjects simply completed the delayed posttest, whereas half were reminded of the identity and characteristics of the source before they completed the posttest. On the delayed measure with no reminder of the source, a significant decay in attitude change was observed for the high-credibility source and no change for the low-credibility source (though a nonsignificant increase in attitude change was observed). A very different pattern of results was obtained for the groups in which subjects were reminded of the source (i.e., for which the cue was reassociated). The high-credibility group showed more and the low-credibility group showed less acceptance than comparable groups for which the cue was not reinstated (see fig. 3.8). Weber (1972) has found essentially the same pattern of results by making the cue either easy or difficult to dissociate from the message. He did this by repeating the source's name either two (easy dissociation) or twenty-two (difficult dissociation) times during the initial testing session. Subjects exposed to the easy dissociation cue showed converging attitudes similar to those shown in figure 3.8, whereas subjects exposed to the difficult dissociation cue showed persisting attitudes characterized by those illustrated for the reinstatement groups in figure 3.8.

Figure 3.8

Attitude change measured immediately and three weeks after the communication, with and without reassociating the sources and the advocated position. (Adapted from Kelman & Hovland (1953). Copyright by the American Psychological Association. Used with Permission.)

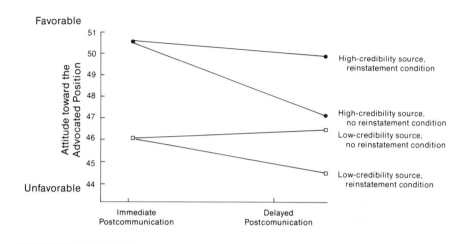

These studies, however, failed to obtain a significant *increase* in attitude change with the passage of time, which is the test for an *absolute* sleeper effect (Cook, Gruder, Hennigan, & Flay, 1979). Intensive searches for the absolute sleeper effect were instituted, and after seven different experiments failed to find it, Gillig and Greenwald (1974) proposed that it was time to "lay the sleeper effect to rest."[5]

The sleeper effect was down, but not out. A group of researchers at Northwestern University sought to arouse the sleeper effect (Cook, 1971; Cook & Flay, 1978; Cook et al., 1979). They examined the model proposed by Hovland and his colleagues and proclaimed that everyone had been looking in the wrong places for the effect. The Northwestern group reasoned that the message-learning approach predicted that a sleeper effect could be found only when: (a) the message alone had a substantial initial impact on attitudes, (b) this immediate attitude change was totally suppressed by association with a discounting cue, (c) the discounting cue and the message conclusion were dissociated with the passage of time, and (d) this dissociation occurred more quickly than did the forgetting and dissociation of the message content and conclusion. Finally, it was important that the cue and the message content affect attitude change separately and that they not affect one another.

With their route thus marked, Cook and colleagues set out to find the sleeper effect (Cook et al., 1979; Gruder, Cook, Henningan, Flay, Alessis, & Halamaj, 1978). Subjects read a 1,000-word message that contained strong arguments supporting its conclusion, thereby meeting the first requirement, (a), above. *After* reading the message, some subjects were exposed to a discounting cue. For instance, in their first experiment the discounting cue consisted of a "Note to the Reader" stating that the conclusion of the message was false. Moreover, it said that the message had been refuted because it was "inaccurate and wrong" (Gruder et al., 1978, p. 1065). Not surprisingly, subjects who read this "Note" indicated no attitude change on an immediate posttest. However, when their attitudes were measured again five weeks later, these subjects indicated a significant *increase* in attitude change—that is, their attitudes showed an absolute sleeper effect.

How well does the dissociative-cue hypothesis fare, then? The study by Gruder et al. (1978) suggests it fares very well. But now that the sleeper effect has been aroused, it is appearing in a variety of places (Greenwald, Baumgardner, & Leippe, 1979; Watts & Holt, 1979), occasionally in ways unanticipated by the dissociative-cue hypothesis. For instance, Greenwald et al. (1979) were able to turn the sleeper effect on and off: It was obtained when the discounting cue *followed* the message, but not when the cue *preceded* the message. This result suggests that the assumption regarding the separate lives of the cue and message is, in many instances, incorrect (Watts & Holt, 1979). Indeed, as we mentioned previously, several studies have demonstrated that a person's interpretation and retention of a message is affected by source cues when the source is identified *before* rather than following the message (Husek, 1965; Mills & Harvey, 1972; Norman, 1976; see also Eagly & Chaiken, 1975). That is, people who know the source of and circumstances surrounding a message prior to rather than following its delivery respond differently to the message and its conclusion. When this occurs, it becomes meaningless to speak of dissociating the "cue" from the "message," since the meaning of each can be interpreted only in light of the other.

In sum, the dissociative-cue hypothesis may work only when the cue is introduced following the message in such a manner that it cannot alter the meaning of the message or how the message is encoded. For instance, imagine that you are exposed to a persuasive message about eliminating the delivery of mail on Saturdays. Imagine also that a discounting cue is associated with the message— you are told that the arguments contained in the message have been found to be completely unsubstantiated or false. If the discounting cue is introduced before rather than following your exposure to the message arguments, the way in which you might think about the message arguments and the emergence of attitude change as a function of having read the message could be quite different. If the discounting cue is introduced before the message, you would probably pay very little attention to the arguments, and little attitude change would result. If the cue is introduced after the message, however, it comes at a time when you may have already done a considerable amount of thinking about the communication. In chapter 8 we specifically address the issue of how knowledge of the source can affect how a person thinks about the message arguments.

Retrospective

In this chapter, we have focused on a second major approach that developed to attitudes and persuasion. This approach, which was advanced by Carl Hovland and his associates at Yale University during the 1940s and 1950s, postulates that message learning is a fundamental determinant of attitude change. These researchers examined how different variables (e.g., source, message, recipient, channel) affected a person's attention to, comprehension of, yielding to, and retention of the arguments contained in a persuasive message. The working assumption underlying this approach was that message learning portended attitude change, particularly when incentives were provided in the persuasive message for accepting the recommended position. In the remaining chapters of this book, we discuss some of the judgmental, motivational, and cognitive processes that influence attitudes and persuasion. These processes often uniquely transform objective stimuli (e.g., the message arguments) into a more comfortable, functional, or meaningful psychological reality for the individual. The later approaches to persuasion owe much to the important work by Hovland and his associates, who identified a large number of important factors and interesting effects in persuasion. The subsequent approaches evolved in most instances to explain more simply, completely, and/or accurately the psychological processes underlying these effects (e.g., message repetition enhancing persuasion) and to specify in greater detail the circumstances that would lead to their emergence, nonemergence, and reversal.

Notes

[1]Asch (1948) has provided an alternative account of this prestige-suggestion effect. He posits that the nature of the source actually alters how people interpret the recommendation. In other words, he proposes that the recommendation is perceived to *mean* something more favorable when it comes from a prestigious rather than a nonprestigious source. Whether or not the context in which something is presented can affect its meaning ("meaning shift") is currently the subject of much controversy (Kaplan, 1975; Ostrom, 1977; Zanna & Hamilton, 1977).

[2]In chapters 5 and 6, we shall describe circumstances in which a compliant behavior can cause a person to internalize a new and consistent attitude.

[3]The notion that a person's own idiosyncratic thoughts about a message were an important mediator of persuasion (Smith, Bruner, & White, 1956) was not foreign to Hovland and his associates. In 1949, Hovland, Lumsdaine, and Sheffield suggested that an audience may protect itself against persuasion by going over their own arguments against the advocacy. Hovland (1951) later emphasized that the best way to study the internal process of attitude change was to have subjects "verbalize as completely as possible their thoughts as they responded to the communication" (p. 430). Nevertheless, Hovland focused most of his research efforts on situational factors as they pertained to attitude change.

[4]There has been some disagreement recently regarding the term *sleeper effect*. Hovland et al. (1949, 1953), Katz (Stotland, Katz, & Patchen, 1959), McGuire (1969), Cook (Cook & Flay, 1978), and others have used the term, as we have here, to denote any facilitative delayed action effect on attitude change. Others use the term to refer to the increase in persuasion over time that results from messages initially associated with low-credibility source (Gillig & Greenwald, 1974).

[5]A *relative* sleeper effect is tested by finding a significant interaction between time of attitude measurement and the cue manipulation (e.g., high- or low-source-credibility). Thus, a relative sleeper effect does not have to include a significant increase for the low credibility appeal but may result from any *relative persistence* of the low compared to the high-credibility message. For example, the low-credibility message may not decay as fast as the high-credibility appeal. These relative sleeper effects have not been so elusive (Cook & Flay, 1978; Cook et al., 1979).

Judgmental Approaches

4

Have you ever wondered why the first 60° F (16° C) day after a bitterly cold winter seems quite *warm*, but the first 60° F day after an intensely hot summer seems rather *cool*? Clearly, how we judge something depends upon what we are comparing it to. Our evaluations of social objects are also affected by our comparison points, and the theme of this chapter is that all evaluative judgments (including belief and attitude judgments) are relative. In other words, how positive or negative something feels or how it is rated on some attitude scale depends upon what our frame of reference is. For example, when college men were asked to judge the physical attractiveness of a potential date, the date was rated as significantly less attractive if the men had just finished watching a television program starring three very attractive women ("Charlie's Angels") than if they had watched a control program (Kenrick & Gutierres, 1980).[1] All of the approaches to attitudes and persuasion that we will consider in this chapter share the same view: the psychophysical principles of human judgment that are used to explain why one light is rated as brighter than another, and why one line is rated as longer than another, can be used to understand why one person is more influenced than another, why one message is more persuasive than another, and why one object is rated more favorably than another.

Adaptation Level Approach

The underlying postulate of judgmental theories, including adaptation level theory as elaborated by Helson (1959; 1964), is that all stimuli can be arranged in some meaningful order. Thus, weights can be arranged from the lightest to the heaviest, and attitudes toward some object or issue can be arranged from the most negative (unfavorable) to the most positive (favorable). The theory gets its name from that point on the dimension of judgment that corresponds to the psychological neutral point, called the *adaptation level*. For example, if you were to put your hand in a bucket of very cold water, eventually your hand would adapt to the water temperature so that the cold water would feel neutral or normal. Subsequent judgments of how cold or warm another bucket of water felt would be made relative to the water temperature to which your hand had previously adapted. More formally, the adaptation level is defined as a weighted geometric *average* of all the stimuli that a person takes into account when making a particular judgment (a geometric average gives relatively greater weight to smaller values). The adaptation level is of considerable importance because other stimuli are judged in relation to it. A *contrast effect* is said to occur when some new stimulus being judged is displaced away from the adaptation level. This contrast effect can be experienced very easily with physical stimuli. For example, if you were to place your right hand in a bucket of ice water, and your left hand in a bucket of hot water, and then place both hands in a bucket of medium water, your right (ice water) hand would feel warm, whereas your left (hot water) hand would feel cool. The judgments of the medium water have been displaced from the initial adaptation level. Another way to view this is that as the adaptation level moves toward the value of a new stimulus, the judgment of every other stimulus in the series moves in the opposite direction. As the adaptation level of your hand becomes "colder" by placing it in the ice water (i.e., the ice water comes to feel neutral or normal), the experience of every other temperature in the series (including the medium water) becomes "warmer." Likewise, as the adaptation level of your hand becomes "warmer" by placing it in hot water, the experience of every other temperature in the series becomes "colder." The medium water can simultaneously feel warm and cool because your two hands have different adaptation levels serving as *anchors* or reference points. You can easily see, then, how adaptation level theory can explain how a 60° F day can seem warm if you have adapted to very cold temperatures, but it will seem cool if you have adapted to very hot temperatures. Similarly, a moderately attractive person can seem less attractive if you have adapted to very attractive people but more attractive if you have adapted to very unattractive people.

A large number of studies have accumulated demonstrating that contrast effects can occur in the judgments of social stimuli as well as physical stimuli. For example, Pepitone & DiNubile (1976) asked college students to judge the severity of a crime, assuming that the judgment of a first crime would shift the adaptation level in its direction. Thus, the judgment of a second crime that was very discrepant from the first should show a contrast effect. Specifically, if a very severe crime (homicide) was judged after a more minor crime (assault), it should be rated as more severe than if it was judged after another severe crime. Likewise, if a minor crime was judged after a severe crime, it should be seen as less severe than if it was judged after another minor crime. These contrast effects were obtained only when the judges were required to publicly record their judgments of the first case before proceeding to the second, not when the second case was judged after simply reading the first. The public commitment manipulation apparently enhanced the importance of the first judgment as an anchor or comparison point. In addition to affecting the ratings of crime severity, the order of crime judgment also affected the prison sentences that committed judges handed out in the second case. Thus, a homicide case judged after another homicide case drew an average of twenty-two years of punishment, but a homicide judged after an assault drew thirty-three. Similarly, an assault case judged after another assault case drew eight years, whereas an assault judged after a homicide drew only five.

In an intriguing application of adaptation level theory, Brickman, Coates, and Janoff-Bulman (1978) tested the proposition that extremely positive events do not increase one's overall level of happiness. For example, say that a person wins one million dollars in the Irish Sweepstakes. Brickman et al. suggest that this should raise the person's adaptation level so that more common, mundane events become less pleasurable than they used to be. To test this hypothesis, people who had won from $50,000 to $1,000,000 in the Illinois state lottery were asked to rate how pleasant they found seven ordinary events like watching television, eating breakfast, and hearing a funny joke. A control group of nonwinners was also asked the same questions. In support of the adaptation level predictions, lottery winners rated these events as less pleasant than the controls. This effect could not have been due to the fact that lottery ticket buyers are in general less happy than nonbuyers (and that is why they buy lottery tickets), because a second study found no differences in pleasure ratings between these two groups. It was only the lottery *winners* who devalued the simple pleasures. When asked to rate their overall current happiness, there were no differences in ratings between winners and controls. It is as if the extra pleasure of winning the money is offset by the decline in pleasure from other ordinary events.[2]

Dermer, Cohen, Jacobsen, and Anderson (1979) have obtained conceptually similar findings in an experimental laboratory study. Instead of examining pre-existing groups of people who had experienced very positive or negative outcomes, they had subjects imagine and describe their reactions to either four very positive hypothetical events (e.g., that they were winners of an all expenses paid tour of Europe), or four very negative events (e.g., that they were severely burned and disfigured). Subjects who wrote about very positive events subsequently rated their present life satisfaction as lower than subjects who wrote about very negative events.

As we have just seen, an attitudinal contrast effect may be observed when subjects are asked to judge some test stimulus in the context of either very positive or very negative stimuli. In typical demonstrations of the contrast effect, including those that we have just described, the contextual material designed to influence the adaptation level is presented prior to, or in conjunction with, the test stimulus. Manis and Moore (1978) demonstrated that a contrast effect can also be obtained if the contextual material is presented immediately *after* the crucial test stimulus to be judged. For example, in some of the conditions of their study, subjects heard a message that was either very favorable or very unfavorable toward national health insurance after they had heard a neutral message about national health insurance. Immediately following the positive or negative context messages, subjects were asked to summarize the neutral message. A separate group of judges rated each subject's summary in terms of how favorable it (and presumably the neutral message it represented) was to the topic. Analyses of the judges' ratings revealed that subjects produced summaries that were more positive toward national health insurance when they had heard the anti- rather than the pro-context message.

In summary, we now know that contrast effects can occur not only for physical stimuli but for social stimuli such as persuasive messages. In addition, the contextual stimuli that the test stimulus is displaced away from may be presented either before, during, or immediately after exposure to the test stimulus, as long as the judgment of the test stimulus occurs while the contextual stimuli are still salient. One major implication that adaptation level theory has for attitude judgments is that when an object or issue is evaluated in the context of very positive stimuli, it will be rated less favorably along the same dimension of judgment than if it is evaluated in the context of very negative stimuli.

But how are adaptation level theory and the contrast effect relevant to social influence or persuasion situations? In an early study employing adaptation level principles, Blake, Rosenbaum, and Duryea (1955) attempted to influence the amount of money that graduate students would donate to a secretary who was leaving the University of Texas. Some students were approached and merely asked to donate what they would like, whereas others were approached and allowed to see a clipboard that presumably contained the contributions of previous students. When no information about other donations was provided, the average student's contribution was seventy-five cents. When the clipboard indicated an average donation of twenty-five cents, however, the typical donation received for the secretary was only thirty-two cents. According to adaptation level theory, presumably the subject's subjective neutral point for an appropriate contribution (not too generous but not too cheap) was shifted toward twenty-five cents from seventy-five cents. Because of this shift in adaptation level toward the "cheap" end of the scale, contributing seventy-five cents would now seem far *too generous* and a smaller, more appropriate contribution would be decided upon. Of course, although the adaptation level interpretation is possible, other explanations for the observed conformity are plausible. For instance, students may still have felt that seventy-five cents was reasonable and twenty-five cents was cheap, but they decided to give a smaller contribution because they could get away with it without embarrassment.

Adaptation level theory has not led to much research on social influence or attitude change, and to date there is not a single persuasion study that can be explained exclusively by adaptation level principles. Because of this, we turn now to a judgmental approach that has generated considerably more persuasion-relevant research.

The Social Judgment—Involvement Approach

Social judgment theory (as introduced by Sherif and Hovland, 1961; and elaborated upon by Sherif, Sherif, and Nebergall, 1965; and Sherif & Sherif, 1967) represents an ambitious attempt to derive specific persuasion predictions by the application of judgmental principles. Like adaptation level theory, the social judgment theory approach assumes that people tend to arrange stimuli in a meaningful order on a psychological dimension (i.e., people may be arranged from the youngest to the oldest, shortest to the tallest, least likable to the most likable). Judgments about physical as well as social stimuli are thought to be subject to two judgmental distortions—contrast and assimilation. As we already noted, *contrast* refers to a shift in judgment *away* from an anchor or reference point. *Assimilation*, on the other hand, refers to a shift in judgment *toward* an anchor.

An early study by Sherif, Taub, and Hovland (1958) demonstrated both of these processes. Students were asked to judge how heavy various different weights felt by assigning them a number from one, "the lightest," to six, "the heaviest." At first, subjects were asked to lift each weight, without being able to see it, and assign it to a category. There were actually six different weights ranging from 55 to 141 grams. The weights were presented in a haphazard order, and subjects were given a total of fifty trials with each weight. The top panel of figure 4.1 graphs the average number of weights that subjects assigned to each category. Subjects were quite accurate at the task, assigning about fifty weights to each category. The next two panels of figure 4.1 graph the results when subjects were asked to categorize the same set of weights with an anchoring stimulus introduced. The data in the middle panel were obtained by having subjects lift a weight of 141 grams (to be labeled "6") prior to each judgment. The data from the bottom panel were obtained by having subjects lift a weight of 347 grams (which again was to be labeled "6") prior to each judgment. In the middle panel, when the anchoring stimulus was right at the end of the range of stimuli to be judged, ratings of the other weights were *displaced toward the anchor* (assimilation). In the bottom panel, when the anchoring stimulus was far removed from the range of the other weights, the judgments of these weights were *displaced away from the anchor* (contrast).

In the realm of attitudes, one's own attitude is thought to serve as a powerful anchor, and the opinions and attitudes expressed by others may be displaced either toward or away from one's own position. Attitudes that are relatively close to one's own are assimilated (seen as closer than they actually are), but attitudes that are very discrepant from one's own are contrasted (seen as further than they actually are).[3]

Figure 4.1

Assimilation and contrast in the judgment of weight. (Adapted from Sherif, Taub, & Hovland (1958). Copyright by the American Psychological Association. Used with permission.)

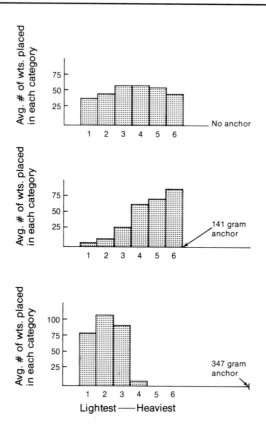

An interesting example of assimilation and contrast in attitudinal judgments is provided by Granberg and Brent's (1974) analysis of the 1968 presidential election. The data from a national election survey were analyzed in order to determine how one's own attitudes on the Vietnam War affected preceptions of the candidates' positions on the war. Figure 4.2 presents the data for voters who favored Democratic candidate Hubert Humphrey. In this election, Humphrey voters tended to be relatively liberal, Nixon voters were generally conservative, and Wallace voters tended to be extremely conservative. Figure 4.2 graphs the perceived attitudes of the candidates as a function of the voters' own attitudes

Figure 4.2

Assimilation and contrast in Humphrey voters' perceptions of Humphrey (HH) and Wallace (GW) in the 1968 election. No distortion of Nixon (RN) occurs. (Adapted from Granberg & Brent (1974). Copyright by the American Psychological Association. Used with permission.)

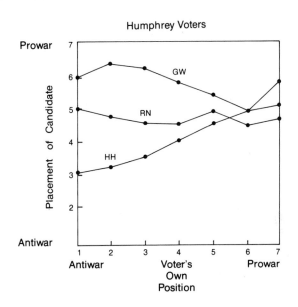

Humphrey Voters

on the issue of the Vietnam War. The figure indicates that the more prowar the Humphrey voter was, the more prowar they perceived the liberal Democrat Humphrey to be (an assimilation effect) but the more antiwar they perceived the ultraconservative independent candidate George Wallace to be (a contrast effect). Perceptions of Republican candidate Richard Nixon's position on the war were not affected by the Humphrey voters' own attitudes. Interestingly, just as this study provides evidence for the view that people sometimes *distort* the candidates' positions, other evidence suggests that the candidates sometimes *modify* their positions as they speak to different audiences in different parts of the county (see box 4.1).

How close must another's expressed attitude be to one's own in order to be assimilated and how far from one's own must it be in order to be contrasted? According to social judgment theory, an attitudinal dimension is composed of three categories or latitudes. The *latitude of acceptance* includes the person's most preferred position but also includes the range of other opinions on an issue that the person finds acceptable. The *latitude of rejection* comprises the range

Box 4.1

If one's major goal is to be liked, there is a lot to be gained by tailoring a message to an audience. People will presumably like a speaker who agrees with them better than one who disagrees with them (Byrne, 1969). Surprisingly, listeners also like speakers who deliver attitudinally consistent information more than speakers who deliver attitudinally discrepant information, even when it is clear that the speaker does not necessarily endorse the information he provides (Manis, Cornell, & Moore, 1974). It is as if the negative feelings elicited by the bad news, or the positive feelings elicited by the good news, become conditioned to the person transmitting the news. In a series of experiments, Tesser and Rosen (1975) have documented the reluctance of people to transmit bad news (called the MUM effect). This may indicate that people are aware that the bearer of bad tidings is disliked.

In any case, it is clear that speakers might effectively tailor their messages to an audience in order to enhance liking for either themselves of their cause. On the other hand, Newtson and Czerlinsky (1974) have suggested that, rather than attempting to gain favor with the audience, speakers may tailor their messages in order to "correct" for an expected contrast effect. For example, since an extremely liberal audience is likely to view a discrepant speaker's opinion as less liberal than it really is, a speaker might present himself as more liberal to this group in order to correct for the expected judgmental distortion (see also Dawes, Singer, & Lemons, 1972).

Although there may be some controversy about whether the tailoring of a message to an audience is motivated by ingratiation or accuracy motives, there is little controversy about the fact that message tailoring is an ever-present part of our culture. For example, politicians are often accused of saying different things to different audiences. An analysis of former President Johnson's statements about the Vietnam war by Miller and Sigelman (1978) suggests that the charge might be true. These authors had judges rate the statements that President Johnson made about the war to various groups on a five-point hawk-dove scale. For example, a statement made by the president on 23 July 1968 that "Everybody in America wants peace. Our government wants peace, our men in Vietnam want peace, your president wants peace," was rated as (2), or "dovish." On the other hand, the president's 12 December 1967 statement that, "We will hold the line against aggression as it has been drawn by the Congress and the president. We will not now nullify the word of Congress or the people as expressed in the SEATO treaty," was rated as (4), "hawkish." Miller and Sigelman divided the audiences

of opinions that the person finds objectionable. Finally, the *latitude of noncommitment* comprises those positions that the person finds neither acceptable nor unacceptable (see box 4.2 for a procedure for measuring these latitudes). If the position advocated by a communication falls within a person's latitude of acceptance, assimilation occurs, but a position that falls within the latitude of rejection addressed by the president between 1 July 1967 and 20 January 1969 into two groups: *hawkish* (consisting of audiences like the Veterans of Foreign Wars or the First Cavalry Division) and *non-hawkish* (consisting of such groups as the Young Democrats and the American Milk Producers). The mean rating of the president's addresses to the hawkish audiences was 4.06, whereas the mean rating of the speeches to the non-hawkish audiences was 3.19 ($p < .001$). The character of the audiences addressed by President Johnson had a significant impact on the nature of his remarks, even when extraneous variables were held constant (like the fact that the president tended to become less hawkish and to address less hawkish audiences over time).

As another example of tailoring a message to an audience, note the advertisement below. This ad was prepared by the prosmoking Tobacco Institute and contains one message for smokers and one for nonsmokers. If the messages have been tailored to the audience, we would expect the message to smokers to be more harsh in its characterization of antismokers than the message to nonsmokers. Judge for yourself if this is the case. (Courtesy of the Tobacco Institute.)

is contrasted. Assimilation presumably increases the likelihood that an advocated position will be accepted, since it is seen as closer to one's own view; whereas contrast, which causes the advocated position to be seen as further from one's own view, increases the likelihood of rejection. Whether or not the advocated position of a communication falls within a person's latitude of acceptance or rejection will thus be a primary determinant of whether or not persuasion will occur.

The Method of Ordered Alternatives for Assessing Attitude Structure (Latitudes of Acceptance, Rejection, and Noncommitment)

In order to measure the latitudes of acceptance, rejection, and noncommitment, subjects are presented with a list of attitude statements that represent the entire range of positions on the issue. The statements chosen are ones that can be reliably ordered from one extreme to another. No assumptions are made about the intervals between the statements. Below are nine statements used by Hovland, Harvey, and Sherif (1957) to measure latitudes about the prohibition of alcohol. Subjects might be asked to underline the position that they find most acceptable and circle those statements that are also acceptable. These statements form the *latitude of acceptance* (LOA). Subjects would then be asked to place an *X* next to those statements that are objectionable. These statements form the latitude of rejection (LOR). The unmarked statements form the *latitude of noncommitment* (LNC).

LOR
- ✗. Since alcohol is the curse of mankind, the sale and use of alcohol, including light beer, should be completely abolished.
- ✗. Since alcohol is the main cause of corruption in public life, lawlessness, and immoral acts, its sale and use should be prohibited.
- ✗. Since it is hard to stop at a reasonable moderation point in the use of alcohol, it is safer to discourage its use.

LNC
- 4. Alcohol should not be sold or used except as a remedy for snake bites, cramps, colds, fainting, and other aches and pains.
- 5. The arguments in favor of and against the sale and use of alcohol are nearly equal.

LOA
- ⑥ The sale of alcohol should be so regulated that it is available in limited quantities for special occasions.
- 7. The sale and use of alcohol should be permitted with proper state controls, so that the revenue from taxation may be used for the betterment of schools, highways, and other state institutions.
- ⑧ Since prohibition is a major cause of corruption in public life, lawlessness, immoral acts, and juvenile delinquency, the sale and use of alcohol should be legalized.

LNC
- 9. It has become evident that man cannot get along without alcohol; therefore there should be no restriction whatsoever on its sale and use.

Figure 4.3

The curvilinear relationship between message discrepancy and attitude change. Notice that the deflection point in the curve occurs at a higher level of discrepancy for the high than for the low credible source. (Adapted from Bochner & Insko (1966). Copyright by the American Psychological Association. Used with permission.)

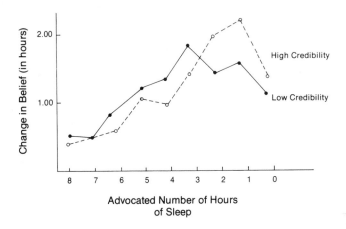

Communication Discrepancy

Communication *discrepancy* refers to the distance between the position advocated in the persuasive message and the attitudinal position of the message recipient. According to social judgment theory, the greater the discrepancy within the latitude of acceptance, the greater the attitude change that will result; but the greater the discrepancy in the latitude of rejection, the less the attitude change that will result. Overall, then, attitude change should show an inverted-U relationship with discrepancy, with the maximum amount of persuasion occurring somewhere in the latitude of noncommitment (which separates the acceptance and rejection regions). An inverted-U pattern of results has been reported in several studies (Aronson, Turner, & Carlsmith, 1963; Bochner & Insko, 1966; Insko, Murashima, & Saiyadain, 1966; Johnson, 1966; Peterson & Koulack, 1969), but not universally (cf. Eagly, 1974). For example, figure 4.3 presents the data obtained by Bochner and Insko (1966). In this study, subjects were presented with a message that advocated that the average young adult should get either eight, seven, six, five, four, three, two, one, or zero hours of sleep per night. The message was attributed to either a Nobel prize-winning physiologist (high-credibility source) or to a Y.M.C.A. director (low-credibility

Figure 4.4

Top panel: Theoretical interaction of credibility with discrepancy as predicted by social judgment theory. *Bottom panel:* Theoretical interaction of involvement with discrepancy as predicted by social judgment theory.

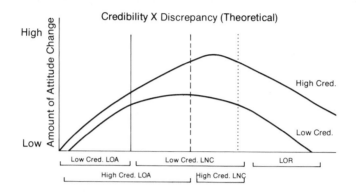

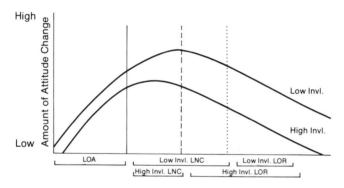

source). With each source, belief change increased up to a point and then began to decrease. The point of maximum change occurred at a greater advocated discrepancy for the high- than for the low-credibility source. The different inflection points for different sources would be inconsistent with social judgment theory unless it was assumed that increasing source credibility increases the latitude of acceptance (Sherif & Sherif, 1967; see top panel of fig. 4.4).

Although this study and others that found a general curvilinear relationship between discrepancy and persuasion appear to be consistent with social judgment theory, experiments testing more specific social judgment theory predictions on discrepancy have not been as supportive. For example, Eagly and Telaak (1972) exposed procontraception subjects who had either narrow, medium, or wide latitudes of acceptance on the issue to an anticontraception message that was either slightly, moderately, or strongly discrepant from their own positions. For all three levels of discrepancy, subjects with wide latitudes of acceptance showed greater attitude change than did subjects with either narrow or medium latitudes of acceptance. Suprisingly, subjects with a narrow latitude of acceptance showed a slight negative reaction to the slightly discrepant message even though it fell within their latitude of acceptance, and subjects with a wide latitude of acceptance showed a positive reaction to the strongly discrepant message even though it fell within their latitude of rejection. These specific results are clearly not consistent with social judgment theory despite the overall inverted-U relationship between discrepancy and persuasion showed by narrow and wide latitude subjects. Eagly (1981) suggests that the size of the latitude of acceptance on an issue may be a better predictor of *general susceptibility* to persuasion on the issue than it is of susceptibility to messages of a specified level of discrepancy.

Ego Involvement

Social judgment theory emphasizes the importance of one additional factor in determining the amount of persuasion that a message will produce—the person's level of ego involvement with the issue. Sherif and Hovland originally defined the level of ego involvement in terms of a person's group memberships. Thus, a member of the United Auto Workers Union would be more "involved" than a member of the American Medical Association concerning a speech advocating the government takeover of the Chrysler Corporation. In general, a person can be considered to have a high amount of ego involvement with an issue when the issue has "intrinsic importance" (Sherif & Hovland, 1961), "personal meaning" (Sherif, Kelly, Rodgers, Sarup, & Tittler, 1973), or when people expect the issue "to have significant consequences for their own lives" (Apsler & Sears, 1968).[4]

There are generally two ways to tell how involved a person is with an issue. One method—called the *own-categories procedure*—requires the person to sort a large number of diverse attitude statements into any number of piles or categories with the criterion that all items in any one category "belong together." Highly involved subjects will use fewer categories than less involved subjects (Sherif & Hovland, 1953). A second way to assess involvement comes from the method of ordered alternatives described in box 4.2. Highly involved persons have larger latitudes of rejection than less involved individuals. Both of these effects are presumably due to the fact that a person's own attitude acts as a stronger anchor under high involvement conditions. Thus, assimilation and contrast effects are greater for highly involved individuals. Items that are relatively close to the person's own position are lumped together, and objectionable items are lumped together with very little discrimination, which results in fewer overall categories. Also, items that would appear in the latitude of noncommitment for uninvolved individuals fall within the latitude of rejection for involved persons. Not suprisingly then, there are a number of implications for attitude change of increased issue involvement.

First, since involved persons have larger latitudes of rejection, they should generally be more resistant to persuasion than less involved persons, because any given message has a greater probability of falling in the rejection region for them. As Sherif and Sherif (1967, p. 133) have strongly stated it: "Regardless of the discrepancy of the position presented, we predict that the more the person is involved in the issue, the less susceptible he will be to short-term attempts to change his attitude." Involvement should also interact with other variables. For example, the bottom panel of figure 4.4 diagrams the theoretical interaction of involvement with message discrepancy. The inflection point in the inverted-U curve relating discrepancy to persuasion occurs at a more discrepant advocacy for persons of low rather than high involvement.

There have been several approaches to empirical study of the effects of ego involvement on persuasion. In much of the early research, involvement was investigated by examining preexisting groups thought to differ in their level of involvement. An important problem with this approach, however, is that involvement is confounded with every other characteristic that differentiates the groups. Typically, the involved groups also had more extreme attitudes than the uninvolved groups and may have been more (or less) intelligent, well-adjusted, and so forth (see Kiesler et al., 1969, for a further discussion). A preferable procedure for testing whether involvement affects persuasion as predicted by social judgment theory is by experimental manipulation of involvement. In some experimental studies, the subjects, drawn from the same pool, are randomly assigned to hear a message on a highly involving topic or on a different topic that is noninvolving (Rhine & Severance, 1970; Sherif et al., 1973; Watts & Holt, 1979). Although characteristics of the subjects are held constant with this procedure (because of the random assignment), characteristics of the message are confounded with the involvement manipulation, and any observed effects might therefore be attributed to irrelevant message characteristics (e.g., quality, complexity) rather than to the level of involvement.

Various procedures have been used to manipulate involvement but keep subject and message characteristics constant. For example, Miller (1965) attempted to involve half of his subjects with a message concerning fluoridation of public water supplies. Subjects in the "involved" group received information stressing the importance of the fluoridation issue; they were made aware of groups who supported their opinions on the issue; they were asked to list reasons to support their attitudes; and they committed themselves to distributing literature in support of their attitudes. Consistent with the social judgment prediction, involved subjects showed less attitude change in response to the fluoridation message than subjects who went through the involvement manipulation on an unrelated issue. But contrary to social judgment theory, the involvement manipulation did not increase subjects' latitudes of rejection. Halverson and Pallak (1978) attempted to increase involvement with an issue by having subjects publicly commit themselves to their initial positions (i.e., subjects gave their names and read a speech supporting their initial attitudes in front of a video camera, believing that their speech would be seen by fellow students). Subjects who were above the median in the extremity of their attitudes were unaffected by the involvement manipulation. Subjects who were below the median in extremity, however, showed significantly less persuasion under high involvement and also showed extended latitudes of rejection. Subjects with extreme attitudes already had large latitudes of rejection, and the involvement manipulation employed was ineffective in extending it further. Sherif (1976) suggests that manipulations of commitment (Kiesler, 1971) may be effective in *temporarily* increasing the level of involvement with an issue for persons who are initially uninvolved.

Evaluation of Social Judgment Theory

Unlike adaptation level theory, which has seen little application to persuasion, the social judgment-involvement approach has generated a considerable amount of research. In fact, enough research has accumulated to indicate that some of the specific predictions of the theory are clearly incorrect. For example, recall that Eagly and Telaak (1972) found that people's latitudes of acceptance and rejection were more predictive of their general persuasibility than of how they would respond to messages at specific discrepancy levels. Further, take the notion (presented in the last section) that increased involvement should invariably reduce persuasion. There are already several studies indicating that increased issue involvement may sometimes be associated with *increased* persuasion (Apsler & Sears, 1968; Eagly, 1967; Petty & Cacioppo, 1979a, 1979b; see chap. 8 for a further discussion). For example, Pallak, Mueller, Dollar and Pallak (1972) presented subjects who were either publicly committed (high involvement) or privately committed (low involvement) to their initial attitudes with information that either contradicted their opinions or was consistent but more extreme. They found that involvement increased resistance to the countercommunication, but it facilitated change toward the position advocated by the extreme consonant message. Interestingly, it is possible to explain the reaction to the consonant message using social judgment theory. If the consonant message fell within the subjects' latitudes of acceptance, then the publicly committed group should perceive the communication as closer to their own positions than the privately committed group, since increased involvement strengthens the anchoring properties of one's own attitude. What are the implications for persuasion of this assimilation effect? Is there less pressure to change one's attitude under high involvement because the message is seen as even closer to one's own view (as suggested by Kiesler et al., 1969), or is there more pressure to change one's own attitude toward a position that is perceived to be very close to one's own (as implied by Pallak et al., 1972)?[5]

This ambiguity demonstrates one of the major weaknesses of social judgment theory. Although the theory is quite clear about predicting the judgmental distortion effects—assimilation and contrast—it is less clear about how and why these processes affect attitude change. To date, there is no convincing evidence that assimilation and contrast effects *precede* (and thus potentially cause) the observed attitude changes, as required by the theory. Assimilation and contrast may come after and be a result of the attitude change, they may in some instances substitute for attitude change (a large assimilation effect may obviate the need for any attitude change at all; see Lammers & Becker, 1980), or they may be totally independent of the attitude change. Until these problems are resolved, social judgment theory will be more adequate as a theory of human judgment than as a theory of persuasion (Insko, 1967).

The Variable Perspective Approach

Unlike the other two approaches that we have just discussed, the variable perspective approach as outlined by Upshaw (1969) and Ostrom and Upshaw (1968) distinguishes between the content of an attitude and the judgmental language a person uses to describe his or her attitude. The *content* of an attitude refers to all of the various ideas, beliefs, images, and other elements associated with the attitude object or issue. The *rating* of an attitude refers to how the person presents his position on an evaluative dimension (e.g., pro-con; favorable-unfavorable; positive-negative). Mediating the relationship between the content and the rating of one's attitude is one's *perspective,* which refers to the range of content alternatives that an individual takes into account when an attitude object is rated. For any attitude issue, then, an individual's perspective would be defined by what he considers to be the most positive and the most negative content positions that are reasonable. These extreme content points serve as the endpoints (and anchors) of the person's attitude rating scale. An interesting feature of perspective theory is that two people can describe their attitudes in an identical manner on an attitude rating scale, but they can have different content positions in mind when they do so (see box 4.3). This is possible because different people may have different perspectives and may take a different range of content positions into account when making attitudinal judgments.

The rating of an attitude is a function of the content of the attitude and one's perspective. This idea is expressed in the formula,

$$R = f\left(\frac{C - L}{U - L}\right)$$

Box 4.3

Same Attitude Rating but Different Underlying Content

The scales below provide an example of two people who profess the same attitude (as measured by the rating scale) but who have different attitude content. This is possible because the two people have different perspectives. Person A considers positions that are more favorable to the church than does person B when rating his attitude.

Person A

	X			
Attitude Rating:	**Very Prochurch**	**Prochurch**	**Antichurch**	**Very Antichurch**
Attitude Content:	The church is the greatest institution in America today.	The church is a powerful agency for promoting social and individual welfare.	The church serves a useful need for some people.	Church services are not always completely interesting.

Person B

	X			
Attitude Rating:	**Very Prochurch**	**Prochurch**	**Antichurch**	**Very Antichurch**
Attitude Content:	The church serves a useful need for some people.	Church services are not always completely interesting.	The church seeks to impose worn-out dogmas on individuals.	The church represents shallowness, hypocrisy, and prejudice.

---

where R is the attitude rating, C is the attitude content, and U and L refer to the upper and lower perspective end anchors. This formula suggests that there are at least two ways to get a person to change his or her attitude rating on an issue. One involves getting the person to change the content (C) of the attitude without changing his or her perspective (U and/or L). Most persuasion attempts probably involve this approach. For example, the arguments in a message are designed to get a person to adopt more favorable beliefs about an issue, and as a result of this, the person should come to rate himself or herself as more favorable toward the issue. The formula also implies, however, that a second way to get the person to change his or her attitude rating is to change the person's perspective without changing the content of the attitude. This implication is particularly

Effect of Perspective on Attitude Content and Rating

Solid Downward Arrows

Assume that a person favored three years in prison for the defendant (attitude content) and initially considered himself to be slightly lenient (a 4 on the initial rating scale). If this person shifts perspectives so that instead of considering the range 1–8 years, he only considers 1–5 and maintains his belief in three years in prison for the defendant, he will now view himself as slightly stern (a 6 on the rating scale in the narrow perspective condition). This is demonstrated by projecting a line from three years in prison on the underlying stimulus continuum down onto the rating scale for the narrow perspective. On the other hand, if the person's perspective is increased rather than decreased (the person now considers a range of 1–17 years), but the attitude content remains at three years in prison, the person would now rate himself as extremely lenient (a 2 on the rating scale in the wide perspective condition). This is demonstrated by projecting a line from three years in prison on the underlying stimulus continuum down onto the rating scale for the wide perspective. Thus, a change in perspective can produce a rating scale shift without any change in the person's underlying attitude content.

Dotted Upward Arrows

Assume that the person initially views himself as slightly lenient (a 4 on the initial rating scale) and advocates a prison term of three years. If this person shifts perspectives so that, instead of considering the range of 1–8 years, he only considers 1–5 and maintains his view of himself as slightly lenient, he will now advocate only two years in prison (this is determined by projecting rating scale position 4 on the narrow perspective rating scale onto the attitude content continuum above). On the other hand, if he now considers a range of 1–17 years and maintains his self-rating as slightly lenient, he will now advocate a prison term of about six and one-half years (representing a projection of position 4 on the wide

intriguing, because it suggests that a change on an attitude rating scale may not always represent a true change in the underlying content of the person's attitude, but merely a change in the way a person *describes* an attitudinal position.

An example of this latter effect is provided in a study by Ostrom (1970). College students read a case history about a Mr. R. K. who had been found guilty of threatening to bomb a large metropolitan hospital. After reading the case history, the students were asked to indicate how many years they felt that Mr. R. K. should be imprisoned for his crime. In addition, they were asked to write a brief paragraph justifying their positions. The number of years assigned was taken as an indicant of the students' attitude *content,* and the justifying paragraph was introduced in an attempt to commit the students to their content positions. Next, the students received the perspective manipulation. Half of them perspective rating scale onto the attitude content continuum above). Thus, a change in perspective can produce a shift in attitude content with no accompanying change in the person's self-description.

Solid downward arrows show how an underlying content position (in years in prison) can be translated onto a nine-point rating scale (ranging from maximally lenient to maximally stern). The dotted upward arrows show how the rating scale position can be translated back into an attitude content position.

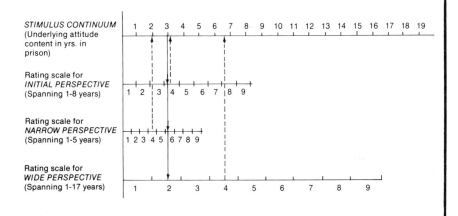

Note: On the rating scales, 1 = maximally lenient, 2 = extremely lenient, 3 = very lenient, 4 = slightly lenient, 5 = medium, 6 = slightly severe, 7 = very severe, 8 = extremely severe, and 9 = maximally severe.

learned that the maximally lenient punishment allowable for this crime was one year and the maximally stern punishment was five years. The other half also were told that the maximally lenient sentence was one year but were told the maximally stern punishment was thirty years. After this, the students were asked to rate themselves on a lenient-stern scale with nine categories: maximally lenient, extremely lenient, very lenient, slightly lenient, moderate, slightly stern, very stern, extremely stern, and maximally stern.

Assuming that the commitment induction was successful and subjects maintained their content positions, what effect should the perspective manipulation have on self-rating of sternness or leniency? The solid arrows in box 4.4 demonstrate the effect of perspective on an attitude rating scale when content remains constant. In this particular instance, students exposed to the narrow perspective

Figure 4.5

Top panel: Effect of perspective change on attitude rating scale. *Bottom panel:* Effect of perspective change on attitude content. (Data from Ostrom, 1970.)

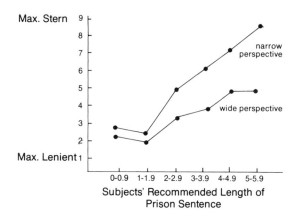

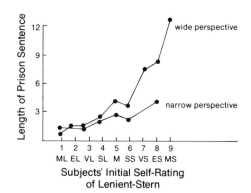

should rate themselves as more stern than subjects exposed to the wide perspective, even though they have not changed the content of their attitude (their belief in the number of years that Mr. R. K. should serve in prison). (Consult box 4.4 for the full explanation.) The top panel of figure 4.5 shows that the predicted results were obtained.

Just as one's response to an attitude rating scale depends upon content and perspective, an algebraic transformation of the perspective theory formula shows that attitude content is a function of rating and perspective.

$$C = f[L + R(U - L)]$$

One can therefore produce a change in content by getting the person to change his or her attitude rating without changing the perspective or by getting the person to change his or her perspective without changing the attitude rating. In a second study, Ostrom (1970) tested the latter proposition. A different group of subjects read the same case of Mr. R. K. In this second study, however, the students first rated themselves on the stern-leniency scale and wrote a paragraph justifying their position (thus committing themselves to their scale rating). Next, the students received either the narrow (one to five years) or the wide (one to thirty years) perspective induction. Finally, they were asked to assign Mr. R. K. to whatever number of years in prison that they felt was appropriate. The dotted upward arrows in box 4.4 demonstrate the effect of perspective on attitude content when the rating scale response remains constant. Students exposed to the narrow perspective should advocate fewer years in prison than subjects exposed to the wide perspective, even though they both would still describe their attitude positions as the same. The bottom panel of figure 4.5 shows that the predicted results were obtained. (See box 4.5 for further examples of the perspective theory approach.)

Indirect Influence

Steele and Ostrom (1974) have proposed that a perspective shift for one attitude issue can mediate *indirect* attitude change toward another issue sharing a comparable reference scale. In a test of this hypothesis, students were asked to read a felony case and render a judgment as to how many years the defendant should serve in prison. After making a judgment, the subjects were exposed to the prison term presumably handed down by the actual judge in the case. The judge's sentence was made to be considerably more severe than the sentences of the subjects, so that their perspectives on punishment would be increased. After reading the judge's sentence, subjects were asked to make another judgment in the same case. On the average, subjects increased their sentences (a direct influence effect), which would be expected even if subjects maintained their same rating scale responses (see box 4.4). Of particular interest, however, is that when subjects were later asked to judge an unrelated but similar case, subjects who had been exposed to the judge's sentence in the first case gave longer prison sentences than subjects who were not aware of the judge's sentence. This indirect influence effect would be the expected result if the judge's sentence in the first case produced a perspective shift that also influenced judgments in the second case.

Another possible explanation for the indirect influence effect is that subjects simply shifted toward the position that they expected the judge to take in the second case. This anticipatory shift would prevent them from being proven "wrong" when they were exposed to the real judge's decision. It is unlikely that this alternative explanation provides a complete account of the indirect influence

Box 4.5

Perspective Theory

The attitude expressed about an object or issue depends upon one's perspective. In the cartoon above, Chip attempts to change his mother's description of his room by increasing her perspective.

Comparative ads like the one below rely in part on perspective theory principles for their effectiveness. The goal of the ad is to set the anchors of your rating scale for tar content at 8 mg. (very low tar) and 19 mg. (very high tar). A rating scale anchored at the extreme values in the ad (8 and 19) would lead one to rate L&M long lights as the "lowest" in tar. This conclusion would not be correct to the extent that there are cigarettes (not mentioned in the ad) with even lower tar content that should anchor your rating scale.

Courtesy of Liggett & Myers Tobacco Company, Inc.

effect, however, since a recent study by Saltzstein and Sandberg (1979) demonstrated that an indirect influence effect still occurred when the subjects were told that they would never hear the judge's ruling in the second case. If the judge's opinion in the second case was not available, subjects would presumably be more willing to give their true opinions rather than opinions that would appear "correct" to the investigator.

Unresolved Issues in Perspective Theory

We have so far presented a fairly objective presentation of the perspective theory approach. Although perspective theory deals with the same type of phenomena as adaptation level theory and social judgment theory, a major difference among these theories is where the attitude rating scale is anchored. Adaptation level theory posits that the subjective neutral point on the scale is the most important anchor; social judgment theory holds that the person's own attitude is the most important anchor; and perspective theory contends that the extreme end points of the scale serve as anchors. As we have already seen, there is persuasive evidence indicating that a rating scale is anchored at *all* of these places (Ostrom & Upshaw, 1968).

A more interesting difference among these approaches is that, while adaptation level theory and social judgment theory view judgmental distortions (assimilation and contrast) as representing a fundamental shift in the perception of an object or issue (the weight actually feels heavier; the girl actually appears prettier), perspective theory views these distortions as representing only a change in response language (the weight feels the same, but is described as being heavier; the girl looks the same, but is described as prettier). Box 4.6 shows how perspective theory can account for assimilation and contrast effects as shifts in judgmental language.

As we have already noted, perspective theory distinguishes between attitude content and attitude rating. Although the conceptual distinction between these two concepts should be clear to you by now, the operationalization of these concepts in research has proven quite problematic (Kinder, Smith, & Gerard, 1976; Upshaw, 1976) and has led Upshaw (1978) to revise his thinking in several respects. The results of a recent experiment by Upshaw (1978) are illustrative. In this study, subjects read the details of a manslaughter case and then read the recommended sentence of the prosecuting attorney in the case. Control subjects who did not read the prosecutor's recommendation advocated a prison sentence of about three years. Experimental subjects read that the prosecutor recommended either one, six, eleven, twenty-one, or thirty-one years. Following this, subjects were asked to recommend an appropriate sentence and then to rate themselves in terms of leniency-sternness. Unlike Ostrom's (1970) studies employing similar procedures, no attempt was made to commit subjects to either the content of their attitudes (recommended sentence) or their attitude rating (leniency-sternness).

Box 4.6

A Perspective Theory Analysis of Assimilation and Contrast

In the diagram below, Panel A represents the underlying stimulus continuum or the underlying content of the attitude. Panel B represents a person's initial attitude rating scale, which has six response alternatives. You can see that an attitude content at point *X* on the underlying stimulus continuum receives a rating of 3 on the scale in Panel B. Panel C represents a scale with the same number of response alternatives as in Panel B but with an increased end anchor point. Scale C has been extended to accommodate a new extreme stimulus. This extension of the rating scale, without increasing the number of response alternatives, causes content position *X* to be displaced away from the new extreme stimulus. Position *X* now receives a rating of 2 instead of 3, a *contrast effect*. Panel D presents a scale with eight response alternatives that covers the same stimulus range as Scale B. Content position *X* receives a rating of 4 on this scale, an *assimilation effect*. On Scale D content position *X* is displaced in the direction of the added response categories. Thus, in the present example, a contrast effect resulted from a change in a stimulus anchor, while an assimilation effect resulted from a change in the response alternatives. Neither effect involved a change in the perception of content position X, only a change in the language used to describe it. In addition to the methods shown here for accounting for assimilation and contrast effects in terms of perspective theory, other accounts are also possible (Upshaw, 1978).

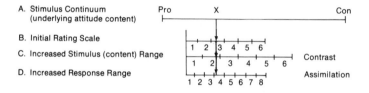

A. Stimulus Continuum
   (underlying attitude content)

B. Initial Rating Scale

C. Increased Stimulus (content) Range

D. Increased Response Range

Thus, there are several different predictions that might be made for the results, depending upon what assumptions are made. If we assume that the underlying content of subjects' attitudes was unaffected by the prosecuting attorney's recommendation but the subjects' perspectives were increased, then we would expect that as the prosecuting attorney's recommended sentence increased, there would be an increasing contrast effect on subjects' ratings of leniency-sternness. The more severe the punishment advocated by the prosecutor, the more lenient the subjects should rate themselves (see solid downward arrows in box 4.4). On the other hand, if we assume that subjects were more committed to their leniency-sternness positions, then an increase in perspective should yield a change in the content of the subjects' attitudes. Specifically, the greater the sentence that the judge advocated, the greater the sentence that the subjects should advocate (see dotted upward arrows in box 4.4). Upshaw (1978) found the latter effect. The prosecutor's recommendation had no effect on the subjects' leniency-sternness ratings but did significantly affect the number of years of punishment that the subjects recommended for the defendant. The results of this study appear to be an example of an increase in perspective modifying the content of the attitude without changing the person's self-description (as measured by the leniency-sternness rating scale).

Upshaw (1978) does not interpret his data in this manner, however. Upshaw prefers to advocate that no change in the underlying attitude of subjects has been produced as a result of the prosecuting attorney's influence. How can this be? Upshaw acknowledges that he cannot make this claim without reformulating some operational definitions. In previous research on perspective theory employing the criminal case study materials, the number of years assigned to prison was taken as a measure of attitude content, and the leniency-sternness measure was taken as the rating scale response that presumably reflected the underlying attitude content. Upshaw (1978) contends that this procedure (advocated in Ostrom & Upshaw, 1968) is incorrect. Upshaw now prefers to view both the leniency-sternness scale and the number of years in prison measure as self-descriptive rating scale measures that reflect an underlying attitude toward the defendant. Returning to box 4.6 may help to clarify this new interpretation. Assume now that Scale A represents an underlying attitude toward the defendant and that point X represents a particular point on that continuum. Now assume that scale B represents the subject's initial rating scale for the number of years in prison to which he feels the defendant should be sentenced (in this case three). Further assume that if the subject learns that the prosecuting attorney has advocated that the defendant spend eight years in prison, the number of response alternatives spanning the same stimulus range (i.e., with no change in perspective) has been increased from six to eight (see Scale D), and an assimilation effect is predicted. Subjects should move toward the new response categories. What had been called a direct influence effect and assumed to represent a change in the underlying content of an attitude (Ostrom, 1970) has now been interpreted as merely a change in response language representing no true change in attitude content!

It is very important to note at this point that the implications of Upshaw's modification of perspective theory are in the research operations rather than in the nature of the theory itself. Thus, the conceptual predictions of the theory are the same as we have already discussed in the preceding sections: (1) if there is no change in perspective, then a change in either attitude content or rating will normally bring about a change in the other; and (2) if there is a change in perspective, then it is possible to obtain either a scale or a content change with no change in the other. Although Upshaw's modification in the methodology of the theory may prove to be valuable, it does pose some problems. Namely, the theory is now left without an appropriate means for assessing attitude content, and previous research that was taken as supportive of the theory may now be irrelevant and would, in some cases, be difficult to reconcile with the new formulation. Nevertheless, perspective theory remains intriguing because of its caution that what may appear to be "true" attitude change in some studies may actually represent only a change in a person's self-description. Another judgmental approach, *accentuation theory*, that makes this same fundamental point, but for different reasons, is discussed briefly in box 4.7.

Box 4.7

Accentuation Theory

Like perspective theory, accentuation theory as developed by Eiser and his colleagues (Eiser & Stroebe, 1972) deals with situations in which an attitude *rating* may change, but the change does not reflect any true change in the underlying *content* of the attitude. According to the theory, an attitude rating is a joint outcome of a person's true attitude and the *evaluative connotations of the particular words that are used to label the extremes of the response scale.* For example, if you wanted to use a scale to measure how freely somebody thinks that another person spends money, you could anchor the response scale with the words "stingy" and "extravagant," or you could anchor the response scale with the words "thrifty" and "generous." If you get different ratings with these scales, however, you cannot assume that you are measuring different underlying attitudes. The first set of words has a negative connotation, whereas the second set of words has a positive connotation. Eiser and his colleagues have shown that the words you choose to anchor the rating scale can affect in a predictable manner how polarized subjects' judgments are.

For example, Eiser and Osmon (1978) have argued that words with negative connotations imply more *extreme* positions than do words with positive connotations. Thus, if we were to place the four words above on a continuum from "spends sparingly" to "spends freely," the words might rank order as indicated below:

SPENDS SPARINGLY	stingy	thrifty	generous	extravagant	SPENDS FREELY

What are the implications, then, of anchoring a scale with two negative or two positive anchors? Eiser and Osmon found that subjects' judgments were more polarized on the positive than on the negative scale. The diagram on the right shows how accentuation theory accounts for this effect.

Comparison of Approaches: Perception versus Description

Adaptation level theory and social judgment theory share the view that assimilation and contrast effects represent a fundamental shift in how an object or issue is *perceived*. Perspective theory and accentuation theory view assimilation and contrast effects as a shift in how an object or issue is *described*. Enough evidence has now accumulated to suggest that *all* assimilation and contrast effects cannot be attributed to mere changes in judgmental language. For example, earlier we described a study by Pepitone and DiNubile (1976) in which

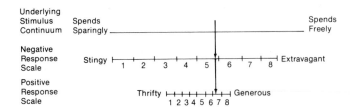

Because the positive anchors correspond to a smaller stimulus range than do the negative anchors, a polarization effect is observed. The underlying content that rates a 5 on the negative response scale receives a more extreme rating of 7 on the positive scale.

If the positive and negative anchors are *mixed*, then subjects will give the more polarized rating when the end of the scale that they favor has the positive rather than the negative label (Eiser & Mower-White, 1974; 1975). This effect is demonstrated below for a person whose own attitude falls on the "spends sparingly" side of the scale (Person A), and for a person whose own attitude falls on the "spends freely" side of the scale (Person B).

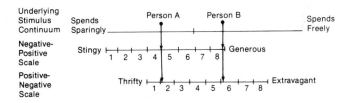

Notice that Person A gives the most polarized rating when his side of the scale (spends sparingly) is characterized by a positive (thrifty) rather than a negative (stingy) label. Similary, Person B also gives the most polarized rating when his side of the scale (spends freely) is characterized by a positive (generous) rather than a negative (extravagant) label.

subjects in some conditions judged a very severe crime (homicide) after a more minor crime (assault). Recall that these subjects rated the homicide as more severe than subjects who judged the homicide after judging another homicide (a contrast effect). In addition, though, recall that the contrast effect subjects also advocated longer prison sentences for the crime than non-contrast subjects. This result suggests that the contrast effect was not confined to a shift in the language used to describe the severity of the crime, but that it also occurred in the actual perception of the crime itself. Since the crime actually seemed more severe, a longer prison sentence was assigned (see also Simpson & Ostrom, 1976).

Another weakness of perspective theory is that studies providing support for it have for the most part relied on hypothetical and uninvolving attitude issues (though this is not exclusively the case; see Judd & DePaulo, 1979). On the other hand, adaptation level and social judgment theories have explored more involving and personally relevant attitude topics.

Social judgment theory—the most ambitious of the approaches in relation to persuasion—deals with two very important variables (discrepancy and ego involvement), but the attempt to expand the scope of the theory to incorporate additional variables has not been impressive. For example, the attempt to explain the persuasion facilitating effect of high source credibility by arguing that it extends the latitude of acceptance appears post hoc and circular. Furthermore, it is important to note that there are many variables that are known to affect the persuasion process that are not addressed by any of the judgmental theories (see chap. 3 for a long list of such variables).

Retrospective

The approach to attitudes and persuasion that we have discussed in this chapter highlights the notion that judgmental processes are important in understanding attitudes and persuasion. How a person judges the position of an incoming message (is it extreme, or close to one's own attitude) is therefore hypothesized to be a crucial determinant of the nature and amount of attitude change that results. The judgmental theories presented in this chapter also share the notion that the previous attitudinal positions to which the person has been exposed are unique determinants of the individual's reference scale and the attitude positions that anchor it. Each of the theories differs, however, in defining the attitudinal positions that anchor the reference scale. Nevertheless, the emphasis on different anchors does not prevent each theory from predicting and explaining the two judgmental distortion effects—*assimilation* (movement toward an anchoring stimulus), and *contrast* (movement away from an anchoring stimulus). Each of the theories in this chapter provides a respected and valuable approach to understanding human judgmental processes, some of which involve attitudes. And, although each theory provides some unique and interesting insights into attitudinal processes, none yet provides a comprehensive approach to the study of persuasion. A full understanding of persuasion requires the discussion of human motivations in the next chapter, and human information processing in the remaining chapters.

Notes

[1]Of course it might be that men who like to watch programs with very attractive women have higher standards of attractiveness or are generally more negative toward women than men who like to watch other programs. To eliminate this possibility (caused by the inability to randomly assign subjects to conditions in a naturalistic study), Kenrick and Gutierres (1980) replicated the study in a controlled laboratory environment and found the same effects even when the men could be randomly assigned to conditions.

[2]In another test of adaptation level theory, Brickman et al. (1978) predicted that victims of tragic misfortune (a crippling accident that leaves the person paralyzed) would show an increase in ratings of common events. This did not occur, probably because all activities were now more difficult for the accident victims. On the other hand, the victims of misfortune did overestimate how happy they were in the past in comparison to controls. The accident victims showed a contrast effect by idealizing their past.

[3]See Parducci and Marshall (1962) and Helson (1964) for the argument that assimilation and contrast effects are complementary processes that are consistent with adaptation level principles. One's own attitude may in fact serve as a subjective neutral point.

[4]Ego involvement or "issue involvement" can be compared with what has been labeled "task" or "response involvement" (Sherif & Hovland, 1961). In the latter type of involvement, the attitudinal issue is not particularly important to the person, but adopting a position that will maximize the immediate situational rewards is. If the situational rewards favor persuasion, then increasing involvement will enhance attitude change (e.g., Zimbardo, 1960), but if the rewards favor resistance, increasing task involvement will decrease persuasion (e.g., Freedman, 1964). The interested reader may wish to consult Greenwald (1981) for even further distinctions about the "involvement" concept.

[5]Although social judgment theory may account for involvement increasing persuasion for consonant messages, research indicating that involvement can sometimes increase persuasion for messages that are clearly *counterattitudinal* provides more difficulties for the theory (Chaiken, 1980; Petty & Cacioppo, 1979b). We return to this issue in chapter 8.

Motivational Approaches

5

In the present chapter, we survey theory and research on attitude change that results from motivational rather than learning or judgmental processes. The impact of motivational forces on attitudes is illustrated by the observations of three social psychologists who joined a doomsday group to find out what happens when a group's belief is disconfirmed (Festinger, Riecken, & Schachter, 1956).

The group was a private and cohesive band of individuals who believed that the world would end by flood before the sun rose on 21 December. This belief was based upon a "message" received from aliens on the planet Clarion by the group's leader, Mrs. Keech. The aliens also indicated that they would use their flying saucer to save the members of the group on the eve of the flood. Following the flood, the group would be returned to earth to create a better world.

The eve of the great flood arrived. The eve turned to night, then to early morning. The aliens and flood failed to materialize, and the group was downcast. Suddenly, Mrs. Keech received another "message" from the aliens saying that the world had been spared because of their faith. Hearing this, the group members rejoiced, reaffirmed their faith in their purpose, and set out to recruit new members for the group. The undeniable disconfirmation of their beliefs left them not only unshaken, but more convinced of their truth than ever before (Festinger et al., 1956, p. 3). As illustrated in this case, people sometimes think, feel, and act in ways that don't appear plausible. People sometimes hold or change attitudes *despite* the objective facts.

We saw in the preceding chapter that perceptual processes can cause a person to distort judgments and thereby influence attitudes. Here we review several motivational theories that posit an automatic, homeostatic system, akin to a central heating system in a house, that maintains an internal state of harmony (equilibrium) within a person.

Cognitive Elements and Systems

The internal mapping of a person's world consists of elements of knowledge called cognitions. These cognitions are interconnected and organized into cognitive systems. For instance, the word "bread" probably reminds you of the word "butter." This is because the cognitive elements of bread and butter are located close together within a cognitive system. In this example, the bond between these two elements is *positive:* bread and butter go together because one follows from (or goes on top of) the other. Other kinds of connections between elements can exist as well. The word "love" may call to mind the word "hate," but these two elements do not follow (typically) from one another—indeed, hate is the opposite of love. Hence, these cognitions, though related, are *negatively bonded.* Finally, two elements might be so distant from or unrelated to one another that the elements are *irrelevant* to one another.

In sum, this internal mapping and organizing serves to structure an individual's world and make it comprehensible and predictable. The elements of this mapping, called cognitions, are numerous and are interconnected to form organized and efficient systems of elements. The systems formed by these interconnections, however, are not as inflexible as the steel girders of a high-rise structure, but rather change to accommodate new information. When the new information disrupts the preexisting equilibrium among the elements, motivational forces come into play to readjust the system of elements so that they are again in harmony.

The Motive to Maintain Cognitive Consistency

The general notion underlying consistency theories of attitudes is that there is a strong tendency for people to maintain consonance (consistency) among the elements of a cognitive system. Suppose you were opposed to the building of nuclear power plants *and* you willingly spoke in favor of constructing nuclear power plants to a group of high school students. These two cognitions—your feeling of opposition to nuclear plants and your knowledge that you spoke in favor of them—are elements within a system of elements about nuclear power plants. Focusing for the moment on just these two elements, you will notice that they imply different things about your attitude toward nuclear power plants— that is, the elements are *inconsistent* regarding the attitude object, nuclear power plants. According to consistency theories of attitudes, this inconsistency causes you to feel uncomfortable and motivates you to somehow resolve this inconsistency. You might resolve this inconsistency, for instance, by deciding that you actually favor the building of at least some nuclear power plants.

There are several characteristics that consistency theories of attitudes have in common: each (a) describes the conditions for equilibrium and disequilibrium among cognitive elements, (b) asserts that disequilibrium motivates the person to restore consistency among the elements, and (c) describes procedures by which equilibrium might be accomplished.

The three major theories of cognitive consistency and attitudes—balance, congruity, and cognitive dissonance—are described in the following sections. Our discussion of balance theory focuses on Heider's (1946, 1958) original formulation and on the research it generated. Congruity theory, which is more limited in scope than balance theory, is described as formulated by Osgood and Tannenbaum (1955; Tannenbaum, 1968). Cognitive dissonance theory is then surveyed in its original form (Festinger, 1957) and in its contemporary form (Wicklund & Brehm, 1976). Finally, we examine two different kinds of "consistency" theories: impression management theory (Tedeschi, Schlenker, & Bonoma, 1971), which was proposed as an alternative to many of the theories reviewed in this chapter, and reactance theory (Brehm, 1966).

Balance Theory

Heider (1958) wrote about the operation of consistency, which he termed *balance,* in dyads (two elements) and triads (three elements). We will focus on triads since most of the research has centered on this configuration. Ever present in Heider's work was his emphasis on the person's own point of view about these elements and their connections. Balance, Heider asserted, was a harmonious, quiescent state in which all of the elements appeared to the individual to be internally consistent. Balance was the most pleasant, desirable, stable, and expected state of relationships among any set of elements to which a person attended. People tend to assume and prefer balanced over imbalanced relations among elements.

Terminology

Heider labeled the elements of the triad as *p,* which represented the subject or self (e.g., you); *o,* which stood for another person; and *x,* which symbolized some stimulus or event. Heider went on to describe two relations that might exist in *p*'s judgment between any two of these elements. The first he termed the *sentiment relation,* which is an attitude. If the attitude is favorable, it is symbolized by *L* (for liking); an unfavorable attitude (e.g., *p* does *not* like *o*) is symbolized by *nL.* Thus, *p* L *x* means that the person likes the stimulus or event, whereas *o* L *x* means that the person *thinks* that the other person likes the stimulus or event.

The second relation discussed by Heider is the *unit relation,* which designates the extent to which two elements are perceived as being associated or dissociated. A positive unit relation, symbolized by *U,* exists when two elements, like opposite magnetic poles, are drawn together (e.g., husband and wife). A negative unit relation, symbolized by n*U,* exists when two elements repulse one another like two similar magnetic poles (e.g., an ex-husband and wife). Of course, a null unit relation can exist between two elements, which means that from the given information we do not know whether the elements are associated or dissociated (Cartwright & Harary, 1956; Insko & Schopler, 1967), and therefore the elements are not pertinent to the same cognitive system of elements. An example of a null unit relation is the case in which *p* and *o* are unmarried. From this information, we simply can not determine whether *p* and *o* are associated, dissociated, or unrelated.

Determining Imbalance in a Cognitive System

The eight possible configurations that can exist among three cognitive elements are displayed in figure 5.1. Regardless of whether the relations are sentiment, unit, or some combination, there are eight possible configurations. More complex analyses using a larger number of elements and relations have been calculated (Cartwright & Harary, 1956), but the fundamental operation of balance is the same as for cognitive systems consisting of two and three elements with one relation between each element.

There are four easy steps in determining whether a triad of elements is balanced or imbalanced. (1) Specify the relevant elements that constitute the cognitive system to the person. (2) Specify the relation between each pair of elements within the system. (3) Assign each positive relation the value of $+1$ and assign each negative relation the value of -1. (4) Multiply all of the values that you assigned to the relations. The product should be either ± 1, since you are multiplying only ± 1s together. When the product is $+1$, the system of elements is balanced; when the product is -1, the system is imbalanced.[1] Balance occurs, for instance, when you agree with a person you like and you disagree with a person you dislike. Imbalance occurs when you agree with a person you dislike and you disagree with a person you like (see box 5.1).

Consequences of Imbalance

As noted earlier, Heider posited that imbalance induces an unpleasant state of tension. He described imbalance as motivational in the sense that the unpleasant tension tended to cause a restoration of balance among the elements (Heider, 1946). Nonetheless, he asserted that imbalance could be tolerated. Imbalance may make a person feel uncomfortable, but it would not irreparably harm the person if not resolved forthwith. In this respect, imbalance differed from traditional motivational constructs such as hunger and thirst.

How is balance restored in an imbalanced system of elements? Rosenberg and Abelson (1960) suggested the reasonable answer that balance is restored in the easiest way possible. Some relations are formed securely between elements whereas others are formed less assuredly, and the latter are more likely to change.

Procedures for eliminating imbalance have been described using a number of terms (transcendence, bolstering, misconstrual, autism). These procedures are manifested in one of three changes in the triad. Recall that the elements in a system are balanced when the product of the signs of their connections to each

Figure 5.1

Balanced and imbalanced "*p-o-x*" triads. *P, o,* and *x* represent you, another person, and an object or issue, respectively; a plus sign denotes a positive relation between two elements, whereas a minus sign denotes a negative relation.

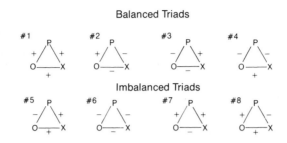

Balanced Triads

#1 #2 #3 #4

Imbalanced Triads

#5 #6 #7 #8

other is positive. A negative product becomes positive by any number of changes in the system of elements, including: (a) reversing the sign of one of the sentiment or unit relations (Tyler & Sears, 1977); (b) changing a sentiment or unit relation to a null relation, in which case what constitutes a system of elements changes (Steiner & Rogers, 1963); or (c) differentiating the positive and negative attributes of an object or person (Stroebe, Thompson, Insko, & Riesman, 1970). For example, suppose that you like to drink coffee, but your doctor (who you also like and trust) tells you that too much coffee is harmful to you. This is an imbalanced state of affairs, since you like both the doctor and coffee, but the doctor does not like the coffee you are drinking because it contains caffeine. To balance this situation, you might differentiate the concept of coffee into caffeinated and decaffeinated types. Balance could be restored then by drinking (and liking) decaffeinated coffees and avoiding (and disliking) caffeinated coffees.

Empirical Research

The most common method of testing the predictions of balance theory involves asking subjects questions about hypothetical social situations usually involving three elements: oneself, another person, and an inanimate object or issue (the *p-o-x* triad—see Mower-White, 1979, Zajonc, 1968). One of the following research strategies is typically used: (a) subjects' reactions (e.g., ratings of pleasantness, consistency) to a *p-o-x* triad are obtained when all of the relations among the elements have been specified; (b) subjects predict how one or more of the relations in a *p-o-x* triad might change after some time has passed; (c) subjects try to memorize and later recall the *p-o-x* triads; and (d) subjects are asked to specify the nature of the third relation when two have been specified

Balance theory furnishes an explanation for the persuasive effectiveness of ads such as this one. You or any other reader of the ad would be *p*, the tennis pro, John Newcombe, would be *o*, and the Cannon AE-1 camera would be *x*. There is a positive relation between Newcombe and the camera (*o-x*), because we learn from the ad that he uses and likes the camera.

Courtesy of Canon USA, Inc. Used with permission.

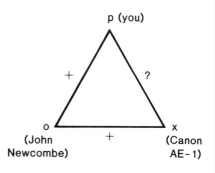

The advertiser is counting on you to form a positive attraction to (or already having a positive attraction to) John Newcombe (*p-o*), leaving only the *p-x* relation unspecified. According to balance theory, you should evaluate *x* (the camera) positively in order to attain balance in the *p-o-x* triad. However, recall from your reading of conditioning (chapter 2) and associational (chapter 3) approaches that there are other explanations besides the balance interpretation that can account for the effectiveness of this ad.

by the experimenter (Burnstein, 1967; Cottrell, Ingraham, & Monfort, 1971; Rossman & Gollob, 1976).

The first test of balance theory was reported by Jordan (1953) using the *p-o-x* triad. Jordan presented the eight triads displayed in figure 5.1, specifying either sentiment, unit, or both sentiment and unit relations among the elements. Students rated each triad along a pleasant-unpleasant scale (high numbers indicated greater unpleasantness). The results of Jordan's study are presented in table 5.1. As predicted, Jordan found that balanced triads (triads 1–4) were

Table 5.1

Perceived Pleasantness of p-o-x Triads

| | p-o-x Triad Number | | | | | | | |
	1	2	3	4	5	6	7	8
Relation								
p-o	+	+	−	−	−	−	+	+
p-x	+	−	+	−	+	−	+	−
o-x	+	−	−	+	+	−	−	+
Rating								
Mean Pleasant- ness*	26.2	39.5	62.4	55.3	58.4	54.8	57.0	58.2

Data from Jordan, 1953.

*Lower numbers indicate greater perceived pleasantness in the triad. Triad numbers refer to those illustrated in figure 5.1.

generally judged to be more pleasant ($M = 45.85$) than imbalanced triads (triads 5–8; $M = 57.10$).

Two additional configurations of the elements undetected by Jordan also influenced the pleasantness ratings, however. First, an *attraction effect* emerged: subjects judged triads in which the p-o relation was positive (triads 1, 2, 7, and 8) as more pleasant ($M = 45.23$) than triads in which the p-o relation was negative (triads 3–6; $M = 57.73$). Second, an *agreement effect* was contained in Jordan's data: Subjects judged triads as more pleasant when the signs of the relations between p-x and o-x were in agreement (triads 1, 2, 5, and 6; $M = 44.73$) than when they were in disagreement (triads 3, 4, 7, and 8; $M = 58.23$). Thus, Jordan (1953) obtained three different cognitive effects (attraction, agreement, and balance) that influenced the perceived pleasantness of the triads.

Zajonc (1968) noted that balance theory as described by Heider and Newcomb did not anticipate the operation of the attraction and agreement effects but rather expected only the balance effect. Nonetheless, the attraction, agreement, and balance effects can be found repeatedly in the literature in which subjects provide data about the pleasantness (e.g., Fuller, 1974; Miller & Norman, 1976), stability (Burnstein, 1967; Crano & Cooper, 1973), consistency (Gutman & Knox, 1972), harmony (Insko & Adewole, 1979), or memorability (Zajonc & Burnstein, 1965) of the triads.

Determinants of Balance, Agreement, and Attraction Effects

Two major explanations have been proposed to account for the emergence of attraction, agreement, and balance effects. The first is that these effects each involve three elements and relations, some of which are experimenter-specified (e.g., *p* likes *x*) and some of which subjects generate on their own (e.g., *p* likes *p*—one likes oneself). According to this account, attraction and agreement effects are really complex balance effects. For instance, triads might be rated as more pleasant when *p-x* and *o-x* agree rather than disagree, because subjects assume that the agreement implies that they (*p*) are similar to the other person (*o*). This subject-generated similarity bond constitutes a positive *p-o* unit relation. What is called an agreement effect therefore might actually be a three-signed balance effect involving three experimenter-specified elements (*p, o,* and *x*), two experimenter-specified relations (*p-x* and *o-x*), and one subject-generated relation (*p-o*) *that subjects use in place of the experimenter-specified p-o relation.* When the *p-o* relation is positive, then agreement is balanced and disagreement is imbalanced. This and other balance interpretations of attraction and agreement effects have been proposed and tested by Insko and his colleagues (Insko & Adewole, 1979; Tashakkori & Insko, 1979).

The second explanation for attraction, agreement, and balance effects holds that they are *not* the consequences of equally complex analyses of the triads (as might be expected if each is a three-sign balance effect), but rather that they differ in the extent of thought required to obtain each, with attraction effects requiring the least and balance effects requiring the most thought about the triad (Cacioppo & Petty, 1981a; Mower-White, 1979; Zajonc, 1968). Recall that (a) the attraction effect requires only that a subject think about one of the three relations (i.e., the *p-o* relation) that exists in the *p-o-x* triad; (b) the agreement effect involves two of the three relations (i.e., *p-x* and *o-x* relations); and (c) the balance effect necessarily involves thought about all three of the relations constituting the triad. According to this account, people have learned to spontaneously direct their attention to particular and increasingly complex aspects of social situations when determining how they feel about or judge the situations. That is, people have learned that in triads the single most important relation is that which exists between themselves and another person (the *p-o* relation); the single most important pair of relations is that which indicates whether agreement or disagreement with another person exists (the *p-x* and *o-x* relation); and the only complex triad of relations is that which involves them *(p),* the other person *(o),* and the object or issue *(x).* The tendency for people to organize their conceptual worlds in positive ways, a tendency called the *positivity bias* (Boucher & Osgood, 1969), might lead people who think minimally about the triads to prefer those that contain a positive rather than a negative *p-o* relation. With further thought about the triad and after noticing the *p-o* relation, the *p-x* and *o-x* relations may become salient. Agreement, in contrast to disagreement, between these relations might be judged more pleasant, because agreement between dyads regarding their attitudes has been associated with more rewards in the past than has disagreement (Byrne & Clore, 1971). Finally, all three relations and elements constituting the triad might require yet more thought about the triad, and the balance effect as initially described by Heider (1946), would emerge.

Recent experimental evidence is consistent with the notion that attraction, agreement, and balance effects emerge at varying levels of thinking about the *p-o-x* triads (Cacioppo & Petty, 1981a). For instance, in one experiment, subjects were given either a brief (ten seconds) or a moderate (thirty seconds) amount of time to view and judge each of the eight *p-o-x* triads along the pleasantness dimension. The results indicated that providing thirty seconds to judge the triads produced, when compared to ten seconds, an equally strong attraction effect, a slightly stronger agreement effect, and a markedly stronger balance effect; indeed, the balance effect did not emerge when subjects were given only ten seconds to judge each of the triads.

Summary

The accumulated research supports balance theory, though additional cognitive biases not anticipated by Heider have emerged (agreement and attraction effects). Heider stressed that balance is a preferred and stable state of elements within a system, and, further, he asserted that balance exists in the person's mind rather than in objective fact. His discussion of this point focused primarily on how relations among elements were defined. The point is equally applicable, however, to defining which elements and relations in the triad are the most salient to a person. When all three elements and relations in a *p-o-x* triad are salient, balance theory predicts that its pleasantness, stability, and so forth are maximal when the product of the relations is positive. This tendency is termed the balance effect.

People, however, do not always take all of the experimenter-specified information into account when judging the triads or real-life social situations. The one sign (*p-o*) attraction effect emerges, for instance, when people have little time or motivation to think extensively about the experimenter-specified elements and relations. The two-sign (*p-x* and *o-x*) agreement effect is found with slightly more thought about the triads.

Congruity Theory

One of the major criticisms of Heider's balance theory is that there are no provisions for *degrees* of liking or belongingness between elements. A positive *p-o* sentiment is scored simply $+1$, whether the couple are casual friends or madly in love. Congruity theory, first proposed by Osgood and Tannenbaum in 1955, overcomes this objection by quantifying gradations of liking and can thus be considered as a special case of balance theory. Its range of application is more limited than that of balance theory, but congruity theory does make very specific, quantitative predictions about the effects of imbalance (incongruity).[2]

The Domain of Congruity Theory

Congruity theory focuses on two elements, the *source* and a *concept,* and one relation, the *assertion* made by the source about the concept. The effect of a movie star asserting in a commercial that a brand of toothpaste is best falls within the domain of congruity theory. This domain can be subsumed by balance theory as follows: (a) the source is the other person, *o;* (b) the concept is, in balance theory, the inanimate object *x;* and (c) whoever hears or reads and responds to the source's assertion about the concept is the person under study, *p.* We have, then, a *p-o-x* triad in which the relation between *o* and *x* is specified. Congruity theory makes predictions about the changes in *p-x* and *p-o* relations as a result of specifying the *o-x* relation. Similarly, both congruity and balance theory assert that *p*'s perception of elements and relations is more important than is the objective state of the elements and relations. Congruity theory therefore operates like a balance theory applied to the effects of sources making assertions (or persuasive appeals) regarding objects or issues (Feather, 1965). On the other hand, congruity theory goes further than Heider's balance theory in that it accommodates gradations of liking. Osgood and Tannenbaum (1955) measured subjects' attitudes toward sources and concepts using the semantic differential to quantify the degree of liking (see chap. 1 for a description of the semantic differential).

Determining and Resolving Disequilibrium (Incongruity)

Incongruity is a state of cognitive disequilibrium that is characterized by a pressure toward congruity or cognitive equilibrium. Perfect congruity is achieved only when a source is associated with a concept that is evaluated identically to the source (e.g., both the source and concept are rated $+1$) or when a source is dissociated from a concept that is evaluated exactly opposite (e.g., the source is rated $+1$ and the concept is rated -1). In most instances, therefore, when a source is linked to a concept, some degree of incongruity arises. The degree of incongruity (and amount of pressure that exists to restore congruity) is a function of how differently an associated source and concept are evaluated and how similarly a dissociated source and concept are evaluated.

Several aspects of congruity theory are noteworthy at this point. First, pressures exist that motivate the person to restore congruity by changing attitudes toward *both* elements. If the Supreme Court rules on the legality of capital punishment, pressures exist to change one's attitude toward both the Supreme Court *and* capital punishment. Second, if a person feels more strongly about one of the elements, that element will change less than the other.

The Mathematics of Congruity Theory

Osgood and Tannenbaum developed mathematical formulae with which to predict the changes in attitudes toward a source and concept when an assertion between them causes incongruity. The point of congruity resolution for the object is obtained using the following formula:

$$R_o = \frac{|A_o|}{|A_o| + |A_s|} A_o + (d) \frac{|A_s|}{|A_o| + |A_s|} A_s$$

where R_o is the point of resolution of the object, A_o is the prior attitude toward the object, A_s is the prior attitude toward the source, and d is the direction of the assertion ($+1$ if favorable and -1 if unfavorable). The point of resolution for the source is obtained from the following formula: $R_s = R_o (d)$. An example of an incongruity resolution is illustrated in figure 5.2.[3]

Empirical Research

Typically, congruity theory is tested by asking subjects to rate on semantic differentials a long list of sources and concepts. This provides the researcher with the needed information about each subject's initial attitude toward each element. At some later time subjects read or hear about one of these sources speaking either in support of or in opposition to one of the concepts. Following this linking, subjects are again asked to rate the sources and concepts on semantic differentials, and comparisons are then made between the attitudes toward each as predicted by congruity theory and as actually observed (Osgood & Tannenbaum, 1955; Tannenbaum, 1968).

Two criteria have been used in these comparisons to judge the merits of congruity theory (Zajonc, 1968). The strictest criterion is to compare how closely the predicted values for attitudes toward the source and concept match the actual values obtained. Congruity theory on the whole appears to perform poorly when applying this strict criterion (Norris, 1965; Stachowiak & Moss, 1965). A second, more lenient criterion is to test whether the attitude that was predicted to show the greatest change did in fact change the most and in the proper direction. Congruity theory appears somewhat more successful using this more lenient criterion, although there are important exceptions (Tannenbaum, 1967; Tannenbaum & Gengel, 1966; Tannenbaum, Macaulay, & Norris, 1966).

The failure of congruity theory to consider the unit relation between the source and concept is another problem. Take the case of a television commercial for a particular brand of basketball shoe. In one version of the commercial, a famous socialite advocates the purchase of the shoe; in another version, an equally famous basketball star promotes the shoe. The socialite and the basketball star have

Figure 5.2

Congruity Theory. **I**: Initial Attitudes—This person has a high regard for the Supreme Court (SC = +3) but is mildly against legalizing capital punishment (CP = −1). **II**: If the Supreme Court ruled that capital punishment was just and legal, pressures to restore congruity should lead to the person liking capital punishment more and the Supreme Court less than initially. Note that congruity is restored following an associative assertion by assigning the same numerical value and sign to the source and concept (in this case, the source = concept = 2.0). **III**: If the Supreme Court ruled that capital punishment is illegal, the person should dislike both more than initially. Note that congruity is restored following a dissociative assertion by assigning the same numerical value but opposite signs to the source and concept (in this case, the source = +2.5, concept = −2.5). Check these values by working through the equations in the text. (Note that these are the values obtained prior to making the assertion and incredulity corrections described in Note 3.)

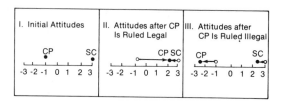

formed an associative assertion between themselves and the basketball shoe; and each may be evaluated equally when people are simply expressing their attitudes toward each source (before their appearance in the commercial). But the basketball star has a strong, positive unit bond to the basketball shoe, which presumably has carried him to stardom. The socialite, on the other hand, has a null unit bond to the basketball shoe, at best. Evidence from Kerrick (1958) indicates that an endorsement by the basketball star rather than the socialite is indeed more likely to induce liking for the shoe. Congruity theory however predicts that, since the sources were evaluated similarly to begin with, they would be equally effective in changing an attitude.

In conclusion, congruity theory can be considered a special case of the more general but less quantified balance theory (Feather, 1964; Tashakkori & Insko, 1979). Congruity theory improves on Heider's balance theory by specifying precise, directional, and testable predictions and by quantifying sentiment toward another person (source) and object (concept) (but see note 2). Furthermore, the congruity theory formulae have some nonobvious implications. For instance, one nonobvious implication is that when a liked source derogates a disliked concept, both the source and the concept may be devalued.

Cognitive Dissonance Theory

Cognitive dissonance theory, first proposed by Leon Festinger in 1957, has generated more research and debate in social psychology than balance and congruity theory put together (or any other single theory in this text). Cognitive dissonance theory is similar in many respects to those other consistency theories.

Although his specification of a cognitive element was less precise than Heider's or Osgood and Tannenbaum's, Festinger also considered two elements as either consistent, inconsistent, or irrelevant to one another. According to Festinger, two elements are consistent (consonant) when one follows from the other. Liking Woody Allen movies and going to see a Woody Allen movie are consonant pieces of knowledge, or cognitive elements; and one would be expected from the other (Aronson, 1969). Festinger said two elements are inconsistent (dissonant) when knowledge of one suggests the opposite of the other. A violation of a person's expectancy might lead to dissonance between the two elements (Aronson, 1969; Brehm & Cohen, 1962). For instance, a doomsayer has dissonant cognitions when a belief that the world is to end by a great flood at sunrise is disconfirmed when the sun completes its uneventful rise over the land.

Finally, two elements can be irrelevant when knowledge of one tells you nothing about what you might expect regarding the other. Knowing that the sun rose this morning and that a movie is premiering tonight would be irrelevant cognitions for most people. We say "for most people" because, just as we found for balance and congruity theory, relations among elements in dissonance theory are determined by a person's subjective expectations regarding them rather than by their logical interrelationships.

These similarities aside, dissonance theory is unique to other consistency theories in some important ways.

First, other consistency theories can simultaneously consider the interrelationships among a number of elements to determine whether or not the structure of elements is balanced (Cartwright & Harary, 1956). Dissonance theory, on the other hand, considers only pairs of elements at a time. The magnitude of the dissonance within a set of many elements is determined by (a) the proportion of relevant elements that are dissonant and (b) the importance of the elements to the person. For example, let's say that you have to choose between two jobs. At one job, the people are friends of yours but the pay is low. The other job has higher pay but everyone is a stranger to you. There is a dissonant consequence of selecting either alternative (i.e., working with strangers versus low pay). If you had a third job offer where you had both friends with whom to work *and* high pay, then the *magnitude* of dissonance created by choosing this, rather than the former two alternatives, would be much less. It would be less because this alternative has all of the positive and none of the negative elements that characterizes the other alternatives. The proportion of dissonant elements therefore is low.

Festinger also used his dissonance theory to make a number of nonobvious predictions regarding attitude change. The nonintuitiveness of these predictions, coupled with the creative (though sometimes questionable) methods used to confirm these predictions (Chapanis & Chapanis, 1964; Johnson & Watkins, 1977), did much to stimulate research in this area. We turn next to Festinger's statements regarding the effects of cognitive dissonance. Some of the surprising implications of this theory should become apparent shortly.

Effects of Cognitive Dissonance

Festinger described dissonance as essentially a motivational state that energized and directed behavior. "Just as hunger is motivating, cognitive dissonance is motivating. Cognitive dissonance will give rise to activity oriented toward reducing or eliminating the dissonance. Successful reduction of dissonance is rewarding in the same sense that eating when one is hungry is rewarding" (Festinger, 1957, p. 70).

How do people rid themselves of dissonance? Festinger suggested three modes. First, the person can change one of the elements to make two elements more consonant. For example, the smoker who learns that smoking causes cancer can stop smoking. By changing the behavioral element, the individual has eliminated the dissonance between the cognitions of knowing that "I smoke to enjoy life" and "smoking can make me unhealthy and make life miserable." In many instances, however, a person finds it very difficult to change the behavioral element. The Supreme Court justice who voted to legalize capital punishment, even though he disliked it, will have difficulty changing his public judgment. An easier element to change is his attitude toward capital punishment—dissonance may be reduced by deciding that capital punishment isn't so bad after all.

The addition of consonant cognitions is a second way to reduce dissonance. The person who decides to continue smoking despite evidence that smoking causes cancer may seek out information that is critical of the research. Similarly, the person who likes diet soda and who learns that saccharin causes cancer in laboratory animals may reason that saccharin has different effects on humans than on animals.

Finally, a person can reduce cognitive dissonance by changing the importance of the cognitions. For example, a person who smokes cigarettes or drinks diet soda might decide that the pleasure received from consuming these products more than makes up for any risks of developing cancer by consuming these products. The person might reason that it's more important to enjoy a short life than to struggle through a long one. In other words, living until ninety is not as important as enjoying life until sixty. Each of these modes would reduce the magnitude of dissonance; the mode selected depends upon which offers the least resistance to change.

The principles of cognitive dissonance, then, were stated less precisely than were those of either balance or congruity theory. What constitutes a "cognitive element," how one determines whether or not one element "follows from" another, and which mode of resolution is least resistant to change were left unspecified. As a result, Festinger's theory has served more as a useful heuristic or guiding principle for research than as a precise statement of when and how much attitude change is expected in a given situation. As more was learned about when and how much attitudes changed in laboratory research, dissonance theory was revised to explain the findings. The result of many years of research and several major revisions of dissonance theory (Aronson, 1968; Brehm & Cohen, 1962; Wicklund & Brehm, 1976) is that contemporary dissonance theory is a more precise, limited, and testable theoretical statement than Festinger's original formulation. We examine next some of the implications, evolutions, and refinements of cognitive dissonance theory.

Effect of Disconfirming an Important Belief

People often hold beliefs that are fundamental to them but for which they have no conclusive evidence. The doomsday cult studied by Festinger et al. (1956) believed that the world was to suffer a devastating flood. The cultists' knowledge that they have stated and acted publicly upon the belief that the continent would be flooded is dissonant with the information that there was no flood. Festinger et al. (1956) suggested that, to eliminate this dissonance, the cultists would rationalize their behavior to make the cognitions appear consistent. As you may recall, the cultists did just that—they decided that their faith had caused God to forestall the flooding, and they even sought to convert new members to their group. The disconfirming information about the flood thereby served to *strengthen* rather than weaken the cultists' attitudes and beliefs.

A similar study was reported by Hardyck and Braden (1962). A southwestern evangelical Christian group believed that there was soon to be a devastating nuclear attack. One hundred three members of the group descended into bomb shelters so that they might survive the attack and build a better civilization. After forty-two days and nights in the bomb shelters, the members surfaced, accepting the fact that no nuclear attack had occurred as expected. But rather than accepting the obvious conclusion that they had erred in their prediction, group members proclaimed that their beliefs had been instrumental in stopping the nuclear attack. Although the members of this group did not participate in active proselytizing following the disconfirmation of their belief (which, you will recall, Festinger et al., 1956, found members of Mrs. Keech's group did), their postdisconfirmation reaction of reinterpreting the events to maintain their beliefs replicated Festinger et al.'s (1956) observations. Hardyck and Braden (1962) indicated that the people who served as subjects in their study may not have proselytized following emergence from the bomb shelter because the Christian group was very cohesive, and the community at large did not ridicule the group members.

Of course, disconfirming information about a belief does not always have the paradoxical effect observed in the doomsday cults. Interaction with our environment often causes us to modify our cognitions to bring them more in line with reality. Nevertheless, disconfirming information *can* have the opposite effect, as illustrated by the above studies. What conditions must be present for this dissonance effect? Festinger et al. (1956, p. 216) specified the following: (a) there must be a firm conviction; (b) there must be public commitment to this conviction; (c) the conviction must be amenable to unequivocal disconfirmation; (d) such unequivocal disconfirmation must occur; and (e) social support for the changed beliefs must be available to the believer after the disconfirmation.

The first four conditions specify what must exist for the arousal of cognitive dissonance. People must possess a personally significant cognition that has been publicly proclaimed, and this cognition must be followed by the opposite of what was expected by it. The fifth condition specifies what must be present for attitude change to serve as the most likely mode of dissonance reduction (see also Batson, 1975).

In sum, information that disconfirms a personally significant belief or expectation can cause a person to seek justification for the initial belief. When social support is available, the person may actually become a more ardent believer than he or she was before the disconfirming event ("my belief must be true if others still agree with me").

Dissonance and the Decision Process

People seldom have their personally significant and publicly proclaimed beliefs disconfirmed. Most everyone, however, has to make small daily decisions and larger life-decisions by choosing from among the available alternatives. Consider the student who is trying to decide whether to major in psychology or accounting. There are advantages and disadvantages in choosing either alternative. Studying psychology may be more interesting than studying accounting, but getting a job may be easier with a degree in accounting. Whichever major is chosen, the student foregoes the advantages of the unchosen alternative and accepts the disadvantages of the chosen alternative. According to cognitive dissonance theory, a person experiences dissonance following a decision because of the psychologically uncomfortable selection that meant giving up the unique advantages of the unchosen alternative and accepting the unique disadvantages of the chosen alternative. In decisionmaking, dissonance is aroused to the extent that the decison (a) is important to the person, (b) means giving up relatively attractive features of the unchosen alternative or accepting unattractive features of the chosen alternative, and (c) concerns alternatives that are dissimilar in their attributes but similar in their desirability.

Festinger suggests four methods of reducing the dissonance aroused by making a decision: revoking the decision; increasing the attractiveness of the chosen alternative and/or decreasing the attractiveness of the unchosen alternative; or viewing the consequences of the alternatives as similar. Most studies of postdecision dissonance use highly dissimilar alternatives and disallow a subject from revoking the decision. That leaves subjects with the possibility of increasing the attractiveness of the chosen alternative and/or decreasing the attractiveness of the unchosen alternative to reduce dissonance. In fact, subjects typically use both of these strategies, which results in a postdecisional spreading of the alternatives. The chosen alternative becomes more highly regarded and the unchosen alternative becomes less highly regarded following a decision than they were before the decision.

The first study demonstrating postdecisional spreading of alternatives was reported by Brehm (1956). Women students were told that a number of manufacturers were interested in determining potential customers' reactions to their products. In addition, they were told that as payment for their participation they would be given one of the products. The women then rated the desirability of a number of consumer products such as a stop watch, silk screen print, portable radio, and fluorescent lamp.

Three conditions were then established. In the control condition, subjects were given one of the products selected by the experimenter; that is, the women made no decision and therefore had no dissonance to reduce. In the high-dissonance condition, the women were asked to choose between an item that had previously been rated as highly desirable and another rated just below it in desirability. In the low-dissonance condition, the women chose between two items that were rated as quite different in desirability.

Following the selection of a product, the women read reports about some of the products and again rated the desirability of each product. As predicted by dissonance theory, the women who chose between two nearly equally-liked products spread apart their postdecisional judgments of these alternatives more than the other women did. Even the women in the low-dissonance condition, though, tended to rate the chosen product as more desirable following their decision than did women who were given one of the products (i.e., who made no decision).

It is possible that this spreading of the alternatives is a logical response to the objective facts about the products that the person notices following the decision. According to dissonance theory, however, this spreading occurs even when there are no objective facts on which to base the reevaluations of the alternatives. Dissonance theory contends that the spreading of the alternatives results from a person's attempt to reinstate cognitive consistency per se. This notion that people rationalize their choices was put to a test by interviewing people at the Canadian National Exhibition (Younger, Walker, & Arrowood, 1977). Younger et al. interviewed people just before or just after they placed a twenty-five-cent bet on a game of chance (bingo, birthday game, or wheel of fortune). Since the outcome of these games is determined solely by chance, further thought about one's decision cannot uncover objective facts that support the alternative selected. According to dissonance theory, of course, there should still be a spreading of the alternatives following a decision. The results (see fig. 5.3), as predicted by

Figure 5.3

The mere act of choosing an alternative can cause changes in how a person views, thinks about, and feels toward the selection. (Data from Younger, Walker, & Arrowood, 1977.)

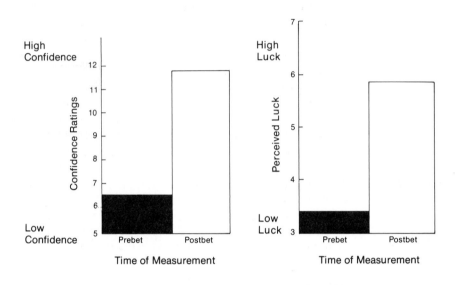

dissonance theory, show that people were more confident in their bet and felt luckier after making their bet than before making it. This same kind of rationalizing has been observed in betters at the two-dollar window of a horse racetrack (Knox & Inkster, 1968). These studies, which were conducted in naturalistic rather than laboratory settings, lend support to Festinger's explanation for the postdecision spreading of alternatives, namely, that rationalizing one's choice of alternatives serves to reduce the cognitive dissonance produced by foregoing the good features of the unchosen alternative and accepting the bad features of the chosen alternative.

Insufficient Justification

Both the disconfirmation of personally significant expectations and the postdecision spreading of alternatives can be cast in terms of *insufficient justification*. Insufficient justification means that a cognition following from another cannot be explained or justified by either the preceding or any other apparent cognition (Gerard, Connolley, & Wilhelmy, 1974). Research illustrating this notion shows that choosing between two equally valued alternatives leads to greater attitude change than choosing between two alternatives that are valued quite differently. The latter decision can be justified by the relative abundance of positive attributes and absence of negative attributes for the chosen compared to the unchosen alternative. There is much less justification for choosing one alternative over another, however, if each is highly regarded to begin with. Insufficient justification for the person's selection of one over the other alternative therefore causes a great deal of dissonance among the apparent cognitive elements.

The notion that insufficient justification leads to more attitude change than sufficient justification has led to some of the most controversial studies conducted in social psychology. Recall from chapters 2 and 3 that, according to several theories of attitude change, the more reward associated with some attitude or behavior, the greater the change in attitude toward that position that should occur. According to dissonance theory, however, the opposite is predicted to occur in some instances. Specifically, when people do something contrary to their attitudes, their attitudes are hypothesized to change toward consistency with the behavior to the extent that they are *underpaid* for engaging in the attitude-discrepant behavior.

The classic study on this question was conducted by Festinger and Carlsmith (1959). Subjects were required to perform several very boring and trivial tasks as part of a study on "measures of performance." In one task, subjects turned each peg on a board of pegs one-quarter turn; then, starting with the first peg, they again turned each peg one-quarter turn. Subjects continued this task for some time before they were asked to take the spools off another pegboard, then place the spools back onto the board, and so on.

After completing the "experiment," a third of the subjects were asked simply to report to a secretary about how interesting they found the experiment to be (control condition). The remaining subjects were asked to convince a waiting subject that the experiment was "exciting and fun." The experimenter explained to these subjects that usually an accomplice would do this, but the accomplice had failed to show up. The experimenter told the subjects that they would be paid for serving as accomplices. Some subjects were told that they would earn one dollar, whereas other subjects were told they would earn twenty dollars for telling the waiting subject that the experiment was interesting. Afterwards, they too were asked to tell the secretary how interesting they thought the experiment was, which served as the measure of attitude toward the task.

The prediction from dissonance theory is that insufficient monetary justification (e.g., one dollar) should produce more liking for the experiment than sufficient monetary payment (e.g., twenty dollars). This prediction is based upon the assumption that dissonance is aroused by telling a believing other person that an incredibly boring experiment is interesting. Since this dissonance would be difficult to reduce by denying the behavior, subjects are left with either changing their attitude about the experiment or explaining their behavior using other cognitive elements. The more money they knew they were being paid when they made their decision, the more easily they could explain their actions by saying they did it for the money. Being paid one dollar rather than twenty dollars makes this reasoning less likely to occur; hence, subjects paid one dollar are left only with changing their attitude toward the experiment as a means of reducing the dissonance created by their behavior. The results of this study, which are displayed in figure 5.4, support the dissonance prediction.

Insufficient Justification: Does Less Really Lead to More?

The Festinger and Carlsmith study and many conceptual replications (see box 5.2) show that less justification produces more attitude change. Initially, this finding may appear to be inconsistent with the predictions from hedonic (reward and incentive) theories of attitude change (e.g., Elms, 1967).

The research surveyed in chapter 2 shows that when people advocate positions that they do not believe, they become more likely to believe the advocated position as the reward that follows the advocacy increases. This reward may be a monetary payment (Rosenberg, 1965), or it may derive internally from the success in persuading another person in a debate (Scott, 1957). Further, when people listen to rather than generate a persuasive message, they are likely to accept the advocated position to the extent that they see incentives and rewards for doing so (see chap. 3). How then do we explain the apparent contradiction of these hedonic (incentive) effects and the counterhedonic effects of the dissonance research?

Many years of research show that the clash between dissonance and hedonic theories of attitude change is more apparent than real. Festinger's theory of cognitive dissonance predicts that *under certain conditions* insufficient justification should arouse dissonance and more attitude change than sufficient justification. Exactly what these conditions are was unclear from Festinger's original statement of dissonance theory, however; and as a result, dissonance theory has been revised periodically since 1957 to better specify the necessary conditions for the arousal of cognitive dissonance (cf. Greenwald & Ronis, 1978). As these conditions became better specified, researchers found that most of the circumstances faced by people in their daily lives lacked one or more of these conditions. As a result, incentive effects are observed more often than dissonance effects (Staw, 1974). For instance, most advertising firms continue to use attractive, well-liked sources for their persuasive messages, because these sources are typically more effective in gaining the attention and acceptance of an audience than obnoxious sources.

Nonetheless, when the conditions necessary for the arousal of cognitive dissonance exist, a counterhedonic relationship between reward and attitude change results. Moreover, the research we surveyed in the preceding sections and in box 5.2 illustrates how pervasive these counterhedonic effects on attitudes *can* be. For instance, under the proper conditions, an unattractive source can be more effective in changing people's attitudes than an attractive source, even though

Figure 5.4

Low rather than high incentives can lead to greater attitude change. (Data from Festinger & Carlsmith, 1959.)

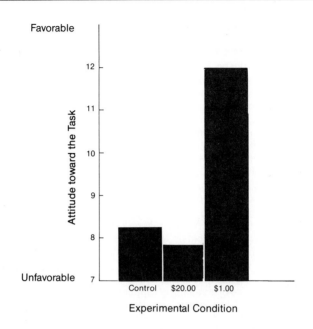

the message delivered by each is identical (Cooper, Darley, & Henderson, 1974; Jones & Brehm, 1967). This occurs, of course, because under certain conditions (specified below) people feel a need to justify their listening to an unattractive source.

Necessary Conditions for Dissonance Arousal

What are the requisite conditions for dissonance arousal? The presumed necessary conditions appear to be ever changing (Converse & Cooper, 1979; Higgins, Rhodewalt, & Zanna, 1979; cf. Greenwald & Ronis, 1978), but fundamentally, dissonance is avoided as long as there are "neutralizing cognitions" available (Aronson, 1969). Unless a person's actions are clearly inconsistent with an existing attitude, for instance, the person should not judge these elements as necessarily dissonant (Fazio, Zanna, & Cooper, 1977). Even when people exhibit some behavior that clearly does not follow from their attitude, they can prevent any dissonance arousal by deciding that (a) there was *no choice* but to act as they did (Linder, Cooper, & Jones, 1967; Sherman, 1970); (b) no one could

---

Box 5.2

Insufficient Justification: Conceptual Replications

The Festinger and Carlsmith study led to a deluge of replications, some using the same procedure (called the "induced compliance paradigm") with different amounts of monetary inducement (Cohen, 1962; Rosenberg, 1965), and others using very different procedures (Aronson & Carlsmith, 1963; Aronson & Mills, 1959). For example, Aronson and Carlsmith (1963) studied the effects of threat on children's preferences for playing with toys. Children who received a *mild threat* for not playing with a toy they initially liked (insufficient justification) later devalued the toy more than children who received a *severe threat* for not playing with the toy (sufficient justification).

In a quite different test of dissonance theory, Zimbardo, Weisenberg, Firestone, and Levy (1965) found that subjects who were induced to eat grasshoppers by a *disliked source* (insufficient justification) came to value them more than subjects induced to eat them by a liked source (sufficient justification). Cooper, Darley, and Henderson (1974) similarly demonstrated that if they can induce people to listen to them, deviant-appearing campaigners can be more persuasive to voters than conventional-appearing campaigners.

Aronson and Mills (1959) extended dissonance theory to the realm of *effort justification.* They found that women who had to go through an embarrassing initiation to join a boring group (insufficient justification) later rated the group as more interesting than women who went through a simple and nonembarrassing initiation to join the group (sufficient justification).

These studies open new domains of application for dissonance theory and illustrate the creativeness of the dissonance researchers through the years.

---

identify them with the discrepant behavior, so they could deny that they seriously meant what they said or did (Brehm & Cohen, 1962; Riess & Schlenker, 1977); or (c) the actions for which they are responsible caused no harm to anyone (Calder, Ross, & Insko, 1973; Collins & Hoyt, 1972; Cooper & Worchel, 1970; Goethals & Cooper, 1975). Wicklund and Brehm (1976) summarized these conditions as follows:

> When an individual has no foresight, or hint, that his commitments might have discrepant implications, he is thereby not a causal agent in the cognitive inconsistency. . . . recent research has made it abundantly clear that dissonance reduction as we know it takes place only when the dissonant elements have been brought together through the personal responsibility of the individual who experiences dissonance. [P. 7.]

Dissonance, then, is aroused only when a person is forced to conclude that he or she is the willing causal agent of some discrepant and personally significant decision that leads predictably to some form of negative consequences.

The operation of both hedonic and counterhedonic effects on attitudes is evident is a study reported by Staw (1974). During the Viet Nam war, young men were being drafted to serve in the armed forces. A number of students wanted to avoid the draft, and one common tactic to do so was to join the U.S. Army Reserve Officer's Training Corps (ROTC) at their campus. Some of these students simply enrolled for a year. Others signed a contract committing themselves to attend ROTC training for the duration of their college careers *and* to serve several years in the Army Reserve after graduation.

On 13 March 1969, then-President Nixon proposed that the U.S. Selective Service System choose draftees by the use of a lottery. The lottery would assure draftees were selected randomly and would allow young men to anticipate their chances of being drafted. Men receiving a draft number ranging from 1–122 were described as likely draftees, whereas men receiving a number ranging from 245–366 were described as unlikely draftees (the numbers were assigned on the basis of date of birth).

The lottery for people born prior to 1951 was held in December of 1969, and the lottery for people born during 1951 was conducted in July of 1970. Staw studied the attitudes of students who joined ROTC in the fall of 1969—before receiving a draft number but *after* learning that they would obtain one. Staw reasoned that if a student received a low draft number (1–122), then the incentive for belonging to the somewhat unpopular ROTC organization would be greatly enhanced, since joining the ROTC program would prevent their being drafted into the active Armed Forces. Students who received a high draft number, as it turned out, need not have joined the ROTC program to avoid the draft. They knew when they decided to join, moreover, that the lottery may be all that they needed to avoid the draft. These individuals would therefore be especially susceptible to dissonance arousal.

Consider first the students who had not committed themselves to continuing their participation in ROTC. These students were initially justified in joining ROTC because of the *chance* that they might receive a low draft number and be drafted. Once numbers were assigned, students with low numbers had even more justification for belonging in the ROTC program. However, students who received high numbers no longer could justify their participation in terms of avoiding the draft. These students *could* avoid dissonance, however, by discontinuing their participation in ROTC. This, in fact, is what generally happened (Staw, 1974). That is, when noncommitted students received low numbers (enhanced incentives for participating), they became more likely to continue their participation in ROTC. Noncommitted students who received high numbers (reduced incentives for participation), however, became less likely to continue their participation in the organization (March & Simon, 1958). This hedonic relationship between incentive (reward) and attitude change occurred when students were not committed to their attitude-discrepant behavior.

Consider, though, the students who had signed a multi-year contract to participate in ROTC and to serve in the Army Reserve. Students who subsequently received a low draft number were redeemed; their "foresight" was going to keep them out of the draft. The students who received a high draft number, however, faced a more dissonant set of circumstances. As predicted by dissonance theory, the students who received high draft numbers became *more* positive toward and performed better in the ROTC program than those who received low draft numbers. This, of course, is counterhedonic: the rewards of belonging to the ROTC program were greater for students with low numbers than for students with high numbers.

Temporal Characteristics of Dissonance Reduction

The timing of the occurrence of dissonance is one final aspect of Staw's (1974) study that warrants comment here. The students enrolled in the ROTC program in the fall of 1969, but the lotteries were not held until months later. Nevertheless, dissonance was aroused by the lottery assignment if it indicated a negative consequence of the earlier decision. Goethals and Cooper (1975) have shown that people who anticipate the possibility of negative consequences following a decision suffer no dissonance until the negative consequences are seen as inevitable. They found also that if negative consequences appear inevitable at the time of the initial decision, dissonance reduction begins immediately.

These results are compatible with Festinger's (1957) outline of dissonance reduction, which he conceived as an active though biased form of information processing. Further evidence for the notion of dissonance as a form of active information-processing activity can be found in studies showing that distracting a person from thinking about the dissonant elements stalls or stops dissonance reduction (Allen, 1965; Zanna, 1975). Moreover, should dissonant cognitions exist when the person is motivated and able to think about them some time later, the person begins *at that time* to search for modes by which to resolve the dissonance (Higgins, Rhodewalt, & Zanna, 1979; Riess & Schlenker, 1977).

In sum, when dissonant cognitive elements become apparent to a person, the person becomes motivated to find a cause or label for the dissonance (Zanna & Cooper, 1976). The person first attempts to explain away the cognitive inconsistency by finding possible external causes, which require little or no cognitive reorganization on the part of the person ("I had no choice but to do it"—Riess & Schlenker, 1977). When no "neutralizing cognitions" can be found that are convincing to the person, internal readjustments of cognitive elements must occur (e.g., attitude change).

The Nature of Cognitive Dissonance

In our discussion of dissonance, we have thus far focused on the antecedents and consequences of cognitive dissonance. Indeed, throughout the many years of research on cognitive dissonance, there has never been a "manipulation check" for the arousal of dissonance.[4] One could tell if dissonance was aroused only by observing whether or not the predicted mode of dissonance reduction occurred (attitude change). When the predictions from a study were not confirmed, the researcher did not know whether dissonance was not aroused by those particular conditions (Wicklund & Brehm, 1976, pp. 29–48), dissonance failed to have the predicted consequences (Freedman & Sears, 1965), or dissonance was reduced through some unmeasured mode (Gaes, Kalle, & Tedeschi, 1978).

How might cognitive dissonance be identified? Festinger (1957, p. 3) described dissonance as a motivational tension that is unpleasant. This description points to three dimensions along which dissonance might be characterized: the motivational, physiological, and phenomenological (subjective) dimensions.

Traditional motivational constructs such as hunger or thirst create a drive that facilitates the learning of simple responses but disrupts the learning of complex responses (Spence & Spence, 1966). If cognitive dissonance produces a motivational state, then the experimental manipulation of dissonance should have these effects on learning simple and complex responses. Though the data are not in complete agreement on this issue (Pallak & Pittman, 1972), most of the studies indicate that putting people in high dissonance conditions causes them to perform better on simple tasks and worse on complex tasks (Kiesler & Pallak, 1976; Wicklund & Brehm, 1976, chap. 6). Dissonance therefore seems to serve as a motivational drive with general energizing effects on simple and dominant responses.

The physiological effects of dissonance are not yet very well understood. The dissonance created by deciding between two attractive alternatives leads to a constriction of the blood vessels in the outer portions of the body—a response typically found when persons are under stress (Gerard, 1967). What dissonance "looks like" physiologically when aroused by other means is unknown at this time, so it is not known whether dissonance generally appears physiologically as a stress reaction or whether it varies in its physiological appearance depending upon the procedures used to arouse it.

Finally how does dissonance feel to the person? The subjective nature of dissonance has been examined using a number of procedures (Cooper, Zanna, & Taves, 1978; Cooper, Fazio, & Rhodewalt, 1978), but the most common means of study is based upon the notion that people search external cues first to label an unexplained internal state (e.g., tension or arousal—Schachter & Singer, 1962). People sometimes *misattribute* the cause of an internal state to something that seems a reasonable cause at the time. For instance, a person who awakens on a rainy day feeling fatigued may attribute this feeling to the weather when, in fact, it is caused by the late hours of socializing in which the person engaged the night before. Of course, if the person had awakened to a beautiful sunny day, he or she could not have misattributed the feeling of fatigue to the weather. Misattribution can occur only when the external event has the same kind of effects on the person as is being experienced at the moment.

Zanna and Cooper (1974) used this reasoning to study how dissonance felt to people. They gave people a pill to ingest. The subjects believed that the researchers were investigating the effects of the drug on learning. Some of the subjects were told that the drug had no side effects, others were told that it might cause them to feel tense, and still others were told that it might cause them to feel relaxed. Further, subjects were told that any side effects would occur quickly, though the effects of the drug on learning were not to occur for some time. Subjects were asked, while waiting for the drug to take full effect, to assist the experimenter in another study, in which they would write an attitude-discrepant message under conditions of choice (dissonance group) or no choice (no dissonance).

Zanna and Cooper had, in fact, given all of the subjects a placebo—a pill made of milk powder. The pill, of course, had absolutely no side effects, but some of the subjects *believed* that the pill might cause them to feel a certain way (i.e., tense or relaxed). If dissonance caused subjects to feel tense, then only the group of subjects who believed the pill might cause them to feel tense would be able to misattribute this internal state to the pill.

How do you know whether or not the person misattributes the dissonance to the pill? Let's go back to the example of the person who awakens feeling fatigued. If the weather is beautiful and sunny, then the person can't misattribute the fatigue to the weather and must continue thinking about other possible causes of the fatigue. Should this person decide that the prior night's activity caused the fatigue, then he or she may decide to make some changes in late night habits. On the other hand, if the person awakens to a rainy day and decides that the fatigue is due to the weather, then the person won't make any changes in his or her attitudes or *behavior,* even though he or she may continue to feel fatigued that day. Any cognitive reorganization to reduce the unpleasant feeling is blocked, since the unpleasant feeling is supposedly caused externally and therefore is only temporary (see also Fazio, Zanna, & Cooper, 1979).

This reasoning now allows us to make predictions regarding the outcome of Zanna and Cooper's study. Typically, subjects who engage in attitude-discrepant behavior under choice conditions are forced to realign their attitudes with their dissonant behavior (Linder et al., 1967). But if subjects misattribute the dissonance-created feelings to the pill, then they should show no attitude change, since they no longer have responsibility for doing anything about these feelings. These subjects by their misattribution have decided that the tension is caused externally (by the pill) and is only temporary. Hence, the subjects in the high-choice tension-producing conditions should show *no* attitude change (just like the subjects in the low-choice conditions). The results of Zanna and Cooper's study (displayed in fig. 5.5) support these predictions. The authors concluded that dissonance feels something like "tension." Notice that when subjects experiencing dissonance expected to feel "relaxed" rather than tense, they showed an especially high level of attitude change. Presumably, this is because the felt dissonance was most apparent and least explicable in terms of an external source under these conditions.

Figure 5.5

The attitude change normally produced by an attitude-discrepant behavior under high-choice conditions was affected by the possible "side effects" of a placebo. (Data from Zanna & Cooper, 1974.)

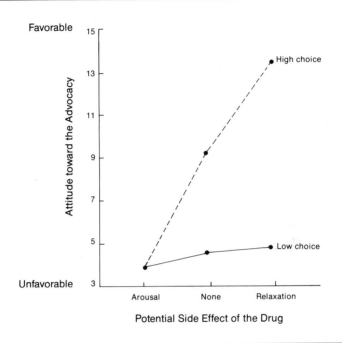

In a number of studies that followed Zanna and Cooper's (1974) study, dissonance was thought to create a feeling of unpleasant arousal in a person (Cooper, Fazio, & Rhodewalt, 1978; Cooper, Zanna, & Taves, 1978; Zanna & Cooper, 1976). One question remained: was dissonance simply *unpleasant,* or was it felt to be *arousing* as well? Several studies suggested that dissonance felt arousing, but the results could be explained if dissonance simply induced feelings of unpleasantness (e.g., Cooper, Zanna, & Taves, 1978).

To answer this question, Higgins, Rhodewalt, and Zanna (1979) conducted a study similar to the one by Zanna and Cooper (1974). This time, however, subjects were told that the pill might cause them to feel "unpleasantly sedated" (unaroused-unpleasant), "relaxed" (unaroused-pleasant), "tense" (aroused-unpleasant), "pleasantly excited" (aroused-pleasant), or nothing in particular (no side effects control group). These subjects voluntarily wrote an attitude-discrepant message while supposedly waiting for the pill to take effect fully.

The results of Higgins et al. (1979) are displayed in table 5.2. They, like Zanna and Cooper (1974), found that a pill with the possible side effect of

Table 5.2

Immediate Attitude Change for High-Choice Conditions*

| | Possible "Side Effects" of Placebo | | No Side Effects (control condition) |
	Arousing	Calming	
Sensation			
Pleasant	7.3	5.9	4.7
Unpleasant	1.7	0.4	

Data from Higgins, Rhodewalt, & Zanna, 1979.
*Higher scores indicate more acceptance of the counterattitudinal advocacy.

making the person feel "tense" (aroused-unpleasant) lessened attitude change. More important, however, is their finding that a pill described as possibly causing the person to feel "unpleasantly sedated" blocked attitude change even more completely. Overall, the characteristic of unpleasantness was more effective in allowing the misattribution of dissonance to the pill than was the characteristic of arousal (see also Rhodewalt & Comer, 1979). It appears, then, that a high state of cognitive dissonance is best described, from the subject's point of view, as an unpleasant feeling (Shaffer, 1975).

In sum, the experimental manipulations of cognitive dissonance induce (a) a generalized drive similar in some respects to that produced by traditional motivational states, (b) physiological activity similar to that found in individuals under stress, and (c) an unpleasant subjective feeling.

It is evident from the above survey of research that cognitive dissonance theory serves as a heuristic for a wide variety of observations. Occasionally, an alternative explanation has been proposed for some of these observations. We will discuss one of these alternatives in the next section, but we defer discussion of another (Bem's self-perception theory) to the next chapter, since it is not a motivational theory.

Impression Management Theory

Impression management theory deals with how people present an image to others in order to achieve a particular goal (Goffman, 1959). Most analyses of impression management assume that a primary goal in presenting oneself to others is the attainment of social approval (Arkin, 1981). The type of public image presented to people clearly affects the material and social rewards obtained in social interactions (Jones & Wortman, 1973; Schlenker, 1975). During the Watergate scandal, Nixon met with his top aides to discuss what the public should be told about the Watergate burglary and subsequent coverup. The transcripts of Nixon's tapes indicate that he and his advisors went to great lengths to present a public image that would enhance self-esteem and gain approval as much as possible. The tapes also show that Nixon had to concede to the demands of social reality as reporters learned more facts about the coverup. Although Nixon's speeches were designed throughout the investigation to convey an image of innocence and honesty, Nixon finally admitted the possible involvement of his advisors in the coverup when a disclosure of these facts by the press became inevitable (New York Times Staff Editors, 1974; see also box 5.3).

Clearly then, people are often motivated to impress other people, and the manner in which attitudes and beliefs are expressed can be used to create a desired effect on others. For example, people may use complimentary attitude and belief statements to flatter other people and gain their approval. People may also change or report to have changed their beliefs and attitudes in an effort to create a desirable impression on an imaged or real audience (see Schlenker, 1980). Research strongly indicates that impression management *can* affect what people report their attitudes to be (Baumeister, Cooper, & Skib, 1979; Baumeister & Jones, 1978; Gaes et al., 1978; Schlenker, 1975). For instance, Hass (1975) told subjects that they would soon hear a speech made by an expert economist. In addition, subjects were told one of the following: (a) *topic only*—the speech concerned the future U.S. economic situation; (b) *topic and counterattitudinal position*—it concerned the imminence of a U.S. economic depression; or (c) *topic and proattitudinal position*—it concerned the imminence of U.S. prosperity. All subjects were then asked to indicate their own belief about how soon there would be an economic depression in the U.S. (In addition, a control group anticipated no message but simply indicated their belief in the imminence of an economic depression.)

Hass found that subjects stated more neutral attitudes on the issue, even before hearing the speech, when they knew only of the topic of the impending communication. Hass argued that since subjects did not know what position the speaker would take, they adopted a relatively safe, moderate position (see also Cialdini, Levy, Herman, & Evenbeck, 1973). When the subjects expected the speaker to present a view that was opposite to their own, they showed a large shift in the direction of the speaker before hearing the speech. By shifting before the speech, subjects protected themselves from looking inconsistent or indecisive (as they might if they shifted after the speech). Subjects expecting to hear a proattitudinal position showed no anticipatory shifts.

One of the most interesting applications of impression management theory is as an alternative to dissonance theory (Tedeschi, Schlenker, & Bonoma, 1971). Impression management theory holds that:

Irrespective of whether or not people have psychological needs to be consistent . . . there is little doubt that the appearance of consistency usually leads to social reward, while the appearance of inconsistency leads to social punishment [Schlenker, 1980, p. 204].

Box 5.3

Impression Management

On the other hand . . .

The Very Republican Lady from Columbus, Ohio, looked sternly at former Texas Gov. John Connally and asked: "What are your views on the ERA?" "I'm for it," Connally shot back. "I've been for it since 1962." The Very Republican Lady, obviously no fan of the Equal Rights Amendment, glared. After a short, pained silence, Connally began to revise and extend his remarks. "Actually, I have mixed feelings," he said. "If the amendment would weaken or destroy family life, I'd have to take another look. . . . I wouldn't have voted to extend the time for ratification. That was wrong. . . . So for all practical purposes I guess you could say I'm against it today."

Reprinted from the Des Moines Register. Used with permission.

Attempts to impress other people with our attitudes occur often in everyday life. In this news story, John Connally, an unsuccessful candidate for the Republican presidential nomination in 1980, attempts to impress a potential voter with his views on the Equal Rights Amendment to the U.S. Constitution. Although he adopts an attitude that is similar to that of the voters, he does it at the expense of appearing consistent. How impressed do you think the voter is with Connally's position?

People presumably learn to act consistently across social situations early in their lives. When a child's behavior is predictable (i.e., consistent to others) from one moment to the next, the child is easier to deal with and receives more rewards (or less punishment) than when the behavior is unpredictable (i.e., inconsistent across situations and time). This motive is maintained as an adult Schlenker notes because "consistency gives actors a desirable degree of predictability and trustworthiness, and it generates liking and respect" (p. 232).

Thus, impression management theorists (Tedeschi et al., 1971) agree with Festinger that tension is produced when people act publicly in a manner contrary to their attitudes. Tedeschi et al. argue that the tension is not produced by dissonant cognitions but rather by people's knowledge that they *appear inconsistent to others*. These people immediately begin to manage more carefully the impression they are making on others by restoring consistency to their actions or to their expression of attitudes. A person who is induced to advocate raising tuition thus may *report* that they favor an increase in tuition to create the image in others of consistency, dependability, and reliability.

In dissonance theory, then, people are motivated by cognitive inconsistency to set their thoughts and actions in order, whereas in impression management theory, people want to convey, given social constraints, as positive and consistent a public image as possible in order to obtain social rewards. Research clearly demonstrates that impression management affects attitudes, but it also indicates that cognitive consistency (e.g., dissonance) has separate effects on attitudes (Riess & Schlenker, 1977). Snyder and Swann (1976), discussing the relationship between attitudes and behavior, arrived at a similar conclusion:

> an individual in a social setting actively attempts to construct a pattern of social behavior appropriate to that particular context. Diverse sources of information are available to guide this choice, including (a) cues to situational or interpersonal specifications of appropriateness and (b) information about inner states, dispositions, and attitudes (Snyder & Swann, 1976, p. 1035).

The question for future research is not which view is correct, but rather what conditions cause each to operate.

Psychological Reactance Theory

As we have seen, people's attitudes are influenced by a number of motivational forces. The consistency notions of balance, congruity, and dissonance assert that people tend to maintain cognitive equilibrium to minimize intrapsychic tension. Our brief survey of impression management theory further reveals that people are motivated hedonically to convey a positive "face" to those around them. Our discussion of motivational theories of attitude change concludes with consideration of Brehm's theory of psychological reactance.

According to Brehm (1966), threatening to restrict or actually eliminating a person's freedom to act as he or she chooses arouses in that person a motivational drive called *psychological reactance*. This psychological reactance motivates a person to reestablish the lost or threatened free behavior or attitude. When people believe that their freedom to act or hold a certain position may be or has been limited, they try to somehow reinstate this freedom. In essence, then, psychological reactance theory addresses in a more sophisticated manner the phenomenon people sometimes refer to as "reverse psychology" (Gergen, 1973).

What Does It Take to Arouse Reactance?

Brehm (1966) asserted that, to arouse reactance in people, they must first perceive it as likely that they are no longer free to think or do something that they previously could. This restriction of a free behavior is necessary but not sufficient; in addition, the individual must perceive the elimination of free behavior as illegitimate or unjustified (Brehm, 1966, p. 7; Grabitz-Gniech, 1971). For instance, two avid smokers should feel reactance if, while sitting in a restaurant, their waiter told them not to smoke because *he* didn't like it. This same couple, however, should feel little if any reactance if the same instruction was accompanied by a legitimate explanation (that the fire code didn't permit it). The more justified the elimination of a behavior that was previously free, the less reactance aroused within an individual.

Second, the less important the threatened behavior is to an individual, the less reactance aroused by its elimination. Imagine that two people, a heavy smoker and a light smoker, enter the smoking section of a restaurant. As they are seated, a man sitting at an adjacent table turns to the couple and tells them they should not smoke while he is present. Smoking is a free behavior for both smokers, but it is presumably a more important free behavior to the heavy smoker. Hence, the heavy smoker should be especially reactive to the man's admonishment that they not smoke, though both would experience some reactance (Brehm, 1966; Mazis, 1975).

Third, reactance is aroused in direct proportion to the extent to which the free behavior is limited. Imagine that the man told our heavy and light smokers that they should not smoke for the next minute versus the next hour, after which time he would leave and they would again be free to smoke if they wished. Though some reactance should be aroused when the restriction lasted even a minute, substantially more reactance should be aroused when the limitation of their freedom is the more severe one-hour restriction (Brehm & Weinraub, 1977).

Fourth, the extent of reactance arousal depends upon the similarities of the alternatives to the restricted behavior. "When there is considerable qualitative overlap between the alternatives available in a decision, importance of freedom to choose one over another is minimal" (Wicklund, 1974, p. 123). Brehm and Weinraub (1977) found support for this postulate in a study using two-year-old boys. Each child was allowed to play with two toys; one was placed in front of a Plexiglas barrier and one was placed equidistant from the child behind the barrier. In one of the conditions, similar toys were placed in front of and behind the barrier, whereas the toys were dissimilar (but equally preferred) in another condition. When a similar toy was behind the barrier, the child's freedom to play with it was restricted, but the alternative was so similar that little reactance was aroused. Conversely, when a dissimilar toy was behind the barrier, the barrier constituted a more reactance-arousing threat to freedom, since the available and blocked alternatives shared little in common. As predicted by reactance theory, the boys approached the blocked toy more often when it was dissimilar than when it was similar to the easily available toy.

Finally, some research suggests that reactance is not aroused if the individual feels inadequate (Grabitz-Gniech, 1971), incompetent (Wicklund & Brehm, 1976), or controlled by external events (Biondo & MacDonald, 1971). The notion underlying these studies is that some individuals are more responsive to situational cues or are more overwhelmed by the situational demands than other individuals. Individuals easily overwhelmed by situational demands are less assertive about determining their own behavior, are more likely to be influenced, and are less reactive when a free behavior is restricted than are individuals who are not overwhelmed by the situation and who believe they should set their own course of action.

Consequences of the Arousal of Reactance

Brehm (1966, 1972) asserted that reactance is a motivational force that leads a person to try to reestablish the threatened freedom. A clearly predicted consequence of reactance is that the person tries to perform the threatened or restricted behavior or attempts to strengthen his or her hold on the threatened attitude position. The reassertion of a threatened preference has been demonstrated empirically many times (e.g., Brehm and Sensenig, 1966). A limitation on the reactance effect is illustrated in box 5.4.

Interestingly, reactance seems to have a motivational effect whether the restricted freedom is in terms of how a person can *act* or in terms of how a person can *think and feel*. Petty and Cacioppo (1979a), for instance, told some subjects that they were about to hear a message designed to persuade them. The message was on an issue of either high or low personal importance. Other subjects were not told the persuasive purpose of the message. Only the subjects who had been forewarned of the persuasive intent of the message, therefore, should perceive the message as a threat to the way in which they could think and feel, and this should be especially true when the message is on a topic of high importance. As predicted by reactance theory, subjects hearing the high-importance message counterargued and disagreed more with the message than subjects in whom reactance was not aroused. For the low-importance message, the restriction in freedom had no effect on counterarguing or attitudes.

Reactance may also cause a person to reevaluate the threatened behavior or attitude more positively and/or the remaining alternatives more negatively. This consequence, captured in the adage "the grass is always greener on the other side of the fence," is illustrated in a study by Mazis (1975). On New Year's Day 1972, an antiphosphate law went into effect in Miami, Florida, prohibiting the sale, use, or possession of laundry detergents and cleaning products that contained phosphates. Few popular laundry detergents were available at the time that contained no phosphates, so the freedom of Miami residents to choose a laundry detergent was severely restricted. Meanwhile, Tampa, Florida, residents

Box 5.4

Reactance Theory

were unaffected by Miami's antiphosphate law, and they continued choosing whichever detergent they wished (no reactance control group). According to reactance theory, Miami residents should be more motivated than Tampa residents to reestablish the threatened freedom. Although the Miami residents could not legally perform the threatened behavior, they *could* reevaluate the alternatives and change their attitudes about phosphate detergents, nonphosphate detergents, and governmental regulation of their behavior.

The results of Mazis's study are consistent with the view that the Miami residents used these available modes to vent the generalized drive produced by

In this cartoon, Dagwood tries to apply reactance theory to get a raise. According to reactance theory, threatening to eliminate a free behavior tends to make the threatened behavior more valuable—this often leads the person to try and perform the behavior, such as giving out a raise. But Dagwood makes a few mistakes. For instance, from the cartoon we learn that Mr. Dithers didn't want to give Dagwood a raise but felt some pressure, as if he had to give him one. In addition, Dagwood doesn't tell Mr. Dithers that he *can't* give Dagwood a raise (high reactance) but rather that one is not needed.

Regardless of Dagwood's misapplication of reactance theory, he likely would have been unsuccessful in any case; although reactance influences attitudes and persuasion (Brehm, 1972), other factors are also important. For example, the rewards Mr. Dithers can keep for himself by not giving Dagwood a raise may be more than enough to offset any tendency to change an attitude that Dagwood might stimulate using reactance theory.

reactance. Miami residents judged phosphate detergents as more effective than did Tampa residents; moreover, Miami residents were more unfavorable than their Tampa counterparts toward legal restrictions forbidding the sale of products containing phosphates and toward governmental regulations designed to protect the public from water pollution (Worchel, Arnold, & Baker, 1975).[5]

Psychological reactance, then, is created when a person who feels competent in guiding his or her own behavior in a situation perceives an important and unique free behavior, belief, or attitude as threatened. This reactance motivates the person to respond by (a) performing the threatened behavior; (b) counterarguing, often covertly, the reasons for and benefits of the restriction;

and (c) changing attitudes toward the various alternatives, particularly reevaluating more favorably the threatened or eliminated alternative.

Retrospective

The approach to attitudes and persuasion that we surveyed in this chapter focuses on the different human motives as they relate to attitude change. The need or desire to maintain cognitive consistency, or what people consider to be "logical" consistency among their beliefs (i.e., psycho-logic), is addressed by balance and congruity theories of attitude change. The attitudinal effects of the drive to maintain cognitive consistency between pairs of elements, such as between one's attitude and one's behavior, is the focus of cognitive dissonance theory. Dissonance theory is especially intriguing because it correctly predicts that, in certain specifiable instances, our attitudes will change the *less* our newly expressed attitudinal positions are associated with rewards. Another consistency theory of sorts, impression management theory, details how our attitudes are influenced by the desire to maintain a consistency in social behaviors (including attitude expressions) across situations. Finally, psychological reactance theory outlines the effects of threatening or eliminating our freedom to choose freely how to think, feel, and act. Although the research that we have reviewed in this chapter clearly shows that there is utility in viewing some attitude changes as being influenced by strong motivational forces, we shall find in the next chapter that other attitude changes can be viewed as resulting from a cool, detached analysis of the persuasion situation.

Notes

[1]Newcomb (1953, 1968) has developed another version of balance theory that is primarily relevant to interpersonal attraction and communication, so we will not discuss Newcomb's version further here.

[2]There have, however, been attempts to quantify Heider's balance theory. Wiest (1965), for example, allowed each relation to take on a value from -3 to $+3$, and conceptualized the p-o-x triad as a cube in which each of the dimensions represented a different one of the three -3 to $+3$ relations. Connecting the four balanced corners of the cube produces a tetrahedron inside the cube, and Wiest postulated that balanced points would, by and large, exist on the surface of the tetrahedron. Wellens & Thistlewaite (1971) provide mathematical formulae that enable prediction of a value of one relation from specified values of the other two. For example, when relations are rated on a -3 to $+3$ scale, the p-o relation can be predicted from the p-x and o-x relations by the following formula: p-o $= .5[3 - | (p\text{-}x) - (o\text{-}x) |] + .5 [| (p\text{-}x) + (o\text{-}x) | - 3]$. Thus, if you like xylophones a little (p-$x = +1$), and Olivia likes them a lot (o-$x = +3$), your liking for Olivia (p-o) would be: $.5[3 - | 1 - 3 |] + .5 [| 1 + 3 | - 3] = +1$. Research on various tetrahedronic models of balance is only now beginning to accumulate, so it is too early to evaluate their utility, though the early signs are encouraging (see Tashakkori & Insko, 1979, in press).

[3]The empirical research on congruity theory indicates that two corrections need to be made to the basic congruity formulas to achieve a closer correspondence of predicted and obtained values (Osgood & Tannenbaum, 1955). The first is the *assertion constant* that takes into account the tendency for the concept to change more than the source, all else being equal. This constant ($\pm.17$ when a -3 to $+3$ scale is used to assess attitudes) is used to increase the amount of predicted change for the concept. The second is the *correction for incredulity,* which takes into account the finding that people don't always believe everything they read or hear. Specifically, people are especially unlikely to believe a positive assertion linking two elements that are evaluated very differently or a negative assertion linking two elements that are evaluated very similarly. The specific correction (used when attitudes are measured on a -3 to $+3$ scale) is: $i = 1/40\ (A_s^2 + 1)\ (A_o^2 + A_o)$. The value i is used to reduce the amount of change predicted for the source and concept.

[4]A few attempts have been made to assess dissonance arousal using subjective reports of frustration/mental discomfort (Shaffer, 1975; Shaffer & Hendrick, 1974). The interested reader may wish to consult Mackay (1980) as well.

[5]This pattern of results may also be explained by possible Miami/Tampa subject or information exposure confounds or by the fact that Miami residents may have come to like phosphate detergents more because they experienced the ineffectiveness of the nonphosphate brands.

Attributional Approaches

6

In the preceding chapter, we discussed how motivational factors might account for attitude change. In this chapter, we turn to an attributional analysis of attitudes and persuasion. An *attribution* is an inference made about why something happened, why someone did or said something, or why *you* acted or responded in a particular way. The crux of the attributional approach is that people infer underlying characteristics—such as attitudes and intentions—from the verbal and overt behaviors they observe. When there *appears* to be an obvious reason for some behavior, people confidently attribute that behavior to that cause.

A common feature of the various attributional approaches surveyed in this chapter is that an inference about the cause of a response is the most direct antecedent of attitude change. The inference might be that there is something internal to the person that caused an observed behavior, such as the person's attitude or personality, or it might be that there is something external to the person that caused the behavior, such as a threat on the person's life. The former type of inference is called a *dispositional attribution,* whereas the latter is called a *situational attribution.*

For example, consider the case of a door-to-door salesman who appears unable to deliver a sales pitch (see fig. 6.1). From this behavior you might deduce that he is a very poor salesman (a dispositional attribution). You might even buy one of the products being sold to help the individual out. But what if by watching the salesman at your neighbor's house you can see that he acts incompetent in order to evoke sympathy and thereby gain a purchase? You probably would no longer attribute his failure to deliver the standard door-to-door pitch to poor salesmanship but rather to a manipulative or devious intent. These two attributions have very different implications for your susceptibility to the sales pitch. As we shall explain in this chapter, attitude change does indeed depend in part upon the attributions people make about the behavior of others and about their own behavior.

Interest in this approach to attitudes blossomed in 1965, following Daryl Bem's reinterpretation of cognitive dissonance theory using what is now construed in terms of an attributional analysis. Bem suggested that people infer their own attitudes in much the same way as they infer the attitudes of others—by the

Figure 6.1

The attributions we make about a communicator's behavior affect our susceptibility to influence. (Copyright 1979 by King Features Syndicate, Inc. Used with permission.)

behavior they observe. We begin our discussion of attributional approaches with Bem's *self-perception theory,* and we then review some of the spin-offs of the self-perception theory.

Of course, people don't always infer their own attitudes solely on the basis of their behavior. Unlike observers watching your behavior, you are privy to internal cues that provide additional information about how you feel toward some concept. Nevertheless, when these internal cues are weak, you *are* in the same position as an observer when inferring your own attitude (Bem, 1972). In addition, you may sometimes be aware of strong internal cues, such as a surge of arousal, but the cause or meaning of the arousal are ambiguous. In this case, too, you are in a position similar to that of an observer. In the middle section of the chapter, we discuss the influence on attitudes of people's interpretations of and attributions regarding these "internal" sources of information. In the final section, we move from the perspective of an individual inferring his or her own attitude to the perspective of someone inferring a communicator's intent, such as Dagwood is doing in the last panel of figure 6.1.

Self-perception Theory

Bem (1967) reasoned that:

An individual's attitude statements may be viewed as inferences from observations of his own behavior and its accompanying stimulus variables. As
such, his statements are functionally similar to those any outside observer
could make about him. [P. 186.]

Why might people draw inferences in this manner? Bem suggested that children are taught to draw these kinds of inferences. For example, parents have no direct way of knowing how very young children feel, so the parents must infer the children's likes and dislikes (attitudes) by the children's actions. From the children's point of view, their parents treat them as if they approach things they like and avoid things they dislike; the children are treated as if they voluntarily engage in activities they favor or believe in, but they must be made to do things that they do not favor or support. Simply stated, parents teach their children (intentionally or not) that attitudes can be inferred from behavior (White, 1980).

Another and perhaps more important reason why people may infer their own attitudes from their behavior is that people sometimes tend to think illogically; specifically, people tend to draw the erroneous conclusion that because they approach things they like, they like the things they approach (Triandis, 1971). Does such an inference seem reasonable to you? An example may clarify why this kind of reasoning is illogical. Let's say that it is very likely that extremely lazy people are poor. Does this piece of information mean that poor people are extremely lazy? Of course not. People *may* be poor because they are lazy, but they may also be poor for any of a number of other reasons. Perhaps they are hard-working but undereducated or unintelligent. Perhaps they are poor because they have been the object of unfair discrimination or because they have just suffered a major financial setback, such as a large medical expense. Just because extremely lazy people are poor, we cannot logically conclude that poor people are extremely lazy. Similarly, because heroin addicts are very likely to have smoked marijuana, this is no reason to conclude that smoking marijuana makes it very likely that a person will become a heroin addict. It should now be obvious why knowing that we approach things about which we hold a positive attitude does not *logically* lead to the inference that we have a positive attitude toward things that we approach. However, people often *do* make this type of illogical inference, and people may therefore infer their attitudes from their behavior because they do not always think logically.

Salancik and Conway (1975) demonstrated the process of self-perception by very subtly getting students to endorse pro- or antireligious behaviors. Salancik and Conway manipulated the student's pro- and antireligious endorsements by using either the word *frequently* or the word *occasionally* in their questions to the students about their religious activities. For instance, students who Salancik and Conway wanted to act in a *proreligious* manner might be asked whether it was true or false that they *on occasion* attended a church or synagogue, that they *on occasion* refused to step on ants, that they *on occasion* refused to read books by atheist writers, and so forth. Since most students have done these things on occasion, their behavior would appear to be proreligious. Subjects were induced to act in an *antireligious* manner by asking them the same questions, except that the word *frequently* was substituted for the phrase *on occasion.* Since most students do not engage in these behaviors frequently, their behavior would appear to be antireligious. Hence, one group of students kept responding that they engaged in proreligious behaviors, whereas the other group kept answering as if they did not engage in religious behaviors. When Salancik and Conway later asked the students to indicate how religious they were, the students who were induced to endorse proreligious behaviors said they were more religious than the students who were induced to respond in an antireligious manner. That is, how religious students said they were depended partially on their observations of and inferences about the cause of their verbal behavior (e.g., "if I keep saying that I avoid religious activities, then I must not be a religious person").

A number of other studies have shown that external cues can alter the attitudes people infer on the basis of their behaviors. For instance, at the request of the experimenter, subjects in one study agreed to present an unpopular editorial point of view to people on campus (Kiesler, Nisbett, & Zanna, 1969). After agreeing, some subjects heard another "subject" (actually, a confederate of the experimenter) say that he agreed to approach people only because he strongly supported the editorial position he agreed to espouse. The topic of the confederate's editorial differed from that about which the subject had agreed to talk, but nevertheless the confederate's statement provided the subject with an external cue, which signaled to the subject that the cause of his own behavior might be an underlying attitude also. Other subjects heard the confederate say that he agreed to approach people because he was open-minded. These subjects, therefore, were not "cued" that their behavior might be telling them something about their own attitudes. Consistent with self-perception theory, Kiesler et al. found that the subjects who were cued that their attitudes might have caused them to act as they did were more likely to report attitudes that were consistent with their behavior.

The Foot-in-the-door Effect

Another illustration of how self-perception influences attitudes and behavior is provided by the foot-in-the-door technique for inducing compliance. The essence of the foot-in-the-door technique is that people become more likely to perform a large and costly favor for you if they have previously agreed to perform or have performed a smaller favor (though not necessarily for you; Freedman & Fraser, 1966). For example, Freedman and Fraser (1966) had experimenters go door-to-door to speak with homemakers. The experimenters told these people that they represented the Committee for Safe Driving and asked them to sign a petition encouraging senators to support legislation that would make driving safer. As you might expect, almost all of the people that were contacted agreed to sign the petition. Several weeks later, these people were contacted by a different experimenter. This time, however, the experimenter asked them to put in their yard a large, unattractive sign that read "Drive Carefully." The experimenter also made this large request of a sample of homemakers who had not previously been approached. Freedman and Fraser found that over fifty-five percent of the people who had agreed to perform the smaller favor (signing the petition) agreed to put the large sign in their yard, whereas only seventeen percent of the people who had not been asked to perform a smaller favor agreed to place the sign in their yard. This result is consistent with self-perception theory, since the people who had previously acted as if they were concerned, helpful citizens (those who had been induced to perform a small initial favor) were more likely than the other people to act like concerned, helpful citizens when the costs of compliance were raised. Presumably, the former people changed their self-image as a result of their initial behavior (DeJong, 1979).

There are complications, however. First, acceding to the small request must occur in a situation that does not provide obvious external justification for doing the small favor. For instance, Uranowitz (1975) conducted a study in which a man carrying several bulky grocery bags sought help from a woman on the street. All of the women he approached were asked to watch his bags for a moment. Half were given a very good reason for aiding him—he told them he had just lost his wallet. The other half of the women were given little external cause for helping—they were told he had just dropped a dollar in the store. In all cases, the man went into the store and returned smiling a few moments later. He thanked the woman and reported that he found what he had lost. As these women continued down the sidewalk, they encountered another woman (a female experimenter) who "accidentally" dropped a small package in front of them. Uranowitz (1975) found that eighty percent of the women who initially helped the man for little external justification subsequently aided the female experimenter, whereas only forty-five percent of the women who had been given a strong external reason for their initial helpfulness did so. Only thirty-five percent of the women who were only confronted with the opportunity to help the woman who dropped the package did so. According to self-perception theory, only the women who helped the man but who were given little external reason for having helped should have inferred from their behavior that they were very helpful people. The fact that the women who were given the least external justification for the first helping episode helped the most on the second opportunity is consistent with the self-perception analysis.

A second factor that appears important in inducing compliance using the foot-in-the-door technique is the timing of the two requests. People are more likely to comply with a second, larger request only if there is a time delay between their agreement to comply with the initial, small request and the second request (Cann, Sherman, & Elkes, 1975; Cialdini, Cacioppo, Bassett, & Miller, 1978). This research supports the view that when people agree to do a small favor, they think about why they acted that way. When there is no time to think about the causes of the behaviors, they do not change the way they view themselves.

Other factors that are important in inducing compliance using the foot-in-the-door technique are reviewed by DeJong (1979). They include the following:

(a) *Size of the initial request*—According to self-perception theory, the larger the initial favor to which someone accedes, the more likely that they will comply to a second, larger request. This is because larger requests are presumably more likely to induce thought about why the behavior was performed. The evidence suggests support for this prediction except for very large initial requests (Miller & Suls, 1977).

(b) *Agreement versus actual performance of the initial request*—Consistent with self-perception theory, agreement is sufficient, but actual performance of an initial favor, which makes one's agreement to do the favor more salient, increases the strength of the foot-in-the-door effect.

(c) *Effect of noncompliance with the initial request*—People who refuse to do the initial favor generally become less likely to perform the second, larger favor than people not asked to perform the initial request. This occurs because the people who refuse the initial request presumably come to view themselves as people who do not aid strangers. Of course, if the first request is so large that people would not attribute their refusal to help to something about themselves, then the refusal does *not* undermine their likelihood to help later. This is because their initial refusal to help can be attributed to the outrageously large initial request rather than to their unhelpful nature. And

(d) *Effect of explicit social labels*—In some studies, people are explicitly told following their compliance to the initial request that they are generous and helpful (positive label) or that they are miserly and unhelpful (negative label). People become more likely to comply with the second, larger request when their initial compliance is positively labeled and when their initial compliance is negatively labeled if, by performing the larger request, they can refute the claim that they are unhelpful (Gurwitz & Topol, 1978).

Overjustification Effects

We have already noted that the attributional approach indicates that inducing a person to act in a particular manner leads to attitude change to the extent that the person is unaware of the external forces causing the behavior. This is because the person attributes the behavior to an internal attitude. In this section, we review evidence suggesting that when people do things that they enjoy, their enjoyment can be undermined by the presence of obvious external forces that can account for them acting as they do.

An example will help to clarify how plausible external causes for an act can reduce a prior favorable attitude toward the act. Lepper, Greene, and Nisbett (1973) observed three- to five-year-old children and found that the children enjoyed playing with drawing materials (magic markers), and these children drew pictures even though there were no obvious external rewards for their doing so. Lepper et al. promised and gave one group of children "Good Player Awards" for drawing pictures. They promised nothing to a second group of children, but—unbeknownst to the children—they would receive good player awards for pictures they had drawn; and Lepper et al. simply observed how frequently a third (control) group of children played with the drawing materials. From one to two weeks later, the children were given another opportunity to use the materials and the frequency with which the children played with the drawing materials was again determined. They found that the children who had drawn pictures *knowing* that they would get an award now played with the materials less than the children who had drawn pictures in the absence of an obvious external reason. In other words, these data are consistent with the view that the children who were given an external reason for having played with the drawing materials became less likely to view their behavior as reflecting a favorable attitude toward drawing.

This undermining of favorable attitudes by providing too much external justification for an attitude-consonant behavior is called the *overjustification effect,* and it has been found by using promised rewards such as prizes (Ross, 1975), money (Deci, 1971, 1972), tours of psychological laboratories (Kruglanski, Freedman, & Zeevi, 1971), extra course credit (Folger, Rosenfield, & Hays, 1978), and coupons (Scott & Yalch, 1978). Furthermore, rewards that are promised to subjects can undermine their liking a task, whether the rewards are contingent upon some particular level of performance (getting A's in school) or simply upon finishing the task (completing the semester). Moreover, the external justification for performing a behavior need not be a positive reward, but rather can be in the form of surveillance (Lepper & Greene, 1975) and threat of punishment (Deci & Cascio, 1972).

On the other hand, verbal praise as a reward (Anderson, Manoogian, & Reznick, 1976; Deci, 1972)—particularly when delivered in a manner that increases a person's feelings of competence at a task—actually increases the favorableness of a person's attitude toward the task. This finding is consistent with Deci's (1975) view that it is the *controlling* aspect of external forces (e.g., I'm only doing it for the money) that generates undermining effects, whereas the *informational* aspect of external forces (e.g., my salary increase indicates that I'm the best worker) may have the opposite effect. In other words, it is a person's attribution regarding the extent to which an external force determined his or her behavior rather than the external force per se that influences attitudes (see Deci & Ryan, 1980).

In sum, rewards and punishments have both controlling and informational components. When the controlling aspect of a reward or punishment that is administered in a given situation is salient, then a person's intrinsic motivation to perform the task is diminished. When the reward or punishment confers information to the person about his or her competence rather than a fiat regarding what response is best, then intrinsic motivation is enhanced (Deci, 1975; Harackiewicz, 1979).

Effects of Internal Sensations on Self-perception and Attitudes: Dissonance vs. Self-perception

The research on labeling and on overjustification supports Bem's notions of self-perception and the inference of attitudes. People generally seek explanations for their behaviors that provide a plausible account but at the same time that allow them to maintain personal freedom and positive self-regard (Jones & Nisbett, 1972; Monson & Snyder, 1977). In many instances, this means that people first seek explanations outside themselves for their behavior, and when they cannot find a suitable external cause for their behavior, they look to internal causes (e.g., attitudes).

Bem (1965, 1967) reasoned that it was this self-perception process, not the reduction of cognitive dissonance (see chap. 5), that caused people to change their attitudes when they took personal responsibility for advocating a position they had previously rejected. Recall Festinger's (1957) argument that when people were insufficiently justified in performing an act that was contrary to some attitude, they would experience unpleasant internal sensations as a result of the dissonant cognitions. As we suggested in chapter 5, one means by which this unpleasant state of dissonance could be resolved was to align the attitude so that it was consistent with the behavior. Bem (1965), on the other hand, argued that when there was insufficient external justification for people to behave as they did, people deduced that they must have acted as they did because they had a favorable attitude. That is, Bem asserted that people didn't rationalize their behavior to reduce an unpleasant tension, but rather they reasoned what their attitude *must* be for them to have acted as they did.

For example, recall that Festinger and Carlsmith (1959) discovered that giving a subject one dollar to lie about how interesting an experiment was led to more attitude change (more liking for the experiment) than giving the person twenty dollars to lie about the experiment. Bem suggested that when subjects are later asked their attitudes toward the experiment, they act like observers and infer their attitudes from their behavior in that context. Subjects who are given twenty dollars to lie can attribute their behavior to an external cause ("I lied for the money"), so they need not infer any liking for the experiment beyond that which they would deduce had they not lied at all. That is, their attitude-discrepant behavior (telling a lie) can be explained totally in terms of external (situational) causes; hence, the question of why they behaved as they did has a satisfactory (though not necessarily accurate) answer.

On the other hand, subjects who are given one dollar to lie probably find it more difficult to explain their behavior completely in terms of external forces. One dollar is less likely to provide a satisfactory external cause for their lying than twenty dollars. Since there are no obvious external reasons for their behavior, they are forced to infer some internal reason for their acting the way they did. For instance, subjects might reason that "I told the person the experiment was interesting; I guess I liked it." Of course, subjects might also reason that they are the type of person who lies, but this would require a more drastic change in self-perception. Thus, subjects are more likely to view themselves as honest and the task as fairly interesting.

Bem (1965) argued that if subjects in dissonance experiments deduced their attitudes from how they behaved in the situation, rather than from a desire to reduce any internal tension produced by cognitive dissonance, then people observing the behavior should attribute the same attitudes to the subjects as the subjects attributed to themselves. Bem tested his hypothesis by telling students about the various conditions in a dissonance experiment and then asking the students to predict what a subject's attitude might be.

One study Bem (1965) chose to replicate was one conducted by Cohen (cited in Brehm & Cohen, 1962, p. 73). In Cohen's study, Yale students were paid either one dollar or fifty cents to write an essay defending the actions of the New Haven police in a recent clash between the students and police. As predicted by dissonance theory, Cohen found that students who wrote the essay for fifty cents rather than one dollar changed their attitudes more. But Bem obtained the same result simply by asking his students to deduce from the information given (the incentive and behavior) what the attitudes of Cohen's subjects must have been. If observers could correctly infer what the subjects' attitudes toward the New

Haven police must have been for them to have written an essay in support of the police, Bem reasoned, then subjects in Cohen's study may have determined their attitude by the same cool, detached, attributional process as was used by his own student observers. In this way, both Bem's theory of self-perception and Festinger's theory of cognitive dissonance became capable of explaining the research on insufficient justification and attitude change.

Deciding between these theories proved difficult, and many attempts to do so failed (Greenwald, 1975; Kiesler & Munson, 1975). Fazio, Zanna, and Cooper (1977) then proposed that both theories were accurate, but that each applied to different domains. According to their analysis, self-perception processes are operative when a person's behavior is generally consistent but not in total agreement with the initial attitude—that is, when the behavior falls within the person's latitude of acceptance (see chap. 4). Fazio et al. reasoned that, in these instances, the person does not experience the unpleasant internal sensations postulated in cognitive dissonance theory. Hence, the person is not motivated to reduce any internal tension, but rather is able to employ the calm, detached reasoning process of self-perception to deduce his or her attitude toward the issue. Cognitive dissonance theory applies, however, when a person acts without sufficient external justification in a manner opposite to what would be expected from the relevant (prior) attitude—that is, when the person's behavior falls within his or her latitude of rejection. In these instances, the person experiences an unpleasant internal state of tension that initiates rationalizing (rather than inferential) processes and attitude change.

To test their reasoning, Fazio et al. (1977) obtained latitude measures from a group of students. This required that each student indicate what he or she considered to be unacceptable and acceptable positions and what each considered to be the most acceptable position on a liberal-conservative continuum (see box 4.2 in chap. 4). Next, each student was induced to write an essay supporting either the most extreme position they labeled as acceptable (within their latitude of acceptance) or the least extreme position they labeled as unacceptable (within their latitude of rejection). Some of the students wrote their essays believing they had freely chosen to do so (low external justification), whereas others believed they had no choice but to write the assigned essay (high external justification).

Fazio et al. (1977) used the misattribution procedure that we discussed in chapter 5 to distinguish whether self-perception or cognitive dissonance was causing attitude change in the high-choice conditions. They did this in the following way. Half of the students in the high-choice conditions were simply asked to write the essays, as we described above. If these students experienced the tension that characterizes the state of cognitive dissonance, they would have nothing to attribute it to except their decision to write the essay. Hence, they might be expected to change their attitude to reduce their felt tension. The other half of the subjects in the high-choice (low external justification) conditions were led to believe that the *booth* in which they were sitting might cause them to feel tense and uncomfortable. The instruction about the booth provided the subjects with the opportunity to misattribute to the booth any felt unpleasant tension created by their decision to write the essay, thereby saving them the effort of reorganizing their attitudes and beliefs about the issue.

The results of the Fazio et al. (1977) study are displayed in figure 6.2. First, note that, as predicted by both self-perception and cognitive dissonance theory, high-choice subjects in the "no booth" conditions changed their attitudes more than low-choice subjects. More importantly, look at what happens to attitude change when subjects in the high-choice conditions had the chance to misattribute to the booth any tension produced by their decision. Students who believed they chose to write an essay supporting a position they previously had accepted (within their latitudes of acceptance) changed their attitude regardless of what they were told about the booth. This result suggests that their decision caused these subjects no tension or discomfort, but rather that they used their behavior to infer what their attitude must be for them to have acted as they did. The opportunity to misattribute tension had very different effects on the subjects who believed they chose to write an essay supporting a position that they had previously rejected (within their latitude of rejection). As you can see in figure 6.2, subjects who, following their decision to endorse a position they had previously rejected, were given a plausible external cause for feeling tense or uncomfortable, changed their attitudes less than subjects who had no external factors to which to attribute their tension. Overall, then, Fazio et al.'s study supported the notion that choosing to support a previously unacceptable position leads to attitude change because of the arousal of cognitive dissonance, whereas choosing to support an acceptable position leads to attitude change by the process of self-perception. Of course it is not sufficient to engage in a behavior in one's latitude of rejection for dissonance processes to occur. The behavior must also meet all of the criteria outlined in chapter 5. These conditions were met in the Fazio et al. study (see also Shaffer, 1975).

In sum, Bem's theory of self-perception holds that, to the extent that plausible external causes for an act are absent or nonobvious, the person who engaged in the act (the "actor") infers his or her attitude toward the topic on the basis of his or her behavior. This attributional approach to attitudes helps to explain the subtle adjustments in attitudes that follow acts that are generally consistent with a prior attitude, but it does not account as well for attitude change following insufficiently justified behavior that is highly discrepant from the person's initial attitude. Attitude change in these latter instances appears at least in part to be motivated by felt internal tensions and sensations, to which only the actor has access. Finally, these internal sensations are unambiguous in the sense that they are clearly unpleasant (see chap. 5). Nevertheless, the fact that people can misattribute the cause of these internal cues when a plausible external cause is salient indicates that people are not as good at knowing their internal states as they might believe.

Figure 6.2

The presence of a misattributional cue (the booth) prevented attitude change only when subjects believed they freely chose to endorse a position they previously rejected. (Data from Fazio, Zanna, & Cooper, 1977.)

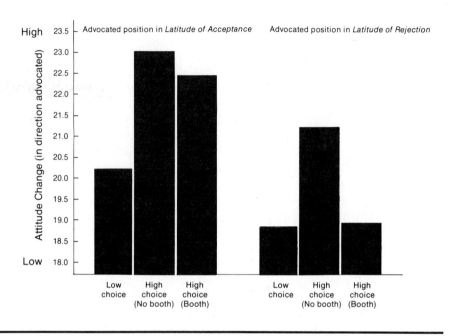

Effects of Ambiguous Internal Cues on Attitudes

Still, not every sensation that you detect from your body is clearly pleasant or unpleasant. You might, for example, suddenly notice that your heart is beating rapidly without knowing why and without feeling either more pleasant or less pleasant by its rapid beat. These cues are experienced as ambiguous signals from the body. In this section, we survey the research on and describe the effects of these ambiguous internal cues on attitudes.[1]

Emotional Plasticity

Schachter and Singer (1962) reasoned that when people experience an unexplained and diffuse change in their bodily responses, such as a surge of arousal, they search for external cues that might help them to identify what these changes mean. If the situation in which they find themselves contains cues indicating that they are angry (other people were becoming angry in the same situation), then they surmise that the unusual bodily responses they are feeling are due to their being angry. If, however, the situation contains cues indicating that they are happy, then they deduce that they must be happy.[2]

Schachter and Singer (1962) tested their theory by injecting subjects with a small amount of epinephrine (adrenalin). Some subjects knew that the injection would make them aroused, whereas other subjects did not. Subjects then were placed individually in a room with another person (a confederate of the experimenter), and both were asked to complete questionnaires. Just about the time that the drug began to take effect, the confederate began acting as if filling out the questionnaire had made him either very angry or very euphoric (happy). Schachter and Singer expected that the subjects who knew their arousal was due to the injection would not be affected greatly by the situational cues (the confederate's behavior). But subjects who experienced unexplained arousal were expected to use the situational cues to determine what they were feeling. Consistent with this notion, subjects who were paired with the "angry" confederate believed themselves to be more angry when they did not know the injection would cause arousal than when they did know the injection had caused their felt arousal.

Contrary to Schachter and Singer's expectations, though, whether or not subjects knew in advance that the injection would cause them to feel aroused did not especially affect them if they were paired with the "euphoric" confederate. This latter result suggests that a sudden onset of unexplained arousal may not be experienced as neutral but rather as distress or apprehension (Maslach, 1979). This point has been the topic of debate, and resolution regarding whether an injection of epinephrine causes a person to feel pleasantly, neutrally, or unpleasantly aroused has not yet been resolved (Marshall & Zimbardo, 1979; Schachter & Singer, 1979).

Nonetheless, the fundamental concept of emotional plasticity espoused by Schachter and Singer is that experiencing unexplained and neutral arousal causes one to search the situational context for cues to determine the meaning of the felt arousal. The evidence supporting this formulation is weak, but the formulation has certainly been important in drawing attention to the influence of attributional processes in attitudes and emotions (Zillmann, 1978).

Effects of Bogus Physiological Feedback

A major thrust of research that developed out of Schachter and Singer's (1962) work concerned the effects on attitudes of receiving bogus (false) feedback about what a person's body is doing. Valins (1966) suggested that people need not perceive actual physiological changes in order to be affected by these cues but need only to *believe* that their bodily responses changed.

As evidence for this proposition, Valins (1966) did a study in which men were asked to look at pictures of *Playboy* centerfolds. They listened to what they believed was their heart rate as they looked at the pictures. While viewing half of the pictures their heart rate seemed to beat steadily. In addition, half of the men heard their "heart rate" increase and half heard their "heart rate" decrease while they looked at the remaining pictures. Afterwards, the men were asked to rate the attractiveness of each picture. Valins found that men rated as most attractive the pictures that were accompanied by bogus feedback indicating that their heart rate had changed (either increased or decreased). Valins (1967) replicated this finding and demonstrated further that the ratings by relatively emotional men were more affected by the false physiological feedback than were the ratings by nonemotional men. These observations hinted that bogus feedback about changes in physiological arousal enhances the positive regard for pleasant stimuli.

Similarly, research has shown that believing one's bodily responses were altered by attending to an unpleasant stimulus leads to more negative evaluations of the unpleasant stimulus (e.g., pictures of accident victims; Hirschman, 1975; Stern, Botto, & Herrick, 1972). Moreover, the impact of the bogus feedback on attitudes is again more apparent in relatively emotional than in nonemotional people (Hirschman & Hawk, 1978).[3]

In each of the above studies, the bogus feedback that signified a change in bodily functioning was probably sufficiently unexpected that it piqued the subjects' interest. Subjects searched their environment for an explanation and particularly focused on the stimulus whose presentation was associated with their "arousal." In other words, subjects may have attended to and thought more about a stimulus that was introduced at or near the same moment in time as information that their body's responses (heart rate) had changed unexpectedly (e.g., increased by 20 bpm). The enhanced thought about stimuli makes likable stimuli (e.g., attractive photographs) more likeable and dislikable stimuli (e.g., photographs of automobile accidents) more dislikable (Tesser, 1978; we discuss this further in chap. 8.).

The bogus feedback studies that we have described so far all involve shifting one's attitude to a position that was generally consistent with but more extreme than a previous attitude. Box 6.1 illustrates yet another example of how bogus physiological feedback can serve as a cue that (a) piques the subjects' curiosity regarding its cause and (b) causes subjects to search and think about aspects of their environment that covaried with the unexpected change in physiological feedback and may therefore have accounted for the change.

On occasion, however, decisions made in a given situation have such important consequences for individuals that they are moved to be circumspect about the stimulus, whether or not they receive bogus feedback about an unexpected change in bodily processes (Janis & Mann, 1977). Taylor (1975) provides an interesting illustration of this point. She obtained ratings of the attractiveness of ten men from her subjects (all of whom were women) by approaching them individually in their dormitory rooms. One week later, the subjects participated in an experiment in which three of the ten photographs of the men were presented while the women were attached to physiological recording apparatus. (Subjects saw their most-preferred, medium-preferred, and least-preferred pictures.) One-third of the subjects then simply heard that clear results had been obtained in the physiological recordings, which constituted the *no-feedback condition.* The remaining subjects overheard the experimenter say that they had reacted noticeably and strongly to "David." For the subjects in the *attitude-congruent condition,* "David" referred to the man in their most-preferred photograph, whereas for the subjects in the *attitude-incongruent condition* "David" referred to the man in their medium-preferred photograph.

Next, the experimenter introduced the manipulation of future consequences. The subjects were told that there was a second part to the study in which they would again be seeing the photographs of the three men. Subjects were instructed to look as long as they wished at each photograph and to evaluate each. Subjects in the *no-future-consequences conditions* were told that after viewing the pictures, their attitudes toward psychology experiments would be assessed. Subjects in the *future-consequences conditions,* however, were told that they were to select from among the three men the one whom they wanted invited to a social gathering to which they were also invited. Taylor found that when there were no future consequences involved as a result of their evaluating the photographs, the women tended to elevate their liking for the man whose picture purportedly "aroused" them. But when their evaluations would determine whether or not they would have the chance to meet the man they most preferred (in the future-consequences condition), bogus feedback did not significantly influence their evaluations of the men.

In sum, the research on bogus physiological feedback provides several important qualifications to the attributional approach to attitudes. First, self-perception theory must be broadened to encompass perceived internal cues and accord them the same theoretical status as behavioral and environmental cues in the attitude-inference process. Second, you might recall that the research on behavioral cues revealed that self-perception processes best accounted for adjustments in attitudes that involved movement to positions that, though not preferred, were somewhat acceptable initially (i.e., attitude-congruent; Brown, Klemp, & Leventhal, 1975). Research on the effects of bogus physiological feedback (Taylor, 1975; Valins, 1966) and general "arousal" (Maslach, 1979; Schachter & Singer, 1962) suggests also that self-perception processes are operative primarily when the attitudes involved are on issues that are low in personal relevance or importance.

Recipients' Attributions Regarding the Cause of a Communicator's Behavior

In the preceding sections, we surveyed the attitudinal effects of the attributions that a person made about behaviors they produced themselves (overt actions, physiological "arousal"). We noted that whether people attributed a behavior to

Bem (1972) suggested that internal cues typically are too weak or ambiguous to be utilized in the same manner as are behavioral cues in self-perception. Research on bogus physiological feedback, however, suggests that perceived "internal" cues do play a role in the self-perception of attitudes. An interesting demonstration of their influence is provided by Pittman, Cooper, and Smith (1977). They conducted a study in which subjects manually maneuvered the distance between two metal rods to move a metal ball up an inclined plane. Each subject was given ten trials at the task to accumulate as many points as possible. Electrodes were attached to each subject presumably so that the experimenters could measure "arousal." The experimenters then varied the internal and external cues available to subjects while they performed their task. A control group was told nothing additional about the task, whereas subjects in a second group were promised money (extrinsic reward) for their performance on the task. Pittman et al. found that subjects who expected to earn money for playing the game subsequently showed less interest in the game than subjects who did not expect to earn money. This, you will recall, is the overjustification effect.

Pittman et al. (1977) tested two additional groups of subjects. Subjects in these groups expected to earn money on the basis of their performance on the task, just as had subjects in the second group described above. But these new subjects were stopped after performing five of the trials and were told that their bodily readings from the electrodes indicated that they were "aroused." Subjects from one group were told that the arousal signified their personal involvement and interest in the *game*, whereas subjects from the other group were told that the arousal reflected their interest in *money*. That is, some subjects were given "internal" cues (false physiological feedback) that pointed to intrinsic reasons for

themselves or to the situation determined what attitude was inferred. In this section, we survey the application of the attributional approach to situations in which the person focuses on the behavior emitted by a *communicator*.

This application requires that we shift from an actor's (the person performing the behavior) perspective to an observer's perspective. This change in perspective on a person's behavior can lead to very different inferences about the cause of behavior. In general, actors attempt initially to attribute their counterattitudinal behaviors to the situation; only when suitable external causes are not available do actors attribute their behaviors to something intrinsic to themselves, such as their attitudes. Observers, on the other hand, are in most instances more likely than actors to attribute the cause of the behavior to something intrinsic to the actor (Jones & Nisbett, 1971; Ross, 1975; cf. Monson & Snyder, 1977).

There are two general attributional principles, proposed by Kelley (1972, 1973), that have guided much of the attribution research on the perspective of

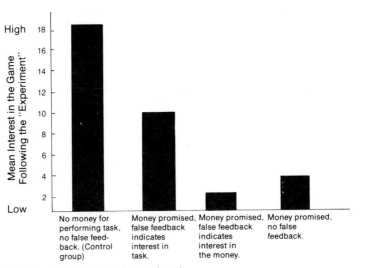

| No money for performing task, no false feedback. (Control group) | Money promised, false feedback indicates interest in task. | Money promised, false feedback indicates interest in the money. | Money promised, no false feedback. |

Data from Pittman, Cooper, & Smith (1977).

playing with the game, whereas the "internal" cues given to other subjects highlighted external reasons for playing with the game. As you can see in the figure, what subjects were told about the import of their "arousal" determined whether or not the money undermined their interest in the game. When the "internal cues" were said to reflect interest in the game, intrinsic motivation to play the game was maintained to some degree. But when the "internal cues" were said to index their interest in the money, intrinsic motivation to play the game was undermined.

observers. First, there is the *discounting principle,* which states that to the extent that a response (or effect) has a number of plausible causes, the viability of any single cause is discounted or weakened. Second, the *augmentation principle* states that a response that is unexpected (i.e., unique) given the contextual cues is especially likely to be attributed to something unique about the actor. Let's look at how these principles might be used to account for a persuasion effect.

In chapter 3, we noted that a communicator who argues against his or her own vested interests is more persuasive than a communicator who argues for his or her own vested interests. Eagly, Wood, and Chaiken (1978) have presented an attributional analysis of this effect by focusing on the inferences made by subjects when their expectations prior to receiving the message are violated.

Eagly et al. reasoned that message recipients generally expect communicators to argue *for* their own vested interests. If a communicator does indeed advocate a position that favors his own interests, he confirms the recipients' premessage expectation. The recipients can attribute the communicator's support for his advocated position to several factors: his veridical view of the world, his biased (unrepresentative) body of information on the topic (referred to as a "knowledge bias"), or his concealment of issue-relevant information to obtain personal gains (referred to as a "reporting bias"). If message recipients draw the first attribution (that the communicator is expressing a veridical view of the world), they will be susceptible to influence; but since there are a number of alternative explanations for the communicator's appeal (knowledge or reporting biases), the recipients tend to discount the possibility that the message arguments reflect the true state of the world. This discounting makes the recipients more resistant to the communicator's persuasive appeal.

If, however, the communicator disconfirms the recipients' premessage expectations by advocating a position that is contrary to his own best interests, then *augmentation* occurs: recipients have few if any explanations for the communicator's behavior except that external reality is as he describes; and the unexpected nature of the communicator's behavior enhances the likelihood that the recipients shall attribute the communicator's behavior to something about him (e.g., his unique understanding of the issues). One consequence of this attribution is that the recipients become particularly susceptible to the communicator's persuasive appeal. Eagly and her colleagues have provided substantial support for this attributional analysis of the effects of message sources when the communicator violates some premessage expectation on the part of the recipient (Eagly & Chaiken, 1975; Eagly, Chaiken, & Wood, 1981). It is important to note, however, that in many persuasion situations recipients have no firm expectations regarding the communicator or the message, and this formulation would not apply in these instances.

A body of related literature deals with the inferences drawn by recipients about the communicator's true attitude. For instance, have you ever wondered whether or not the husky football player really felt as positively toward the product he was endorsing (e.g., a popcorn maker) as he said he felt? A capsule survey of this research is provided in box 6.2.

Retrospective

The attributional approach to attitudes and persuasion characterizes people as active problem solvers and focuses on changes in attitudes that result from reasoned (though not necessarily logical) inferences. The notion common to attributional theories is that a person's inferences or attributions about the cause of a behavior are the most important determinants of the resulting attitude change. These inferences might concern the communicator's behavior ("why is he or she saying or doing that?") or they might concern the person's own behavior ("why did I say or do that?"). We reviewed evidence that indicates that an individual's behavior within a particular setting provides one source of information that is used when the individual deduces his or her attitude. In other words, we have seen that people sometimes infer their attitudes from their be-

Inferences Regarding a Communicator's Attitude

Consider the following situation. Your teacher assigns a classmate of yours to argue as persuasively as possible that nuclear power plants be constructed and licensed as a means of dealing with the energy crisis. Although you have seen this student in your class, you haven't spoken with her and you don't know how she personally feels about nuclear energy. She argues for nuclear energy, as requested by your teacher. What do you think her true attitude is toward nuclear energy? This type of question has been addressed by social psychologists. They have found that even though people know that a communicator was *arbitrarily* assigned to present a particular stand on an issue, they nevertheless infer that the communicator personally agrees somewhat with this position (Jones & Harris, 1976; Miller, 1976). This effect does not emerge until the communicator actually delivers the assigned presentation (Jones, Worchel, Goethals, & Grumet, 1971), but then it appears whether or not observers are exposed to it (Brockner & Nova, 1979), or whether or not the message is persuasive (Snyder & Jones, 1974).

A study by Ajzen, Dalto, and Blyth (1979) indicates that the background information people have about the communicator also influences what inference is likely to be drawn. If the background information is ambiguous, people tend to assume that the communicator is espousing his or her true attitude; if the background information is unambiguous and inconsistent with the position espoused by the communicator, the tendency for people to draw this erroneous inference is attenuated or eliminated (Zanna, Klosson, & Darley, 1976).

Finally, a study by Miller, Baier, and Schonberg (1979) indicates that communicators are aware that audiences tend to assume they support a position that they were forced to endorse.

haviors. However, there are many other sources of information that can be and are used. In the next chapter, we discuss how more complex reasoning processes covering information other than the cause of one's own or another's behavior might relate to attitude change.

Notes

[1]We should note that research has also shown that changes in the body can have effects on attitudes, even though these changes are not salient to the person. For example, Rhodewalt and Comer (1979) found that, relative to people who wrote a counterattitudinal essay with their faces in a neutral position, subjects whose faces were subtly manipulated into a frown reported a more negative mood and changed their attitudes significantly more toward the position taken in their essays, whereas subjects whose faces were subtly manipulated into a smile reported a more positive mood and changed their attitudes significantly less (see also Comer & Rhodewalt, 1979; Laird, 1974). In chapter 8 we will see how changes in heart rate that are undetected by subjects can affect attitudes (Cacioppo, 1979). These effects are reviewed further in Cacioppo and Petty (in press).

[2]The search for an explanation described by Schachter and Singer (1962) may sound similar to those we have described in our discussion of cognitive dissonance theory and self-perception theory. The following distinctions can be drawn: (a) According to cognitive dissonance theory, the internal cues are clearly unpleasant rather than neutral initially; and (b) according to self-perception theory, internal cues are largely unimportant, whereas one's behavior in a particular situation is paramount.

[3]Actual physiological changes sometimes follow the bogus feedback regarding a change in a person's physiological arousal (Stern et al., 1972). These changes in *actual* physiological functioning, however, do not appear to be necessary for obtaining the reported effects of bogus physiological feedback on attitudes (Harris & Katkin, 1975; Kerber & Coles, 1978; Leibhart, 1979).

Combinatory Approaches

7

Two of your friends have asked you to describe the professor that you had for American history last semester. To one friend, you describe the professor using two extremely positive traits: brilliant and witty. To the other friend, you describe the professor using two extremely positive traits, but you also use one trait that is only moderately positive: prompt, brilliant, and witty. Which of your friends will form the most favorable attitude toward the professor?

The theme of this chapter is that a person's attitude about some person, object, or issue is determined by the information the person has about the stimulus and by how that information is *combined* or *integrated* to form one overall impression. In our example, the information consists of the traits that have been associated with the professor. But how is this information put together? If the information is *added,* then the friend who heard the three positive traits would have a more favorable attitude than the friend who heard the two traits, but if the information is *averaged,* then the friend who heard only the two extremely positive traits would have the most favorable attitude. In this chapter we will focus first on the different types of information that we can have about people, objects, and issues; and then we will present three different approaches to the study of attitude change that emphasize how people combine information. (We will return to our adding vs. averaging dilemma later in the chapter in box 7.3).

Fishbein and Ajzen (1975) have distinguished among three different types of information that we may have about attitude objects. The first kind of information associates an attribute with an object on the basis of direct personal experience and has been called a *primitive belief* (Rokeach, 1968) or a *descriptive belief* (Fishbein & Ajzen, 1975). Since these beliefs comprise our basic truths about the world, attitudes based on descriptive beliefs are very difficult to change. Also, as we saw in chapter 1, attitudes based on descriptive beliefs (i.e., attitudes based on direct contact with the object of judgment) correlate highly with behaviors toward that object (Fazio & Zanna, 1981). A second kind of information consists of beliefs that go beyond directly observable events and are called *inferential beliefs*. For example, if you believe that *Alice runs faster than Barbara* on the basis of direct observation, and that *Barbara runs faster than Clara* on the basis of direct observation, you would likely infer that *Alice runs faster than*

Clara, even though you never observed them in the same race. Finally, some knowledge that we have about objects is neither directly observed nor inferred, but it is provided to us by the verbalizations of others. These beliefs, formed by accepting information from external sources, are called *informational beliefs.* According to the combinatory theories, the beliefs that we have about objects, persons, or issues are the basis of our attitudes about them. Since most of the information that children have about the world comes directly from their parents, it is not surprising that children's beliefs, and thus their attitudes, are initially very similar to those of their parents. For example, it is well documented that children tend to share their parents' racial prejudices, religious preferences, and political party affiliations (Epstein & Komorita, 1966; Jennings & Niemi, 1968). As the child grows up and begins to receive more information from outside sources, the information provided in school and by peers assumes a more important role (Coleman, 1961; Hess & Torney, 1967), as does information provided by the mass media (Lambert & Klineberg, 1967). Interestingly, some mass media advertisements emphasize information heavily, whereas others downplay it considerably (see box 7.1).

In the remainder of this chapter we will discuss three different combinatory approaches to the study of belief and attitude change. The first approach is based on the rules of probability and formal logic ("probabilogical"—McGuire, 1981) and deals with the issue of how changes in one belief can lead to inferential changes in other beliefs. The next two approaches examine how beliefs form the basis of attitudes. One model contends that attitudes are best represented by a sum of beliefs, whereas the other contends that attitudes are best represented by an average of beliefs. In many respects the combinatory approaches that we present in this chapter are the most direct descendents of Hovland's message-learning approach described in chapter 3. Rather than concentrating on simply learning beliefs from external sources, however, the approaches in this chapter tend to emphasize the individual meaning that the information has to each recipient and how this information is integrated into a general attitude.

Probabilogical Approaches to Belief Change

The nature and structure of belief systems is important from the perspective of an informational theorist because beliefs are thought to provide the cognitive foundation of an attitude. In order to change an attitude then, it is presumably necessary to modify the information on which that attitude rests. It is generally necessary, therefore, to *change* a person's beliefs, *eliminate* old beliefs, or *introduce* new beliefs. One popular approach to the structure of beliefs is to view them as existing in an interconnected syllogistic network containing both a vertical and a horizontal structure (Bem, 1970; Jones & Gerard, 1967; McGuire,

1960b). A belief *syllogism* is a set of three statements, two of which serve as *premises* that lead psycho-logically to a *conclusion*.[1] For example:

Syllogism 1
{
First premise: Reading *Time* magazine keeps one informed.
Second premise: A magazine that keeps one informed is valuable.
Conclusion: *Time* magazine is valuable.
}

The conclusion is an *inferential* belief that is derived or makes sense on the basis of the two premises. This syllogism does not exist in isolation in the belief system, however. It is likely that the premises of this syllogism serve as the conclusions of other syllogisms in the belief structure. For example, the first premise in Syllogism 1 might be the conclusion of the following syllogism.

Syllogism 2
{
First premise: My best friend Bill reads *Time* magazine to stay informed.
Second premise: Bill is always well-informed.
Conclusion: Reading *Time* magazine keeps one informed.
}

Furthermore, it is likely that the premises of this syllogism serve as the conclusions of still other syllogisms. For example:

Syllogism 3
{
First premise: Bill always knows the platforms of candidates running for office.
Second premise: Anyone who knows the candidates' platforms is well-informed.
Conclusion: Bill is well-informed.
}

Syllogisms 2 and 3, which are part of the psycho-logical chain leading to the final conclusion that "*Time* magazine is valuable," form the *vertical structure* of that belief. Notice that if a belief high up in the vertical structure changed, it would have implications for beliefs that are further down the chain of reasoning.

In addition to a vertical structure, belief systems are thought to possess a *horizontal structure* as well. The horizontal structure of a belief refers to the fact that the conclusion of one syllogism may also serve as the conclusion of other syllogisms. For example, Syllogism 4 might be part of the horizontal structure of the belief that "*Time* magazine is valuable."

Syllogism 4
{
First premise: *Time* magazine has the best movie reviews of any weekly publication.
Second premise: Weekly movie reviews are very valuable.
Conclusion: *Time* magazine is valuable.
}

Box 7.1

Informational Appeals

Compare the two advertisements on the left with the two on the right. The ads for the stereo equipment are laden heavily with facts and figures to impress the potential purchaser. The ads for the liquor, on the other hand, present very little information about the product. In fact, the product is almost lost in the majestic scenery. Which type of ad do you think is most effective—one that is heavy on content or one that attempts to associate the product with a desirable cue? We will address this issue in chapter 9.

Courtesy of Fisher Corporation.

Courtesy of Zenith Radio Corporation.

The more extensive the horizontal structure of a belief (the more syllogisms that have the belief as its conclusion), the less susceptible a belief will be to change when one of the premises in its vertical structure is changed. Thus, if Syllogism 4 did not exist, and if there were no other syllogisms providing a horizontal structure for the belief that "*Time* magazine is valuable," then it should be quite easy to change the belief by modifying a premise in the vertical structure. For example, in the next election, if you found out that Bill did not know the candidates' platforms, you might reason that Bill is not well-informed (Syllogism 3), that reading *Time* magazine does not keep one informed (Syllogism 2), and that *Time* magazine is not valuable (Syllogism 1).

McGuire (1960b, 1981) and Wyer (1970, 1974) have developed probability models of syllogistic reasoning that take into account the fact that a person's

Courtesy of Brown-Furman Distillers.

Because you enjoy going first class.

In Paris or at home, life's more satisfying when you're enjoying the best. That's Passport. Enjoyed worldwide because it's made of Scotland's finest whiskies. Ask for Passport—go first class.

Passport Scotch.

Courtesy Calvert Distillers Company.

belief in the premises of a syllogism are not necessarily all or none. For example, in Syllogism 1 the person may not have complete confidence in the first premise, feeling that there is only a seventy percent chance, or a 0.7 probability that *Time* magazine keeps one informed. If the premises are not held with complete confidence (a probability of 1), then the conclusion should not be held with complete confidence either.[2] Consider the following simple syllogism:

Syllogism 5

First premise: If Governor Smith is reelected, state aid to education will be increased.
Second premise: Governor Smith will be reelected.
Conclusion: State aid to education will be increased.

Changes in Central Beliefs

The more *central* a belief is (the greater the number of other beliefs that follow from it), the greater the change in an entire cognitive system that will occur when the belief changes. Religious conversions represent a dramatic example of a person's entire approach to life changing as a result of one change in a central belief. Usually, these conversions are the product of an intense emotional experience (Frank, 1974), but this need not be the case. Consider the person who does not believe in a supreme being, because there is no concrete evidence of the existence of a supernatural power, who comes across the article below in the morning paper. To the extent that the person comes to believe that tangible proof now exists, this one belief change is likely to have far-reaching effects on the person's entire cognitive system.

Shroud Of Turin Called Real

WOONSOCKET, R.I. (UPI) — Thomas D'Muhala, leader of the scientific team which studied the Shroud of Turin in Italy last year, says all evidence collected so far indicates the authenticity of the material reputed to have been Jesus Christ's burial cloth.

"Every one of the scientists I have talked to believes the cloth is authentic. Some say maybe this is a love letter, a tool he (Christ) left behind for the analytical mind," D'Muhala said.

The president of Nuclear Technologies Corp. in Amston, Conn. made his comments at a meeting of the Full Gospel Businessmen's Fellowship.

There is growing circumstantial evidence the image was "projected" on the cloth — perhaps by a brief flash of radiation emanating from all parts of the body, D'Muhala said.

If the probability of the conclusion is designated $p(B)$ and the probability of the second premise is designated $p(A)$, then the first premise should be designated $p(B/A)$. The latter is read as the probability of B given A and is a *conditional probability*. Based on the laws of probability, Wyer and Goldberg (1970) used Equation 1 to describe how the probability of the conclusion should be derived from the two premises.

$$p(B) = p(B/A)\,p(A) + p(B/\bar{A})\,p(\bar{A}) \tag{1}$$

The only new terms in this equation are $p(\bar{A})$ and $p(B/\bar{A})$. The former is the probability that *not A* is true (the probability that Governor Smith will not be reelected). The latter is the conditional probability that B is true given *not A* (that state aid to education will be increased if Governor Smith is not reelected). For example, if you thought that $p(A) = 0.75$, $p(\bar{A}) = 0.25$, $p(B/A) = 0.8$, and $p(B/\bar{A}) = 0.6$, then $p(B)$ should equal $(0.80 \times 0.75) + (0.60 \times 0.25) = 0.75$. This is summarized in table 7.1. There is now considerable evidence that the actual judgments people make of the probability of the conclusion of a

Table 7.1

Determining the Probability of a Syllogistic Conclusion from the Two Premises

$p(A)$ = The probability that Governor Smith will be reelected = 0.75
$p(\bar{A})$ = The probability that Governor Smith will not be reelected = 0.25
$p(B/A)$ = The probability that state aid to education will be increased if Governor Smith is reelected = 0.80
$p(B/\bar{A})$ = The probability that state aid to education will be increased if Governor Smith is not reelected = 0.60
$p(B)$ = The probability that state aid to education will be increased = 0.75

The first four probabilities are subjective, and the fifth is calculated from Equation 1, as demonstrated below.

$$p(B/A)\, p(A) + p(B/\bar{A})\, p(\bar{A}) = p(B)$$
$$(0.80)\,(0.75) + (0.60)\,(0.25) = p(B)$$
$$0.60 + 0.15 = p(B)$$
$$0.75 = p(B)$$

syllogism can be predicted reasonably well from mathematical probability laws like that specified in Equation 1 (Henniger & Wyer, 1976; Rosen & Wyer, 1972; Wyer, 1972, 1973; Wyer & Carlston, 1979).

A better test of the utility of Equation 1 as a descriptor of the structure of a belief system, however, is whether or not it can correctly predict the effects that a *change* in a premise will have on the conclusion. For example, if a person received a message that argued convincingly that there was a very low probability that Governor Smith would be reelected ($p(A) = 0.15$ instead of 0.75), and the person accepted this information (a change in a premise occurred), then Equation 2 can be used to predict the change in $p(B)$ that should result.

$$\triangle p(B) = \triangle [\, p(B/A)p(A) + p(B/\bar{A})\, p(\bar{A})\,] \qquad (2)$$

Assuming that $p(\bar{A}) = 1 - p(A)$, and the $p(B/A)$ and $p(B/\bar{A})$ are unaffected by the change in $p(A)$, then Equation 2 simplifies to Equation 3.

$$\triangle p(B) = \triangle p(A)\, [p(B/A) - p(B/\bar{A})] \qquad (3)$$

Working through the equations indicates that if $p(A)$ changes from 0.75 to 0.15 (i.e., $\triangle p(A) = 0.75 - 0.15 = 0.60$), then $\triangle p(B) = 0.60\,[0.80 - 0.60] = 0.12$. Thus, $p(B)$ should change 0.12, or from 0.75 to 0.63. In order to test the predictive utility of Equation 3, Wyer (1970) described nine hypothetical situations (like the one described in Syllogism 5) to subjects. In each case they were provided with information about the likelihood of $p(A)$, $p(\bar{A})$, $p(B/A)$, and $p(B/\bar{A})$. As we noted already, Equation 1 predicted subjects estimates of $p(B)$ very accurately. After making probability estimates on the basis of the initial information, however, subjects received a persuasive message that was designed to change their belief in $p(A)$. According to the model, a change in $p(A)$ should also produce a change in the inferential belief, $p(B)$. In support of the model, the persuasive message produced considerable change in $p(A)$ and also affected $p(B)$. Figure 7.1 graphs the obtained changes in $p(B)$ as a function of the predicted changes from Equation 3. The average discrepancy between predicted and obtained values was only 0.003.

McGuire (1960b) earlier proposed a very similar syllogistic model of belief organization.[3] One interesting feature of McGuire's model is that he postulates a need for *hedonic consistency* as well as *logical consistency* in belief structures. McGuire recognizes that Equation 1 (or his version of it in footnote 3) describes a person's belief structure only insofar as it is perfectly logical and does not consider the fact that the subjective probability that a person assigns to a belief may also be affected by the *desirability* of that belief. Hedonic consistency, or "wishful thinking," refers to the fact that there is a tendency for individuals to see things as consistent with their personal desires and wishes. They might therefore tend to see conclusions and premises as more likely the more desirable they are, even if this goes against pure logic.

In order to test the notion that syllogistic inferences are affected by both logical and hedonic consistency, McGuire (1960a) asked subjects to rate both the subjective probability and the desirability of the premises and conclusions of sixteen syllogisms. The correlation between the desirability and the subjective likelihood across the forty-eight propositions was 0.40, providing evidence for the hedonic consistency postulate. The correlation between the predicted probability of the conclusion (based on the laws of probability) and the actual probability assigned by subjects was 0.48, providing evidence for the logical consistency postulate. When this correlation was recomputed to take into account both logical and hedonic consistency (this was done by partialing out or holding constant the rated desirability of the conclusion and the mean of the desirability ratings of the two premises), the correlation increased to 0.85. In another study (McGuire, 1960b), the logical consistency correlation increased from 0.74 to 0.96 when desirability was taken into account (i.e., controlled for by computing a partial correlation). These data strongly suggest that belief structures are governed by both logical and hedonic factors. Interestingly, two studies (Dillehay, Insko, & Smith, 1966; Watts & Holt, 1970) found that hedonic consistency was relatively more important for less intelligent or less educated subjects.

Like Wyer, McGuire (1981) has also addressed the notion of *changes* that occur in belief systems. One type of change that has been documented is called the *Socratic effect* (McGuire, 1960a). This refers to the tendency for belief structures to become more logically consistent simply as a result of asking people to express their beliefs. Presumably, when a person's beliefs about an issue become salient, the strain toward logical consistency increases. Operationally, the Socratic effect has been demonstrated by showing that the correlation between the obtained and predicted ratings of the probability of a conclusion is greater in a

Figure 7.1

Mean obtained changes in newly formed beliefs (ΔP_B) as a function of mean predicted values based upon Equation 3. Prediction is perfect when dots fall on the solid line. (Adapted from Wyer (1970). Copyright by the American Psychological Association. Used with permission.)

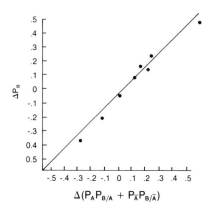

second rating than in an initial one (Henniger & Wyer, 1976; Rosen & Wyer, 1972).

The second type of change addressed by McGuire (1981) deals with changes induced by outside sources. We have already seen how a communication designed to change one belief (a premise) can also lead to changes in an unmentioned conclusion. McGuire further postulates two qualifications on the amount of inferential belief change that will occur. First, the *spatial inertia* postulate holds that the actual impact on a syllogistic conclusion of changing a logically related belief will fall progressively more short of that required by Equation 1 as the changed premise becomes more removed from the conclusion. Thus, the higher up in the vertical structure of a belief system you begin to produce a change, the greater the chance that the amount of change produced on the conclusion will fall short of that required by Equation 1. Second, the *temporal inertia* postulate holds that the impact of an induced change on a premise filters down to the inferential conclusion gradually over time. A change in a syllogistic conclusion as a result of a change in a premise should therefore be smaller on a measure taken immediately after the induced change in the premise than on a delayed measure. The spatial and temporal inertia postulates have generally received support in empirical tests (McGuire, 1981).

The most important contributions of the probabilogical models of Wyer and McGuire are: (1) that there is a strain toward hedonic as well as logical consistency in beliefs; and (2) that an induced change in one belief is capable of producing a change in a logically related belief, even though the related belief is never mentioned or attacked directly by a persuasive message. The causes of the initial belief change are not addressed by the models, however, and thus they would be inadequate as general theories of persuasion. Additionally, Wyer and Hartwick (1980) argue that the probabilogical models of belief inference are most likely to be employed by people when the proposition being judged is nonevaluative. When the proposition being judged is evaluative (e.g., whether state aid to education *should* be increased rather than whether state aid to education *will* be increased), Wyer and Hartwick suggested that beliefs may be integrated via other combinatory principles. The next two approaches we discuss provide two such combinatory possibilities. These approaches specifically relate beliefs to attitudes and, in addition, attempt to deal with the underlying dynamics of attitude change.

The Theory of Reasoned Action

Fishbein and Ajzen (1975, 1981) have proposed a theory of reasoned action that specifies in a mathematical way the relationship among beliefs, attitudes, and behaviors. The theory is quite intriguing because its authors argue that most human behaviors can be predicted and explained almost exclusively in terms of individual beliefs and attitudes. Like the other approaches in this chapter, the theory is based on the assumption that "humans are rational animals that systematically utilize or process the information available to them" and that "the information is used in a reasonable way to arrive at a behavioral decision" (Fishbein, 1980).

According to the theory, the immediate determinant of a person's overt *behavior* (B) is the person's *intention* (I) to perform (or not to perform) that behavior. So, if you knew what a person's intention was regarding some object or person (e.g., does the person intend to vote for Candidate A or B; does the person intend to purchase Brand X or Brand Y), this would be the single most important piece of information that you could have in attempting to predict the person's eventual behavior.[4] Often, however, we are not privy to a person's intentions. We can predict a person's intentions, however, by knowing two things: (1) the person's *attitude* toward the behavior (A_B) and (2) the person's *subjective norm* (SN). The first component is already quite familiar to you and of course refers to the person's positive or negative feelings about engaging in the behavior. The second component refers to the person's perceptions of the social pressures to perform or not perform the behavior in question. Generally, people will perform behaviors that they value highly and that are popular with others and will refrain from behaviors that they do not regard favorably and that are unpopular with others.

Attitude

As we discussed in chapter 1, it is possible to assess a person's attitude toward performing some behavior directly by asking the person to rate the performance of the behavior on a series of evaluative semantic differential scales (good-bad, favorable-unfavorable, etc.). According to the theory of reasoned action, however, attitudes are a result of the information that a person has about the attitude object. An alternative procedure for assessing attitudes, then, would be to measure the *salient* (readily available) beliefs that a person has about the attitude object. For example if we wanted to know a person's attitude about buying a new foreign car, we could ask the person to list his beliefs about the consequences of buying the car. Fortunately, the theory of reasoned action specifies how the different salient beliefs are combined to arrive at an overall evaluation of the behavior under consideration.[5] The integration process is described by Equation 4:

$$A_B = \sum_{i=1}^{N} b_i e_i \qquad (4)$$

In the equation, A_B refers to the person's attitude toward the behavior; b refers to the beliefs that the person has about the act's consequences in terms of the subjective probability that the act truly leads to each consequence; and e refers to the evaluations of the consequences. The i in the equation refers to the specific belief number where beliefs are numbered from 1 to N. Thus, according to the model, a person's attitude toward a behavior can be predicted by multiplying the evaluation of each consequence associated with an act by the subjective probability that the act really leads to that consequence and by summing the products. A specific example should make this clearer.

Suppose that Anne believes that the purchase of the foreign car she wants will lead to: (1) getting better gas mileage than she is getting now, (2) owning a prestigious car, (3) having less money in her bank account, and (4) paying higher insurance premiums. Let's also assume that we had asked Anne to rate the likelihood that buying the foreign car would lead to each of these consequences on a 7-point scale anchored at -3 by "unlikely" and at $+3$ by "likely"; assume also that we had her evaluate each of the consequences on a 7-point scale anchored at -3 by "bad" and at $+3$ by "good." Table 7.2 demonstrates how Anne's attitude toward the act of buying the foreign car would be determined. The calculations indicate that Anne would have a positive attitude ($+5$) toward buying the foreign car. Notice that by using a bipolar scale to assess likelihood, likely consequences that are evaluated positively and unlikely consequences that are evaluated negatively contribute to a favorable attitude toward the act. On the other hand, likely consequences that are evaluated negatively and unlikely consequences that are evaluated positively contribute to an unfavorable attitude toward the act.[6]

Table 7.2

Determining Attitude (A) from b_i and e_i

i Consequences of Buying the Foreign Car	Belief (b)		Evaluation (e)		(b_i) (e_i)
1. better gas mileage	(+3)	$\times$	(+3)	$=$	+9
2. prestige	(+1)	$\times$	(+3)	$=$	+3
3. less money in bank	(+3)	$\times$	(−2)	$=$	−6
4. higher insurance premiums	(+1)	$\times$	(−1)	$=$	−1
					+5

$$A = \sum_{i=1}^{N} b_i e_i = +5$$

Adapted from Fishbein (1980). Copyright by the University of Nebraska Press. Used with permission.

Although in the "theory of reasoned action" Equation 4 is used to predict attitudes toward behaviors, the formula may also be used to assess attitudes toward people, objects, and issues. For example, if A in the formula $A = \sum_{i=1}^{N} b_i e_i$ referred to a person's attitude about some object, then b would refer to the beliefs that the person had about the object's attributes in terms of a subjective probability that the object truly possessed each attribute, and e would refer to the evaluations of the attributes. Other investigators have proposed similar *additive models* of attitudes (Peak, 1955, Rosenberg, 1956), and there is now considerable evidence supporting them. In the typical demonstration of the utility of Equation 4 for predicting attitudes, a correlation is computed between a direct measure of attitude toward some object or behavior (as on a series of evaluative semantic differential scales) and the predicted value obtained based on a person's beliefs about the behavior or object. For example, in the initial test of Equation 4, Fishbein (1963) had a preliminary group of subjects list all of the attributes that they believed characterized Negroes. Some of the attributes listed were: dark skin, athletic, friendly. A list of the ten most frequently mentioned attributes was then presented to a second group of subjects who rated each attribute on the likelihood (b) and evaluation (e) dimensions. The estimate of the subjects' attitudes obtained by summing the product of b and e for each attribute correlated 0.80 with a more direct semantic differential measure of their attitudes toward Negroes. Either component employed alone did not correlate as well with the attitude measure ($r = 0.47$ for e_i; $r = 0.65$ for b_i), indicating that both components are important. Similar high correlations between a direct measure of attitudes and the predictions from the additive belief model have been obtained across a wide variety of people, issues, and behaviors, including such attitude objects as: presidential candidates (Fishbein & Coombs, 1974; Fishbein & Feldman, 1963), using birth control pills (Jaccard & Davidson, 1972), and allowing free speech for communists (Rosenberg, 1956).

Subjective Norm

According to the "theory of reasoned action," the second predictor of a behavioral intention is the person's subjective norm (SN). As was the case with attitude, it is possible to measure the subjective norm directly or by assessing the specific beliefs that comprise it. For example, a direct measure of Anne's subjective norm about buying a foreign car could be obtained by having her rate the following statement on a 7-point likelihood scale, where -3 indicated "unlikely" and $+3$ indicated "likely": "People who are important to me and whose opinions I value think I should buy the foreign car." According to the theory of reasoned action, this general subjective norm is based on the person's *normative beliefs* (NB)—her expectations that important reference groups or individuals endorse performing the behavior—and her *motivation to comply* (MC) with each of the referent persons or groups. This information is integrated into a general subjective norm as specified by Equation 5.

$$SN = \sum_{i=1}^{M} (NB)_i \, (MC)_i \tag{5}$$

Thus, according to the model, a person's general subjective norm can be predicted by multiplying one's assessment of another's endorsement of performing the behavior (NB) by one's motivation to comply (MC), and summing the product obtained for each referent, where referents are numbered from 1 to M. Again, an example should clarify matters. Suppose that Anne believes that there are four other people who have relevant opinions about her next car purchase: her husband, her father, her neighbor Sam, and her daughter Jane. Further assume that Anne rated the likelihood that each relevant person favored her purchase of the foreign car on a 7-point scale anchored at -3 by "unlikely" and $+3$ by "likely" and that she also rated her motivation to comply with each person on a 7-point scale anchored at -3 by "I generally do not want to do what (Referent i) thinks I should do" and $+3$ by "I generally want to do what (Referent i) thinks I should do." Table 7.3 demonstrates how Anne's subjective norm would be determined from her individual beliefs. The calculations indicate that Anne would have an unfavorable subjective norm ($SN = -8$) about buying the foreign car.

Finally, we note that just as attitudes correlate highly with a combination of b_i and e_i as specified by the model, the general subjective norm has been predicted very well by NB and MC. For example, Bowman and Fishbein (1978), in an attempt to predict how people would vote on an election initiative concerning nuclear power plant construction, showed that a direct assessment of the subjective norm (SN) correlated 0.79 with $\sum_{i=1}^{M} NB_i \, MC_i$.

Table 7.3

Determining Subjective Norm (*SN*) from Normative Beliefs (*NB*) and Motivation to Comply (*MC*)

i Important Referents	NB_i		MC_i		$(NB_i)\,(MC_i)$
1. my spouse	(-2)	$\times$	$(+3)$	$=$	-6
2. my father	$(+1)$	$\times$	$(+1)$	$=$	$+1$
3. my neighbor Sam	(-3)	$\times$	$(+1)$	$=$	-3
4. my daughter Jane	$(+3)$	$\times$	$(\ 0)$	$=$	$\underline{\ \ 0}$
					-8

$$SN = \sum_{i=1}^{M} (NB)_i\,(MC)_i = -8$$

Behavioral Intention

Equation 6 presents the full model for relating behavioral intentions to attitudes and subjective norms. Equation 7 presents the short form.

$$I = W_1\,[\sum_{i=1}^{N} b_i e_i] + W_2\,[\sum_{i=1}^{M} (NB)_i\,(MC)_i] \qquad (6)$$

$$I = (W_1)\,(A_B) + (W_2)\,(SN) \qquad (7)$$

The only new aspect of the equations is the introduction of weights W_1 and W_2. These weights represent the fact that attitudes and norms will not always be weighted equally in forming behavioral intentions. If Anne weighted both components equally, then we would predict that her behavioral intention would be unfavorable toward buying the foreign car, since $I = (5) + (-8) = -3$. On the other hand, if Anne weighted her own attitude twice as much as her subjective norm, then her behavioral intention would be favorable, since in this case $I = 2(5) + (-8) = +2$. Different people might have characteristically different weights that they apply to each component, or different types of issues might lead to differential weighting of the components.

Accumulated research has provided rather consistent support for the notion that behavioral intentions can be predicted from attitudes and subjective norms as specified by the theory of reasoned action. For example, McArdle (1972) used the model to predict the behavioral intentions of alcoholics to sign up for treatment in a veterans' hospital program. She obtained measures of the subjects' attitudes toward signing up for the alcoholic treatment program as well as their normative beliefs and motivation to comply with the following referents: spouse, doctor, parents, clergyman, and close friends. The multiple correlation of attitude and subjective norm with intention to join the program was 0.74. Other behavioral intentions predicted with success by the model include intention to perform various leisure time activities (Ajzen & Fishbein, 1969), cheating in college (DeVries & Ajzen, 1971), and having a baby (Davidson & Jaccard, 1975).

The accumulated research has also indicated that both the attitude and subjective norm components uniquely contribute to the prediction of intentions, although their relative importance may vary with people and issues. For instance, in predicting college students' intentions to engage in premarital sex, Fishbein (1966) found that for females, the *attitude* component was more important in determining intentions than the *subjective norm,* but for males, the *subjective norm* component was more important than *attitude.* Thus, females were guided more in their intentions by their own view of the consequences of premarital sex, whereas males were guided more in their intentions by others' views on premarital sex.[7]

Behavior

Of course, the ultimate goal of the theory of reasoned action is not to predict behavioral intentions per se but to predict and understand the determinants of actual behavior. In some of the studies we have already mentioned, behaviors as well as behavioral intentions were monitored. For example, McArdle (1972) found that the correlation between intending to sign up for an alcoholic treatment program and actually signing up was 0.76. Similarly, Fishbein & Coombs (1974) found that the correlations between intentions to vote and actual voting behavior in the 1964 presidential election were 0.89 for Goldwater and 0.78 for Johnson.

Davidson and Jaccard (1979) used the full model in an attempt to determine whether having a baby could be predicted from attitudes and subjective norms. In the initial phase of their investigation, 270 women completed a questionnaire assessing their attitudes and subjective norms about having a baby within the next two years. The women rated various outcomes of having a baby in the next two years (making my marriage stronger, restricting my freedom, etc.) on both the likelihood (b_i) and the evaluation (e_i) dimensions. The women also rated the likelihood that important reference persons favored the idea of their having a child in the next two years (NB) and their motivation to comply with each referent (MC). Two years later, 244 of the women were located again in order to determine whether or not they actually had a child in the intervening period. The multiple correlation between the model's predictive components ($\sum_{i=1}^{N} b_i e_i$ and $\sum_{i=1}^{M} (NB)_i (MC)_i$) and actual birth was 0.51. The correlation between the components and birth or *attempted conception* was a significantly larger 0.60. The second correlation is higher, of course, because not all of the women who tried to get pregnant were successful in doing so. (See Ajzen & Fishbein, 1980, for further examples.)

Recently, Fishbein (1980) has noted that, although a person's intention to perform a given behavior is the best *single* predictor of whether or not the person will perform the behavior, predictions may sometimes be improved by measuring intentions (and/or the underlying attitudes and subjective norms) with respect to *all* of the person's alternative courses of action. In our example then, if we were really trying to accurately predict whether or not Anne will buy the foreign car, it might not be sufficient to know her intentions regarding it. We might also need to know her intentions regarding the other cars she is considering. Let's assume that, as described previously, Anne's intention regarding the foreign car (calculated from Equation 6) is -3. Initially, it appears that it is not very likely that she will purchase the car. However, what if you now learned that Anne's intentions regarding two other American cars she is considering were -7, and -9 respectively? If Anne were only considering these three cars, it now appears very likely that she will purchase the foreign car. On the other hand, if you learned that her intentions regarding the alternative cars were $+3$, and $+6$, it would be very unlikely that you would predict that she would purchase the foreign car. In any case, it seems clear that, under some circumstances, behavioral predictions can be improved by assessing intentions for each of the alternative courses of action. We suggest that a difference score between intentions toward the target behavior and intentions toward alternative behaviors could be used as an improved predictor of the target behavior (e.g., $I = I_{target} - [\sum_{i=1}^{p} I_{alternative \ i}/P]$; where salient alternative behaviors are numbered from 1 to p).

The importance of considering a person's beliefs about alternative courses of action may be especially important when attempting to predict habitual behaviors such as smoking, drinking, or gambling. For example, it has long been an embarrassment to attitude researchers who emphasize rational processes in behavior determination that millions of Americans can agree that it is very likely ($b_i = +2$) that smoking increases the risk of lung cancer ($e_i = -3; b_i e_i = -6$) but yet continue to smoke. In fact, if a sample of people were asked to list the *consequences of smoking,* it is likely that a number of negative outcomes could be listed by both smokers and nonsmokers (it causes breathing problems, it is offensive to others, it leads to bad breath, it is expensive, etc.). According to a theory of *reasoned* action, then, how can it be that some people continue to smoke while others do not. The answer to this dilemma may lie in the *consequences of not smoking* that would be listed by smokers and nonsmokers. Nonsmokers would undoubtedly list a number of very positive consequences of not smoking, but smokers might list a number of very negative consequences of not smoking (they would become less relaxed and more tense and nervous, they would gain weight, etc.). Ultimately, then, a decision to smoke is actually quite reasonable if the decision maker believes that the net effects of smoking are (relatively) more positive than the net effects of not smoking. Data supporting this analysis have been collected by Fishbein, Loken, Roberts, and Chung (cited in Fishbein, 1980).[8]

Summary of the Theory

The theory of reasoned action specifies that the single best predictor of behavior is the behavioral intention regarding that behavior. The behavioral intention is viewed as a function of two other factors: (1) the person's attitude toward the behavior and (2) the person's subjective norm with respect to the behavior. A person's attitude about a behavior is a function of his or her salient beliefs about performing the behavior, including the likelihood that the behavior produces certain consequences (b_i) and the evaluation of those consequences (e_i). The subjective norm is a function of the person's perception that particular referents think the behavior should or should not be performed (NB_i) and the person's motivation to comply with these referents (MC_i). According to the model, any *other* variable (e.g., sex, personality) can only indirectly affect behavior. For example, if men smoke more than women, it must be because men have different beliefs that produce different behaviors. A summary diagram of the theory of reasoned action is presented in figure 7.2. Finally, it is important to note that behavioral *prediction* is *not* increased by assessing anything other than behavioral intentions. Knowing a person's attitude, subjective norm, or individual beliefs will not enhance prediction over that obtained solely by knowing the behavioral intention. (In fact, the theory would be incorrect if behavioral prediction could be enhanced!). On the other hand, as Fishbein (1980) notes, the goal of science is to *understand* the determinants of human behavior, not merely to predict them. It is for this latter purpose that the concepts of attitude, subjective norm, and the various beliefs that comprise them assume importance in the theory.[9]

Changing Beliefs, Attitudes, Norms, Intentions, and Behaviors

The theory of reasoned action makes it clear that any influence attempt—whether the goal is to change an attitude, norm, intention, or behavior—must always be directed at one or more of the individual's beliefs. The beliefs that serve as the fundamental determinants of the variable that one is trying to change are called *primary beliefs*. The beliefs that the influence attempt is designed to change are called *target beliefs*. For example, a persuasive message will be successful in changing someone's attitude about smoking to the extent that the target beliefs the communication is designed to change correspond to the primary beliefs that serve as the foundation of the person's attitude toward smoking. It is also possible that a communication may produce changes in *external beliefs*—beliefs that do not correspond to any of the informational items provided in the message. For example, Al, who is an avid smoker, hears an antismoking message that argues that smoking produces bad breath. Al knows that his new girlfriend, Sara, despises bad breath, and he reasons that Sara also despises smokers. Be-

Figure 7.2

The theory of reasoned action. (Adapted from Fishbein (1980). Copyright by the University of Nebraska Press. Used with permission.)

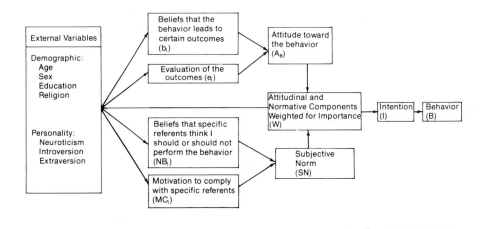

cause of Al's strong desire to comply (MC) with Sara's wishes (NB), it is possible that Al's intention to smoke might significantly decrease, even though the message might be unsuccessful in changing Al's personal attitude about smoking. This suggests that, in research, the choice of a dependent measure of influence is extremely important. The person constructing the message was attempting to change Al's attitude by getting him to associate (b_i) a negative (e_i) attribute (bad breath) with smoking. Instead, the information had an impact on an external belief—a subjective norm in this case. Since according to the Fishbein and Ajzen model, subjective norms are a component of behavioral intentions and not of attitudes, a measure of intentions would be more likely to show an effect of the message than a measure of attitudes (assuming that the nature of one's breath was not a relevant primary belief underlying Al's attitude toward smoking).

In any case, it is clear that, to change a person's attitude, it is necessary to know the salient primary beliefs on which the attitude is based, and then to construct a message that provides information either to change the person's subjective probability that the attitude object has certain attributes (b_i) or to influence the evaluations of those attributes (e_i). Likewise, a subjective norm can be changed by attacking either the specific normative beliefs relevant to each important reference person (NB) or the motivation to comply with a given referent (MC). By changing the beliefs underlying either attitudes or subjective norms, changes in behavioral intentions—and thus behaviors—could also be induced (Ajzen, 1971; Ajzen & Fishbein, 1972).

Fishbein and Ajzen (1975) have speculated about the factors that influence the likelihood that the beliefs in a persuasive message will change the audience's beliefs. Equation 8 states that the probability that a person will completely accept ($p(a)$) a belief statement in a message in an inverse function of the discrepancy (D) between the source's belief and the subject's belief. The greater the discrepancy from the person's own position, the less likely the person is to accept it.

$$p(a) = 1 - D \qquad (8)$$

Of course, many variables other than discrepancy may influence the probability of acceptance, as we have seen in the previous chapters of this book. In any given persuasion situation, other facilitating factors may affect the likelihood of accepting any particular advocated belief. These facilitating factors may be associated with the communicator (e.g., source credibility), the message (e.g., the number of arguments employed), or the audience (e.g., recipient intelligence). Equation 9 inserts a variable *"f"* into Equation 8 to represent these facilitating factors.

$$p(a) = (1 - D)^{1/f} \qquad (9)$$

This equation generates the family of acceptance curves in the left panel of figure 7.3. In the figure, it can be seen that as the overall facilitating factors decline (e.g., the source becomes less credible), the probability of acceptance is hypothesized to decrease dramatically with increasing discrepancy. On the other hand, as facilitation reaches very high levels, the probability of acceptance remains very high, even at very large discrepancy levels.

Although Equation 8 specifies that the probability of completely accepting a source's belief is an inverse function of discrepancy, the *potential amount of change* that can be produced in a subject's belief is a *direct* function of discrepancy. In other words, the more discrepant the advocated position, the more potential there is for change. Considering both of these observations, Fishbein and Ajzen (1975) contend that *actual change* (*C*) in the advocated direction is a function of potential change (as indexed by discrepancy) and the probability of complete acceptance. This is shown in Equation 10.

$$C = p(a)D \qquad (10)$$

The right panel of figure 7.3 graphs the predicted amount of change that would occur as a function of discrepancy *and* acceptance gradients, with facilitation values as specified in the left panel of the figure. At most levels of facilitation, the relationship between predicted belief change and discrepancy shows an inverted-U pattern, with the point of inflection at higher discrepancy levels the greater the amount of overall facilitation.

Although Fishbein and Ajzen's (1975) speculations about the factors determining the amount of belief change that would be produced under various conditions are quite interesting, the specific model proposed has not been subjected to empirical tests; and reinterpretations of existing data provide only mixed

Figure 7.3

Left panel: Family of acceptance gradients for different degrees of facilitation: $p(a) = (1 - D)^{1/f}$. *Right panel:* Change in the advocated direction as a function of discrepancy and acceptance gradients with varying *f* values: $C = p(a)D$. (From Fishbein & Ajzen (1975). Copyright by Addison-Wesley Publishing Company, Inc. Reprinted with permission.)

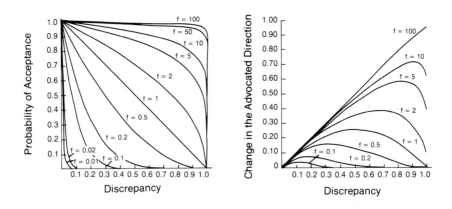

support for the model. For example, if source credibility was examined as a facilitating factor, the higher the source credibility, the greater the *f* value should be in the prediction equations. The right panel of figure 7.3 could then represent the predicted relationship between discrepancy and sources at different credibility levels. In this instance, the predicted pattern matches quite well the patterns actually obtained in several investigations. With higher credibility (facilitation), the inflection point in the inverted-U occurs at a higher level of discrepancy (Aronson et al., 1963; Bochner & Insko, 1966; see the discussion of discrepancy in chap. 4).

In other instances, however, the predictions from the model do not seem to be supported. For example, one implication of the model is that if overall facilitation is already at a high level, a manipulation designed to increase facilitation will not have much effect on acceptance (see the left panel of fig. 7.3). Fishbein and Ajzen (1975, p. 464) use the following example: ". . . When the receivers are not involved with the issue, . . . the initial level of overall facilitation will be very high. The acceptance gradient will therefore remain relatively unchanged, whether the communicator has high or low credibility." In other words, source credibility should have a smaller persuasive impact on unimportant or uninvolving issues than on important or relevant ones, because it should be generally easier to change people's attitudes on issues they don't care about; and an expert source should add little when overall facilitation is already high. The empirical research to date, however, appears to indicate that just the opposite is true.

Credibility has a larger impact on uninvolving than involving issues (Petty, Cacioppo, & Goldman, in press; Rhine & Severance, 1970; see chaps. 8 and 9 for a further discussion).

The equations relevant to belief change in the Fishbein and Ajzen model (Equations 8–10) are of more recent vintage than the equations relating beliefs to attitudes, norms, intentions, and behaviors (Equations 4–7). Thus, it is not surprising that the latter have developed to the point where they are highly respected and valuable formulations, whereas the former have not yet demonstrated their usefulness. The equations relating beliefs to behaviors (as mediated by attitudes and norms) are important tools for the applied attitude researcher who may be interested in predicting voting patterns, consumer choices, and jury decisions; at the same time, they are also valuable to theoretical researchers interested in understanding and explaining the bases of these same behaviors. At present, the equations relevant to belief change have not been shown to predict existing data accurately, and they do not yet appear to be very promising tools for explaining and understanding the persuasion process. The model neither gives insight into what kinds of variables should be facilitating factors, nor does it provide any indication of *why* these variables would be facilitating. Nevertheless, Fishbein and Ajzen have provided the most complete informational analysis of attitudes and, of equal importance, have provided a coherent and highly useful model of the relationships among beliefs, attitudes, and behaviors.

Information Integration Theory (Cognitive Algebra)

Norman Anderson (1971; in press) has proposed a general combinatory theory of human judgment and decision called *information integration theory,* which has considerable relevance to the study of attitudes and persuasion. A basic tenet of information integration theory is that much of human judgment and decision, including attitude judgment, obeys simple algebraic models (this is referred to as *cognitive algebra*). We have already seen examples of the use of algebraic models of belief inference in the last two sections. In this section we will discuss Anderson's *weighted averaging* model, which he has most often employed in the study of attitude judgments. Anderson (1974) has employed other algebraic models (multiplicative, additive) in other judgmental domains, however.

According to the information integration theory, attitude judgments will ordinarily be determined by several beliefs.[10] The belief information may be generated from memory or may be provided by external sources. In either case, each piece of information is represented by two parameters—a scale value (s) and a weight (w). The scale value (like Fishbein & Ajzens's e_i component) represents how favorable or unfavorable the person is toward the information, and the weight represents how important the information is to the person (this is analogous to Fishbein & Ajzen's b_i component). In attitude judgments, the person's initial attitude is always one piece of information that is considered along with any other salient information. In cases of attitude formation (where the person has no previous information about the attitude object), the person's initial attitude will usually receive a scale value of neutrality (zero), but it still may receive a large weight if the person's neutrality is very important. When some new information becomes salient, the person's new attitude will be the average of his prior attitude and the newly salient information. This weighted averaging model of attitudes is expressed in Equation 11.

$$A = \frac{[w_o s_o + \sum\limits_{i=1}^{N} w_i s_i]}{w_o + \sum\limits_{i=1}^{N} w_i} \tag{11}$$

In this equation, w_o and s_o represent the weight and scale value of the original attitude, and w_i and s_i represent the weights and scale values of the newly salient information, where each piece of new information is numbered from 1 to N.

Let's say that you were interested in how a person would judge four different cars if only two pieces of information were provided about each car: make and color. The four cars to be judged are a red Ford, a blue Ford, a red Chevrolet, and a blue Chevrolet. In order to predict the person's attitude toward each of the cars, we would need to know how he evaluates (s_i) the attributes red, blue, Ford, and Chevrolet; and we would need to know how he weights the importance (w_i) of make and color in evaluating cars. Table 7.4 provides an example of possible weights and scale values that might be applied in this instance, along with the evaluations that would be predicted by the weighted averaging model. (For simplicity we will assume that the initial attitude has a weight of zero and thus does not enter into the judgment.) The weighted averaging model would predict that the blue Ford would be liked the best and the red Chevy the least.

One way to test the utility of the averaging model in prediction would be to correlate the predicted attitudes (as demonstrated in table 7.4) with those obtained on a more direct measure of attitude (e.g., semantic differential) toward each of the four cars. This would require that subjects provide estimates of their weights and scale values. However, Anderson (1976, 1981) suggests another means of testing the averaging model based on the *parallelism theorem*, which does not even require that weight and scale value parameters be obtained from subjects. The parallelism theorem can be applied whenever a factorial experimental design has been employed, meaning that every level of one variable intersects with every level of every other variable. In the example in table 7.4, there are two variables—make and color—and each make (Ford and Chevrolet) is paired with each color (red and blue). The parallelism theorem states that if the attitude data from a factorial experiment are graphed and the data plot as parallel lines, then the data provide joint support for three conclusions:

1. The averaging model is correct.
2. Each piece of information has the same weight and scale value regardless of what other piece of information it is paired with (referred to as *meaning constancy*), and
3. The attitude rating response is on an equal-interval scale (Anderson, 1981).

Figure 7.4 graphs the data in table 7.4. Clearly, parallelism is obtained.[11] Finally,

Table 7.4

Hypothetical Weights and Scale Values Assigned to Four Kinds of Cars and the Evaluations Predicted from Anderson's Weighted Averaging Model of Attitudes

	W	s	s	s	s
COLOR	1	Red (+2)	Red (+2)	Blue (+4)	Blue (+4)
MAKE	3	Ford (+4)	Chevy (+2)	Ford (+4)	Chevy (+2)
$\dfrac{\Sigma w_i s_i}{\Sigma w_i}$		$\dfrac{(1\times2)+(3\times4)}{1+3}$	$\dfrac{(1\times2)+(3\times2)}{1+3}$	$\dfrac{(1\times4)+(3\times4)}{1+3}$	$\dfrac{(1\times4)+(3\times2)}{1+3}$
		$\dfrac{2+12}{4}$	$\dfrac{2+6}{4}$	$\dfrac{4+12}{4}$	$\dfrac{4+6}{4}$
ATTITUDE =		3.50	2.00	4.00	2.50

NOTE: In this example, the person has weighted make of car as being 3X as important as color. The person also likes blue twice as much as red and Fords twice as much as Chevys.

once parallelism has been demonstrated, it is possible to estimate the weights and scale values used by subjects in making their judgments, and the procedure used to do this is called *functional measurement* (Anderson, 1977; in press).

The parallelism theorem has been supported in a number of experiments in which subjects made belief and attitudinal judgments. For example, in one study (Sawyers & Anderson, 1971) subjects read two paragraphs about United States presidents and were instructed to integrate them into an overall evaluation. There were four different kinds of paragraphs presenting either highly favorable information about the president (H), moderately favorable (M+), moderately unfavorable (M−), or highly unfavorable information (L). Figure 7.5 presents the mean attitudes of the subjects who were exposed to the various combinations of paragraphs. The six graphs follow the parallelism prediction quite closely. The parallelism prediction has been upheld in evaluation judgments of a wide variety of stimuli (e.g., attitudes about outstanding women, Simms, 1976; about consumer products, Troutman & Shanteau, 1976).

The information integration model in Equation 11 has also been applied to a wide variety of variables that have been shown to affect persuasion (Anderson, 1981; in press). The model is capable of accounting for various source, message, receiver, and context factors. We have already seen how a message variable (quality of the arguments presented) could affect attitudes toward presidents through the *s* parameter. As further examples, let us see how a source and a recipient factor could affect information integration and, thus, attitudes.

Figure 7.4

Attitude rating of four cars (data from table 7.4). Parallelism is consistent with Anderson's averaging model.

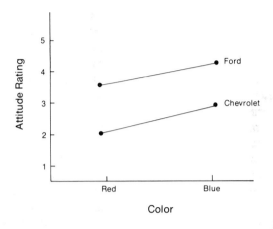

Figure 7.5

Attitudes toward U.S. presidents as a function of stimulus information. Each panel represents one 2 × 2 design. (Adapted from Sawyers & Anderson (1971). Copyright by the American Psychological Association. Used with permission.)

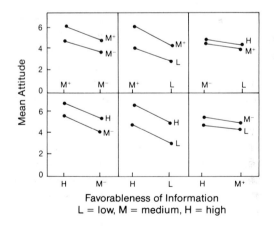

Box 7.3

Adding vs. Averaging

When attempting to form an attitude about a person, object, or issue, do we *add* or *average* the information we have. An additive approach is used in the cartoon.

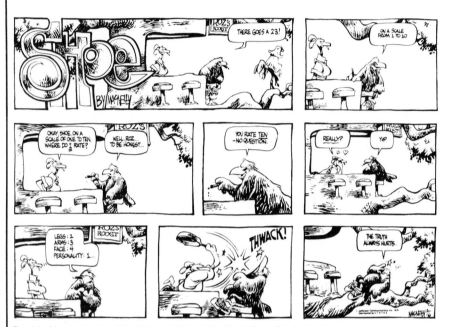

Reprinted by permission of the Chicago Tribune-New York News Syndicate, Inc.

Assume that a long time friend of yours moves next door to you. You have always liked this person ($s_o = +10$), and you hold this attitude with great confidence ($w_o = +9$). One day while shopping at the supermarket, you hear the local gossip state that she saw your friend stealing a can of beans. You dislike stealing ($s_1 = -6$), but the town gossip is not a very credible source, and so you assign little weight to the information ($w_1 = 1$). The result of hearing this news on the evaluation of your friend, as predicted from Equation 4, would be as follows:

$$\frac{(w_o)\,(s_o) + (w_1)\,(s_1)}{(w_o) + (w_1)} = A = \frac{(9)\,(10) + (1)\,(-6)}{(9) + (1)} = 84/10 = 8.4$$

There have been several attempts to devise crucial tests of adding versus averaging models of information integration. For example, consider that two people were described to you: one person was described by three traits of equal favorability (say $+2$ as rated by a group of judges); another person was described by four traits, each having a $+2$ rating. At first glance it would appear that an adding model would predict that you would like the second person $(2+2+2+2 = 8)$ better than the first $(2+2+2 = 6)$, whereas the averaging model would predict that you would like both people equally, since the average of the traits would be $+2$ for both people (assuming equal weights for each trait in the Anderson model and subjective probabilities of 1 in the Fishbein model). Experimental tests of these notions (Anderson, 1965) have indicated that the second person (with four $+2$ traits) is actually liked better. This finding is referred to as the *set size* effect. These data do not unequivocally support the adding formulation, however, because if it is assumed that people also integrate an initial neutral impression (S_o) with the new information, the averaging model would also predict that the second person $(0+2+2+2+2/5 = 1.6)$ would be liked better than the first $(0+2+2+2/4 = 1.5)$.

Another attempt to distinguish between the two models has been made in the following manner. This time assume that a person has been described to you who has two $+3$ traits (as determined by a separate group of judges). If this person was compared to another who also possessed the two $+3$ traits but who also possessed a trait that a group of judges had rated as $+1$, which person would you like better? At first glance, it would appear that the adding model would predict that the first person $(3+3 = 6)$ would be liked less than the second $(3+3+1 = 7)$, whereas the averaging model would predict that the second person $(0+3+3+1/4=1.75)$ would be liked less than the first $(0+3+3/3 = 2)$. In this case, experimental tests have indicated that the second person is liked less than the first (Anderson, 1965). These data do not unequivocally support the averaging formulation, however. It could be argued that, although naive judges rated the third trait as $+1$, subjects who must rate this mildly positive trait in the context of *very* positive traits, might actually perceive it as relatively negative (-1). This, of course is the *contrast effect* that we discussed in chapter 4. If this contrast phenomenon occurs in this situation, then the adding model would also predict that the second person $(3+3-1 = 5)$ would be liked less than the first.

In sum, there is no convincing evidence to date that unequivocally supports either the adding or averaging formulation.

The evaluation of your friend would drop slightly from $+10.0$ to $+8.4$. On the other hand, if you heard the same information from Dan Rather on the "CBS Evening News," you might assign considerably more weight to the information (say $+8$), and the evaluation of your friend would drop dramatically to $+2.5$ $\left[\dfrac{(90) + (8)(-6)}{(9) + (8)} = 42/17 = 2.5. \right]$ You can see, then, that the traditional effect of source credibility on persuasion can be explained by how the source information affects the weight parameter.

For purposes of the example, assume now that your mother also heard the town gossip make the disparaging remark about your friend. She initially liked your friend as much as you $(s_o = 10)$, disliked stealing as much as you

$(s_1 = -6)$, and gives the remark little weight ($w_1 = 1$). However, the remark has a very strong impact on her attitude, because she held her initial attitude less confidently than you ($w_0 = 1$). In this case, the effect is to change your mother's attitude from 10.0 to 2.0 $\left[\dfrac{(1)(10) + (1)(-6)}{(1) + (1)} = \dfrac{4}{2} = 2.0 \right]$. In this example, information integration theory accounts for the effects of issue involvement on persuasion by contending that more involved persons give their own initial attitudes greater weight than less involved persons and thus are harder to persuade.

Of course, information integration theory can also account for the effects, observed occasionally, that moderately credible sources produce more persuasion than highly credible ones (Sternthal, Dholakia, & Leavitt, 1979) and that highly involved persons are sometimes more susceptible to persuasion than less involved persons (Petty & Cacioppo, 1979b). (These effects are discussed further in the next chapter). The weighted averaging model can account for these data by postulating that in some circumstances highly credible sources are given less weight than sources of low credibility and that involved persons sometimes weight their own attitudes less than uninvolved persons. The power of the model to account for opposite effects stems, in part, from its post hoc application and the flexibility in the s and w parameters. By allowing these parameters to take on all values, including negative ones, almost any pattern of data can be found to "fit" the model. Furthermore, if an averaging model does not prove adequate, Anderson (1974) has suggested that other algebraic models can be employed (e.g., multiplicative). It is clear that some algebraic model will be able to account for virtually any data set after it is collected; and an important weakness of Anderson's *cognitive algebra,* therefore, is its inability to anticipate many effects in advance (Ostrom & Davis, 1979).

It is typical procedure for information integration theorists to find a reliable persuasion effect first and then find an algebraic model to fit the data. With a wide enough variety of models and post hoc assumptions about what scale values and weights subjects "must have" used in order to produce a certain pattern of data, it becomes impossible to ever disconfirm information integration theory (cognitive algebra) notions. Nevertheless, integration theory and the cognitive algebra notions it employs remain impressive tools for *describing* a wide variety of persuasion effects. In comparison with Fishbein and Ajzen's additive model of attitudes, it may be concluded that, although the additive model is not as flexible as Anderson's information integration theory, the theory of reasoned action has three major advantages: (1) it is disconfirmable, (2) it emphasizes understanding and prediction of attitudinal phenomena rather than description, and (3) it relates attitudes and beliefs to overt behaviors. Nevertheless, on the important question of whether people combine the information that goes into their attitude judgments by adding or averaging, there is not yet truly compelling evidence for either process (see box 7.3).

Retrospective

In this chapter we have presented an approach to persuasion that focuses on the role of information in changing peoples' attitudes and on how people combine the information they receive into an overall impression. Common to all of the theories covered in this chapter is the view that an attitude is based on the information or beliefs that a person has about the attitude object. The probabilogical theories with which we began our discussion emphasized the interrelationships among a person's beliefs and how the change in one belief could lead to a change in others. These belief changes were shown to be governed by both logical and "wishful" thought processes. The theory of reasoned action viewed an attitude as a weighted *sum* of the information that a person had about an attitude object; and it further indicated that a person's behaviors were based on a consideration of one's own attitude and one's perceptions of the views of important other people. The theory of information integration was shown to allow description of a wide range of attitudinal phenomena with the fundamental principle that an attitude was best represented as a weighted *average* of information about an attitude object. The next chapter also emphasizes the role of information in persuasion but focuses on the information that people generate themselves rather than on information presented by external sources.

Notes

[1] The term psycho-logic is used to imply that the actual syllogisms comprising a person's belief structure do not necessarily follow the formal rules of logic and probability. Instead, the conclusion of the syllogism may "follow from" the premises only in the mind of the person (Abelson & Rosenberg, 1958).

[2] The probability of an event can range from 0 (no chance of occurring) to 1 (certain to occur). In this instance, it is impossible to assign an objective probability to the event, and therefore a subjective probability is employed. Thus, different people might assign different probabilities to the same event.

[3] McGuire labels the probabilities associated with the two premises p(a) and p(b) and the probability associated with the conclusion p(c). Thus, $p(c) = [p(c/(a \& b)) \, p \, (a \& b)] + [p \, (c/(a \& b)) \, p \, (a \& b)]$ (McGuire, 1981). Although McGuire's and Wyer's models make the same predictions, Wyer's (1975) notation is somewhat easier to use.

[4] Of course, intentions will not predict behaviors perfectly because some behaviors are not under the complete control of the actor. For example, Fred may *intend* to marry Ethel, but whether he does or not depends on Ethel's intentions also.

[5] Fishbein and Ajzen (1975) argue that although a person may hold a very large number of beliefs about any given attitude object, only a relatively small number of *salient* beliefs (5-9) will generally serve as determinants of attitude at any given moment in time. Of course given more time or incentive, a greater number of beliefs may be taken into account.

[6]In some research that tests the theory or reasoned action, the belief component is assessed on a unipolar scale (with no negative numbers) following the argument that subjective probabilities should not take on both negative and positive values (Davidson & Jaccard, 1979). Although it is strictly true that a probability can only range from 0 to 1, it also seems true that if some act were highly unlikely to lead to some positive consequence, this would be seen psychologically as a strike *against* performing the behavior, whereas if some act were highly unlikely to lead to some negative consequence, this would be seen psychologically as a point *in favor of* performing the behavior. The unipolar scoring method would lead to the opposite conclusion (the former would be counted as favorable toward the behavior, and the latter would be counted as unfavorable toward the behavior). Fishbein and Ajzen (1975) suggest that when the unipolar assessment of belief is used, a measure of subjective probability and evaluation of the *negation* of the belief (e.g., that buying the foreign car will *not* lead to better gas mileage) should also be included (see Fishbein and Ajzen, 1975, pp. 82–86, for an extended discussion and justification).

[7]In research employing Equations 6 and 7, the weights of the attitudinal and normative components are empirically determined by a statistical procedure known as multiple regression.

[8]The increase in behavioral prediction by including ratings of not smoking stems from the potential lack in symmetry in the b_i ratings of the consequences of smoking and not smoking. For example, a smoker might rate being relaxed as a *somewhat likely* consequence of smoking (+1) but rate being relaxed as an *extremely unlikely* consequence of not smoking (−3). Similarly, assessing the subjective norm component for not smoking might also enhance prediction if there were asymmetry in the normative belief (*NB*) ratings.

[9]The causal model in figure 7.2 has not been without its detractors, however. For example, Bentler and Speckart (1979), in a test of the theory of reasoned action against alternative causal models, have claimed support for the view that attitudes can have a *direct* effect on behavior that is not mediated by intentions. They also found support for the view that past behaviors could affect future behaviors without being mediated by intentions (see also Bearden & Woodside, 1977; Triandis, 1980). But even though the causal sequence among attitudes, norms, intentions, and behaviors has not been firmly established, the great bulk of existing data provides impressive support for the Fishbein and Ajzen model.

[10]Anderson distinguishes between *attitude* and *attitude judgment*. Whereas an attitude is a general affective reaction toward some person or object (e.g., do you like the president?), an attitude judgment refers to an evaluation along a specific dimension (e.g., do you like the president as a statesman? a friend? an actor?).

[11]If any of the three conclusions above is incorrect, parallelism will not likely be obtained (parallelism is supported by obtaining a nonsignificant interaction in an analysis of variance on the data). Anderson argues that the parallelism test is better than one based on correlations because extremely high correlations can be obtained even though a model is incorrect, and discrepancies from the model can be detected more easily as nonparallelism. Anderson recognizes, however, that parallelism is not absolute proof that the three conclusions are correct, because it is possible that two incorrect premises could counteract each other. Furthermore, obtaining parallelism provides no unique support for an *averaging* model of information integration. An *additive model* would also provide parallelism in the data. Graph the sum of the evaluations for each car in table 7.4 to demonstrate this for yourself. See box 7.3 for more on adding versus averaging.

Self-persuasion Approaches

Have you ever been insulted by someone whom you considered a friend? Initially, you are probably surprised and upset, and as you continue to think about the incident, you might become even more upset—how could that person *say* that to you?—and further thought might even lead to intense hatred and rage. On the other hand, has a friend ever done something especially nice for you? At first, you are pleasantly surprised. As you think more about the good deed, it may begin to seem even nicer—very few other people would have been so kind—and your attitude toward the other person may soon become extremely favorable. In both of these examples, the phenomenon of *self-persuasion* is occurring—thinking about some incident or issue causes your attitude to become more extreme or *polarized*. The attitude change that occurs is not the result of a message that originates externally but rather is the result of thoughts, ideas, and arguments that you generate yourself (see box 8.1).

In this chapter, we will first focus on research in which an attempt is made to change attitudes by having people generate their own messages on some issue. Next, parallels between the self-persuasion approach and the dissonance theory approach (discussed in chap. 5) are addressed. Finally, we discuss the importance of a person's own thoughts in inhibiting and facilitating attitude changes that result from exposure to externally originated messages. The theme of this chapter is that virtually all persuasion effects can be thought of as self-persuasion.

The Role-playing Approach: Active Participation vs. Passive Exposure

Janis and King (1954) reported one of the earliest investigations in which the effects of actively presenting arguments on an issue were compared with the effects of passively listening to arguments presented by another person. In this study, subjects participated in groups of three. In any one session, an individual subject was to present a talk on one topic and listen to the two other subjects present speeches on two different topics. The subjects were led to believe that

Messages That We Generate Ourselves Can Be Highly Persuasive

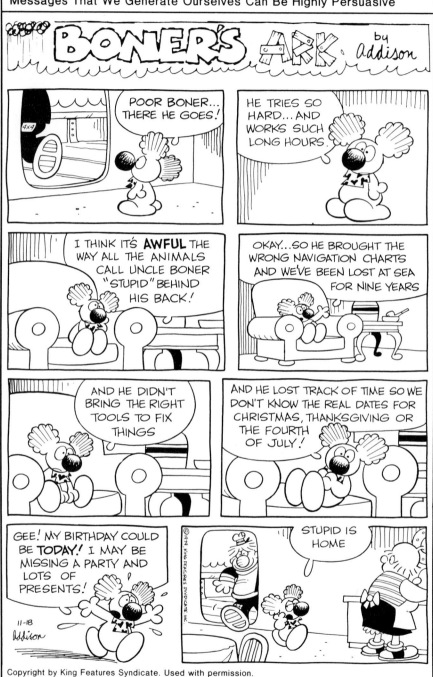

they were helping the investigator to develop an aptitude test for assessing oral speaking ability. Each of the subjects was given an outline of arguments that might be used in making a speech on all three topics. In every case, the speeches that the subjects were to make took positions different from that which they had endorsed on an opinion survey four weeks earlier. After the subjects had given their own speeches and listened to the speeches of the two other subjects, another measure of attitude was taken. For two out of the three issues, subjects who had actively presented the arguments were more influenced by them than subjects who were passively exposed to exactly the same arguments. On the third issue, there were no differences between the active and passive exposure groups.

Why did active subjects show more change for two of the issues but not for the third? After carefully comparing the conditions in which active participation produced more change than passive exposure (topics 1 and 2) with the condition in which it did not (topic 3), Janis and King discovered that active participants giving speeches on topics 1 and 2 appeared to improvise more (i.e., went beyond their prepared outlines) and were more satisfied with their talks than active participants giving speeches on topic 3. This suggested that the enhanced influence produced by the active role playing may have been due to either *improvisation* (the fact that active participants were persuaded by the unique arguments that they generated during their speeches) or *satisfaction* (the fact that the positive feelings resulting from the role playing generalized to or became associated with the attitude issue).

In a second experiment, King and Janis (1956) attempted to determine which of these two possibilities was the most likely mediator of the observed effect. All subjects were exposed to a discrepant communication arguing that over ninety percent of college students would be drafted one year after graduation and that they would serve in the military for at least three years. There were three experimental conditions in the study: in the *control* condition, subjects simply read the discrepant communication to themselves silently; in the *non-improvisation* condition, subjects read the communication aloud into a taperecorder, and finally, in the *improvisation* condition, subjects gave an extemporaneous talk based on the written communication but without having access to it during their speech. When attitudes were assessed, it was found that a greater percentage of improvisation subjects changed in the direction of the discrepant communication than subjects in the other two conditions (which did not differ from each other). The fact that improvisation subjects showed the most attitude change as a result of their role-playing experience, but that the nonimprovisation subjects reported more satisfaction with their performances than improvisation subjects, indicates that improvisation and not satisfaction is a more likely explanation for the increased persuasion that results from active role playing. Later research has shown role playing to be an effective technique for changing attitudes on a wide variety of issues as long as people have enough background information on the issue to permit improvisation of arguments (Janis & Mann, 1977).

The Persistence of Attitude Changes Produced by Role Playing

We have seen how role playing can be an effective persuasion technique. Interestingly, there is now sufficient evidence to conclude that not only can improvisational role playing be a more effective technique than passive exposure to arguments in producing initial persuasion, but it may also be more effective in producing *persisting* persuasion. For example, in a carefully designed experiment, Watts (1967) had subjects either read a communication or actively generate a passage on an assigned topic. The persuasive messages employed in the experiment were developed in pretesting so that they would produce the same amount of initial attitude change as would the self-generation of a communication. The pretesting was apparently successful to the extent that subjects who passively read the communications showed an amount of initial attitude change equivalent to that of subjects who generated their own messages. Both groups showed significantly more attitude change than controls who neither received nor generated messages. On a delayed measure of opinion taken six weeks later, however, subjects in the self-generated conditions showed total persistence of attitude change, but subjects in the passive reading conditions were no longer different from the control subjects.

Elms (1966) conducted a conceptually similar study. After reading a brief antismoking pamphlet, some subjects in his study were asked to play the role of a person who had a serious disease and had given up smoking. These subjects were told that it was their job to generate a message that would convince their best friend to quit smoking. Finally, these subjects were asked to write down all of the reasons they could for giving up smoking. Another group of subjects passively listened to the messages generated by the active subjects after they too had read the antismoking pamphlet. These subjects were asked to write down all of the reasons that the role-playing subjects had given to stop smoking. On the immediate test of opinion about smoking, active subjects showed slightly (but not significantly) more attitude change in the antismoking direction than passive exposure subjects. On a measure taken three weeks later, however, the active subjects were considerably (and significantly) more antismoking than the passive group. Again, active improvisation led to greater persistence of the induced attitude change than passive exposure.

Why Is Role Playing So Effective?

Janis (1959, 1968) has argued that when a person agrees to espouse a discrepant position, a *biased scanning* of the arguments on the issue occurs:

> . . . when a person accepts the task of improvising arguments in favor of a point of view at variance with his own personal convictions, he becomes temporarily motivated to think up all the good positive arguments he can and

at the same time, suppresses thoughts about the negative arguments which are supposedly irrelevant to the assigned task. This "biased scanning" increases the salience of the positive arguments and therefore increases the chances of acceptance of the new attitude position. [Janis & Gilmore, 1965, pp. 17–18]

In an explicit test of the biased scanning hypothesis, O'Neill and Levings (1979) recruited some high school students for a study that presumably investigated "debating techniques". The students were told that they would be assigned to one side of an issue and would have to debate that side with another group of students. The debate teams were composed of three members. Prior to the debate, all teams were allowed forty minutes of preparation time. Before the preparation time began, all of the teams were told about the issue that they were going to debate, but only half of the subjects were additionally informed of the *side* of the issue that they were to debate. The other half did not learn their side until after the preparatory discussion (but before the debate of course). All of the discussion sessions were tape recorded, since the investigators were interested in whether or not biased scanning of information would occur prior to the debate in the informed groups. These tapes were later rated by judges who counted the number of arguments mentioned in the discussion on both sides of the issue. Students who had been informed of the side they were to debate prior to the discussion generated arguments primarily on the side of the issue they were to debate; whereas uninformed students were more open-minded, generating arguments on both sides of the issue. Thus, in anticipation of role playing, people apparently do engage in a *biased information search,* and this biased information search may contribute to the attitude changes produced by role playing. In the O'Neill and Levings study, subjects did show more attitude change toward their assigned positions when they had an opportunity for biased scanning of information than when they did not. This effect occurred both when attitudes were measured after the discussion but before the debate and when attitudes were measured after the debate.

It is not clear, however, that this biased scanning process can completely account for the attitudinal affects of role playing. First of all, we have already seen, in one of the earliest studies on role playing (Janis & King, 1954), that people who actively generated and presented the arguments were more influenced by the arguments than people who were passively exposed to the *same* information. Since everyone was exposed to exactly the same information (both active and passive subjects were exposed to the same biased sample of arguments), there must be some other process contributing to the effectiveness of active over passive participation.[1] Secondly, it is not clear how the biased scanning hypothesis accounts for the greater persistence of persuasion found with active as opposed to passive participation.

A study by Greenwald and Albert (1968) suggests answers to both of these dilemmas. In their study, college students were asked to write five statements in favor of either a general or a specialized college education. The subjects were randomly assigned to take one side of the issue or the other with the rationale that "since there are many valid arguments to be made on both sides of the issue, we feel that no one will be disappointed by this arbitrary assignment" (p. 31). In order to help them generate their five statements, five thought-questions were provided (e.g., "in what way does a general (or specific) education prepare a college graduate to meet the rapid changes characteristic of modern life?"). In addition to generating arguments on one side of the issue, all subjects were also exposed to five arguments that were generated by another subject who had been assigned to argue the opposite position. Subjects were given a chance to generate their arguments either before or after they had been exposed to the arguments of another subject. Several measures were taken. First, subjects were asked to rate each of the arguments (their own and the other subject's) on an eleven-point originality scale. Then, after an intervening task that took about twenty minutes (and allowed some forgetting of the arguments to occur), subjects were asked to give their own opinion on the issue and attempt to recall as many of the arguments that they had read (their own and the other subject's) as they could. Consistent with the previously described literature on role playing, subjects were more influenced by the arguments that they generated themselves than by the arguments to which they were passively exposed. Of greater interest, however, was that subjects rated their own arguments as being more original than the arguments that they received from the other subject. Of course in any individual comparison, the arguments that the subject generated may have been of higher quality or more original than the arguments of the other subject, but the procedure employed in the experiment ensured that, over the whole sample of subjects, differences in quality would balance out. Thus, even though the arguments in the whole sample did not differ objectively, subjects perceived their own arguments to be of greater merit (more original) than the arguments to which they were exposed from another person. This suggests that even when active and passive participants have identical information, the generators of the arguments may be more influenced by their own arguments because they perceive them to be of higher quality. Perloff and Brock (1980) refer to this tendency as the *ownness bias*.

The second interesting effect obtained in the Greenwald and Albert investigation was that subjects were able to recall significantly more of the arguments that they generated themselves than they recalled of the arguments generated by another person (see also Slamecka & Graf, 1978). This provides a possible explanation for the fact that active participation leads to more enduring persuasion than passive exposure. After a long delay period, active participants are better able to recall the reasons for the initial change than are passively exposed groups, and this most likely contributes to the more enduring attitude change observed in the former group.

In sum, we can conclude that: (1) role playing is an effective procedure for changing attitudes because people engage in a biased information search when asked to role-play, (2) role playing is more effective than passive exposure because people tend to value the arguments that they generate more than the arguments generated by others, and (3) role playing produces more persisting attitude change than passive exposure because people can better remember the arguments that they generate than the arguments generated by others.

Can Dissonance Theory Account for Role-playing Effects?

Astute readers of this text have probably recognized certain similarities between the role-playing procedures described in this chapter and the procedures employed by dissonance theorists discussed in chapter 5. We have just described a number of studies in which people were asked to make verbal statements or write essays that conflicted with their true opinions. According to the early dissonance theorists, when a person engaged in a behavior (made a speech or wrote an essay) that was inconsistent with a prior attitude, dissonance was aroused. One means of reducing the dissonance was to change one's attitude to bring it into line with the discrepant behavior. At first glance, then, dissonance theory appears to provide a plausible account of the effects of counterattitudinal role playing on attitude change.

A number of studies were conducted in the 1960s in an attempt to distinguish the dissonance theory explanation from the "biased scanning" formulation that we presented earlier in this chapter. Most of these studies compared role-playing conditions carried out under either high or low incentive. According to dissonance theory, the greater the incentive for counterattitudinal role playing, the less attitude change that should be produced because the incentive serves to justify the discrepant action. According to the biased scanning formulation, however, the greater the incentive, the greater the attitude change that should occur. This is because subjects who role-play under high incentive conditions should be more motivated to generate more and/or better arguments than subjects who role-play with little or no incentive (Elms & Janis, 1965; Janis & Gilmore, 1965). Support for the biased scanning hypothesis has come from a number of studies. For example, Rosenberg (1965) asked students at Ohio State University to write essays in favor of the highly counterattitudinal position of banning the football team from playing in the Rose Bowl, even though they were the current Big Ten champions. The students were offered either fifty cents, one dollar, or five dollars for writing their essays. A measure of attitude taken after the essays were written indicated that the subjects paid the most money were most influenced by the arguments that they had generated. In further support of the biased scanning hypothesis, Rosenberg reports that when a group of naive judges rated the persuasiveness of the essays produced, it was found that the five-dollar subjects had written the highest quality papers. In a similar study, Rosenberg (1968) had subjects engage in a six-minute counterattitudinal role-play for either fifty cents or two and one-half dollars. The greater the payment, the greater the number of arguments the subjects put forth during the role-play, and the more they came to support the position they advocated.

None of these data suggest that dissonance theory is incorrect—just that it is an unlikely explanation for the role-playing studies that we have discussed in this section. As we noted in chapter 5, there is widespread agreement that the original dissonance formulation was too general and that the dissonance effect is obtained in a much narrower set of circumstances than was originally believed. Those specific circumstances are outlined in chapter 5. Interestingly, even before the limiting conditions on the dissonance effect were fully documented, Rosenberg (1968) suggested that the context in which the role-playing experience was presented to subjects had a lot to do with whether dissonance or incentive effects would be obtained. He noted that dissonance effects are more likely to be obtained when the role-playing experience is presented as a means of deceiving, tricking, or cynically persuading another person of something that the role-player did not believe. We would add that if a dissonance effect is to be observed, the role player should also feel that the role playing is likely to bring about some foreseeable harmful consequence. Under these limited conditions, the smaller the incentive for role playing, the more the attitude change. The greater attitude change under low incentive results from the role player's desire to reduce the discomfort that results from engaging in the counterattitudinal act. On the other hand, Rosenberg (1968) noted that the typical role-playing study is carried out under conditions that are unlikely to instill dissonance. The role playing is usually presented to subjects as a "self-exploration" or as a task that will help the investigator learn about verbal abilities or debating. In this context, which is void of the necessary preconditions for dissonance arousal (see chap. 5), the greater the incentive, the more effective the role playing will be (in terms of the number and/or quality of the arguments generated), and the more attitude change that will result.

Mere Thought as a Determinant of Attitude Polarization

Our review of the role-playing effect indicated that if people were specifically asked to play a certain role and to argue for a particular position, their attitudes would probably change as a result. As we noted in the introduction to this chapter, however, sometimes our attitudes about something will change simply as a result of thinking to ourselves. When we think about something, we may generate information that we did not consider when our initial attitudes were formed (see box 8.1).

Tesser (1978) has provided the most extensive analysis of attitude changes that result from "mere thought." Tesser makes three assumptions in deriving the prediction that simply thinking about some object can make one's attitudes more extreme. The three assumptions are:

1. For various stimulus domains, persons have naive theories or *schemas* that make some attributes of the stimuli salient and provide rules for inferences regarding other attributes;
2. Thought, under the direction of a schema, produces changes in beliefs, and these changes are often in the direction of greater schematic . . . consistency;
3. Attitudes are a function of one's beliefs. [Tesser, 1978, p. 290.]

A *schema* is a prexisting bias a person has that provides a framework or structure for beliefs on a particular issue. In addition to organizing beliefs, a schema can be viewed as a subjective theory that guides a person in processing information. The schema helps the person decide what to attend to and what to ignore and tells the person how different pieces of information should be related.[2] For example, one very general schema that we have already encountered in chapter 5 is the balance schema (Sentis & Burnstein, 1979). If you like football and meet someone new whom you like, you will probably assume that the person likes football also. Furthermore, once you like someone, you will probably also infer that the person has a number of other desirable characteristics in the absence of contrary information. Thus, a schema guides the "filling in" of information that may be unavailable. Assumption 2 specifies that the more you think about something, the more your thoughts are likely to become more consistent with the schema. After all, the presumed purpose of a schema is to guide and organize thinking. Thus, the more you think about a basically likable person, the more you would tend to ignore negative features of the person and concentrate on positive ones. Your thoughts would become more consistent with an evaluative consistency theme: likable people have positive characteristics, dislikable people have negative characteristics. Given assumption 3—that attitudes are based on beliefs (see chap. 7 for an extended justification)—it follows that mere thought can lead to more extreme attitudes. The idea of a schema guiding thinking is important because without a schema, all thoughts would be equally relevant, and no selective adding, reinterpreting, or ignoring of information would occur. We now turn to some of the research conducted by Tesser and his colleagues on attitude changes that result from mere thought.

Empirical Research on Mere Thought

In one of the first in a series of studies on mere thought, Sadler and Tesser (1973) introduced subjects to either a likable or a dislikable partner. Unknown to the subject, the partner was simulated with one of two tape recordings. The likable partner was very pleasant, describing himself in complimentary terms but without appearing to brag. The dislikable partner criticized the subject and was generally arrogant and insulting. After listening to one of the partners, some of the subjects were instructed to think about him while other subjects were given an irrelevant distraction task to work on. The distraction task would presumably keep them from thinking about their partner. Finally, subjects rated their partners on a series of attitude scales and listed their thoughts about him. Nondistracted subjects evaluated the likable partner more favorably and generated more positive thoughts about him than distracted subjects. Also, nondistracted subjects evaluated the dislikable partner more unfavorably and generated more negative thoughts about him than did distracted subjects. Mere thought apparently was responsible for more schema-consistent beliefs being generated than in the distraction conditions, and thus more extreme attitudes resulted with thought than with distraction. Later work has further shown that the more time a person is given to think about some issue or object, the more polarization that results (Tesser & Conlee, 1975).

Of course there has to be some limit to the amount of polarization that can occur as a result of thinking. For example, Konecni (1975) found that angered subjects who were given an opportunity to think displayed more aggression toward the person who insulted them than did distracted subjects after seven minutes, but this difference was not present after eleven minutes. Tesser (1978) suggests that after a relatively brief period, all of the thinking that can be accomplished is done and no further polarization can result. In fact, if the attitude becomes too polarized too quickly, "this increasing affect may act as a kind of danger signal that causes the individual to engage in a *reality search*" (p. 302). This more realistic or objective processing would presumably inhibit—and perhaps even reverse—the polarization process.

There is some evidence that attitude polarization may be inhibited by reality constraints. Tesser (1976) reasoned that attitude polarization would be easier in situations in which the person is not confronted by the actual presence of the object of thought. The physical presence of the object would presumably limit the kinds of thoughts the person could generate. When the object is not present, it is a lot easier to generate a number of thoughts that are consistent with one's schema, but that may objectively be quite unrealistic. In order to test this hypothesis, Tesser (1976) asked subjects to rate slides of paintings. They were then shown a particular painting under one of three conditions. In the *distraction* condition, subjects worked on some problems designed to distract them from thinking about the painting. In the *object-present* condition, they were asked to think about the painting while the painting was displayed. Finally, in the *object-absent* condition, they thought about the painting without its being present. The data for the female subjects supported the "reality constraint" hypothesis. On the second rating of their attitude toward the paintings, females in the object-absent condition showed the most extreme attitudes, followed by females in the object-present and distraction conditions. For male subjects, however, the experimental manipulations made little difference on attitudes. Tesser suggests that this may have occurred because females, having a greater interest in and appreciation of art (Tyler, 1965), may have had a more extensively developed schema or framework guiding the generation of art-relevant thoughts than did the male subjects. Later research (Tesser & Leone, 1977) has supported the view that mere thought leads to more extreme attitudes only when people have a schema (or bias) to guide their thinking.

Other Determinants of Mere Thought

In the research by Tesser and his colleagues described in the preceding section, mere thought was induced by directly asking people to think about a particular object or issue. Although this induction is interesting from a theoretical point of view, and there are real world instances in which someone specifically asks us to think about something, it would be interesting to know what other kinds of manipulations are likely to lead to further thought.

Exposure to the Opinions of Others
It is a well-known finding in social psychology that when people are confronted with the opinions of others who disagree with them, there is considerable pressure to go along with the group (Asch, 1956). For example, in a field study, White (1975) exposed students to the opinions of eight other students on a variety of different issues. On one issue, subjects were asked to sign their names and give their opinion about the optimal size for college classes on a survey sheet that already contained the names and opinions of eight other students. In the various different experimental conditions, the average opinions of the other students ranged from an optimal class size of twenty-seven to an optimal class size of eighty. The subjects who gave their own opinions after examining the survey sheet were greatly influenced by the opinions of the other students. The greater the average class size endorsed by the eight preceding students, the greater the average class size endorsed by the subjects. It is usually referred to as a *conformity effect* when people go along with the opinions or judgments of other people in the absence of any supporting arguments. Various explanations have been suggested for such conformity effects, but a popular one based on Festinger's (1954) social comparison theory contends that people shift toward the majority viewpoint out of a desire to hold a correct opinion.

Burnstein, Vinokur, and Trope (1973) suggested an alternative explanation based on the notion that when people are presented with the conflicting opinions of others, they are motivated to think of the arguments that might have led these other people to hold their discrepant views. "That is to say, knowing [that] others have chosen differently stimulates the person to generate arguments which could explain their choices" (p. 244). This "biased scanning" of arguments might lead to genuine attitude changes. According to Burnstein et al., therefore, what appears on the surface to be conformity might actually be self-persuasion. In order to test the notion that thought about the opinions of others is necessary for attitude change to occur, Burnstein and Vinokur (1975) conducted an experiment with three conditions. In one condition, subjects were exposed to the opinions of other students on some topic and then were given time to generate thoughts on the issue. In a second condition, subjects were exposed to the opinions of others but were asked to generate thoughts on an irrelevant issue. In the third condition, subjects were asked to generate thoughts on the relevant issue, but they were not exposed to the discrepant opinions of the other students. On a subsequent measure of the subjects' own opinions, only the first group showed significant attitude change toward the views expressed by the other students. Mere exposure to the opinions of the others without thought (condition 2) did not produce attitude change nor did mere thought on the issue unguided by the discrepant opinions of others (condition 3). The opinions of the other students apparently served as a schema or bias to guide the subsequent thinking in a particular direction.

Being in a State of Enhanced Self-awareness

In a 1972 monograph, Duval and Wicklund proposed a theory of self-awareness or self-consciousness that has proven relevant to the mere thought issue. According to the theory, conscious attention can be directed either toward the self or toward the environment. For example, if a person is looking into a mirror, being observed by an audience, or listening to his or her own voice on a tape recorder, attention is focused on the self, and a state of enhanced self-awareness results. In such a state, a person's thoughts will be focused on him- or herself. Because a state of self-attention increases thoughts about one's self, it is reasonable to expect that attitudes about one's self or one's mood might be more extreme under conditions of high than low self-awareness.

A study by Ickes, Wicklund, and Ferris (1973) is instructive. In this study, all subjects were given a bogus personality test. Some subjects were given negative feedback about how well they had done on the test, whereas others were given positive feedback. The subjects were then asked to rate their own self-esteem, either while looking into a mirror or without the presence of a mirror. The presence of the mirror tended to polarize subjects' ratings of themselves. Subjects who had received negative feedback showed lower self-esteem with the mirror than without, and subjects who had received positive personality feedback tended to show higher self-esteem with the mirror than without.

There is now a growing body of evidence indicating that attitudes, feelings, and emotions are stronger under conditions of self-attention than under conditions of environment-attention. For example, Scheier and Carver (1977) found that pleasant pictures were rated as more pleasant when self-awareness was increased, but that unpleasant pictures were rated as less pleasant when self-awareness was increased. This data is consistent with the view that stimuli that focus attention on oneself (mirror, camera, audience, etc.) also increase thinking about one's self and one's internal states, and this can lead to more polarized attitudes, feelings, and emotions (see also Carver, 1979; Scheier, 1976).

The Cognitive Response Approach to Persuasion

So far we have seen clear evidence that the thoughts that people generate on their own can be as effective in producing attitude changes as messages that originate externally (sometimes even more effective!). The cognitive response approach takes this reasoning one step further: it contends that even the persuasion that results from exposure to externally originated messages is due to the thoughts that the message recipient generates in response to the communication (see box 8.2). These thoughts generated in response to the communication are called *cognitive responses* and are the end result of information processing activity.

Advocates of the cognitive response approach make the assumption that when a person anticipates or receives a persuasive communication, an attempt is made to relate the information in the message (or the expected message) to the preexisting knowledge that the person has about the topic (Greenwald, 1968; Petty, Ostrom & Brock, 1981). In doing this, the person will consider a substantial amount of information that is not found in the communication itself. These additional self-generated cognitive responses (thoughts) may agree with the proposals being made in the message, disagree, or be entirely irrelevant to the communication. For example, if the president said that we should increase taxes to provide more money for defense, a person might think to him- or herself any one of the following: "What a good idea, we need to keep up with the Russians," or "How stupid, we are already overtaxed!" To the extent that the communication evokes cognitive responses that are supportive (called proarguments or favorable thoughts), the subject will tend to agree with the message. To the extent that the communication evokes antagonistic cognitive responses (called counterarguments or unfavorable thoughts), the subject will tend to disagree with the message. It is also possible that the subject's own antagonistic cognitive responses may be so much more persuasive than the arguments contained in the message that a position *opposite* to that advocated might be adopted (called *boomerang*). In any case, the cognitive response approach holds that the cognitions elicited at the time of message exposure will determine the amount and direction of attitude change that is produced. If the thoughts are primarily favorable (proarguments), persuasion will result; but if the thoughts are primarily unfavorable (counterarguments), resistance will be more likely.

The goal of much cognitive response research, then, is to determine how various features of the persuasion situation influence the amount of pro- or counterargumentation that will occur.[3] We will discuss the empirical research on cognitive responses in four sections. In the first two sections we discuss how information presented to subjects before the message begins can affect the manner

We are not passive recipients of messages but active information processors who generate *cognitive responses* to messages.

LANSKY'S LOOK

" . . . I'm watching a 'talk' show . . . my husband is talking back to commercials . . ."

Courtesy of Copely News Service

in which the communication is processed. In the next section we discuss the effects of various message, context, and recipient variables on cognitive responses and persuasion; and in the final section we present research relevant to a cognitive response analysis of the temporal persistence of attitude changes.

Premessage Inductions That Produce Resistance to Persuasion

Often when we are about to hear a persuasive communication, we have some preliminary information about what to expect. For example, you might read in the morning paper that the governor of your state is going to advocate a twenty percent increase in the state income tax. How does this forewarning affect the impact that the speech will have on your attitude toward the tax increase? Before the governor begins to speak that evening, an aide makes the surprising announcement that the governor has just been awarded the Nobel prize in economics. How does this information about the expertise of the governor on economic matters affect your cognitive responses and your susceptibility to persuasion?

We address these and other questions about premessage inductions in this section and in the next.

Forewarning of Message Content

In the above example, you were warned in the morning that the governor was about to make a counterattitudinal speech that evening on a personally involving topic. McGuire and Papageorgis (1962) suggested that forewarning an audience of an upcoming discrepant communication on an involving topic produces resistance to persuasion by stimulating counterarguments in anticipation of the message. A number of studies have provided support for this view. One type of evidence comes from studies that varied the amount of time between the forewarning and the message. These studies indicate that a forewarning produces resistance to persuasion only when there is a reasonable time delay between the forewarning and the message (e.g. 2 minutes; Freedman & Sears, 1965; Hass & Grady, 1975). If the forewarning comes immediately prior to the message, then there is no time for anticipatory counterarguing to occur.

A second type of evidence comes from studies in which an attempt was made to measure subjects' anticipatory counterarguments. For example, Petty and Cacioppo (1977) conducted a study in which students in an introductory psychology class were led to believe that they would soon be hearing a guest lecture from a psychologist at the university counseling center. Half of the subjects were warned several minutes in advance of the lecture that the speaker was going to advocate that all freshmen and sophomores be required to live in campus dorms. Preliminary testing had revealed that the primarily freshmen audience was strongly opposed to this proposal. The remaining subjects were unaware of the topic of the speech before its delivery. Before hearing the speech, the students were given three minutes to write down (i) either all of the thoughts that had occurred to them in the past few minutes (actual-thoughts groups) or (ii) all of their thoughts on the issue of requiring freshmen and sophomores to live in dorms (topic-thoughts groups). Following this procedure, the guest speaker presented a five minute advocacy on the topic, and then the students' attitudes were measured. The results of the study, presented in table 8.1, indicated that the warning was highly successful in inducing resistance to persuasion. Warned subjects also showed more evidence of thinking about the topic than unwarned subjects. Of special interest is that warned subjects who were asked to write their thoughts on the topic generated more topic-relevant thoughts than unwarned subjects who were asked to write their thoughts on the issue. This suggests that a forewarning gets people to think about the expected message prior to receiving it. Also of interest is that *unwarned* subjects who were asked to write their thoughts about the issue before hearing the message showed resistance to persuasion equivalent to that of the warned groups. In other words, merely being instructed to think about the issue before being presented with a message was sufficient to induce anticipatory counterargumentation and subsequent resistance to persuasion. This suggests that it is not the forewarning **per se** that induces resistance but the

Table 8.1

Effects of Warning and Thought-Listing Instructions on Attitude and Cognitive-Response Measures

Measure	Unwarned		Warned		No Message Control
	Actual Thoughts	Topic Thoughts	Actual Thoughts	Topic Thoughts	
Attitude	6.27	4.60	3.47	4.20	3.23
Counterarguments	0.00	2.67	2.20	3.46	
Favorable thoughts	0.00	1.73	0.27	2.20	
Neutral thoughts	4.93	0.60	2.87	0.27	

Data from Petty and Cacioppo (1977). Copyright by the American Psychological Association. Used with permission.

NOTE: Higher means on the attitude measure indicate more agreement with the speaker's position. Each cell contained 15 subjects. The within-cell correlation between attitude and number of counterarguments generated was -0.46; between attitude and number of favorable thoughts, 0.43; and between counterarguments and favorable thoughts, -0.37.

anticipatory thinking about the topic. The forewarning apparently elicits thoughts consistent with the person's negative attitude about the issue. The fact that warned subjects generate various negative thoughts in anticipation of the message suggests that an attitude measure taken after the warning but prior to the message would show evidence of attitude polarization (recall Tesser's work on "mere thought"). Subjects would become more extreme in the direction of their initial tendency prior to receiving the message. This *anticipatory polarization* effect has been obtained in several studies (Cialdini & Petty, 1981).

In sum, it appears that the forewarning of an impending discrepant communication on a highly involving topic elicits anticipatory counterargumentation, attitude polarization, and then resistance to the subsequent persuasive message. This suggests that the anticipation of an attitudinally congruent communication on an involving topic might lead to anticipatory proargumentation and greater susceptibility to influence. Although there is no research on this matter yet, there is some evidence that advertisers think it might work (see box 8.3).[4]

An "Inoculation" Approach to Resistance

We have just seen that resistance to persuasion could be induced by warning a person in advance of an upcoming counterattitudinal advocacy on an involving issue. We saw in chapter 5 that forewarning an audience of the speaker's persuasive intent on an involving issue would elicit counterargumentation *during*

The text on the other side of this postcard reads:

Dear Friend, In the next few days a very special letter will be arriving in your mailbox. Don't miss it because it offers you an opportunity to get NEWSWEEK magazine at over 40% off our cover price.

Would this forewarning postcard get you to generate cognitions that are favorable to the *Newsweek* offer prior to the arrival of the actual offer?

the persuasive message and thereby produce resistance. When an issue is very involving, people are motivated to defend their attitudes from attack. To the extent that their attitudes are based on a great deal of information, the defense may be relatively simple; but if the person's attitude was without an extensive cognitive foundation, the attitude should be highly susceptible to change. In such cases, a person may need some help in counterarguing the communication. For example, it may be that *hecklers* are so effective in destroying the persuasive effectiveness of a speaker because they provide the audience members with counterarguments that they may not have thought of on their own (Petty & Brock, 1976; Petty, Brock, & Brock, 1978).

One particular issue that has received a considerable amount of research attention because of people's inability to defend their beliefs is the *cultural truism*. Truisms are beliefs that are so widely accepted in a given culture that people are unpracticed in defending them. For example, "you should brush your teeth after every meal," and "mental illness is not contagious" are examples of cultural truisms. Because people have no counterarguments with which to resist a compelling message on these topics, they remain highly vulnerable to influence.

McGuire (1964), using a biological analogy, has suggested that people can be "inoculated" against persuasion on such issues. Just as people can be made more resistant to a disease by giving them a mild form of the germ so that they can develop antibodies, McGuire suggested that people could be made more resistant to a discrepant message by inoculating their initial attitudes. The inoculation treatment consists of exposing people to a few pieces of counterattitudinal propaganda prior to exposure to the threatening message and showing them how to refute this initial discrepant information. The presentation of refuted weak counterarguments presumably produces resistance to subsequent stronger attacks, because the inoculation poses a threat that motivates people to develop bolstering arguments for their somewhat weakened attitude, and it helps them counterargue the attacking message. This practice in generating supportive cognitive responses and refuting attacks enables people to resist subsequent propaganda more effectively than can nonpracticed (or noninoculated) people.

In an early study that tested the effectiveness of inoculation on resistance to persuasion, McGuire and Papageorgis (1961) exposed subjects to three messages attacking three different cultural truisms. Two days earlier, the subjects had received a treatment designed to help them resist two of the messages. For one truism, they were given an "inoculation defense" that consisted of paragraphs presenting and refuting arguments against the truism. For a second truism, they were given a "supportive defense" that consisted of paragraphs containing elaborations of separate arguments in favor of the truism. No defense was provided for the third truism. After the counterattitudinal attacks, subjects rated their attitude on all three truisms and on a fourth truism for which neither a defense nor a subsequent attack was provided. The results, presented in figure 8.1, show that both defenses were helpful in resisting the effects of the counterattitudinal messages, but the inoculation defense was significantly more effective. To test the notion that inoculation defenses motivate subjects to cognitively bolster their attitudes, subjects were asked to list their thoughts in favor of their initial positions one week after being exposed to the defenses. More supportive thoughts were listed in response to the inoculation than to the supportive defense treatment, but this difference was only marginally significant. In any case, it does appear that subjects can be trained to defend their attitudes from attack, even when they are not naturally prepared to do so.

Figure 8.1

Resistance conferred by supportive and inoculation (refutational-same) defenses. (Data from McGuire and Papageorgis, 1961.)

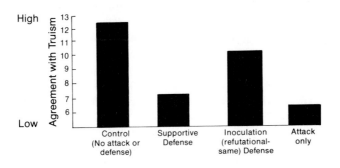

In the McGuire and Papageorgis (1961) study, the arguments used in the counterattitudinal attack were the same arguments that were previously refuted in the inoculation defense (called a "refutational-same" defense). According to McGuire's inoculation theory, however, the effectiveness of an inoculation treatment should not be confined to such cases. Papageorgis and McGuire (1961) found that for inoculation defenses in which arguments other than those used in the subsequent attacking message were refuted (an "inoculation-different" defense), the resistance to persuasion that was produced was equivalent to that in which the identical arguments used in the subsequent attacking message were refuted. Both of the refutational defenses were found to be superior in inducing resistance to a supportive defense.[5]

McGuire has also addressed the question of whether active or passive participation in the inoculation treatment is more effective when preparing people to defend their beliefs. Under active-defense conditions, people were assigned the task of writing a defense (either supportive or refutational) either from an outline or without any assistance. Under passive-defense conditions, people simply read a defense that was previously prepared by the researcher. Because individuals have so little experience in defending their beliefs on cultural truisms, McGuire argues that they are poorly prepared to generate cognitive defenses in the active conditions, and passive defenses will produce more resistance to an immediate attack. McGuire's (1964) research on the inoculation approach has indicated that, although passive defenses tend to be superior when the attacking message occurs very shortly after the defense, active defenses increase in resistance conferral when the attack occurs at a later point in time (e.g., after one week). McGuire argues that, since people initially perform so poorly in the active defense conditions, they become more motivated to defend and bolster their beliefs over time than do people provided with a passive defense.

Although there is no systematic research that applies the inoculation approach to issues for which people's cognitive structures are more elaborate than they are on cultural truisms, it is reasonable to suspect that an active inoculation defense is superior to a passive one on both immediate and delayed measures for such issues. If people value their own arguments more than the arguments provided by others (Greenwald & Albert, 1968), it makes sense to hypothesize that they would also overvalue their own counterarguments (if they could only generate some!).[6]

Premessage Inductions That Affect the Motivation to Process a Message

In the research just discussed, we saw that certain premessage inductions could get people to resist an impending advocacy by enabling them to generate counterarguments to the message either before or while it was being delivered. In this section we discuss some variables that appear to either increase or decrease a person's motivation to process the content of a persuasive communication in a more objective manner.

Issue Involvement

The first of these variables—the degree to which the message addresses a personally relevant issue—is one that we have encountered already. In chapter 4 we noted that social judgment theory proposed that the greater the personal involvement with an issue, the more difficult it would be to change people's attitudes because the larger their latitudes of rejection were likely to be. We also saw that the social judgment formulation was not completely successful in explaining the effects of issue-involvement on persuasion because of studies indicating that high involvement sometimes led to *more* persuasion than low involvement.

The instances in which high involvement increased persuasion were primarily those in which the messages advocated proattitudinal positions (Eagly, 1967; Pallak et al., 1972). To explain this finding, Petty and Cacioppo (1979b) hypothesized that increasing a person's involvement with an issue also increases that person's motivation to think about the information being presented in the persuasive message. The more important the issue is to somebody, the more important it is to have an informed attitude. Under most circumstances people will generate primarily favorable thoughts when they think about the content of a proattitudinal message (since the message is likely to present ideas with which the subject will agree); and they are likely to generate primarily counterarguments when they think about the content of a counterattitudinal advocacy (since the message is likely to present ideas with which the subject will disagree). To the extent that increased involvement is associated with increased thinking, increasing involvement would be expected to enhance the production of favorable thoughts for a proattitudinal message, but it would enhance the production of counterarguments for a counterattitudinal message. This reasoning explains how involvement could enhance persuasion for proattitudinal messages and reduce it for counterattitudinal ones. However, if involvement actually enhances thinking about the content of a message, rather than enhancing thoughts that are consistent with a person's pre-existing attitude, it should be possible to construct counterattitudinal messages for which increased involvement increases persuasion and to construct proattitudinal messages for which increased involvement decreases persuasion. The former was attempted in a study reported by Petty and Cacioppo (1979b).

In this study, subjects listened to a message advocating that seniors be required to take a comprehensive exam in their declared major as a prerequisite to graduation (a position that is strongly counterattitudinal for most college students). Half of the college student subjects were led to believe that the speaker was advocating that the proposal go into effect at their own institution (and thus they would be affected personally by the proposal); and the remaining subjects were led to believe that the speaker was advocating that the proposal go into effect at a distant university. Additionally, half of the subjects were exposed to eight compelling arguments in favor of the issue, and half were exposed to eight rather specious arguments. The strong arguments were developed in pretesting so that they would elicit primarily favorable thoughts on the part of subjects, whereas the weak arguments were pretested to insure that they would elicit primarily counterarguments. An example of a strong argument was that "graduate and professional schools show a preference for undergraduates who have passed a comprehensive exam." An example of a weak argument was that "by not administering the exams, a tradition dating back to the ancient Greeks was being violated" (p. 1921). The data from this study (presented in table 8.2) show that increasing involvement increased the production of favorable thoughts and persuasion for the strong arguments, but increasing involvement increased the production of counterarguments and reduced persuasion for the weak arguments. Involvement had no significant effect on the number of arguments from the message that subjects could recall. The hypothesis was therefore verified—increasing personal involvement enhanced processing of the message content and led to either increased or decreased acceptance, depending on the quality of the message arguments.

Number of Message Evaluators

A second variable that has been shown to affect a person's motivation to think about the arguments in a persuasive message is the number of other people who are responsible for evaluating the advocacy. For example, when the president of the United States speaks, millions of people are responsible for evaluating what is said, but when a candidate in a small town local election speaks, far fewer people are responsible for the evaluation. How does the number of message evaluators affect cognitive responses and persuasion?

Table 8.2

Attitudes and Cognitive Responses in Relation to Involvement and Quality of Message Arguments

Item	Weak Arguments Involvement		Strong Arguments Involvement	
	Low	*High*	*Low*	*High*
Attitude	-0.24_a	-0.67_b	0.20_c	0.71_d
Counterarguments	2.11_a	3.28_b	2.05_a	1.33_a
Favorable thoughts	0.88_a	1.11_a	1.44_a	2.94_b

Data from Petty and Cacioppo (1979b). Copyright by the American Psychological Association. Used with permission.

NOTE: Means in any given row without a common subscript are significantly different at the .05 level by the Newman-Keuls procedure. Attitudes are expressed in standardized scores.

Many psychological studies have indicated that the more people who are present and available to carry out some *physical* task, the less individual effort any single person spends on the task. This effect has been called "social inhibition" or "social loafing" (Latané, Williams, & Harkins, 1979) and has been shown in a wide variety of settings that range from helping another person in distress (Latané & Darley, 1970), to pulling on a rope (Ingham, Levinger, Graves, & Peckham, 1974), to helping oneself to a coupon for a free lunch (Petty, Williams, Harkins, & Latané, 1977). Based on this research, Petty, Harkins, Williams, & Latané (1977) hypothesized that the more people responsible for some *cognitive* task, the less individual cognitive effort that would be exerted.

The implications of this hypothesis for attitude change are quite direct. If increasing the number of people responsible for message evaluation decreases the amount of thought that any individual gives to the communication, then it should also decrease the importance of message content in producing persuasion. To test this hypothesis, Petty, Harkins, and Williams (1980) had subjects read an essay advocating a counterattitudinal position with each one believing that he or she would be the only person who was going to evaluate the essay or that each would be one of ten people responsible for evaluating the essay's quality. As in the previous study on involvement, the quality of the arguments contained in the essay was systematically varied. Some subjects read strong, compelling arguments, some read weak arguments, and some read very weak arguments. Following this, all subjects expressed their attitudes toward the essay (the attitudinal results are presented in fig. 8.2). When subjects were part of a group that was responsible for the message evaluation, they rated the very weak essay more

Figure 8.2

Mean evaluation of essay in relation to essay quality and number of essay evaluators. (Data from Petty, Harkins, & Williams (1980). Copyright by the American Psychological Association. Used with permission.)

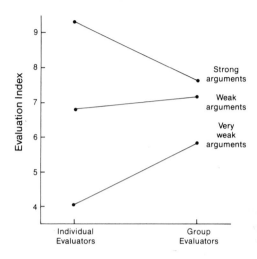

favorably but rated the strong essay less favorably than when they were individually responsible. Also, when evaluating the high-quality essay, individual evaluators generated significantly more favorable thoughts about the essay than group evaluators, but they generated significantly more unfavorable thoughts about the lowest-quality essay than did the group evaluators. These data support the cognitive response hypothesis that people will reduce their cognitive efforts when they are part of a group that is responsible for a cognitive task. The reduction in individual thinking that accompanies an increase in the number of responsible persons can lead to either enhanced or reduced evaluations of a message, depending on the quality of the arguments contained in the message.

Source Expertise

The final premessage induction addressed in this section is the effect of source credibility. The expertise of the source of a message is one of the most important features of the persuasion situation and one of the earliest variables to be investigated. It remains, however, one of the least understood manipulations. Although there is no generally accepted view on how source credibility affects information processing, there has been enough research in the area to suggest a framework for understanding how credibility affects the way in which a person thinks about a message.

In order to understand the effects of source credibility, it is necessary to distinguish two types of persuasion situations. The first involves attitudes for which the person has little cognitive support or has little personal involvement. For these kinds of issues, it appears that people think less about information that comes from expert or credible sources than information that comes from nonexpert sources. For example, Cook (1969) had students read counterattitudinal messages concerning cultural truisms. For some subjects the messages were attributed to low-credibility sources, whereas for other subjects the messages were attributed to high-credibility sources. In the control group, the source of the message was left unspecified. Measures of subjects' thoughts in response to the messages indicated that the high-credibility source condition elicited fewer counterarguments than the low-credibility source and no-source conditions. The latter two conditions did not differ in the number of counterarguments they elicited. This suggests that when people do not have very much prior information about an issue (like a cultural truism), or when involvement is low, messages from sources of high credibility are accepted without much thought. If a highly credible source inhibits the processing and counterarguing that would normally take place during the receipt of a counterattitudinal message, then there should be *no* advantage for highly credible sources if the message recipients are not aware of the credibility information until *after* the message is presented. Presentation of a highly credible source after the message would be too late to inhibit counterarguing. Several research studies support this proposition (Mills & Harvey, 1972; Sternthal, Dholakia, & Leavitt, 1978; see chap. 3).

If a highly credible source leads to less thinking about a counterattitudinal advocacy, the implication is that fewer counterarguments and more persuasion would result than with a source of low credibility. If a highly credible source leads to less thinking about a proattitudinal advocacy, however, the implication is that fewer favorable thoughts and *less* persuasion would result than with a less credible source. In a test of this hypothesis, Sternthal et al. (1978) exposed subjects to a message arguing for the passage of a Consumer Protection Agency bill by the U.S. Senate. For some subjects, the message was attributed to a highly credible source (a Harvard-trained lawyer with extensive experience in consumer issues); and for others, the source was only of moderate credibility (a citizen interested in consumer affairs). When the advocacy was counterattitudinal to subjects, the highly credible source tended to inhibit counterarguing and produced more agreement than the source of moderate credibility. For subjects who initially agreed with the advocacy, however, the highly credible source elicited fewer favorable thoughts and less agreement than the source of moderate credibility (see also Bock & Saine, 1975). It appears, then, that for issues of low involvement or prior knowledge, high source expertise inhibits the generation of thoughts consistent with a preexisting attitude. With low involvement or prior knowledge, subjects are generally not either motivated or able to process the arguments in the communication, and, to the extent that any thinking occurs at all, it will tend to be guided by a preexisting bias (schema).

Since sources of high credibility elicit less thinking than sources of low or moderate credibility, high credibility will facilitate persuasion on counterattitudinal issues (because it tends to inhibit the unfavorable thoughts that would be the likely cognitive responses if subjects were thinking about the issue). On the other hand, the typical credibility effect will be attenuated or reversed for proattitudinal issues (because here it tends to inhibit the favorable thoughts that would be the likely cognitive responses if subjects were thinking about the issue).

The accumulated literature suggests that the situation is very different when the issue is highly involving or when a person has a great deal of prior knowledge about the topic. In this case, the content of the message becomes more important in guiding a person's thinking, since the motivation and ability to think about the content are likely to be high (Petty & Cacioppo, 1979b). Hass (1981) has suggested that for these kinds of issues there is more thinking in response to a highly credible source than to a source of moderate or low credibility. When the issue is important, people are presumably *more* motivated to scrutinize what an expert has to say, perhaps in an attempt to obtain a veridical view of the world. If this is true, then people's thinking about the issue should be guided more by the content of the advocacy than by their preexisting attitude.

Although there are not yet enough experiments in which the proper variables were manipulated in combination with source manipulations to draw a strong conclusion about the effects of source credibility on cognitive responses and persuasion, we suggest that the following postulates are consistent with the available literature.

1. When a message is on an issue of low involvement or prior knowledge, more thinking will occur in response to a source of low credibility than of high credibility, and this thinking will be guided primarily by the person's preexisting attitude on the issue (Cook, 1969; Gillig & Greenwald, 1974).[7]

2. This means that, for issues of low involvement or prior knowledge, highly credible speakers will be more persuasive than speakers of low credibility primarily for counterattitudinal appeals. For proattitudinal appeals, the credibility effect should be attenuated or reversed (Sternthal et al., 1978).

3. The more involving the issue is or the more knowledge that people have about an issue, the more difficult it will be to find any effects of source credibility (Rhine & Severance, 1970). This occurs because when involvement and prior knowledge increase, the message content becomes a more important determinant of persuasion (Petty & Cacioppo, 1979b).

4. Although the effects of source credibility will be minimal for an issue of high-involvement and prior knowledge, more thinking will occur in response to a source of high credibility than of low credibility, and this thinking will be guided primarily by the quality of the arguments presented in the communication (Hass, 1981).

5. This means that for issues of high involvement and prior knowledge, highly credible speakers will be more persuasive than speakers of low credibility primarily for appeals with strong arguments. For appeals with weak arguments or no arguments, the credibility effect should be attenuated or reversed (Norman, 1976; Petty, Cacioppo, & Goldman, in press).

Effects of Message, Context, and Recipient Inductions

The variables that we discussed in the last section were ones that gave people a set to process the message in a certain way *prior* to exposure. We saw that increasing the personal relevance of a message increased peoples' motivation to think about the communication but that increasing the number of people who were responsible for evaluating the message reduced peoples' motivation to think about the communication. We also suggested that increasing the expertise of the message's source would increase thinking if the message were on a topic of high involvement or knowledge, but it would decrease thinking if the message were on a topic of low involvement or knowledge.

The variables that we discuss in this section also affect the processing of the message during exposure, but they consist of features of the message itself, the message context, or the recipients of the message. According to a cognitive response analysis, message, context, and recipient factors should affect persuasion primarily by affecting a person's motivation or ability to think about the message being presented. If the manipulation facilitates the production of favorable thoughts, or if it inhibits the production of counterarguments, increased persuasion should result. On the other hand, if counterarguments are facilitated or favorable thoughts inhibited, decreased persuasion should result.

The Effects of Distraction

Petty, Wells, and Brock (1976) hypothesized that a moderate amount of distraction during a message would inhibit a person's dominant cognitive response to the message arguments, thereby possibly leading to either enhanced or reduced persuasion, depending upon the type of cognitive responses that would normally have been dominant. For example, let's assume that an atheist is attending a Billy Graham crusade. Normally, the atheist would be counterarguing the message that is delivered. But what if the atheist was distracted from thinking about the message because a poor speaker system was intermittantly delivering a shrill noise throughout the speech. This noise might disrupt the chain of negative thoughts that usually helps the atheist resist persuasion. The effects of distraction might be very different, however, on a long-term advocate of evangelical Christianity. This person would normally be generating very favorable thoughts during the speech. In this case, the shrill noise might disrupt the chain of positive thoughts that usually occurs, leaving the person less influenced by the speech.

In two studies testing this hypothesis, Petty, Wells, and Brock manipulated the likely dominant cognitive response to a speech by varying the quality of the message arguments used to support the advocacy. Consistent with the cognitive response formulation, when the dominant cognitive response to a low-distraction or no-distraction version of the speech was favorable (i.e., the message contained strong arguments), increasing distraction inhibited the production of favorable thoughts and reduced agreement with the message. However, when the dominant cognitive response to a low-distraction or no-distraction version of the speech was unfavorable (i.e., the message contained weak arguments), increasing distraction inhibited the production of counterarguments and increased agreement with the message (see fig. 8.3).[8]

Message Repetition

Distraction reduces a person's ability to think about the arguments in a message. Cacioppo and Petty (1979b) reasoned that if a person were already motivated to think about a message, repeating the message several times (a favorite technique of advertisers) would give people a greater opportunity to think about the implications of the message. If the message contained compelling arguments of some complexity, people might generate additional favorable implications of the arguments with each repetition.[9] In order to test this hypothesis, university students were exposed to eight cogent arguments for increasing expenditures at their university. Half of the subjects were led to believe that the money for the increased expenditures would come from a tuition increase, making the context of the message a counterattitudinal one. The remaining subjects were led to believe that the money for the increased expenditures would come from a tax on visitor services, making the context of the message a proattitudinal one. The second manipulation in the study was the number of times the message was repeated for the students. Some of the students heard the message only once, some heard it three times, and some heard it five times. After hearing the message, all of the students rated the extent to which they endorsed the proposal to increase university expenditures, and they listed their thoughts about the issue. The results for these measures are displayed in the top panel of figure 8.4. Repeating the messages three times led to more agreement with the advocacy than only one presentation. The cognitive response data supported the view that with more presentations of the good arguments (and more opportunity for further thinking), the students generated more favorable and fewer unfavorable implications of the arguments. Interestingly, when the number of repetitions of the message increased to five, agreement with the advocacy declined. Cacioppo and Petty (1979b) suggested that, at this high level of message repetition, tedium and/or reactance may have set in, motivating the subjects to cognitively attack the now offensive communication. In fact, at the highest level of repetition, counterargumentation increased, and the production of favorable thoughts decreased.

Cacioppo and Petty argued that these data could best be explained by a two-stage attitude modification process in which moderate levels of message repetition provide more opportunities to elaborate cognitively upon the message arguments. At moderate levels of repetition, this elaboration is fairly objective. If the message arguments are cogent (as in the study above), greater elaboration would likely lead to the production of more favorable thoughts and increased persuasion. If the message arguments are weak, however, the greater opportunity for thinking allowed by repeating the message would likely lead to the production of more

Figure 8.3

Top panel: Mean attitude scores in relation to message and level of distraction for Experiment 1. Bottom panel: Mean attitude scores in relation to message and level of distraction for Experiment 2. Attitudes are expressed in standardized scores. In Experiment 1, a counterattitudinal position was advocated by the speaker (increasing tuition), and in Experiment 2 a proattitudinal position was advocated (reducing tuition). (Adapted from Petty, Wells, & Brock, (1976). Copyright by the American Psychological Association. Used with permission.)

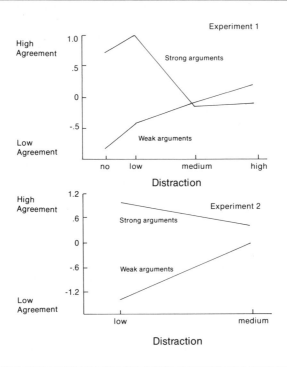

unfavorable thoughts and decreased persuasion (see Cacioppo and Petty, 1981c, for a demonstration of the latter effect; data presented in the bottom panel of fig. 8.4). In the second phase of processing, initiated when the repetition reaches tedious levels, objective processing ceases, and the person becomes motivated to reject the message regardless of its quality.

Heart Rate

One rather unusual recipient characteristic that appears to affect a person's ability to process the arguments in a communication is the person's heart rate. A number of psychophysiological studies have demonstrated that the performance of complex cognitive tasks leads to an elevation in heart rate (Cacioppo

Figure 8.4

Top panel: The effects of preexposure position and message repetition on agreement and cognitive response, Experiment 2. (Adapted from Cacioppo & Petty (1979b). Copyright by the American Psychological Association. Used with permission.) *Bottom panel:* The effects of argument quality and message repetition on agreement. (Adapted from Cacioppo & Petty, 1981c.)

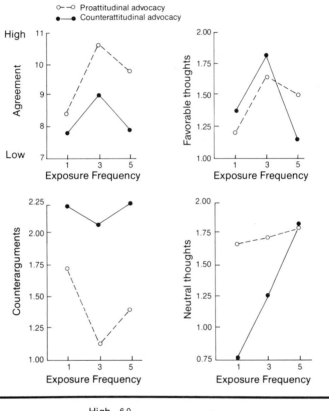

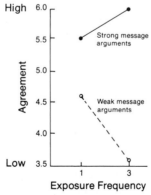

and Sandman, 1978; Lacey, Kagan, Lacey, and Moss, 1963), suggesting that all else being equal, an accelerated heart rate may facilitate cognitive elaboration (Cacioppo and Petty, in press; Lacey and Lacey, 1958). In an attempt to test this hypothesis and its implications for attitude change, Cacioppo (1979) recruited pacemaker patients who were visiting their cardiologist for a checkup. These patients had a certain kind of pacemaker that normally kept the patient's heart rate at seventy-two beats per minute. However, when a magnet was placed over a reed of the pacemaker, heart rate was increased to eighty-eight beats per minute. This technique provides a means of changing a person's heart rate without changing other bodily processes and without the person's awareness that a change has occurred. In an initial study, Cacioppo found that the patients performed better on a reading comprehension test when the test passage was read at eighty-eight rather than seventy-two beats per minute. This suggests that an accelerated heart rate facilitates cognitive ability. In a second study, a different group of patients read highly counterattitudinal messages (e.g., advocating that social security and medicare programs be eliminated) that contained some rather specious arguments. The messages were read while the pacemaker was set at either seventy-two or eighty-eight beats per minute. After hearing the messages, subjects were asked to speak their thoughts about the messages into a tape recorder. Subsequent analyses of the tapes revealed that the messages read at eighty-eight beats per minute elicited significantly more counterarguments than the messages read at seventy-two beats per minute. Furthermore, as expected, the number of counterarguments generated showed a significant negative relationship with the amount of agreement with the message (see also Cacioppo, Sandman, & Walker, 1978). Although it has not yet been done, it would be interesting to demonstrate that an accelerated heart rate could *increase* persuasion if the arguments in a message were strong rather than weak. In this case, the greater cognitive ability allowed by the accelerated heart rate should facilitate the production of favorable rather than unfavorable thoughts.[10]

The Number of Arguments and Sources of a Message

Two of the most basic features of any persuasion situation are the number of arguments presented in support of a position and the number of sources advocating a particular view. In chapter 3, we reported a study by Calder et al. (1974) showing that the more arguments associated with a particular position, the greater the persuasion that resulted.[11] Specifically, Calder et al. varied the number of prodefense and proprosecution arguments that they gave subjects in a hypothetical jury trial. Before making their decisions on guilt or innocence, however, the subjects were asked to list their thoughts about the case. The manipulation of the number of defense and prosecution arguments to which the subjects were exposed affected the thoughts that they listed as being relevant to the case. Not surprisingly, the more defense arguments that subjects had seen, the more thoughts that they listed favorable to the defense; and the more prosecution arguments that they had seen, the more thoughts that they listed favorable to the prosecution. Each new compelling argument for the defense (or prosecution) that is presented gives the subject one more opportunity to generate a thought favorable to the defense (or prosecution). The more good arguments presented, the more favorable thoughts generated, and the more persuasion. The cognitive response approach would expect just the opposite result if the arguments presented were weak, however. The easier it is to counterargue statements presented, the more unfavorable thoughts that would be generated, and the more resistance to persuasion that would result.

There has been relatively little investigation of the effects of the number of sources on persuasion, even though there are many instances in which a message is presented by multiple people (e.g., multiple testimonials for a product, multiple character witnesses for a defendant). There has probably been so little work on this question because the well-documented *conformity effect*—the more people who agree with some position, the more likely it is that other people will go along—is universally accepted (see any introductory psychology book). These conformity effects occur whether or not the subjects are actually exposed to the different people presenting their views. It is usually sufficient for a person merely to know how many other people support a particular position for a conformity effect to occur (White, 1975). Harkins and Petty (1981) were interested in whether or not there was any persuasive advantage to actually being exposed to the different sources rather than just learning of their existence (see box 8.4).

To explore this notion, Harkins and Petty exposed college students to one or three arguments in favor of instituting comprehensive exams at their university. Furthermore, the arguments came from one or three sources. Crossing these two variables created four experimental conditions: (a) hearing one argument from one source, (b) hearing the same argument from three different sources, (c) hearing three different arguments from one source, and (d) hearing three different arguments, each presented by a different source. In addition, two control conditions were created. In the attitude-control group, subjects simply gave their opinions about the senior comprehensive exam issue. In the conformity-control group, subjects gave their opinions on the issue after learning that three fellow students had each recorded three arguments in favor of the proposal: they were not actually exposed to any of the sources or arguments, however. The results of this study are presented in table 8.3. First, notice that students in the conformity-control condition show significantly more agreement with the comprehensive exam proposal than students in the attitude-control condition. Simply knowing that others have endorsed the proposal was sufficient to increase agreement (a conformity effect). The experimental cells provide information about the effects of actual exposure to the sources and arguments. Subjects in all of the experimental cells showed significantly more agreement with the exam proposal than subjects in the attitude-control, but subjects in only one of the experimental groups showed more agreement than subjects in the conformity-control condition—multiple sources presenting multiple arguments. The enhanced persuasion produced in the multiple source-multiple argument condition cannot be attributed to mere exposure to the three different arguments (since the one source-multiple argument condition did not show enhanced agreement), nor can the increased

Box 8.4

Exposure to Souces and Arguments

Look at the two different advertisements below for Merit cigarettes. The ad on the top provides some statistical evidence on the number of people who like Merit cigarettes and their reasons why. The ad on the bottom simply presents various reasons generated by different people. Which ad do you think is the most effective and why? Does your conclusion and reason agree with that provided in the text?

Courtesy of Phillip Morris, U.S.A.

Table 8.3

Effects of Multiple Sources and Multiple Arguments on Attitudes and Thought Generation

Condition	Attitude	Favorable Thoughts
Three sources–three arguments	1.88_a	3.75_a
Three sources–one argument	0.30_b	2.20_b
One source–three arguments	0.04_b	1.85_b
One source–one argument	0.03_b	1.50_b
Conformity control	0.12_b	1.95_b
Attitude control	-2.38_c	0.70_c

Data from Harkins and Petty (1981). Copyright by the American Psychological Association. Used with permission.

NOTE: Attitudes are expressed in standardized scores. Means in each column without a common subscript are significantly different from each other, $p<.05$, by the Newman-Keuls procedure.

persuasion be attributed to mere exposure to the three different sources (since the one argument-multiple source condition did not show enhanced persuasion). Finally, the effect cannot be attributed to the additive combination of the separate effects of sources and arguments, because there were no separate effects to add (i.e., neither increasing sources nor arguments *alone* increased persuasion over the conformity control cell).

Harkins and Petty proposed that there was something unique about multiple sources presenting multiple arguments that led to enhanced processing of the information provided. Specifically, they proposed that each time a new source is introduced, the subject "gears up" to process the message. If it is a new speaker, and a new argument, the recipient thinks about the argument's implications. However, if the same speaker appears again, even though with new arguments, the recipient puts less effort into processing the argument because this source has been heard already. Likewise, if new speakers are presented, but all give the same argument, little additional processing takes place—after all, the recipient has heard this argument before. Consistent with this reasoning, it was found that subjects in the multiple source-multiple argument condition generated more favorable thoughts about the issue than subjects in any other condition.[12]

One interesting implication of the cognitive response interpretation of the multiple-source multiple-argument effect is that if the arguments presented by multiple sources were weak rather than compelling, there would be less persuasion the more speakers who endorsed the proposal. In a test of this hypothesis, Harkins and Petty (1981) had subjects read three compelling arguments that were attributed to either one or three people, or they read three weak arguments that were attributed to one or three people. Again, background information about the number of people and arguments that existed in support of the advocacy was held constant. Checks on the effectiveness of the background information indicated that subjects in all conditions made the same inferences about the number of people who endorsed the proposal.[13] Nevertheless, subjects who read the three compelling arguments purportedly produced by three different people generated more favorable thoughts—and expressed more agreement with the proposal—than subjects who read the same high quality arguments presumably generated by one person. Subjects who read the three weak arguments purportedly produced by three different people, however, generated more counterarguments—and expressed less agreement with the proposal—than subjects who read the same weak arguments presumably generated by one person. In summary, the number of sources who provide arguments in support of an advocacy appears to have an effect on persuasion over and above that which would be expected, based on the research on conformity. This "extra" effect occurs because the different arguments receive greater elaboration when they come from multiple sources rather than when they come from a single source.

The Use of Rhetorical Questions

As a final example of how a variable can affect message elaboration, we examine the use of rhetorical or "tag" questions in a persuasive communication. Television attorneys are famous for their use of the dramatic rhetorical question. Instead of phrasing a closing argument in a statement form ("it is clear that John Smith was nowhere near the scene of the crime"), a rhetorical form is often preferred ("isn't it clear that John Smith was nowhere near the scene of the crime?). Zillmann (1972) argued that the use of rhetorical questions enhanced persuasion because an audience expects the rhetorical form to be associated with powerful arguments. Zillmann had subjects listen to the defense attorney's closing arguments to the jury in a hypothetical criminal case. The defense attorney's summation was presented either completely in statement form or with ten argument-condensing persuasive statements transformed to rhetorical form. Subjects who heard the rhetorical form of the message recommended a shorter prison sentence for the defendant than subjects who heard the statement form.

Petty, Cacioppo, and Heesacker (1981) presented a cognitive response analysis of the use of rhetorical questions in persuasion. They argued that for issues of low personal relevance (like the hypothetical defense summation used in the Zillmann study), the use of rhetoricals would focus more attention on the message arguments used, leading to greater elaboration of them. If the arguments were cogent (as in the Zillmann study), rhetoricals would increase the generation of favorable thoughts and enhance persuasion; but if the arguments were weak, the use of rhetoricals would increase the generation of unfavorable thoughts and reduce persuasion. On the other hand, these authors hypothesized that the effect of rhetoricals would be very different if people were already highly motivated to think about the arguments in a message. For example, if the message was on a topic of high personal relevance, and a person was already processing the message diligently (Petty and Cacioppo, 1979b), the use of rhetoricals would likely disrupt the person's natural train of thoughts. For highly involving issues, therefore, the use of rhetoricals would reduce persuasion for cogent messages (because the production of favorable thoughts would be disrupted), but it would increase persuasion for weak messages (because the production of unfavorable thoughts would be disrupted).

To test this cognitive response hypothesis, Petty et al. (1981) had college students listen to a counterattitudinal message in which the major arguments were summarized in either a statement or a rhetorical form. In addition, the personal relevance of the issue and the quality of the arguments used in the message were varied. The results of the study were exactly as would be expected on the basis of the cognitive response hypothesis. The use of rhetoricals enhanced elaboration of the arguments when the issue was of low personal relevance, but it disrupted elaboration when the issue was of high personal relevance (see fig. 8.5).

Summary

We have just seen how the various features of the persuasion situation can affect the nature of the thoughts elicited by a communication and thereby affect persuasion. We have generally seen that the different variables can affect a person's motivation and/or ability to think about an advocacy. Furthermore, we have seen that this thinking can proceed in either a fairly objective manner or in a biased manner. Some variables have been shown to affect a person's motivation to process a message in a fairly objective manner (e.g., the personal relevance of the message, the number of people responsible for evaluating the message, the number of sources of a message). Others have been shown to affect a person's motivation to process a message in a biased manner (e.g., making salient the persuasive intent of the speaker). Still other variables have been shown to affect a person's ability to process a message in a fairly objective manner (e.g., distraction, accelerated heart rate, moderate message repetition), whereas others have been shown to affect a person's ability to process a message in a biased manner (e.g., inoculation treatments). In some cases, the effects of a particular variable have been shown to be quite complex, having one effect when combined with some variables but having a different effect when combined with other variables (e.g., source expertise, rhetorical questions).

The variables that have affected processing in a biased manner have tended to work by increasing a person's motivation and/or ability to counterargue a message regardless of its quality. On the other hand, the variables that have affected processing in a more objective manner have tended to work by making people more (or less) sensitive to the quality of the message. These variables could therefore increase persuasion by increasing the motivation and/or ability to think about strong arguments or by decreasing the motivation and/or ability to think about weak arguments. Similarly, these variables could decrease persuasion by increasing the motivation and/or ability to think about weak arguments or by decreasing the motivation and/or ability to think about strong arguments.

Figure 8.5

Effects of involvement, argument quality, and message style on persuasion. Attitudes are expressed in standardized scores. (Adapted from Petty, Cacioppo, & Heesacker (1981). Copyright by the American Psychological Association. Used with permission.)

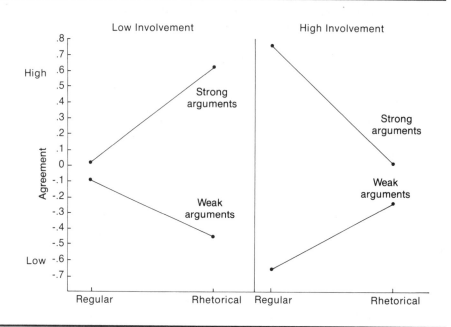

The Postmessage Persistence of Persuasion

As we have seen, at the root of the cognitive response approach is the notion that the initial attitude change produced by a message will depend on the extent to which favorable or unfavorable thoughts are generated by the message recipient at the time of message exposure. Greenwald (1968) has proposed that the *persistence* of persuasion depends on the extent to which people rehearse the cognitive responses elicited at the time of message exposure. If a message initially elicits many favorable thoughts, and if the message recipient rehearses these favorable thoughts so that they are transferred from short-term to long-term memory, persistence of persuasion is likely. The cognitive response approach thus holds that the generation of favorable thoughts leads to initial persuasion, and—to the extent that these favorable thoughts are still salient at a later point in time—the initial persuasion is likely to persist. To the extent that these favorable cognitive responses are forgotten, the initial persuasion is likely to decay.

This position bears some similarity to the persistence model advocated by the Hovland group of researchers (see chap. 3). Hovland proposed that the persistence of persuasion depends upon a person's ability to recall the arguments presented in the persuasive communication. This formulation did not provide an adequate account of persistence effects, however. Although there is some evidence to suggest that attitude change—and the ability to remember the message arguments—decay similarly (Miller and Campbell, 1959), one particularly troublesome finding for a message-learning position is that the observed correlations between attitudinal persistence and the ability to recall message arguments are nonsignificant in most studies (Cacioppo and Petty 1979b; Insko, Lind, and LaTour, 1976).

Love and Greenwald (1978) conducted a correlational test of the cognitive response persistence formulation—that the persistence of attitude change depends on the ability of subjects to recall the favorable thoughts elicited at the time of message exposure. In their study, subjects first received an opinion pretest and then read a message on one of two topics. Each message contained three main arguments, and subjects were asked to write a one-sentence reaction (cognitive response) to each argument. After the communication, subjects' attitudes were measured again, using a different procedure. Additionally, the subjects were unexpectedly given a test for recall of the three main arguments in the message and the three thoughts that they had written. One week later, the subjects returned for what they thought was a different experiment, and the attitude and recall measures were given again. Correlations were computed among the various measures—cognitive response, message recall, and postcommunication attitude—holding constant (partialing out) the subject's initial (precommunication) attitude scores. The correlations provided clear support for the cognitive response persistence hypothesis (see table 8.4). The cognitive responses listed during message exposure significantly predicted both the immediate and delayed posttest. Of greater interest is that subjects' ability to recall their cognitive responses one week later produced significant prediction of the delayed attitude measure, but the ability to recall the message arguments did not.

Further support for the cognitive response view of persuasion persistence comes from an experimental investigation by Petty (1977). In this study, college students read either five strong or five weak arguments in favor of raising the driving age to twenty-one. Control subjects read five neutral statements. Following this, subjects were asked to list five of their own thoughts on the issue. Half of the subjects were than asked to memorize the five arguments or neutral statements that they had read, and half were asked to memorize the five thoughts that they had listed. Subjects were given as much time as they needed to memorize the sentences close to verbatim. An attitude measure was also administered on which subjects could indicate their personal opinions on raising the driving age. One week later, subjects returned and gave a second measure of their attitudes on the issue and also attempted to recall the five message arguments and the five thoughts that they had listed. The results of this study revealed that on the initial attitude measure, subjects exposed to the strong arguments generated more favorable thoughts and showed more attitude change than subjects exposed to the weak arguments or control subjects. Second, the memorization

Table 8.4

Partial Correlations of Cogitive Responses and Argument Recall with Immediate and Delayed Posttest Opinion

	Topic 1		Topic 2	
	Immediate Opinion	**Delayed Opinion**	**Immediate Opinion**	**Delayed Opinion**
1. Cognitive responses during the message	0.47**	0.52**	0.59**	0.48**
2. Recall of cognitive responses				
Immediate	0.22		0.23	
delayed		0.45**		0.30*
3. Recall of message arguments				
Immediate	−0.12		0.19	
delayed		0.15		−0.09

Data from Greenwald (1968). Used with permission of Academic Press.

$*p < .05$, one-tailed

$**p < .01$, one-tailed

NOTE: The cognitive response measure was the number of favorable thoughts minus the number of unfavorable thoughts listed to the arguments. The cognitive response recall measure was the number of favorable thoughts minus unfavorable thoughts correctly recalled. The argument recall measure was the number of arguments out of three correctly recalled.

manipulation was successful—subjects instructed to memorize their thoughts recalled more of their thoughts one week later than subjects instructed to memorize the arguments; whereas subjects instructed to memorize the arguments remembered more of the arguments one week later than subjects instructed to memorize their thoughts. Of most interest, however, is that only the subjects exposed to the strong arguments who memorized their own thoughts at the initial session showed significant persistence at the delayed testing. The subjects who had memorized the message arguments (and who had shown equivalent persuasion to the memorize-thoughts group at the initial testing) were no longer significantly different from controls at the delayed testing.[14] Exposure to sound, reasoned arguments may be sufficient to produce initial attitude change, but this persuasion is likely to decay if the idiosyncratic favorable cognitions elicited at the time of message exposure are no longer as salient. It appears that just at the amount of initial persuasion mirrors the initial cognitive responses elicited, the amount of delayed attitude change mirrors the cognitive responses salient at the delayed testing. The recall of message arguments appears to be relatively unimportant.

An Evaluation of Self-persuasion Approaches

The self-persuasion approaches are united in the view that a person's own thoughts are a more powerful determinant of persuasion than is information that originates externally. This basic principle has received a great deal of research support and has been able to account for the effects of a wide variety of independent variables. Nevertheless, the self-persuasion approaches must rely heavily on many of the other approaches encountered in the previous chapters in this book in order to provide a complete account of the attitude change process (Eagly & Himmelfarb, 1978). It is clear that how a person thinks about an issue or argument is important, but the determinants of *why* a person thinks more or less about some message, or *why* certain kinds of thoughts are generated, appear to reside in some of the other approaches in this text. For example, we saw how a forewarning of persuasive intent could instill *reactance* that would motivate a person to counterargue a message during its receipt (Petty & Cacioppo, 1979a, chap. 5). The counterarguments that the person generates may be the most direct precursors of resistance to persuasion, but without the motivational concept of reactance, there would be no explanation as to why a forewarning of persuasive intent would motivate a certain kind of thinking process. It should also be noted, however, that the reactance concept is completely devoid of explanatory power in this instance without the counterargument mediation. A reactance process is not sufficient to account for the effects of persuasive intent, because research indicates that when the persuasive intent induction is given *after* message receipt, it is ineffective in producing resistance (Kiesler & Kiesler, 1964). Reactance should still be aroused after the message, but it is too late for the reactance to lead to the generation of message counterarguments—the message has already been processed and encoded. Both the reactance and counterargument notions thus appear necessary to explain the effect. A blending of the self-persuasion approach with some of the other approaches in this text holds promise for future research.

A more limiting criticism of the self-persuasion approaches is that they have difficulty dealing with situations in which people appear to be persuaded *without much thought*. For example, Miller, Maruyama, Beaber, and Valone (1976) demonstrated that people are more persuaded by a speaker who talks somewhat faster than normal than by one who speaks at a normal rate. This effect was obtained for a message arguing for the greater use of "hydroponically grown vegetables." It is highly unlikely that the speed-of-speech manipulation affected the manner in which the communication or issue was processed, because people were highly unlikely to have any prior information or thoughts about the topic. Also, the topic had little personal importance, and subjects would not be motivated to devote much cognitive effort to the communication. As Miller et al. noted: "It may be irrational to scrutinize the plethora of counterattitudinal messages received daily. To the extent that one possesses only a limited amount of information-processing time and capacity, such scrutiny would disengage the thought processes from the exigencies of daily life" (p. 623). What accounts for the speed-of-speech effect then? Miller et al. argued that subjects inferred that a fast-talker knows what he is talking about (i.e., is credible), and the enhanced persuasion is due simply to this credibility cue. In the next chapter we present a model of persuasion that specifies the antecedents of cognitive responses and takes into account both attitude changes resulting from effortful thought processes and those resulting from peripheral cues in the persuasion situation.

Retrospective

In this chapter we have focused on the persuasive impact of information that originates internally. This self-generated information can result from a specific role-playing request, from merely thinking about an attitude object, or from specific cognitive responses to the arguments in a persuasive message. Depending on the nature of these self-generated thoughts, a person's attitude can become either more positive or more negative toward the attitude object. Self-persuasion is so potent because people appear to have a higher regard for the information they generate themselves than information that originates externally, and people can better remember arguments that originate internally than externally. Although the self-persuasion approach emphasizes attitude changes that result from a thoughtful consideration of issue-relevant arguments, it is clear that some attitude changes occur without much effortful cognitive activity. In the final chapter of this text we examine both kinds of persuasion and specify the likely determinants of each.

Notes

[1] One yet untested possibility is that active role players may generate arguments that they do not end up presenting in their improvised talks. The role-players may therefore actually have been exposed to more arguments than the passive controls.

[2] "Schemas" (Bartlett, 1932) have also been called "cognitive structures" (Krech & Crutchfield, 1948), "personal constructs" (Kelley, 1955), "frames" (Minsky, 1975), "scripts" (Abelson, 1976), and "themes" (Lingle & Ostrom, 1981), among other terms.

[3] A procedure for measuring and categorizing a person's cognitive responses to a persuasive message has been developed by Brock (1967) and Greenwald (1968). The procedure involves giving subjects a specified period of time (e.g., 3 minutes) in which to list the thoughts that they had while reading or listening to the message. Subjects are given a lined sheet of paper on which they are to list one thought per line. These thoughts are then coded by judges as to whether they represent ideas that are favorable or unfavorable to the position advocated in the persuasive communication. This "thought-listing" procedure, as well as other methods for assessing cognitive responses, are described and evaluated in Cacioppo and Petty (1981d).

[4]Cacioppo and Petty (1979a) forewarned subjects of an impending pro- or counterattitudinal advocacy and found that elevated speech muscle (EMG) activity accompanied the expectation of the counterattitudinal but not the proattitudinal message. The speech-muscle EMG measure presumably reflects the extent or depth of cognitive preparation for the impending appeal (Cacioppo & Petty, 1981b). These data, of course, suggest that cognitive preparation is more extensive for counter-rather than proattitudinal messages. No anticipatory attitude measures were taken in this study to assess polarization, however, and there were no unwarned groups for comparison purposes, since the study was not designed to address the polarization issue. Finally, we note that n this section we have only discussed the effects of forewarning when the issue is of high personal relevance. We discuss the very different effects that occur when people are forewarned on issues of low personal relevance in chapter 9.

[5]Research on how long-lasting these inoculation effects are over time has indicated that both the supportive and refutational-same defenses decay in effectiveness over time but that the refutational-different defense first increases—and then decreases—in effectiveness with time (McGuire, 1964).

[6]There has been research, however, on the effectiveness of supportive vs. refutational defenses for nontruism topics. Unlike the research with truisms, which finds superiority for refutational over supportive defenses (McGuire & Papageorgis, 1961; Suedfeld & Borrie, 1978), the research on nontruism topics has tended to find that the defenses are equal in effectiveness (Adams & Beatty, 1977; Pryor & Steinfatt, 1978). When the issue employed is not a cultural truism, so that people are probably not operating under the assumption that their belief is invulnerable, the refutational defense would not be expected to have any unique motivating power.

[7]Of course, if the source is of *extremely* low credibility, no thinking may occur, as the entire message is discounted.

[8]If the amount of distraction is so high that message comprehension is severely impaired, these effects are not obtained. Rather, a general decrease in persuasion occurs (Haaland & Venkateson, 1968; Romer, 1979), as would be expected from the Yale model of opinion change (see chap. 3). An argument must be understood before its implications are realized.

[9]If the arguments were very simple or very familiar, it would be unlikely that new favorable implications would be generated with repetition.

[10]It is important to emphasize that these effects were obtained when heart rate was manipulated without changing other bodily responses. Thus, this research does not suggest that you can increase your cognitive ability by running around the block!

[11]Calder (1978) has argued and provided evidence for the view that the number-of-arguments effect is limited by the capacity of a person's short-term memory. "If the capacity of short-term memory is exceeded (by presenting too many arguments at once), additional cognitive responses cannot be represented, and thereby cannot affect attitude" (p. 631).

[12]At first glance, these results may appear to conflict with what we have previously said about persuasion being increased by the number of sources and arguments and by message repetition. The results are not contradictory for these reasons: (1) Previous research on the number of sources and arguments has confounded actual exposure to sources and arguments with the mere knowledge that a certain

number of sources and/or arguments existed that supported a particular view. It has never been clear, then, whether or not actual exposure to sources or arguments alone enhances persuasion over "mere knowledge" conditions. (2) Even if the number of sources and arguments do prove to have separate effects on persuasion, the unique combination of multiple-sources and multiple-arguments would appear to have influence over and above that which would be predicted on the basis of a simple additive model. (3) Finally, message repetition did not have any effect in this study, since the arguments were so simple that it was unlikely that subjects could generate a *new* implication with each exposure (Cacioppo & Petty, 1979b).

[13]In a third study, Harkins and Petty (1981) also demonstrated that subjects make the same inferences concerning the number of arguments that exist in support of the proposal.

[14]However, if the subjects who had memorized the arguments had been instructed to think about them again or were spontaneously motivated to do so, they might have been able to regenerate the cognitive responses that were elicited at the time of initial exposure, which would lead to a return of the initial attitude change.

Epilog: A General Framework for Understanding Attitude Change Processes

You have now read about the major approaches developed by psychologists to study attitudes and persuasion. Each of these approaches was at one time or another thought possibly to provide a very general explanation for why peoples' attitudes change. Because proponents of each approach attempted to explain a wide variety of phenomena, the different approaches often provided *competing* interpretations for the results of a particular experiment, Interestingly, research designed to allow a choice between two different ways to explain some data (crucial experiments) has not led to any of the approaches being abandoned. Instead, the domains of the different approaches have been narrowed. We now know, for example, that rewards do not always increase persuasion and that all changes in attitudes are not based on a consistency motive but that each of these processes applies in some situations.

Fortunately, the failure of one generally accepted approach to attitudes and persuasion to emerge over the last several decades has not inhibited the growth of a significant body of knowledge about attitude change processes. All of the approaches that we have described in this book have contributed significantly to this body of knowledge. Our goal in this chapter is to outline a general framework for thinking about attitude change processes that incorporates many of the major concepts discussed in the previous chapters of this book. As such, the framework takes one step toward a general theory of attitude change.

Central versus Peripheral Routes to Attitude Change

Even though all of the different approaches discussed in the previous chapters have different names, different postulates, and particular "effects" that they specialize in explaining, these different approaches can really be thought of as emphasizing two distinct routes to attitude change. The first route, which we call the *central route,* emphasizes the information that a person has about the attitude object or issue under consideration. Some of these central approaches focus on how the arguments in a persuasive message are comprehended and learned (see chap. 3); other central approaches focus on the information that people generate themselves (see chap. 8); still other central approaches focus on the ways in which people integrate or combine the information available to them (see chap. 7). The view of the persuasion process that emerges from these approaches appears to be a very rational one. The message recipient attends to the message arguments, attempts to understand them, and then evaluates them. Some arguments lead to favorable thoughts, whereas others lead to counterarguments. The person then integrates all of this information into a coherent and reasoned position. Of course the process is not completely objective and/or logical, because what is a good argument to one person may be a bad one to another. But for the most part, under the central route, persuasion is based on a thoughtful consideration of the object or issue at hand.

The second route to attitude change, which we call the *peripheral route,* presents a very different picture of the persuasion process. According to this second view, attitude change is determined by such factors as the rewards or punishments with which the message is associated (see chap. 2), or the judgmental distortions that take place in perceiving the message (see chap. 4), or the simple inferences that a person draws about why a speaker advocated a certain position (see chap. 6). The picture that these peripheral approaches paint of the persuasion process is not a very thoughtful one. If a message is associated with a pleasant smell or an attractive source, it is accepted. If the message takes a position that is too discrepant, it is rejected regardless of the cogency of the arguments presented. People "observe" their own behaviors or physiological responses and infer what their attitudes "must" be.[1]

It is very important to note that the difference between the central and peripheral routes to attitude change is not that the former *actually is* rational and logical whereas the latter is not. We have already noted that the favorable thoughts and counterarguments that a person generates in response to a message need not be logical or rational at all. They only have to make sense to the person who generates them (i.e., they are psycho-logical or psycho-rational). Likewise, it may be perfectly logical and rational in some situations to like things that lead to rewards or to agree with someone simply because of that person's greater expertise on an issue.

The difference between the two routes has to do with the extent to which the attitude change that results from a message is due to active thinking about either the issue or the object-relevant information provided by the message. According to the central view, thinking about issue-relevant information is the most direct determinant of the direction and amount of attitude change produced. On the other hand, according to the peripheral view, attitude change is the result of peripheral *"persuasion cues."* Persuasion cues are factors or motives inherent in the persuasion setting that are sufficient to produce an initial attitude change *without any active thinking about the attributes of the issue or the object under consideration.* These cues (like a very attractive source or the ability to obain a reward) allow a person to evaluate a communication or decide what attitudinal position to adopt without engaging in any extensive cognitive work relevant to the issue under consideration.[2]

Given that there are two basic routes to attitude change, the important questions become: (1) What determines whether the central or the peripheral route will be taken? (2) What are the consequences of each route? (3) How do the traditional approaches to persuasion relate to these routes? Before presenting a model that addresses these questions, let's first briefly examine some research that suggests that these two routes are important.

Anticipatory Attitude Changes

An anticipatory attitude change is one that occurs when a person expects, but has not yet received, a persuasive message. The accumulated research on anticipatory changes indicates that people sometimes become more extreme in their attitudes prior to the receipt of a message, and they sometimes become less extreme. It further appears that whether or not a person becomes more or less extreme depends upon how personally involving the topic of the impending message is to the person. When people expect to receive a message on an issue that is not very personally relevant, attitudes generally become more moderate, but when people expect to receive a message on an issue that has high personal relevance, attitudes become more extreme (see Cialdini and Petty, 1981, for a review of these studies).[3]

Let's briefly examine one study that found evidence for both types of anticipatory changes within one experiment (Cialdini, Levy, Herman, Kozlowski, & Petty, 1976). In the relevant conditions of this study, Cialdini et al. led their college student subjects to believe that, as part of the experiment, they were soon going to discuss a campus issue with another student who took a position opposite to their own. The issue to be discussed was either one that was personally important to the students (e.g., dividing their university into separate graduate and undergraduate campuses next year), or one that would have no personally relevant effects (dividing the university into two campuses in six years). While waiting for the discussion to begin, subjects were asked to list their thoughts about the issue, and they then completed four semantic differential scales assessing their attitudes on the issue. When the issue to be discussed was personally relevant, subjects reported more *polarized* attitudes (more extreme in the direction of their initial tendency) than control subjects (i.e., students on the same side of the issue as the experimental subjects but who did not expect to discuss the issue); and they listed more thoughts in support of their attitudes than did control subjects. On the other hand, when the issue to be discussed was not personally relevant, subjects reported more *moderate* attitudes than controls, and these subjects did not differ from controls in the number of supportive thoughts listed.

Why does one group polarize whereas the other moderates in anticipation of receiving a counterattitudinal message from another person? Cialdini et al. suggested that different motives are operating in the two situations. When the impending discussion is on a topic of low personal importance, the dominant motive of recipients is one of *impression management* (presenting a favorable image to others; recall our discussion of this motive in chap. 5). A moderate position on the topic is adopted because it is easier to defend and/or gives the appearance of open- and broad-mindedness (see also Cialdini et al., 1973; Hass, 1975; and Hass & Mann, 1976). Adopting an attitudinal position for this reason does not require thinking about the merits of the issue. On the other hand, when the impending discussion is on a topic of considerable personal importance, people are more concerned with defending their *true* positions than with creating favorable impressions of themselves. Preparing to defend one's position *does* require issue-relevant thinking. The subjects who polarized therefore followed a central route to attitude change (because the changes were accompanied by issue-relevant thinking), but the subjects who moderated followed a peripheral route to attitude change (because the changes resulted from concerns about non-issue relevant matters).

An interesting feature of the Cialdini et al. (1976) study is that after the subjects' initial anticipatory shifts were monitored, all of the subjects were told that they would *not* be engaging in a discussion on the issue after all. The subjects had only to complete a final attitude scale. On this second measure of attitudes, taken after the expectation of discussion had been cancelled, an intriguing result was obtained. The subjects who had initially polarized in anticipation of discussion (high-involvement subjects) remained polarized relative to controls, but the subjects who had moderated in anticipation of discussion (low-involvement subjects) were no longer any more moderate than controls. These subjects had returned to their original attitude positions. These data suggest one important consequence of the different routes to attitude change: that the central route produces more *permanent* changes than does the peripheral route.

The Relative Importance of Source and Message Factors in Persuasion

In the research on anticipatory shifts, subjects are never actually exposed to a persuasive communication. Nevertheless, when the issue about to be discussed is highly involving, issue-relevant concerns mediate the attitude changes observed. But when the issue about to be discussed is not very involving, features of the persuasion situation that are irrelevant to the issue are responsible for the attitude changes. These same effects can be observed in the more common attitude change situation in which a persuasive message is presented to subjects.

Petty, Cacioppo, and Goldman (in press) had college students listen to a communication advocating that seniors be required to take a comprehensive exam in their major prior to graduation. Three variables were manipulated in this study: (1) *personal consequences*—for half of the subjects the speaker advocated that the policy begin next year (high consequences), and for half the speaker advocated that the policy take effect in ten years (low consequences); (2) *message arguments*—for half of the subjects the message contained eight highly persuasive arguments (strong), and for half the message contained eight specious arguments (weak); and (3) *source expertise*—for half of the subjects the source was described as a professor of education at Princeton University (expert source), and for half the source was described as a junior at a local high school (nonexpert source). The attitude data from this study are presented in figure 9.1. Under high-consequences conditions, subjects' attitudes about comprehensive exams were determined primarily by the nature of the issue-relevant arguments in the message. Strong arguments produced significantly more attitude change than weak ones; the expertise of the source had no significant influence. On the other hand, under low-consequences conditions, attitudes were determined primarily by source expertise; the quality of the arguments presented had little effect. Just as in the anticipatory attitude change research, where no persuasive message is actually delivered (Cialdini et al., 1976), the primary determinant of attitude change when a persuasive communication is presented depends on whether the issue under consideration is of high or low personal relevance. Under high relevance, factors central to the issue are more important; under low relevance, peripheral factors become more potent.

Chaiken (1980) has obtained data relevant to the persistence of attitude changes induced under different source and message characteristics. In her study, college students read a persuasive message on one of two topics (e.g., changing the university calendar from a two-semester to a trimester system). Three variables were manipulated: (1) *personal consequences*—half of the subjects thought that they were going to be interviewed about the issue that they had read about (high consequences), and half thought that they would be interviewed about a different issue (low consequences); (2) *message arguments*—half of the subjects received a message containing six cogent arguments, and half received a message containing two cogent arguments (randomly selected from the six); and (3) *source likability*—half of the subjects read that the communicator had insulted students at their university (unlikable source), and half read that the communicator had complimented students at their university (likable source). The attitude data for this study (for the two issues combined) are graphed in figure 9.2. In the high-consequences conditions, subjects' attitudes were determined primarily by the number of issue-relevant arguments in the message; the likability of the source had no significant effect. Under low-consequences conditions, however, attitudes were determined primarily by source likability; the number of arguments presented had no significant effect. In addition to the initial measure of attitude, though, Chaiken took a second measure about ten days later. Although there was a trend for all subjects to show less persuasion on the second testing, the decay in attitude change was *less* for high-consequences subjects (whose initial attitude changes were based primarily on their responses to the issue-relevant arguments) than for low-consequences subjects (whose initial attitude changes were based primarily on their responses to the characteristics of the source).

Figure 9.1

Top panel: Attitude change as a function of source expertise and perceived consequences. *Bottom panel:* Attitude change as a function of argument quality and perceived consequences. (Adapted from Petty, Cacioppo, & Goldman, in press. Copyright by the American Psychological Association. Used with permission.)

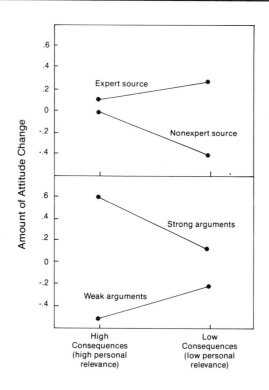

The Relative Importance of Recipient and Message Factors in Persuasion

We have just seen that people will generally be more motivated to think about issues that are highly involving, and that their motivation to think about an issue can be increased if they expect to be interviewed about the topic. There is some evidence that, all else being equal, people are more motivated to think about messages taking counterattitudinal positions than about messages taking proattitudinal positions. For example, in their study on message repetition (discussed in chap. 8, fig. 8.4), Cacioppo and Petty (1979b) exposed subjects to the same arguments in support of either a counter- or a proattitudinal position. Subjects generated more issue-relevant thoughts when the arguments were used to support

Figure 9.2

Top panel: Attitude change as a function of source likability and perceived consequences. *Bottom panel:* Attitude change as a function of number of arguments and perceived consequences. (Adapted from Chaiken (1980). Copyright by the American Psychological Association. Used with permission.)

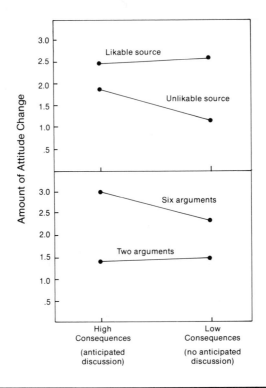

the counter- rather than the proattitudinal position. Also, after the message, subjects were able to recall more of the message arguments when they were used to support the counter- rather than the proattitudinal position. This is what would be expected if the counterattitudinal arguments elicited greater thinking (Craik & Lockhart, 1972). Counterattitudinal arguments probably elicit greater scrutiny than proattitudinal ones because the consequences of accepting them are greater.

Cacioppo and Petty (1980b) used this reasoning to test a hypothesis about when sex differences would emerge in attitude change research. Based on Sistrunk and McDavid's (1972) study (discussed in chap. 3), there is now widespread agreement that the sex differences observed in most investigations (women being easier to persuade than men) have been due to the fact that women were less familiar with the issue under consideration than men were. When men are less familiar with the issue than women, however, men are easier to persuade. Does this mean that explanations of the sex difference based on the social roles of men and women (i.e., that women are socialized to be cooperative and men to be independent; Eagly, 1978; Eagly, Wood, & Fishbaugh, in press) are never responsible for persuasion differences between men and women? Cacioppo and Petty (1980b) hypothesized that if a sex difference due to a person's social role were to be found, it would most likely be observed in situations that have few important consequences for the person (as when a message takes an agreeable position). But when consequences are high (as when a message takes a disagreeable position), attitude change should be determined more by the person's ability to react to the issue-relevant information provided than by one's social role.

To test this hypothesis, two kinds of stimuli were developed—pictures of current fashions and pictures of football tackles. Preliminary work indicated that women were more familiar with and had more knowledge about the former stimuli, whereas men were more familiar with and had more knowledge about the latter. In the high-consequences conditions, the subjects were exposed to the statements of others about the fashions and tackles that were *inaccurate*. In this case, the subjects would be motivated to defend their own views of reality, and agreement would depend on the subjects' ability to defend their own opinions. It was expected—and found—that, under the high-consequences conditions, men agreed more with the inaccurate opinions of others on the fashions but that women agreed more with the inaccurate opinions of others on the football tackles. In the low-consequences conditions, the subjects were exposed to the *accurate* statements of others about fashions and football tackles. In this case, there is no need to defend one's own view, and it was hypothesized that agreement would be determined more by the person's social role (something clearly peripheral to the issue under consideration). Under the low-consequences conditions, women agreed more with the opinions of the others than men did for both the fashion and the football pictures. It appears that the female role to be cooperative and/ or the male role to be independent is most likely to affect the extent of influence when the personal consequences of agreement are low. When the consequences of agreement are increased, the extent of influence is determined more by the person's ability to process the issue-relevant information presented.

The Elaboration Likelihood Model

In summary, we have proposed that there are two basic routes to attitude change. One route—the central one—is taken when persuasion results from thinking about the issue or arguments under consideration. The other route—the peripheral one—results when persuasion results from non-issue-relevant concerns such as impression management motives, the attractiveness of the message's source, or one's social role. Furthermore, if the new attitude results from effortful issue-relevant cognitive activity (central route), the new attitude is likely to be relatively enduring. But if the new attitude results from various persuasion cues in the situation (peripheral route), the attitude change is likely to exist only so long as the cues remain salient. Recent reviews of attitude change studies measuring persistence (Cook & Flay, 1978; Petty, 1977b) have supported the view that the active cognitive involvement of the person in the persuasion situation is crucial for the production of enduring attitude changes. In studies where issue-relevant cognitive activity was likely to be intense (e.g., role-playing studies, experiments employing personally relevant issues, etc.), the attitude changes produced have been found to be relatively enduring. On the other hand, in studies where issue-relevant cognitive activity was likely to be weak (e.g., experiments employing issues of little personal relevance), the initial attitude changes produced have been relatively short-lived.

Enduring attitude change, then, appears to depend on the likelihood that an issue or argument will be elaborated upon (thought about). As we noted at the end of chapter 8, it doesn't make sense for a person to think carefully about every message received daily. Most of the messages that we receive, in fact, are on issues that are relatively trivial, and it is not worth our time and energy to scrutinize them carefully. In figure 9.3 we present an elaboration-likelihood model of attitude changes that result from exposure to persuasive communications. The model maps both the central and the peripheral routes to attitude change and thus specifies the manner in which enduring—rather than temporary—shifts are produced. In the remaining sections of this chapter, we focus on the components and implications of the elaboration-likelihood model.

Motivation and Ability to Process the Message

As we have already noted, two factors will determine whether or not a person will think about a persuasive message—motivation and ability. We can begin our mapping, then, of the two routes to persuasion with the question: *Is the person motivated to process the communication?* People will not be motivated to think about every message they receive. For example, in chapter 8 we saw how people become less motivated to think about a message when many other people are also evaluating it (Petty, Harkins, & Williams, 1980). On the other hand, we saw how people become more motivated to think about a message that has high personal relevance (Petty & Cacioppo, 1979b). In this chapter, we saw that people could become more motivated to think about the content of a message if they were told that they were going to be subsequently interviewed about the issue (Chaiken, 1980). We also saw that people would sometimes be more motivated to think about incongruent than congruent information (Cacioppo & Petty, 1979b, 1980b; in press). In any case, there are many variables that can affect a person's motivation to elaborate upon the content of a message. For

Figure 9.3

The elaboration-likelihood model of attitude change.

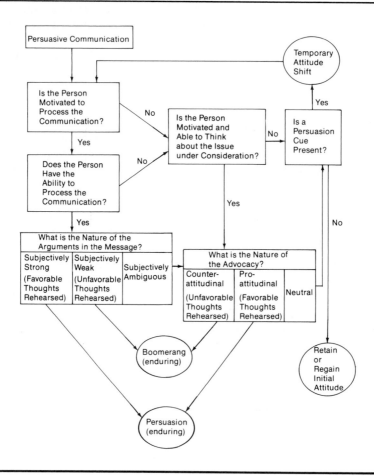

example, in chapter 6 we saw that unexpected physiological feedback might enhance thinking about the stimulus associated with the arousal. Recipient variables, like a person's "need for cognition" (Cohen, 1957), probably affect the motivation to elaborate. If the person generates his or her own message, the amount of dissonance produced by the message should determine the person's motivation to think about the arguments he or she has generated (see chap. 5).

Motivation to think about a message is not sufficient for message elaboration to occur, however. The person must also have the ability to process the message. So assuming the motivation is present, our next question becomes: *Does the person have the ability to process the communication?* As we have seen, many variables can affect elaboration ability. The more a message is repeated, for example, the greater the opportunity the person has to think about the message content (Cacioppo & Petty, 1979b; 1980a). The more distracted a person is, the less thinking about the message that can occur (Petty et al., 1976). Written messages provide people with a greater opportunity for elaboration than audio messages because people can process written messages at their own pace (Chaiken & Eagly, 1976; Wright, 1981). If the message is incomprehensible (Eagly, 1974) or if the person has no schema or framework for relating the message to his or her existing beliefs, then no processing can occur, even if sufficient motivation was present.

If both motivation and ability are present, then message elaboration will occur. The nature of that elaboration will be determined primarily by the subjective quality of the arguments presented in the communication, so our next question becomes: *What is the nature of the arguments in the message?* If the person perceives the message to contain strong, compelling arguments, then thinking about the arguments will cause favorable thoughts to be rehearsed—and enduring persuasion will result; but, if the person perceives the message to contain weak arguments, thinking about the arguments will cause counterarguments to be rehearsed, and it is possible for the person to move in a direction away from that advocated in the communication (boomerang). This is the central route to attitude change. According to the model, if a person is motivated and able to think about the message arguments, the following sequence of events will occur: *Attention, comprehension, elaboration, integration,* then *enduring attitude change.* The processes of attention and comprehension were emphasized in chapter 3, the process of elaboration (cognitive responses) in chapter 8, and the process of integration in chapter 7. In addition, the rationalizing process of dissonance reduction (described in chap. 5) can be viewed as an elaboration process producing an enduring attitude change (Collins & Hoyt, 1972).

Motivation and Ability to Think about the Issue

Sometimes a person will be either unmotivated or unable to think about the persuasive message, and in these situations an important question becomes: *Is the person motivated and able to think about the issue under consideration?* For example, if the issue is very important to the person but the person doesn't understand the arguments being presented in the message, or if no arguments are actually presented, then elaboration of the arguments cannot occur. Attention and comprehension of the arguments are prerequisites for argument elaboration. Nevertheless, the person may still be able to think about the *issue.* In this case, instead of the person's thoughts being guided by the subjective quality of the arguments in the message, the person's thoughts will be guided by his or her preexisting attitude on the issue. If the attitude is positive, with further thought the person is likely to generate and rehearse favorable thoughts and adopt an even more positive attitude. But if the attitude is negative, with further thought the person is likely to generate and rehearse unfavorable thoughts and adopt an even more negative attitude (Tesser, 1978). Thus, in these situations, the important question is: *What is the nature of the advocacy?* If the person's thoughts are guided by a preexisting attitude rather than by the arguments in the message, then it will appear that people are persuaded by proattitudinal messages but show resistance or boomerang to counterattitudinal messages. Thus, when a person is either not motivated or able to think about the arguments in a message but is motivated and able to think about the issue, the nature of a person's thoughts will be guided more by a preexisting attitude than by the nature of the arguments presented in the message. According to the elaboration-likelihood model, though, the attitude changes that result from issue elaboration will be just as enduring as those that result from message-argument elaboration.

There is another situation in which a person's thoughts will be guided more by an initial attitude than by the arguments presented. This occurs when a person is motivated and able to process the message arguments, but the arguments presented are neither subjectively strong nor weak. In this case, argument processing leads to no preponderance of favorable or unfavorable thoughts. Rather than remain in this ambiguous situation, we suggest that after an initial period of argument processing, the message recipient will begin to generate cognitions that are consistent with a prior attitude in an attempt to end the ambiguity. This will lead subjects to become more extreme in their own views when presented with ambiguous, inconclusive, or contradictory messages that they are attempting to process (Lord, Ross, & Lepper, 1979). Furthermore, this polarization is likely to be relatively enduring.

The Central Route: A Difficult Way to Change Attitudes

Clearly, the elaboration-likelihood model indicates that it is quite difficult to produce an enduring attitude change by exposing people to a persuasive communication. The recipient of the message must have both the motivation and the ability to process the information contained in the communication, and the information presented must elicit favorable cognitive responses that are rehearsed and stored in long-term memory. Favorable cognitive responses will be elicited only if the message recipient finds the message arguments to be compelling. In experimental work on the basic persuasion process, it is fairly easy to construct highly persuasive arguments by fabricating information (e.g., "Long term studies at Yale medical school show that people who sleep 6 hours per night live 4.2 years longer than people who sleep 8 to 9"). In the real world, the problem of constructing a highly persuasive message is much more difficult. If the arguments you construct turn out not to be compelling, people may counterargue your message; or if the arguments are compelling—but too complex to be understood fully—people's thoughts will be guided by their preexisting attitudes (which may be antagonistic) rather than by your arguments. In many cases, however, the problem is even more basic—just motivating people to attend to and think about what you have to say! It's no wonder that, given the difficulty of the central route to persuasion, the peripheral route is often tried.

The Peripheral Route: Attitude Change without Issue-relevant Thinking

We have seen, in several chapters of this text, how attitudes can be changed by peripheral means. The most obvious peripheral route is to associate the advocated position with other things that your target already feels positively towards, like food or money (see chap. 2). Or you might associate the advocated position with an expert, an attractive, or a powerful source (see chap. 3). Or you might present your advocacy after you have presented several other irrelevant advocacies that your subject truly despises. In comparison, the crucial advocacy might not seem so bad (this is the contrast effect discussed in chap. 4). Although all of these techniques have been successful in producing attitude changes, the elaboration-likelihood model suggests that all of these changes will not be very permanent. Furthermore, these techniques are not likely to be very successful in changing people's attitudes when they have a lot of prior information about the issue or if the issue is very involving to them. When people have a lot of prior information about an issue and the issue has personal relevance, they will be motivated to process the issue-relevant information presented, and peripheral aspects of the persuasion situation will be less important.

In many "real world" instances, however, people are not interested in changing our attitudes about such involving issues. They are interested in getting us to like Brand X more than Brand Y, or they want us to like Candidate A more than Candidate B. For example, if we don't have very much prior information about these issues, or if we don't perceive the issues to have very much personal relevance, then the peripheral approach will probably have some success. The success will be short-lived, however, so it will be necessary for the person who is trying to persuade us to constantly remind us of the persuasion cue (reward, attractive source, contextual stimuli) that accompanies the attitude object. These constant reminders may be sufficient to get us to buy certain products or vote for certain candidates. Ironically, once we have made a decision and bought Brand Y or voted for Candidate A, because of the dissonance associated with the choice (see chap. 5) we may then become motivated to think about the product or candidate and generate bolstering cognitions that *then* produce a more permanent change in attitude. Or because we now own the product or feel responsible for the candidate, we may now be motivated to process any subsequent information that we receive about the product and candidate. This, of course, can lead to permanent attitude changes. What begins, then, as a temporary attitude change via the peripheral route, may end up being a more permanent change via the central route.

In practical terms, the model suggests that when a person seeks to change another person's attitudes, the *elaboration likelihood* of the persuasion situation should be assessed (i.e., how likely is it that the other person will be motivated and able to think about the message?). If elaboration likelihood is high, and if there are compelling arguments to present, the central route may be the best strategy to pursue. This is the most ideal strategy, because a relatively permanent change in attitudes will be produced. On the other hand, if the only arguments available are weak, or if elaboration likelihood is low, then the peripheral route will be a more promising strategy.

Retrospective

In this chapter we have suggested that all of the approaches to attitude change discussed in chapters 2–8 of this text can be represented as two distinct routes to persuasion. An elaboration-likelihood model was presented that mapped the two routes, with the *central route* emphasizing a thoughtful consideration of issue-relevant argumentation and the *peripheral route* emphasizing the importance of issue-irrelevant cues. The accumulated literature on persuasion suggests that changes induced via the central route tend to endure, but changes induced via the peripheral tend to decay unless the new attitude is subsequently bolstered by issue-relevant thought.

Notes

[1]Kelman (1961) was one of the first modern social psychologists to propose—and provide evidence for—the view that there were different "kinds" of attitude change (recall from chap. 1 that Aristotle also believed that there were different kinds of persuasion). In Kelman's framework, the kind of persuasion was tied to the source of the message. *Internalization* resulted from accepting information from expert sources. This kind of attitude change was thought to be relatively enduring because it resulted from integrating new information into one's cognitive system. *Identification* was an attitude change produced when a person felt some bond with an attractive or likable source, and this attitude change persisted only so long as the attractive source was still salient. Finally, *compliance* was an attitude change produced by a powerful source. This change persisted only so long as the source retained control over the message recipient in the form of adminstering rewards and punishments. Also, it was necessary for the powerful source to be able to monitor the recipient's attitudes. Internalization would fall under the central route to persuasion if the person changed because of the *information* provided by the source. If the person changed simply because an expert said so, the change would be peripheral. Identification and compliance would fall under the peripheral route.

[2]The distinction that we have made between the central and peripheral routes to attitude change has much in common with the distinctions between "deep" vs. "shallow" processing (Craik & Lockhart, 1972), "controlled" vs. "automatic" processing (Schneider & Shiffrin, 1977); "systematic" vs. "heuristic" processing (Chaiken,

1980); and "thoughtful" vs. "scripted" or "mindless" processing (Abelson, 1976; Langer, Blank, & Chanowitz, 1978). We prefer the present terms as being more descriptive and more encompassing than others (i.e., is the attitude change the result of something central to the issue or peripheral to the issue?). For more details, see Petty and Cacioppo, in press.

[3]If a persuasive message is then actually presented to these subjects after the forewarning, greater persuasion results than for an unwarned group if the message is on a topic of low personal relevance, but less persuasion results than for an unwarned group if the message is on a topic of high personal relevance (Apsler & Sears, 1968).

References

Abelson, R. P. A script theory of understanding, attitude, and behavior. In J. Carroll & T. Payne (Eds.), *Cognition and social behavior.* Potomac, Md.: Erlbaum, 1976.

Abelson, R. P., & Rosenberg, M. J. Symbolic psycho-logic: A model of attitude cognition. *Behavioral Science,* 1958, *3,* 1-13.

Adams, W. C., & Beatty, J. J. Dogmatism, need for social approval, and the resistance to persuasion. *Communication Monographs,* 1977, *44,* 321-325.

Ajzen, I. Attitudinal versus normative messages: An investigation of the differential effects of persuasive communications on behavior. *Sociometry,* 1971, *34,* 263-280.

Ajzen, I., Dalto, C. A., & Blyth, D. P. Consistency and bias in the attribution of attitudes. *Journal of Personality and Social Psychology,* 1979, *37,* 1871-1876.

Ajzen, I., & Fishbein, M. The prediction of behavioral intentions in a choice situation. *Journal of Experimental Social Psychology,* 1969, *5,* 400-416.

Ajzen, I., & Fishbein, M. Attitudes and normative beliefs as factors influencing behavioral intentions. *Journal of Personality and Social Psychology,* 1972, *21,* 1-9.

Ajzen, I., & Fishbein, M. Attitude-behavior relations: A theoretical analysis and review of empirical research. *Psychological Bulletin,* 1977, *84,* 888-918.

Ajzen, I., & Fishbein, M. *Understanding attitudes and predicting social behavior.* Englewood Cliffs, N.J.: Prentice-Hall, 1980.

Allen, V. L. Situational factors in conformity. In L. Berkowitz (Ed.), *Advances in experimental social psychology* (Vol. 2). New York: Academic Press, 1965.

Allport, G. W. Attitudes. In C. Murchison (Ed.), *Handbook of social psychology* (Vol. 2). Worcester, Mass.: Clark University Press, 1935.

Allyn, J., & Festinger, L. The effectiveness of unanticipated persuasive communications. *Journal of Abnormal and Social Psychology,* 1961, *62,* 35-40.

Anderson, N. H. Adding versus averaging as a stimulus combination rule in impression formation. *Journal of Experimental Psychology,* 1965, *70,* 394-400.

Anderson, N. H. Integration theory and attitude change. *Psychological Review,* 1971, *78,* 171-206.

Anderson, N. H. Cognitive algebra: Integration theory applied to social attribution. In L. Berkowitz (Ed.), *Advances in experimental social psychology* (Vol. 7). New York: Academic Press, 1974.

Anderson, N. H. How functional measurement can yield validated interval scales of mental quantities. *Journal of Applied Psychology,* 1976, *61,* 677-692.

Anderson, N. H. Note on functional measurement and data analysis. *Perception and Psychophysics,* 1977, *21,* 201-215.

Anderson, N. H. Integration theory applied to cognitive responses and attitudes. In R. E. Petty, T. M. Ostrom, & T. C. Brock (Eds.), *Cognitive responses in persuasion.* Hillsdale, N.J.: Erlbaum, 1981.

Anderson, N. H. *Information integration theory: A case history in experimental science* (Vol. 1). New York: Academic Press, in press.

Anderson, R., Manoogian, S., & Reznick, J. The undermining and enhancing of intrinsic motivation in preschool children. *Journal of Personality and Social Psychology,* 1976, *34,* 915-922.

Andreoli, V., & Worchel, S. Effects of media, communicator, and position of message on attitude change. *Public Opinion Quarterly,* 1978, *42,* 59-70.

Apsler, R., & Sears, D. O. Warning, personal involvement, and attitude change. *Journal of Personality and Social Psychology,* 1968, *9,* 162-168.

Arenson, S. J., & Morisano, F. A. Effects of partial reinforcement with attitudinal statements on a lever-pressing response. *Personality and Social Psychology Bulletin,* 1977, *3,* 131-134.

Argyle, M. *The psychology of interpersonal behavior.* Baltimore: Penguin Books, 1967.

Aristotle. In R. McKeon (Ed.), *The basic works of Aristotle.* New York: Random House, 1941 (original date unknown).

Arkin, R. M. Self-presentation styles. In J. T. Tedeschi (Ed.), *Impression management: Theory and social psychological research.* New York: Academic Press, 1981.

Aronson, E. Dissonance theory: Progress and problems. In R. P. Abelson, E. Aronson, W. J. McGuire, T. M. Newcomb, M. J. Rosenberg, & P. H. Tannenbaum (Eds.), *Theories of cognitive consistency: A sourcebook.* Chicago: Rand McNally & Co., 1968.

Aronson, E. The theory of cognitive dissonance: A current perspective. In L. Berkowitz (Ed.), *Advances in experimental social psychology* (Vol. 4). New York: Academic Press, 1969.

Aronson, E., & Carlsmith, J. M. Effect of severity of threat on the devaluation of forbidden behavior. *Journal of Abnormal and Social Psychology,* 1963, *66,* 584-588.

Aronson, E., & Mills, J. The effects of severity of initiation on liking for a group. *Journal of Abnormal and Social Psychology,* 1959, *59,* 177-181.

Aronson, E., Turner, J. A., & Carlsmith, J. M. Communicator credibility and communication discrepancy as determinants of opinion change. *Journal of Abnormal and Social Psychology,* 1963, *67,* 31-36.

Asch, S. E. The doctrine of suggestion, prestige, and imitation in social psychology. *Psychological Review,* 1948, *55,* 250-276.

Asch, S. E. Studies of independence and conformities. *Psychological Monographs,* 1956, *70* (9, Whole No. 416).

Atwood, R. W., & Howell, R. J. Pupilometric and personality test score differences of female aggressing pedophiliacs and normals. *Psychonomic Science,* 1971, *22,* 115-116.

Bandura, A. Influence of models' reinforcement contingencies on the acquisition of imitative responses. *Journal of Personality and Social Psychology,* 1965, *1,* 589-595.

Barlow, J. D. Pupillary size as an index of preference in political candidates. *Perceptual and Motor Skills,* 1969, *28,* 587-590.

Bartlett, F. C. *Remembering: A study in experimental and social psychology.* Cambridge, England: Cambridge University Press, 1932.

Batson, C. D. Rational processing or rationalization?: The effect of disconfirming information on a stated religious belief. *Journal of Personality and Social Psychology,* 1975, *32,* 176-184.

Bauer, R. A. The obstinate audience: The influence process from the point of view of social communication. *American Psychologist,* 1964, *19,* 319-328.

Baumeister, R. F., Cooper, J., & Skib, B. Inferior performance as a selective response to expectancy: Taking a dive to make a point. *Journal of Personality and Social Psychology,* 1979, *37,* 424-432.

Baumeister, R. F., & Jones, E. E. When self presentation is constrained by the target's knowledge: Consistency and compensation. *Journal of Personality and Social Psychology,* 1978, *36,* 608-618.

Bearden, W. O., & Woodside, A. G. The effect of attitudes and previous behavior on consumer choice. *Journal of Social Psychology*, 1977, *103*, 129-137.

Bem, D. J. An experimental analysis of self-persuasion. *Journal of Experimental Social Psychology*, 1965, *1*, 199-218.

Bem, D. J. Self-perception: An alternative interpretation of cognitive dissonance phenomena. *Psychological Review*, 1967, *74*, 183-200.

Bem, D. J. *Beliefs, attitudes, and human affairs.* Belmont, Calif.: Brooks/Cole, 1970.

Bem, D. J. Self-perception theory. In L. Berkowitz (Ed.), *Advances in experimental social psychology* (Vol. 6). New York: Academic Press, 1972.

Bentler, P. M., & Speckart, G. Models of attitude-behavior relations. *Psychological Review*, 1979, *86*, 452-464.

Berelson, B., Lazarsfeld, P. L., & McPhee, W. N. *Voting.* Chicago: University of Chicago Press, 1954.

Berger, S. M. Conditioning through vicarious instigation. *Psychological Review*, 1962, *69*, 450-466.

Berkowitz, L., & Knurek, K. A. Label-mediated hostility generalization. *Journal of Personality and Social Psychology*, 1969, *13*, 200-206.

Berscheid, E., & Walster, E. Physical attractiveness. In L. Berkowitz (Ed.), *Advances in experimental social psychology* (Vol. 7). New York: Academic Press, 1974.

Biondo, J., & MacDonald, A. P. Internal-external locus of control and response to influence attempts. *Journal of Personality*, 1971, *39*, 407-419.

Blake, R., Rosenbaum, M., & Duryea, R. Gift-giving as a function of group standards. *Human Relations*, 1955, *8*, 61-73.

Bochner, S., & Insko, C. A. Communicator discrepancy, source credibility, and opinion change. *Journal of Personality and Social Psychology*, 1966, *4*, 614-621.

Bock, D., & Saine, T. The impact of source credibility, attitude valence, and task sensitization on trait errors in speech evaluation. *Speech Monographs*, 1975, *42*, 229-236.

Bostrom, R. N., Vlandis, J. W., & Rosenbaum, M. E. Grades as reinforcing contingencies and attitude change. *Journal of Educational Psychology*, 1961, *52*, 112-115.

Bowman, C. H., & Fishbein, M. Understanding public reaction to energy proposals: An application of the Fishbein model. *Journal of Applied Social Psychology*, 1978, *8*, 319-340.

Bradac, J. J., Bowers, J. W., & Courtright, J. A. Three language variables in communication research: Intensity, immediacy, and diversity. *Human Communication Research*, 1979, *5*, 257-269.

Bradac, J. J., Konsky, C. W., & Davies, R. A. Two studies of the effects of linguistic diversity upon judgments of communicator attributes and message effectiveness. *Communication Monographs*, 1976, *43*, 70-79.

Brehm, J. W. Post-decision changes in desirability of alternatives. *Journal of Abnormal and Social Psychology*, 1956, *52*, 384-389.

Brehm, J. W. *A theory of psychological reactance.* New York: Academic Press, 1966.

Brehm, J. W. *Responses to loss of freedom: A theory of psychological reactance.* Morristown, N.J.: General Learning Press, 1972.

Brehm, J. W., & Cohen, A. R. *Explorations in cognitive dissonance.* New York: Wiley, 1962.

Brehm, J. W., & Sensenig, J. Social influence as a function of attempted and implied usurpation of choice. *Journal of Personality and Social Psychology*, 1966, *4*, 703-707.

Brehm, S. S., & Weinraub, M. Physical barriers and psychological reactance: Two-year-olds' responses to threats to freedom. *Journal of Personality and Social Psychology*, 1977, *35*, 830-836.

Brickman, P., Coates, D., & Janoff-Bulman, R. Lottery winners and accident victims: Is happiness relative? *Journal of Personality and Social Psychology*, 1978, *36*, 917-927.

Brock, T. C. Communicator-recipient similarity and decision change. *Journal of Personality and Social Psychology*, 1965, *1*, 650-654.

Brock, T. C. Communication discrepancy and intent to persuade as determinants of counterargument production. *Journal of Experimental Social Psychology*, 1967, *3*, 269-309.

Brockner, J., & Nova, M. Further determinants of attitude attributions: The perceived effects of assigned behavior on post-behavior attitudes. *Personality and Social Psychology Bulletin*, 1979, *5*, 311-315.

Brown, D., Klemp, G., & Leventhal, H. Are evaluations inferred directly from overt actions? *Journal of Experimental Social Psychology*, 1975, *11*, 112-126.

Bryan, J. H., Redfield, J., & Mader, S. Words and deeds about altruism and the subsequent reinforcement power of the model. *Child Development*, 1971, *42*, 1501-1508.

Bryan, J. H., & Walbek, N. H. Preaching and practicing generosity: Children's actions and reactions. *Child Development*, 1970, *41*, 329-353.

Burnstein, E. Sources of cognitive bias in the representation of simple social structures: Balance, minimal change, positivity, reciprocity, and the respondent's own attitude. *Journal of Personality and Social Psychology*, 1967, *7*, 36-48.

Burnstein, E., & Sentis, K. Attitude polarization in groups. In R. E. Petty, T. M. Ostrom, & T .C. Brock (Eds.), *Cognitive responses in persuasion*. Hillsdale, N.J.: Erlbaum, 1981.

Burnstein, E., & Vinokur, A. Testing two classes of theories about group-induced shifts in individual choice. *Journal of Experimental Social Psychology*, 1973, *9*, 123-137.

Burnstein, E., & Vinokur, A. What a person thinks upon learning he has chosen differently from others: Nice evidence for the persuasive-arguments explanation of choice shifts. *Journal of Experimental Social Psychology*, 1975, *11*, 412-426.

Burnstein, E., & Vinokur, A. Persuasive argumentation and social comparison as determinants of attitude polarization. *Journal of Experimental Social Psychology*, 1977, *13*, 315-332.

Burnstein, E., Vinokur, A., & Trope, Y. Interpersonal comparison versus persuasive argumentation: A more direct test of alternative explanations for group induced shifts in individual choice. *Journal of Experimental Social Psychology*, 1973, *9*, 236-245.

Byrne, D. Attitudes and attraction. In L. Berkowitz (Ed.), *Advances in experimental social psychology* (Vol. 4). New York: Academic Press, 1969.

Byrne, D. *The attraction paradigm*. New York: Academic Press, 1971.

Byrne, D., & Clore, G. L. A reinforcement model of evaluative responses. *Personality: An International Journal*, 1970, *1*, 103-128.

Byrne, D., Ervin, C. R., & Lamberth, J. Continuity between the experimental study of attraction and "real life" computer dating. *Journal of Personality and Social Psychology*, 1970, *16*, 157-165.

Byrne, D., Young, R. K., & Griffitt, W. The reinforcement properties of attitude statements. *Journal of Experimental Research in Personality*, 1966, *1*, 266-276.

Cacioppo, J. T. Effects of exogenous changes in heart rate on facilitation of thought and resistance to persuasion. *Journal of Personality and Social Psychology*, 1979, *37*, 489-498.

Cacioppo, J. T., Harkins, S. G., & Petty, R. E. The nature of attitudes and cognitive responses and their relationships to behavior. In R. Petty, T. Ostrom, & T. Brock (Eds.), *Cognitive responses in persuasion*. Hillsdale, N.J.: Erlbaum, 1981.

Cacioppo, J. T., & Petty, R. E. Attitudes and cognitive response: An electrophysiological approach. *Journal of Personality and Social Psychology*, 1979, *37*, 2181-2199. (a)

Cacioppo, J. T., & Petty, R. E. Effects of message repetition and position on cognitive responses, recall, and persuasion. *Journal of Personality and Social Psychology*, 1979, *37*, 97-109. (b)

Cacioppo, J. T., & Petty, R. E. Persuasiveness of commercials is affected by exposure frequency and communication cogency: A theoretical and empirical analysis. In J. H. Leigh & C. R. Martin (Eds.), *Current issues and research in advertising.* Ann Arbor: University of Michigan, 1980. (a)

Cacioppo, J. T., & Petty, R. E. Sex differences in influenceability: Toward specifying the underlying processes. *Personality and Social Psychology Bulletin*, 1980, *6*, 651-656. (b)

Cacioppo, J. T., & Petty, R. E. Effects of extent of thought on the pleasantness ratings of P-O-X triads: Evidence for three judgmental tendencies in evaluating social situations. *Journal of Personality and Social Psychology*, 1981, in press. (a)

Cacioppo, J. T., & Petty, R. E. Electromyograms as measures of extent and affectivity of information processing. *American Psychologist*, 1981, in press. (b)

Cacioppo, J. T., & Petty, R. E. *Message repetition and persuasion: When more can yield less.* Unpublished manuscript, University of Iowa, 1981. (c)

Cacioppo, J. T., & Petty, R. E. Social psychological procedures for cognitive response assessment: The thought-listing technique. In T. V. Merluzzi, C. R. Glass, & M. Genest (Eds.), *Cognitive assessment.* New York: Guilford Press, 1981. (d)

Cacioppo, J. T., & Petty, R. E. A biosocial model of attitude change. In J. T. Cacioppo & R. E. Petty (Eds.), *Focus on cardiovascular psychophysiology.* New York: Guilford Press, in press.

Cacioppo, J. T., Petty, R. E., & Snyder, C. W. Cognitive and affective response as a function of relative hemispheric involvement. *International Journal of Neuroscience*, 1979, *9*, 81-89.

Cacioppo, J. T., & Sandman, C. A. Physiological differentiation of sensory and cognitive tasks as a function of warning, processing demands, and reported unpleasantness. *Biological Psychology*, 1978, *6*, 181-192.

Cacioppo, J. T., & Sandman, C.A. Psychophysiological functioning, cognitive responding, and attitudes. In R. E. Petty, T. M. Ostrom, & T. C. Brock (Eds.), *Cognitive responses in persuasion.* Hillsdale, N.J.: Erlbaum, 1981.

Cacioppo, J. T., Sandman, C. A., & Walker, B. B. The effects of operant heart rate conditioning on cognitive elaboration and attitude change. *Psychophysiology*, 1978, *15*, 330-338.

Calder, B. J. Cognitive response, imagery, and scripts: What is the cognitive basis of attitude. *Advances in Consumer Research*, 1978, *5*, 630-634.

Calder, B. J., Insko, C. A., & Yandell, B. The relation of cognitive and memorial processes to persuasion in a simulated jury trial. *Journal of Applied Social Psychology*, 1974, *4*, 62-93.

Calder, B. J., & Ross, M. *Attitudes and behavior.* Morristown, N.J.: General Learning Press, 1973.

Calder, B. J., Ross, M., & Insko, C. A. Attitude change and attitude attribution: Effects of incentive, choice, and consequences. *Journal of Personality and Social Psychology*, 1973, *25*, 84-99.

Campbell, D. T., and Stanley, J. C. *Experimental and quasi-experimental designs for research.* Chicago: Rand McNally & Co., 1963.

Cann, A., Sherman, S. J., & Elkes, R. Effects of initial request size and timing of a second request on compliance: The foot in the door and the door in the face. *Journal of Personality and Social Psychology*, 1975, *32*, 774-782.

Carlsmith, J. M., Ellsworth, P. C., & Aronson, E. *Methods of research in social psychology.* Reading, Mass.: Addison-Wesley, 1976.

Cartwright, D. Some principles of mass persuasion. *Human Relations,* 1949, *2,* 253-267.

Cartwright, D., & Harary, F. Structural balance: A generalization of Heider's theory. *Psychological Review,* 1956, *63,* 277-293.

Carver, C. S. A cybernetic model of self-attention processes. *Journal of Personality and Social Psychology,* 1979, *37,* 1251-1281.

Carver, C. S., & Scheier, M. F. Self-focusing effects of dispositional self-consciousness, mirror presence, and audience presence. *Journal of Personality and Social Psychology,* 1978, *36,* 324-332.

Carver, M. E. Listening versus reading. In H. Cantril & G. W. Allport (Eds.), *The psychology of radio.* New York: Harper, 1935.

Chaiken, S. Communicator physical attractiveness and persuasion. *Journal of Personality and Social Psychology,* 1979, *3,* 1387-1397.

Chaiken, S. Heuristic versus systematic information processing and the use of source versus message cues in persuasion. *Journal of Personality and Social Psychology,* 1980, *39,* 752-766.

Chaiken, S., & Eagly, A. H. Communication modality as a determinant of message persuasiveness and message comprehensibility. *Journal of Personality and Social Psychology,* 1976, *34,* 605-614.

Chapanis, N., & Chapanis, A. Cognitive dissonance: Five years later. *Psychological Bulletin,* 1964, *61,* 1-22.

Choo, T. Communicator credibility and communication discrepancy as determinants of opinion change. *Journal of Social Psychology,* 1964, *64,* 1-20.

Cialdini, R. B., Cacioppo, J. T., Bassett, R., & Miller, J. A. The low-ball procedure for producing compliance: Commitment then cost. *Journal of Personality and Social Psychology,* 1978, *36,* 463-476.

Cialdini, R. B., & Insko, C. A. Attitudinal verbal reinforcement as a function of informational consistency: A further test of the two-factor theory. *Journal of Personality and Social Psychology,* 1969, *12,* 342-350.

Cialdini, R. B., Levy, A., Herman, C. P., & Evenbeck, S. Attitudinal politics: The strategy of moderation. *Journal of Personality and Social Psychology,* 1973, *25,* 100-108.

Cialdini, R. B., Levy, A., Herman, P., Kozlowski, L., & Petty, R. E. Elastic shifts of opinion: Determinants of direction and durability. *Journal of Personality and Social Psychology,* 1976, *34,* 663-672.

Cialdini, R. B., & Petty, R. E. Anticipatory opinion effects. In R. E. Petty, T. M. Ostrom, & T. C. Brock (Eds.), *Cognitive responses in persuasion.* Hillsdale, N.J.: Erlbaum, 1981.

Clore, G. L., & Byrne, D. A reinforcement-affect model of attraction. In T. L. Huston (Ed.), *Perspectives on interpersonal attraction.* New York: Academic Press, 1974.

Cohen, A. Need for cognition and order of communication as determinants of opinion change. In C. Hovland, W. Mandell, E. Campbell, T. Brock, A. Luchins, A. Cohen, W. McGuire, I. Janis, R. Feierabend, & N. Anderson (Eds.), *The order of presentation in persuasion.* New Haven: Yale University Press, 1957.

Cohen, A. An experiment on small rewards for discrepant compliance and attitude change. In J. W. Brehm & A. R. Cohen (Eds.), *Explorations in cognitive dissonance.* New York: Wiley, 1962.

Coleman, J. *The adolescent society.* New York: Free Press, 1961.

Coleman, S. R., & Gormezano, I. Classical conditioning and the "law of effect": Historical and empirical assessment. *Behaviorism,* 1979, *7,* 1-33.

Collins, B. E., & Hoyt, M. G. Personal responsibility for consequences: An integration and extension of the "forced compliance" literature. *Journal of Experimental Social Psychology,* 1972, *8,* 558-593.

Comer, R., & Rhodewalt, F. Cue utilization in the self-attribution of emotions and attitudes. *Personality and Social Psychology Bulletin,* 1979, *5,* 320-324.

Converse, J., Jr., & Cooper, H. The importance of decisions and free-choice attitude change: A curvilinear finding. *Journal of Experimental Social Psychology,* 1979, *15,* 48-61.

Cook, S. W., & Selltiz, C. A multiple-indicator approach to attitude measurement. *Psychological Bulletin,* 1964, *62,* 36-55.

Cook, T. D. Competence, counterarguing, and attitude change. *Journal of Personality,* 1969, *37,* 342-358.

Cook, T. D. *The discounting cue hypothesis and the sleeper effect.* Unpublished manuscript, Northwestern University, 1971.

Cook, T. D., & Campbell, D. T. The design and conduct of quasi-experiments and true experiments in field settings. In M. Dunnette (Ed.), *Handbook of industrial and organizational psychology.* Chicago: Rand McNally & Co., 1976.

Cook, T. D., & Flay, B. R. The temporal persistence of experimentally induced attitude change: An evaluative review. In L. Berkowitz (Ed.), *Advances in experimental social psychology* (Vol. 11). New York: Academic Press, 1978.

Cook, T. D., Gruder, C. L., Hennigan, K. M., & Flay, B. R. History of the sleeper effect: Some logical pitfalls in accepting the null hypothesis. *Psychological Bulletin,* 1979, *86,* 662-679.

Cooper, H. M. Statistically combining independent studies: Meta-analysis of sex differences in conformity research. *Journal of Personality and Social Psychology,* 1979, *37,* 131-146.

Cooper, J., Darley, J. M., & Henderson, J. T. On the effectiveness of deviant and conventionally appearing communicators: A field experiment. *Journal of Personality and Social Psychology,* 1974, *29,* 752-757.

Cooper, J., Fazio, R. H., & Rhodewalt, F. Dissonance and humor: Evidence for the undifferentiated nature of dissonance arousal. *Journal of Personality and Social Psychology,* 1978, *36,* 280-285.

Cooper, J., & Worchel, S. Role of undesired consequences in arousing cognitive dissonance. *Journal of Personality and Social Psychology,* 1970, *16,* 199-206.

Cooper, J., Zanna, M. P., & Taves, P. A. Arousal as a necessary condition for attitude change following induced compliance. *Journal of Personality and Social Psychology,* 1978, *36,* 1101-1106.

Corey, S. M. Professed attitudes and actual behavior. *Journal of Educational Psychology,* 1937, *28,* 271-280.

Cottrell, N. B., Ingraham, L. H., & Monfort, F. W. The retention of balanced and unbalanced cognitive structures. *Journal of Personality,* 1971, *39,* 112-131.

Craig, C. S., & McCann, J. M. Item nonresponse in mail surveys: Extent and correlates. *Journal of Marketing Research,* 1978, *15,* 285-289.

Craik, F. M., & Lockhart, R. S. Levels of processing: A framework for memory research. *Journal of Verbal Learning and Verbal Behavior,* 1972, *11,* 671-684.

Crano, W. D., and Brewer, M. D. *Principles of research in social psychology.* New York: McGraw-Hill, 1973.

Crano, W. D., & Cooper, R. E. Examination of Newcomb's extension of structural balance theory. *Journal of Personality and Social Psychology,* 1973, *27,* 344-353.

Cronkhite, G., & Liska, J. A critique of factor analytic approaches to the study of credibility. *Communication Monographs,* 1976, *43,* 51-59.

Darwin, C. *The expression of emotion in man and animals.* London: Murray, 1872.

Davidson, A. R., & Jaccard, J. Population psychology: A new look at an old problem. *Journal of Personality and Social Psychology,* 1975, *31,* 1073-1082.

Davidson, A. R., & Jaccard, J. Variables that moderate the attitude-behavior relation: Results of a longitudinal survey. *Journal of Personality and Social Psychology,* 1979, *37,* 1364-1376.

Dawes, R. M., Singer, D., & Lemons, F. An experimental analysis of the contrast effect and its implications for intergroup communications and the indirect assessment of attitude. *Journal of Personality and Social Psychology*, 1972, *21*, 281-295.

Deci, E. L. Effects of externally mediated rewards on intrinsic motivation. *Journal of Personality and Social Psychology*, 1971, *18*, 105-115.

Deci, E. L. Intrinsic motivation, extrinsic reinforcement and inequity. *Journal of Personality and Social Psychology*, 1972, *22*, 113-120.

Deci, E. L. *Intrinsic motivation.* New York: Plenum, 1975.

Deci, E. L., & Cascio, W. F. *Changes in intrinsic motivation as a function of negative feedback and threats.* Paper presented at the meeting of the Eastern Psychological Association, Boston, April 1972.

Deci, E. L., & Ryan, R. M. The empirical exploration of intrinsic motivational processes. In L. Berkowitz (Ed.), *Advances in experimental social psychology* (Vol. 13). New York: Academic Press, 1980.

DeJong W. An examination of self-perception mediation of the foot-in-the-door effect. *Journal of Personality and Social Psychology*, 1979, *37*, 2221-2239.

Delia, J. G., & Crockett, W. H. Social schemas, cognitive complexity, and the learning of social structures. *Journal of Personality*, 1973, *41*, 413-429.

Dermer, M., Cohen, S. J., Jacobsen, E., & Anderson, E. A. Evaluative judgments of aspects of life as a function of vicarious exposure to hedonic extremes. *Journal of Personality and Social Psychology*, 1979, *37*, 247-260.

DeVries, D. L., & Ajzen, I. The relationship of attitudes and normative beliefs to cheating in college. *Journal of Social Psychology*, 1971, *83*, 199-207.

Dietsch, R. W., Gurnee, H. Cumulative effect of a series of campaign leaflets. *Journal of Applied Psychology*, 1948, *32*, 189-194.

Dillehay, R. C., Insko, C. A., & Smith, M. B. Logical consistency and attitude change. *Journal of Personality and Social Psychology*, 1966, *3*, 646-654.

Dorr, D., & Fey, S. Relative power of symbolic adult and peer models in the modification of children's moral choice behavior. *Journal of Personality and Social Psychology*, 1974, *29*, 335-341.

Dulany, D. E., Jr. The place of hypotheses and intentions: An analysis of verbal control in verbal conditioning. *Journal of Personality*, 1962, *30*, 102-129.

Duval, S., & Wicklund, R. A. *A theory of objective self-awareness.* New York: Academic Press, 1972.

Dysinger, D. W. A comparative study of affective responses by means of the impressive and expressive methods. *Psychological Monographs*, 1931, *41* (No. 187).

Eagly, A. H. Involvement as a determinant of response to favorable and unfavorable information. *Journal of Personality and Social Psychology Monograph*, 1967, *7* (3, Pt. 2).

Eagly, A. H. Comprehensibility of persuasive arguments as a determinant of opinion change. *Journal of Personality and Social Psychology*, 1974, *29*, 758-773.

Eagly, A. H. Sex differences in influenceability. *Psychological Bulletin*, 1978, *85*, 86-116.

Eagly A. H. Recipient characteristics as determinants of responses to persuasion. In R. E. Petty, T. M. Ostrom, & T. C. Brock (Eds.), *Cognitive responses in persuasion*. Hillsdale, N.J.: Erlbaum, 1981.

Eagly, A. H., & Carli, L. Sex of researchers and sex-typed communications as determinants of sex differences in influenceability. *Psychological Bulletin,* in press.

Eagly, A. H., & Chaiken, S. An attribution analysis of the effect of communicator characteristics on opinion change: The case of communicator attractiveness. *Journal of Personality and Social Psychology*, 1975, *32*, 136-144.

Eagly, A. H., Chaiken, S., & Wood, W. An attributional analysis of persuasion. In J. Harvey, W. Ickes, & R. Kidd (Eds.), *New directions in attribution research* (Vol. 3). Hillsdale, N.J. Erlbaum, 1981.

Eagly, A. H., & Himmelfarb, S. Attitudes and opinions. *Annual Review of Psychology,* 1978, *29,* 517-554.

Eagly, A. H., & Telaak, K. Width of the latitude of acceptance as a determinant of attitude change. *Journal of Personality and Social Psychology,* 1972, *23,* 388-397.

Eagly, A. H., & Warren, R. Intelligence, comprehension, and opinion change. *Journal of Personality,* 1976, *44,* 226-242.

Eagly, A. H., Wood, W., & Chaiken, S. Causal inferences about communicators and their effect on opinion change. *Journal of Personality and Social Psychology,* 1978, *36,* 424-435.

Eagly, A. H., Wood, W., & Fishbaugh, L. Sex differences in conformity: Surveillance by the group as a determinant of male nonconformity. *Journal of Personality and Social Psychology,* in press.

Eckstrand, G., & Gilliland, A. R. The psychogalvanometric method for measuring the effectiveness of advertising. *Journal of Applied Psychology,* 1948, *32,* 415-425.

Edwards, A. L., & Kenney, K. F. P. A comparison of the Thurstone and Likert techniques of attitude scale construction. *Journal of Applied Psychology,* 1946, *30,* 72-83.

Eiser, J. R., & Mower-White, C. J. Evaluative consistency and social judgment. *Journal of Personality and Social Psychology,* 1974, *30,* 349-359.

Eiser, J. R., & Mower-White, C. J. Categorization and congruity in attitudinal judgment. *Journal of Personality and Social Psychology,* 1975, *31,* 769-775.

Eiser, J. R., & Osmon, B. E. Judgmental perspective and value connotations of response scale labels. *Journal of Personality and Social Psychology,* 1978, *36,* 491-497.

Eiser, J. R., & Stroebe, W. *Categorization and social judgment.* London: Academic Press, 1972.

Ekman, P. Universals and cultural differences in facial expressions of emotion. In J. K. Cole (Ed.), *Nebraska Symposium on Motivation* (Vol. 18). Lincoln: University of Nebraska Press, 1971.

Ellul, J. *Propaganda: The formations of men's attitudes.* New York: Knopf, 1965.

Elms, A. C. Influence of fantasy ability on attitude change through role-playing. *Journal of Personality and Social Psychology,* 1966, *4,* 36-43.

Elms, A. C. Role playing, incentive, and dissonance. *Psychological Bulletin,* 1967, *68,* 132-148.

Elms, A. C., & Janis, I. L. Counter-norm attitudes induced by consonant versus dissonant conditions of role-playing. *Journal of Experimental Research in Personality,* 1965, *1,* 50-60.

Epstein, R., & Komorita, S. Childhood prejudice as a function of parental ethnocentrism, punitiveness, and outgroup characteristics. *Journal of Personality and Social Psychology,* 1966, *3,* 259-264.

Faison, E. W. J. Affectiveness of one-sided and two-sided mass communications and advertising. *Public Opinion Quarterly,* 1961, *25,* 468-469.

Fazio, R. H., & Zanna, M. P. Attitudinal qualities relating to the strength of the attitude-behavior relationship. *Journal of Experimental Social Psychology,* 1978, *14,* 398-408.

Fazio, R. H., & Zanna, M. P. Direct experience and attitude-behavior consistency. In L. Berkowitz (Ed.), *Advances in experimental social psychology* (Vol. 14). New York: Academic Press, 1981.

Fazio, R. H., Zanna, M. P., & Cooper, J. Dissonance and self-perception: An integrative view of each theory's proper domain of application. *Journal of Experimental Social Psychology,* 1977, *13,* 464-479.

Fazio, R. H., Zanna, M. P., & Cooper, J. On the relationship of data to theory: A reply to Ronis and Greenwald. *Journal of Experimental Social Psychology,* 1979, *15,* 70-76.

Feather, N. T. A structural balance model of communication effects. *Psychological Review*, 1964, *71*, 291-313.

Feather, N. T. A structural balance analysis of evaluative behavior. *Human Relations*, 1965, *18*, 171-185.

Festinger, L. A theory of social comparison processes. *Human Relations*, 1954, *7*, 117-140.

Festinger, L. *A theory of cognitive dissonance.* Stanford: Stanford University Press, 1957.

Festinger, L., & Carlsmith, J. M. Cognitive consequences of forced compliance. *Journal of Abnormal and Social Psychology*, 1959, *58*, 203-210.

Festinger, L., Riecken, H. W., & Schachter, S. *When prophecy fails.* Minneapolis, Minn.: University of Minnesota Press, 1956.

Fishbein, M. An investigation of the relationships between beliefs about an object and the attitude toward that object. *Human Relations*, 1963, *16*, 233-240.

Fishbein, M. *Sexual behavior and propositional control.* Paper presented at the meetings of the Psychonomic Society, 1966.

Fishbein, M. A theory of reasoned action: Some applications and implications. In H. Howe & M. Page (Eds.), *Nebraska Symposium on Motivation* (Vol. 27). Lincoln: University of Nebraska Press, 1980.

Fishbein, M., & Ajzen, I. Attitudes toward objects as predictors of single and multiple behavioral criteria. *Psychological Review*, 1974, *81*, 59-74.

Fishbein, M., & Ajzen, I. *Belief, attitude, intention, and behavior: An introduction to theory and research.* Reading, Mass.: Addison-Wesley, 1975.

Fishbein, M., & Ajzen, I. Acceptance, yielding, and impact: Cognitive processes in persuasion. In R. E. Petty, T. M. Ostrom, & T. C. Brock (Eds.), *Cognitive responses in persuasion.* Hillsdale, N.J.: Erlbaum, 1981.

Fishbein, M., & Coombs, F. S. Basis for decision: An attitudinal analysis of voting behavior. *Journal of Applied Social Psychology*, 1974, *4*, 95-124.

Fishbein, M., & Feldman, S. Social psychological studies in voting behavior: I. Theoretical and methodological considerations. *American Psychologist*, 1963, *18*, 388.

Folger, R., Rosenfield, D., & Hays, R. P. Equity and intrinsic motivation: The role of choice. *Journal of Personality and Social Psychology*, 1978, *36*, 557-564.

Frandsen, K. D. Effects of threat appeals and media of transmission. *Speech Monographs*, 1963, *30*, 101-104.

Frank, J. D. *Persuasion and healing.* Baltimore: Johns Hopkins Press, 1961.

Frank, J. D. *Persuasion and healing: A comparative study of psychotherapy.* New York: Schocken Books, 1974.

Freedman, J. L. Involvement, discrepancy, and opinion change. *Journal of Abnormal and Social Psychology*, 1964, *69*, 290-295.

Freedman, J. L., & Fraser, S. C. Compliance without pressure: The foot-in-the-door technique. *Journal of Personality and Social Psychology*, 1966, *4*, 195-202.

Freedman, J. L., & Sears, D. O. Warning, distraction, and resistance to influence. *Journal of Personality and Social Psychology*, 1965, *1*, 262-266.

Freedman, J. L., Sears, D. O., & O'Conner, E. F. The effects of anticipated debate and commitment on the polarization of audience opinion. *Public Opinion Quarterly*, 1964, *28*, 615-657.

Fuller, C. H. Comparisons of two experimental paradigms as tests of Heider's balance theory. *Journal of Personality and Social Psychology*, 1974, *30*, 802-806.

Gaes, G. G., Kalle, R. J., & Tedeschi, J. T. Impression management in the forced compliance situation: Two studies using the bogus pipeline. *Journal of Experimental Social Psychology*, 1978, *14*, 493-510.

Gardner, D. M. The effect of divided attention on attitude change induced by a persuasive marketing communication. In R. M. Haas (Ed.), *Science, technology, and marketing.* Chicago: American Marketing Association, 1966.

Gerard, H. B., Connolley, E. S., & Wilhelmy, R. A. Compliance, justification, and cognitive change. In L. Berkowitz (Ed.), *Advances in Experimental Social Psychology* (Vol. 7). New York: Academic Press, 1974.

Gerard, J. B. Choice, difficulty, dissonance, and the decision sequence. *Journal of Personality,* 1967, *35,* 91–108.

Gerbing, D. W., & Hunter, J. E. Phenomenological bases for the attribution of balance to social structure. *Personality and Social Psychology Bulletin,* 1979, *5,* 299–302.

Gergen, K. J. Social psychology as history. *Journal of Personality and Social Psychology,* 1973, *26,* 309–320.

Gergen, K. J., & Bauer, R. A. Interactive effects of self-esteem and task difficulty on social conformity. *Journal of Personality and Social Psychology,* 1967, *6,* 16–22.

Gewirtz, J. L., & Stingle, K. C. The learning of generalized imitation as the basis for identification. *Psychological Review,* 1968, *75,* 374–397.

Gibbons, R. X. Sexual standards and reactions to pornography: Enhancing behavioral consistency through self-focused attention. *Journal of Personality and Social Psychology,* 1978, *36,* 976–987.

Gillig, P. M., & Greenwald, A. G. Is it time to lay the sleeper effect to rest? *Journal of Personality and Social Psychology,* 1974, *29,* 132–139.

Goethals, G. R., & Cooper, J. When dissonance is reduced: The timing of self-justificatory attitude change. *Journal of Personality and Social Psychology,* 1975, *32,* 361–387.

Goethals, G. R., & Nelson, R. E. Similarity in the influence process: The belief-value distinction. *Journal of Personality and Social Psychology,* 1973, *25,* 117–122.

Goethals, F. R., & Zanna, M. P. The role of social comparison in choice shifts. *Journal of Personality and Social Psychology,* 1979, *37,* 1469–1476.

Goffman, E. *The presentation of self in everyday life.* New York: Doubleday, 1959.

Goldwater, B. C. Psychological significance of pupillary movements. *Psychological Bulletin,* 1972, *77,* 340–355.

Gormezano, I., & Kehoe, E. J. Classical conditioning: Some methodological-conceptual issues. In W. K. Estes (Ed.), *Handbook of learning and cognitive processes,* Vol. 2: *Conditioning and behavior therapy.* Hillsdale, N.J.: Erlbaum, 1975.

Gorn, G. G., & Goldberg, M. E. Children's responses to repetitive TV commercials. *Journal of Consumer Research,* 1980, *6,* 421–424.

Grabitz-Gniech, G. Some restrictive conditions for the occurrence of psychological reactance. *Journal of Personality and Social Psychology,* 1971, *19,* 188–196.

Granberg, D., & Brent, E. E. Dove-hawk placements in the 1968 election: Application of social judgment and balance theories. *Journal of Personality and Social Psychology,* 1974, *29,* 687–695.

Greenspoon, J. The reinforcing effect of two spoken sounds on the frequency of two responses. *American Journal of Psychology,* 1955, *68,* 409–416.

Greenwald, A. G. Cognitive learning, cognitive response to persuasion, and attitude change. In A. G. Greenwald, T. C. Brock, and T. M. Ostrom (Eds.), *Psychological foundations of attitudes.* New York: Academic Press, 1968.

Greenwald, A. G. On the inconclusiveness of "crucial" cognitive tests of dissonance versus self-perception theories. *Journal of Experimental Social Psychology,* 1975, *11,* 490–499.

Greenwald, A. G. Ego task analysis: An intergration of research on ego-involvement. In A. Hastorf & A. Isen (Eds.), *Cognitive social psychology.* New York: Elsevier North Holland, 1981.

Greenwald, A. G., & Albert, R. D. Acceptance and recall of improvised arguments. *Journal of Personality and Social Psychology.* 1968, *8,* 31–34.

Greenwald, A.., Baumgardner, M. H., & Leippe, M. R. *In search of reliable persuasion affects: III. The sleeper affect is dead. Long live the sleeper affect!* Unpublished manuscript, Ohio State University, 1979.

Greenwald, A. G., & Ronis, D. L. Twenty years of cognitive dissonance: Case study of the evolution of a theory. *Psychological Review*, 1978, *85*, 53-57.

Gruder, C. L., Cook, T. D., Hennigan, K. M., Flay, B. R., Alessi, C., & Halamaj, J. Empirical tests of the absolute sleeper effect predicted from the discounting cue hypothesis. *Journal of Personality and Social Psychology*, 1978, *36*, 1061-1074.

Grush, J. E. Attitude formation and mere exposure phenomena: A nonartifactual explanation of empirical findings. *Journal of Personality and Social Psychology*, 1976, *33*, 281-290.

Grush, J. E. A summary review of mediating explanations of exposure phenomena. *Personality and Social Psychology Bulletin*, 1979, *5*, 154-159.

Gurwitz, S. B., & Topol, B. Determinants of confirming and disconfirming responses to negative social labels. *Journal of Experimental Social Psychology* 1978, *15*, 31-42.

Gutman, G. M., & Knox, R. E. Balance, agreement, and attraction in pleasantness, tension, and consistency ratings of hypothetical social situations. *Journal of Personality and Social Psychology*, 1972, *24*, 351-357.

Haaland, G. A., and Venkatesan, M. Resistance to persuasive communications: An examination of the distraction hypothesis. *Journal of Personality and Social Psychology*, 1968, *9*, 167-170.

Hall, J. A. Voice tone and persuasion. *Journal of Personality and Social Psychology*, 1980, *38*, 924-934.

Halverson, R., and Pallak, M. Commitment, ego-involvement, and resistance to attack. *Journal of Experimental Social Psychology*, 1978, *14*, 1-12.

Hammond, K. R. Measuring attitudes by error-choice: An indirect method. *Journal of Abnormal and Social Psychology*, 1948, *43*, 38-48.

Harackiewicz, J. M. The effects of reward contingency and performance feedback on intrinsic motivation. *Journal of Personality and Social Psychology*, 1979, *37*, 1352-1363.

Hardyck, J. A., & Braden, M. Prophecy fails again: A report of a failure to replicate. *Journal of Abnormal and Social Psychology*, 1962, *65*, 136-141.

Harkins, S. G., & Petty, R. E. Effects of source magnification of cognitive effort on attitudes: An information processing view. *Journal of Personality and Social Psychology*, 1981, *40*, 401-413.

Harris, V. A., & Katkin, E. S. Primary and secondary emotional feedback: An analysis of the role of autonomic feedback on affect, arousal, and attribution. *Psychological Bulletin*, 1975, *82*, 904-916.

Harvey, O. J. Personality factors in resolution of conceptual incongruities. *Sociometry*, 1962, *25*, 336-352.

Haskins, J. Factual recall as a measure of advertising effectiveness. *Journal of Advertising Research*, 1966, *6*, 2-8.

Hass, J. W., Bagley, G. S., & Rogers, R. W. Coping with the energy crisis: Effects of fear appeals upon attitudes toward energy consumption. *Journal of Applied Psychology*, 1975, *60*, 754-756.

Hass, R. G. Persuasion or moderation? Two experiments on anticipatory belief change. *Journal of Personality and Social Psychology*, 1975, *31*, 1155-1162.

Hass, R. G. Effects of source characteristics on the cognitive processing of persuasive messages and attitude change. In R. Petty, T. Ostrom, & T. Brock (Eds.), *Cognitive responses in persuasion*. Hillsdale, N.J.: Erlbaum, 1981.

Hass, R. G., & Grady, K. Temporal delay, type of forewarning and resistance to influence. *Journal of Experimental Social Psychology*, 1975, *11*, 459-469.

Hass, R. G., & Mann, R. W. Anticipatory belief change: Persuasion or impression management. *Journal of Personality and Social Psychology*, 1976, *34*, 105-111.

Hassett, J. *A primer of psychophysiology*. San Francisco: W. H. Freeman, 1978.

Heider, F. Attitudes and cognitive organization. *Journal of Psychology,* 1946, *21,* 107-112.

Heider, F. *The psychology of interpersonal relations.* New York: Wiley, 1958.

Helson, H. Adaptation level theory. In S. Koch (Ed.), *Psychology: A study of a science* (Vol. 1). New York: McGraw-Hill, 1959.

Helson, H. *Adaptation-level theory: An experimental and systematic approach to behavior.* New York: Harper & Row, 1964.

Hemsley, G. D., & Doob, A. M. The effect of looking behavior on perceptions of a communicator's credibility. *Journal of Applied Social Psychology,* 1978, *8,* 136-144.

Hendrick, C., & Seyfried, B. A. Assessing the validity of laboratory-produced attitude change. *Journal of Personality and Social Psychology,* 1974, *29,* 865-870.

Henninger, M., and Wyer, R. S. The recognition and elimination of inconsistencies among syllogistically related beliefs: Some new light on the "Socratic effect." *Journal of Personality and Social Psychology,* 1976, *34,* 680-693.

Hess, E. H. Attitude and pupil size. *Scientific American,* 1965, *212,* 46-54.

Hess, R. D., & Torney, J. V. *The development of political attitudes in children.* Chicago: Aldine, 1967.

Higgins, E. T., Rhodewalt, F., & Zanna, M. Dissonance motivation: Its nature, persistence, and reinstatement. *Journal of Experimental Social Psychology,* 1979, *15,* 16-34.

Hildum, D. C., & Brown, R. W. Verbal reinforcement and interviewer bias. *Journal of Abnormal and Social Psychology,* 1956, *53,* 108-111.

Hirschman, R. Cross-modal effects of anticipatory bogus heart rate feedback in a negative emotional context. *Journal of Personality and Social Psychology,* 1975, *31,* 13-19.

Hirschman, R., & Hawk, G. Emotional responsivity to nonveridical heart rate feedback as a function of anxiety. *Journal of Research in Personality.* 1978, *12,* 235-242.

Hovland, C. I. Human learning and retention. In S. S. Stevens (Ed.), *Handbook of experimental psychology.* New York: Wiley, 1951.

Hovland, C. I., Harvey, O. J., & Sherif, M. Assimilation and contrast effects in reactions to communication and attitude change. *Journal of Abnormal and Social Psychology,* 1957, *55,* 244-252.

Hovland, C. I., & Janis, I. L. (Eds.), *Personality and persuasibility.* New Haven: Yale University Press, 1959.

Hovland, C. I., Janis, I. L., & Kelley, J. J. *Communication and persuasion.* New Haven: Yale University Press, 1953.

Hovland, C. I., Luchins, A. S., Mandell, W., Campbell, E. H., Brock, T. C., McGuire, W. J., Feierabend, R. L., & Anderson, N. H. (Eds.), *The order of presentation in persuasion.* New Haven: Yale University Press, 1957.

Hovland, C. I., Lumsdaine, A. A., & Sheffield, F. D. *Experiments on mass communication.* Princeton, N.J.: Princeton University Press, 1949.

Hovland, C. I., & Mandell, W. An experimental comparison of conclusion-drawing by the communicator and by the audience. *Journal of Abnormal and Social Psychology,* 1952, *47,* 581-588.

Hovland, C. I., & Rosenberg, M. J. (Eds.), *Attitude organization and change.* New Haven: Yale University Press, 1960.

Hovland, C. I., & Weiss, W. The influence of source credibility on communication effectiveness. *Public Opinion Quarterly,* 1951, *15,* 635-650.

Hunter, E. *Brainwashing in Red China.* New York: Vanguard, 1951.

Husek, T. R. Persuasive impacts on early, late, or no mention of a negative source. *Journal of Personality and Social Psychology,* 1965, *2,* 125-128.

Ickes, W. J., Wicklund, R. A., & Ferris, C. B. Objective self-awareness and self-esteem. *Journal of Experimental Social Psychology,* 1973, *9,* 202-219.

Infante, D. A. Richness of fantasy and beliefs about attempts to refute a proposal as determinants of attitude. *Speech Monographs*, 1975, *42*, 75-79.

Ingham, A. G., Levinger, G., Graves, J., & Peckham, V. The Ringlemann effect: Studies of group size and group performance. *Journal of Experimental Social Psychology*, 1974, *10*, 371-384.

Insko, C. A. Verbal reinforcement of attitude. *Journal of Personality and Social Psychology*, 1965, *2*, 621-623.

Insko, C. A. *Theories of attitude change*. New York: Appleton-Century-Crofts, 1967.

Insko, C. A. Balance theory and phenomenology. In R. E. Petty, T. M. Ostrom, & T. C. Brock (Eds.), *Cognitive responses in persuasion*. Hillsdale, N.J.: Erlbaum, 1981.

Insko, C. A., & Adewole, A. The role of assumed reciprocation of sentiment and assumed similarity in the production of attraction and agreement effects in *p-o-x* triads. *Journal of Personality and Social Psychology*, 1979, *37*, 790-808.

Insko, C. A., & Cialdini, R. B. A test of three interpretations of attitudinal verbal reinforcement. *Journal of Personality and Social Psychology*, 1969, *12*, 333-341.

Insko, C. A., Lind, E. A., & LaTour, S. Persuasion, recall, and thoughts. *Representative Research and Social Psychology*, 1976, *7*, 66-78.

Insko, C. A., & Melson, W. H. Verbal reinforcement of attitude in laboratory and non-laboratory contexts. *Journal of Personality*, 1969, *37*, 25-40.

Insko, C. A., Murashima, F., & Saiyadain, M. Communicator discrepancy, stimulus ambiguity, and influence. *Journal of Personality*, 1966, *34*, 262-274.

Insko, C. A., & Oakes, W. F. Awareness and the "conditioning" of attitudes. *Journal of Personality and Social Psychology*, 1966, *4*, 487-496.

Insko, C. A., & Schopler, J. Triadic consistency: A statement of affective-cognitive-connotative consistency. *Psychological Review*, 1967, *74*, 361-376.

Insko, C. A., & Schopler, J. *Experimental Social Psychology*. New York: Academic Press, 1972.

Insko, C. A., Songer, E., & McGarvey, W. Balance, positivity, and agreement in the Jordan Paradigm: A defense of balance theory. *Journal of Experimental Social Psychology*, 1974, *10*, 53-83.

Jaccard, J. J., & Davidson, A. R. Toward understanding of family planning behaviors: An initial investigation. *Journal of Applied Social Psychology*, 1972, *2*, 228-235.

Janis, I. L. Motivational factors in the resolution of decisional conflicts. In M. R. Jones (Ed.), *Nebraska Symposium on Motivation* (Vol. 6). Lincoln: University of Nebraska Press, 1959.

Janis, I. L. Attitude change via role playing. In R. Abelson, E. Aronson, W. McGuire, T. Newcomb, M. Rosenberg, & P. Tannenbaum (Eds.), *Theories of cognitive consistency: A sourcebook*. Chicago: Rand McNally, 1968.

Janis, I. L., & Feshbach, S. Effects of fear-arousing communications. *Journal of Abnormal and Social Psychology*, 1953, *48*, 78-92.

Janis, I. L., & Field, P. B. A behavioral assessment of persuasibility: Consistency of individual differences. *Sociometry*, 1956, *19*, 241-259.

Janis, I. L., & Gilmore, J. B. The influence in incentive conditions on the success of role playing in modifying attitudes. *Journal of Personality and Social Psychology*, 1965, *1*, 17-27.

Janis, I. L., Kaye, D., & Kirschner, P. Facilitating effects of "eating while reading" on responsiveness to persuasive communications. *Journal of Personality and Social Psychology*, 1965, *1*, 181-186.

Janis, I. L., & King, B. T. The influence of role-playing on opinion change. *Journal of Abnormal and Social Psychology*, 1954, *49*, 211-218.

Janis, I. L., Lumsdaine, A. A., & Gladstone, A. I. Effects of preparatory communications on reactions to a subsequent news event. *Public Opinion Quarterly*, 1951, *15*, 487-518.

Janis, I. L., & Mann, L. *Decision making: A psychological analysis of conflict, choice, and commitment.* New York: The Free Press, 1977.

Janis, I. L., & Rife, D. Persuasibility and emotional disorder. In C. I. Hovland & I. L. Janis (Eds.), *Personality and persuasibility.* New Haven: Yale University Press, 1959.

Jaspers, M., et al. Cognitive balance, self-involvement, and anticipation of interaction. *Nederlands Tijdschrift voor de Psychologie en haar Grensgebieden,* 1974, *29,* 535-551.

Jennings, M. K., & Niemi, R. G. The transmission of political values from parent to child. *American Political Science Review,* 1968, *62,* 169-184.

Johnson, H. H. Some effects of discrepancy level on responses to negative information about one's self. *Sociometry,* 1966, *29,* 52-66.

Johnson, H. H., & Watkins, T. Trends in dissonance research and the Chapanis' criticisms. *Personality and Social Psychology Bulletin,* 1977, *3,* 244-247.

Jones, E. E., & Gerard, H. B. *Foundations of social psychology.* New York: Wiley, 1967.

Jones, E. E., & Harris, V. A. The attribution of attitudes. *Journal of Experimental Social Psychology,* 1967, *3,* 1-24.

Jones, E. E., & Nisbett, R. E. The actor and the observer: Divergent perceptions of the causes of behavior. In E. E. Jones, D. E. Kanouse, H. H. Kelley, R. E. Nisbett, S. Valins & B. Weiner (Eds.), *Attribution: Perceiving the causes of behavior.* Morristown, N.J.: General Learning Press, 1972.

Jones, E. E., & Sigall, H. The bogus pipeline: A new paradigm for measuring affect and attitude. *Psychological Bulletin,* 1971, *76,* 349-364.

Jones, E. E., Worchel, S., Goethals, G. T., & Grumet, J. F. Prior expectancy and behavioral extremity as determinants of attitude attribution. *Journal of Experimental Social Psychology,* 1971, *7,* 59-80.

Jones, E. E., & Wortman, C. *Ingratiation: An attributional approach.* Morristown, N.J.: General Learning Press, 1973.

Jones, R. A., & Brehm, J. W. Attitudinal effects of communicator attractiveness when one chooses to listen. *Journal of Personality and Social Psychology,* 1967, *6,* 64-70.

Jones, R. A., & Brehm, J. W. Persuasiveness of one and two-sided communications as a function of awareness there are two sides. *Journal of Experimental Social Psychology,* 1970, *6,* 47-56.

Jordan, N. Behavioral forces that are a function of attitudes and of cognitive organization. *Human Relations,* 1953, *6,* 273-288.

Jowett, B. *The dialogues of Plato (Vol. 1).* New York: Random House, 1937.

Judd, C. M., & DePaulo, B. M. The effect of perspective differences on the measurement of involving attitudes. *Social Psychology Quarterly,* 1979, *42,* 185-189.

Kahle, L. R., & Page, M. M. The deprivation-satiation effect in attitude conditioning without deprivation but with deviant characteristics. *Personality and Social Psychology Bulletin,* 1976, *2,* 470-473.

Kahneman, D. *Attention and effort.* Englewood Cliffs, N.J.: Prentice-Hall, 1973.

Kaplan, M. F. Evaluative judgments are based on evaluative information: Evidence against meaning change in evaluative context effects. *Memory and Cognition,* 1975, *3,* 375-380.

Katz, D. The functional approach to the study of attitudes. *Public Opinion Quarterly,* 1960, *24,* 163-204.

Katz, E., & Lazarsfeld, P. F. *Personal influence.* Glencoe, Illinois: Free Press, 1955.

Kelley, G. A. *The psychology of personal constructs.* New York: Norton, 1955.

Kelley, H. H. Attribution in social interaction. In E. E. Jones, D. E. Kanouse, H. H. Kelley, R. E. Nisbett, S. Valins, & B. Weiner (Eds.), *Attribution: Perceiving the causes of behavior.* Morristown, N.J.: General Learning Press, 1972.

Kelley, H. H. The processes of causal attribution. *American Psychologist,* 1973, *28,* 107-128.

Kelman, H. C. Compliance, identification, and internalization: Three processes of attitude change. *Journal of Conflict Resolution,* 1958, *2,* 51-60.

Kelman, H. C. Processes of opinion change. *Public Opinion Quarterly,* 1961, *25,* 57-78.

Kelman, H. C., & Hovland, C. I. "Reinstatement" of the communicator in delayed measurement of opinion change. *Journal of Abnormal and Social Psychology,* 1953, *48,* 327-335.

Kenrick, D. T., & Gutierres, S. E. Contrast effects and judgments of physical attractiveness: When beauty becomes a social problem. *Journal of Personality and Social Psychology,* 1980, *38,* 131-140.

Kerber, K., & Coles, M. G. The role of perceived physiological activity in affective judgments. *Journal of Experimental Social Psychology,* 1978, *14,* 419-433.

Kerpelman, J. P., & Himmelfarb, S. Partial reinforcement effects in attitude acquisition and counterconditioning. *Journal of Personality and Social Psychology,* 1971, *19,* 301-305.

Kerrick, J. S. The effect of relevant and non-relevant sources on attitude change. *Journal of Social Psychology,* 1958, *47,* 15-20.

Kiesler, C. A. *The psychology of commitment.* New York: Academic Press, 1971.

Kiesler, C. A., Collins, B. E., & Miller, N. *Attitude change: A critical analysis of theoretical approaches.* New York: Wiley, 1969.

Kiesler, C. A., & Kiesler, S. B. Role of forewarning in persuasive communications. *Journal of Abnormal and Social Psychology,* 1964, *68,* 547-549.

Kiesler, C. A., & Munson, P. A. Attitudes and opinions. In M. R. Rosenzweig & L. W. Porter (Eds.), *Annual review of psychology* (Vol. 26). Palo Alto, Calif.: Annual Reviews, 1975.

Kiesler, C. A., Nisbett, R. E., & Zanna, M. P. On inferring one's beliefs from one's behavior. *Journal of Personality and Social Psychology,* 1969, *11,* 321-327.

Kiesler, C. A., & Pallak, M. S. Arousal properties of dissonance manipulations. *Psychological Bulletin,* 1976, *83,* 1014-1025.

Kinder, D. R., Smith, T., & Gerard, H. B. The attitude-labeling process outside the laboratory. *Journal of Personality and Social Psychology,* 1976, *33,* 480-491.

King, B. T., & Janis, I. L. Comparison of the effectiveness of improvised versus non-improvised role-playing in producing opinion change. *Human Relations,* 1956, *9,* 177-186.

Kirk, R. E. *Experimental design: Procedures for the behavioral sciences.* Belmont, Calif.: Brooks/Cole, 1968.

Klapper, J. T. *The effects of mass communication.* Glencoe, Ill.: Free Press, 1960.

Knox, R. E., & Inkster, J. A. Postdecision dissonance at post time. *Journal of Personality and Social Psychology,* 1968, *8,* 310-323.

Konecni, V. J. Annoyance, type, and duration of postannoyance activity and aggression: The cathartic effect. *Journal of Experimental Psychology: General,* 1975, *104,* 76-102.

Krech, D., & Crutchfield, R. S. *Theory and problems of social psychology.* New York: McGraw-Hill, 1948.

Kruglanski, A. W., Freedman, L., & Zeevi, G. The effects of extrinsic incentives on some qualitative aspects of task performance. *Journal of Personality,* 1971, *39,* 606-617.

Kruglanski, A. W., Riter, A., Amitai, A., Margolin, B., Shabtai, L., & Zaksh, D. Can money enhance intrinsic motivation?: A test of the content-consequence hypothesis. *Journal of Personality and Social Psychology,* 1975, *31,* 479-486.

Lacey, J. I., Kagan, J., Lacey, B., & Moss, H. A. The visceral level: Situational determinants and behavioral correlates of autonomic response patterns. In P. H. Knapp (Ed.), *Expression of the emotions in man.* New York: International Universities Press, 1963, 161-196.

Lacey, J. I., & Lacey, B. C. Verification and extension of the principle of autonomic response sterotypy. *American Journal of Psychology,* 1958, *71,* 50-73.

Laird, J. D. Self-attribution of emotion: The effects of expressive behavior on the quality of emotional experience. *Journal of Personality and Social Psychology,* 1974, *29,* 475-486.

Lambert, J. *Social psychology.* New York: Macmillan, 1980.

Lambert, W. E., & Klineberg, O. *Children's views of foreign peoples.* New York: Appleton-Century-Crofts, 1967.

Lammers, H. B., & Becker, L. A. Distraction: Effects on the perceived extremity of a communication and on cognitive responses. *Personality and Social Psychology Bulletin,* 1980, *6,* 261-266.

Langer, E. J., Blank, A., & Chanowitz, B. The mindlessness of ostensibly thoughtful action. *Journal of Personality and Social Psychology,* 1978, *36,* 635-642.

LaPiere, R. Attitudes versus actions. *Social Forces,* 1934, *13,* 230-237.

Latané, B., & Darley, J. M. *The unresponsive bystander: Why doesn't he help?* New York: Appleton-Century-Crofts, 1970.

Latané, B., Williams, K. D., & Harkins, S. G. Many hands make light the work: The causes and consequences of social loafing. *Journal of Personality and Social Psychology,* 1979, *37,* 822-832.

Leibhart, E. H. Information search and attribution: Cognitive processes mediating the effect of false autonomic feedback. *European Journal of Social Psychology,* 1979, *9,* 19-37.

Lemon, N. *Attitudes and their measurement.* New York: Wiley, 1973.

Lepper, M. R., & Greene, D. Turning play into work: Effects of adult surveillance and extrinsic rewards on children's intrinsic motivation. *Journal of Personality and Social Psychology,* 1975, *31,* 479-486.

Lepper, M. R., Greene, D., & Nisbett, R. E. Undermining children's intrinsic interest with extrinsic reward: A test of the "overjustification" hypothesis. *Journal of Personality and Social Psychology,* 1973, *28,* 129-137.

Leventhal, H. Findings and theory in the study of fear communications. In L. Berkowitz (Ed.), *Advances in experimental social psychology* (Vol. 5). New York: Academic Press, 1970.

Libby, W. L., Jr., Lacey, B. C., & Lacey, J. I. Pupillary and cardiac activity during visual attention. *Psychophysiology,* 1973, *10,* 270-294.

Likert, R. A technique for the measurement of attitudes. *Archives of Psychology,* 1932, *140,* 1-55 (whole).

Lind, E. A., & O'Barr, W. M. The social significance of speech in the courtroom. In H. Giles & R. St. Clair (Eds.), *Language and social psychology.* Oxford, England: Blackwells, 1979.

Linder, D. E., Cooper, J., & Jones, E. E. Decision freedom as a determinant of the role of incentive magnitude in attitude change. *Journal of Personality and Social Psychology,* 1967, *6,* 245-254.

Linder, D., & Worchel, W. Opinion change as a result of effortfully drawing a counterattitudinal conclusion. *Journal of Experimental Social Psychology,* 1970, *6,* 432-448.

Lingle, J. H., & Ostrom, T. M. Principles of memory and cognition in attitude formation. In R. E. Petty, T. M. Ostrom, & T. C. Brock (Eds.), *Cognitive responses in persuasion.* Hillsdale, N.J.: Erlbaum, 1981.

Liska, J. Situational and topical variations in credibility criteria. *Communication Monographs,* 1978, *45,* 85-92.

Lord, C. G., Ross, L., & Lepper, M. R. Biased assimilation and attitude polarization: The effects of prior theories on subsequently considered evidence. *Journal of Personality and Social Psychology*, 1979, *37*, 2098-2109.

Lorge, I. Prestige, suggestion, and attitudes. *Journal of Social Psychology*, 1936, *7*, 386-402.

Lott, A. J., & Lott, B. E. A learning theory approach to interpersonal attitudes. In A. G. Greenwald, T. C. Brock, & T. M. Ostrom (Eds.), *Psychological foundations of attitudes*. New York: Academic Press, 1968.

Love, R. E., & Greenwald, A. C. Cognitive responses to persuasion as mediators of opinion change. *Journal of Social Psychology*, 1978, *104*, 231-241.

Lumsdaine, A. A., & Janis, I. L. Resistance to "counterpropaganda" produced by one-sided and two-sided "propaganda" presentations. *Public Opinion Quarterly*, 1953, *17*, 311-318.

Mackay, C. J. The measurement of mood and psychophysiological activity using self-report techniques. In I. Martin & P. H. Venable (Eds.), *Techniques in psychophysiology*. Chichester: Wiley, 1980.

Maier, N. R., & Thurber, J. A. Accuracy of judgments of deception when an interview is watched, heard, and read. *Personal Psychology*, 1968, *21*, 23-30.

Maltzman, I. Theoretical conceptions of semantic conditioning and generalization. In T. R. Dixson & D. L. Horton (Eds.), *Verbal behavior and general behavior theory*. Englewood Cliffs, N.J.: Prentice-Hall, 1968.

Manis, M., Cornell, S. D., & Moore, J. C. Transmission of attitude-relevant information through a communication chain. *Journal of Personality and Social Psychology*, 1974, *30*, 81-94.

Manis, M., & Moore, J. C. Summarizing controversial messages: Retroactive effects due to subsequent information. *Social Psychology Quarterly*, 1978, *41*, 62-68.

March, J. G., & Simon, H. A. *Organizations*. New York: Wiley, 1958.

Marshall, G. D., & Zimbardo, P. G. Affective consequences of inadequately explained physiological arousal. *Journal of Personality and Social Psychology*, 1979, *37*, 970-988.

Maslach, C. Negative emotional biasing of unexplained arousal. *Journal of Personality and Social Psychology*, 1979, *37*, 953-969.

Mazis, M. B. Antipollution measures and psychological reactance: A field experiment. *Journal of Personality and Social Psychology*, 1975, *31*, 654-660.

McArdle, J. B. *Positive and negative communications and subsequent attitude and behavior change in alcoholics*. Unpublished doctoral dissertation, University of Illinois, 1972.

McCroskey, J. C. The effects of evidence as an inhibitor of counterpersuasion. *Speech Monographs*, 1970, *37*, 176-187.

McCullough, J. L., & Ostrom, T. M. Repetition of highly similar messages and attitude change. *Journal of Applied Psychology*, 1974, *59*, 395-397.

McCurdy, H. G. Consciousness and the galvanometer. *Psychological Review*, 1950, *57*, 322-327.

McGinniss, J. *Selling of the president, 1968*. New York: Trident Press, 1969.

McGuire, W. J. Order of presentation as a factor in "conditioning" persuasiveness. In C. I. Hovland et al. (Eds.), *The order of presentation in persuasion*. New Haven: Yale University Press, 1957.

McGuire, W. J. Cognitive consistency and attitude change. *Journal of Abnormal and Social Psychology*, 1960, *60*, 345-353. (a)

McGuire, W. J. A syllogistic analysis of cognitive relationships. In C. I. Hovland & M. J. Rosenberg (Eds.), *Attitude organization and change*. New Haven: Yale University Press, 1960. (b)

McGuire, W. J. Effectiveness of forewarning in developing resistance to persuasion. *Public Opinion Quarterly,* 1962, *26,* 24-34.

McGuire, W. J. Inducing resistance to persuasion: Some contemporary approaches. In L. Berkowitz (Ed.), *Advances in experimental social psychology* (Vol. 1). New York: Academic Press, 1964.

McGuire, W. J. Personality and susceptibility to social influence. In E. F. Borgatta & W. W. Lambert (Eds.), *Handbook of personality theory and research.* Chicago: Rand McNally, 1968.

McGuire, W. J. The nature of attitudes and attitude change. In G. Lindzey & E. Aronson (Eds.), *The handbook of social psychology* (2nd ed., Vol. 3). Reading, Mass.: Addison Wesley, 1969.

McGuire, W. J. The probabilogical model of cognitive structure and attitude change. In R. E. Petty, T. M. Ostrom, & T. C. Brock (Eds.), *Cognitive responses in persuasion.* Hillsdale, N.J.: Erlbaum, 1981.

McGuire, W. J. Communication and social influence processes. In M. P. Feldman, & J. F. Orford (Eds.), *The social psychology of psychological problems.* Sussex, England: Wiley, in press.

McGuire, W. J., & Millman, S. Anticipatory belief lowering following forewarning of a persuasive attack. *Journal of Personality and Social Psychology,* 1965, *62,* 327-337.

McGuire, W. J., & Papageorgis, D. The relative efficacy of various types of prior belief-defense in producing immunity against persuasion. *Journal of Abnormal and Social Psychology,* 1961, *62,* 327-337.

McGuire, W. J., & Papageorgis, D. Effectiveness of forewarning in developing resistance to persuasion. *Public Opinion Quarterly,* 1962, *26,* 24-34.

McNemar, Q. Opinion-attitude methodology. *Psychological Bulletin,* 1946, *43,* 289-374.

Mehrabian, A. Relationship of attitude to seated posture, orientation,and distance. *Journal of Personality and Social Psychology,* 1968, *10,* 26-30.

Melton, A. W. Some behavior characteristics of museum visitors. *Psychological Bulletin,* 1933, *30,* 720-721.

Melton, A. W. Distribution of attention in galleries in a museum of science and industry. *Museum News,* 1936, *13,* 3, 5-8.

Mewborn, C. R., & Rogers, R. W. Effects of threatening and reassuring components of fear appeals on physiological and verbal measures of emotion and attitudes. *Journal of Experimental Social Psychology,* 1979, *15,* 242-253.

Milgram, S. L. *The individual in a social world: Essays and experiments.* Reading, Mass.: Addison-Wesley, 1977.

Milgram, S. L., Mann, L., & Harter, S. The lost-letter technique: A tool of social science research. *Public Opinion Quarterly,* 1965, *29,* 437-438.

Miller, A. G., Baier, R., & Schonberg, P. The bias phenomenon in attitude attribution: Actor and observer perspectives. *Journal of Personality and Social Psychology,* 1979, *37,* 1421-1431.

Miller, C. E., & Norman, R. M. G. Balance agreement, and attraction in hypothetical social situations. *Journal of Experimental Social Psychology,* 1976, *12,* 109-119.

Miller, L. W., & Sigelman, L. Is the audience the message? A note on LBJ's Vietnam statements. *Public Opinion Quarterly,* 1978, *42,* 71-80.

Miller, N. Involvement and dogmatism as inhibitors of attitude change. *Journal of Experimental Social Psychology,* 1965, *1,* 121-132.

Miller, N., & Campbell, D. T. Recency and primacy in persuasion as a function of the timing of speeches and measurements. *Journal of Abnormal and Social Psychology,* 1959, *59,* 1-9.

Miller, N., Maruyama, G., Beaber, R. J., & Valone, K. Speed of speech and persuasion. *Journal of Personality and Social Psychology,* 1976, *34,* 615-625.

Miller, N. E., & Dollard, J. *Social learning and limitation.* New Haven: Yale University Press, 1941.

Miller, R. L., Mere exposure, psychological reactance, and attitude change. *Public Opinion Quarterly,* 1976, *40,* 229-233.

Miller, R. L., & Suls, J. Helping, self-attribution, and size of an initial request. *Journal of Social Psychology,* 1977, *103,* 203-208.

Mills, J., & Harvey, J. Opinion change as a function of when information about the communicator is received and whether he is attractive or expert. *Journal of Personality and Social Psychology,* 1972, *21,* 52-55.

Mills, J., & Jellison, J. M. Effect on opinion change of how desirable the communication is to the audience the communicator addressed. *Journal of Personality and Social Psychology,* 1967, *6,* 98-101.

Minsky, M. A. A framework for representing knowledge. In P. Winston (Ed.), *The psychology of computer vision.* New York: McGraw-Hill, 1975.

Monson, T. C., & Snyder, M. Actors, observers, and the attribution process: Toward a reconceptualization. *Journal of Experimental Social Psychology,* 1977, *13,* 89-111.

Moore, J. W., & Gormezano, I. Classical conditioning. In M. H. Marx & M. E. Bunch (Eds.), *Fundamentals and applications of learning.* New York: Macmillan, 1977.

Mower-White, C. J. Factors affecting balance, agreement, and positivity biases in *POQ* and *POX* triads. *European Journal of Social Psychology,* 1979, *9,* 129-148.

New York Times Staff Editors. *White House transcripts.* New York: Bantam Books, 1974.

Newcomb, T. An approach to the study of communicative acts. *Psychological Review,* 1953, *60,* 393-404.

Newcomb, T. M. Interpersonal balance. In R. P. Abelson, E. Aronson, W. J. McGuire, T. M. Newcomb, M. J. Rosenberg, & P. H. Tannenbaum (Eds.), *Theories of cognitive consistency: A sourcebook.* Chicago: Rand McNally, 1968.

Newtson, D., & Czerlinsky, T. Adjustments of attitude communications for contrasts by extreme audiences. *Journal of Personality and Social Psychology,* 1974, *30,* 829-837.

Nisbett, R. E., & Gordon, A. Self-esteem and susceptibility to social influence. *Journal of Personality and Social Psychology,* 1967, *5,* 268-276.

Norman, R. Affective-cognitive consistency, attitudes, conformity, and behavior. *Journal of Personality and Social Psychology,* 1975, *32,* 83-91.

Norman, R. When what is said is important: A comparison of expert and attractive sources. *Journal of Experimental Social Psychology,* 1976, *12,* 294-300.

Norris, E. L. Attitude change as a function of open or closed-mindedness. *Journalism Quarterly,* 1965, *42,* 571-575.

Norris, E. L. Belief change and stress reduction as methods for resolving cognitive inconsistency. *Dissertation Abstracts,* 1965, *25,* 3706.

Oman, J. C. *Cults, customs, and superstitions of India.* Fountain, Delhi: Vishal Publishers, 1972.

O'Neill, P., & Levings, D. E. Induced biased scanning in a group setting to change attitudes toward bilingualism and capital punishment. *Journal of Personality and Social Psychology,* 1979, *37,* 1432-1438.

Orne, M. T. On the social psychology of the psychological experiment: With particular reference to demand characteristics and their implications. *American Psychologist,* 1962, *17,* 776-783.

Osgood, C. E. Cross cultural comparability of attitude measurement via multilingual semantic differentials. In I. S. Steiner & M. Fishbein (Eds.), *Recent studies in social psychology.* New York: Holt, Rinehart, & Winston, 1965.

Osgood, C. E., Suci, G. J., & Tannenbaum, P. H. *The measurement of meaning*. Urbana, Ill.: University of Illinois Press, 1957.

Osgood, C. E., & Tannenbaum, P. H. The principle of congruity in the prediction of attitude change. *Psychological Review*, 1955, *62*, 42-55.

Oskamp, S. *Attitudes and opinions*. Englewood Cliffs, N.J.: Prentice-Hall, 1977.

Ostrom, T. M. Perspective as a determinant of attitude change. *Journal of Experimental Social Psychology*, 1970, *6*, 280-292.

Ostrom, T. M. Between-theory and within-theory conflict in explaining context effects on impression formation. *Journal of Experimental Social Psychology*, 1977, *13*, 492-503.

Ostrom, T. M., & Davis, D. Idiosyncratic weighting of trait information in impression formation. *Journal of Personality and Social Psychology*, 1979, *37*, 2025-2043.

Ostrom, T. M., & Upshaw, H. S. Psychological perspective and attitude change. In A. G. Greenwald, T. C. Brock, & T. M. Ostrom (Eds.), *Psychological foundations of attitudes*. New York: Academic Press, 1968.

Page, M. M. Social psychology of a classical conditioning of attitudes experiment. *Journal of Personality and Social Psychology*, 1969, *11*, 177-186.

Page, M. M. Demand characteristics and the classical conditioning of attitudes experiment. *Journal of Personality and Social Psychology*, 1974, *30*, 468-476.

Page, M. M., & Kahle, L. R. Demand characteristics in the satiation-deprivation effect on attitude conditioning. *Journal of Personality and Social Psychology*, 1976, *33*, 553-562.

Pallak, M. S., Mueller, M., Dollar, K., & Pallak, J. Effect of commitment on responsiveness to an extreme consonant communication. *Journal of Personality and Social Psychology*, 1972, *23*, 429-436.

Pallak, M. S., & Pittman, T. S. General motivational effects of dissonance arousal. *Journal of Personality and Social Psychology*, 1972, *21*, 349-358.

Papageorgis, D. Warning and persuasion. *Psychological Bulletin*, 1968, *70*, 271-282.

Papageorgis, D., & McGuire, W. The generality of immunity to persuasion produced by pre-exposure to weakened counterarguments. *Journal of Abnormal and Social Psychology*, 1961, *62*, 475-481.

Parducci, A., & Marshall, L. M. Assimilation vs. contrast in the anchoring of perceptual judgments of weight. *Journal of Experimental Psychology*, 1962, *63*, 426-437.

Peak, H. Attitude and motivation. In M. Jones (Ed.), *Nebraska Symposium on Motivation* (Vol. 2). Lincoln: University of Nebraska Press, 1955.

Pepitone, A., & DiNubile, M. Contrast effects in judgments of crime severity and the punishment of criminal violators. *Journal of Personality and Social Psychology*, 1976, *33*, 448-459.

Perloff, R. M., & Brock, T. C. And thinking makes it so: Cognitive responses to persuasion. In M. E. Roloff & G. R. Miller (Eds.), *Persuasion: New directions in theory and research*. Beverly Hills, Calif.: Sage, 1980.

Peterson, P. D., & Koulack, D. Attitude change as a function of latitudes of acceptance and rejection. *Journal of Personality and Social Psychology*, 1969, *11*, 309-311.

Peterson, R. C., & Thurstone. *The effect of motion pictures on the social attitudes of high school children*. Chicago: University of Chicago Press, 1933.

Petty, R. E. The importance of cognitive responses in persuasion. *Advances in Consumer Research*, 1977, *4*, 357-362. (a)

Petty, R. E. *A cognitive response analysis of the temporal persistence of attitude changes induced by persuasive communications*. Unpublished doctoral dissertation, Ohio State University, 1977. (b)

Petty, R. E., & Brock, T. C. Effects of responding or not responding to hecklers on audience agreement with a speaker. *Journal of Applied Social Psychology*, 1976, *6*, 1-17.

Petty, R. E., & Brock, T. C. Thought disruption and persuasion: Assessing the validity of attitude change experiments. In R. E. Petty, T. M. Ostrom, & T. C. Brock (Eds.), *Cognitive responses in persuasion.* Hillsdale, N.J.: Erlbaum, 1981.

Petty, R. E., Brock, T. C., & Brock, S. Hecklers: Boon or bust for speakers? *Public Relations Journal,* 1978, *34,* 10-12.

Petty, R. E., & Cacioppo, J. T. Forewarning, cognitive responding, and resistance to persuasion. *Journal of Personality and Social Psychology,* 1977, *35,* 645-655.

Petty, R. E., & Cacioppo, J. T. Effects of forewarning of persuasive intent and involvement on cognitive responses and persuasion. *Personality and Social Psychology Bulletin,* 1979, *5,* 173-176. (a)

Petty, R. E., & Cacioppo, J. T. Issue involvement can increase or decrease persuasion by enhancing message-relevant cognitive responses. *Journal of Personality and Social Psychology,* 1979, *37,* 1915-1926. (b)

Petty, R. E., & Cacioppo, J. T. Issue involvement as a moderator of the effects on attitude of advertising content and context. *Advances in Consumer Research,* 1981, *8,* in press.

Petty, R. E., & Cacioppo, J. T. *Central and peripheral routes to persuasion: Theory and research.* New York: Springer-Verlag, in press.

Petty, R. E., Cacioppo, J. T., & Goldman, R. Personal involvement as a determinant of argument-based persuasion. *Journal of Personality and Social Psychology,* in press.

Petty, R. E., Cacioppo, J. T., & Heesacker, M. The use of rhetorical questions in persuasion: A cognitive response analysis. *Journal of Personality and Social Psychology,* 1981, *40,* 432-440.

Petty, R. E., Harkins, S. G., Williams, K. D., & Latané, B. The effects of group size on cognitive effort and evaluation. *Personality and Social Psychology Bulletin,* 1977, *3,* 579-582.

Petty, R. E., Harkins, S. G., & Williams, K. D. The effects of group diffusion of cognitive effort on attitudes: An information processing view. *Journal of Personality and Social Psychology,* 1980, *38,* 81-92.

Petty, R. E., Ostrom, T. M., & Brock, T. C. Historical foundations of the cognitive response approach to attitudes and persuasion. In R. E. Petty, T. M. Ostrom, & T. C. Brock (Eds.), *Cognitive responses in persuasion.* Hillsdale, N.J.: Erlbaum, 1981.

Petty, R. E., Wells, G. L., & Brock, T. C. Distraction can enhance or reduce yielding to propaganda: Though disruption versus effort justification. *Journal of Personality and Social Psychology,* 1976, *34,* 874-884.

Petty, R. E., Williams, K. D., Harkins, S. G., & Latané, B. Social inhibition of helping yourself: Bystander response to a cheeseburger. *Personality and Social Psychology Bulletin,* 1977, *3,* 575-578.

Pittman, T. S., Cooper, E. E., & Smith, T. W. Attribution of causality and the overjustification effect. *Personality and Social Psychology Bulletin,* 1977, *3,* 280-283.

Poppleton, P. K., & Pilkington, G. W. A comparison of four methods of scoring an attitude scale in relation to its reliability and validity. *British Journal of Social and Clinical Psychology,* 1964, *3,* 36-39.

Proshansky, J. A projective method for the study of attitudes. *Journal of Abnormal and Social Psychology,* 1943, *38,* 393-395.

Pryor, B., & Steinfatt, T. M. The effects of initial belief level on inoculation theory and its proposed mechanisms. *Human Communication Research,* 1978, *4,* 217-230.

Pryor, J. B., Gibbons, F. X., Wicklund, R. A., Fazio, R. H., & Hood, R. Self-focused attention and self-report validity. *Journal of Personality and Social Psychology,* 1977, *45,* 514-527.

Quigley-Fernandez, B., & Tedeschi, J. T. The bogus pipeline as lie-detector: Two validity studies. *Journal of Personality and Social Psychology,* 1978, *36,* 247-256.

Razran, G. H. S. Conditioned response changes in rating and appraising sociopolitical slogans. *Psychological Bulletin,* 1940, *37,* 481.

Regan, D. T., & Fazio, R. H. On the consistency between attitudes and behavior: Look to the method of attitude formation. *Journal of Experimental Social Psychology,* 1977, *13,* 28-45.

Riess, M., & Schlenker, B. R. Attitude change and responsibility avoidance as modes of dilemma resolution in forced-compliance situations. *Journal of Personality and Social Psychology,* 1977, *35,* 21-30.

Rhine, R. J., & Severance, L. J. Ego-involvement, discrepancy, source credibility, and attitude change. *Journal of Personality and Social Psychology,* 1970, *16,* 175-190.

Rhodewalt, F., & Comer, R. Induced-compliance attitude change: Once more with feeling. *Journal of Experimental Social Psychology,* 1979, *15,* 35-47.

Robinson, J. R., & Shaver, P. R. (Eds.), *Measures of political attitudes.* Ann Arbor, Mich.: Survey Research Center, 1969.

Rogers, R. W. A protection motivation theory of fear appeals and attitude change. *Journal of Psychology,* 1975, *91,* 93-114.

Rogers, R. W., & Mewborn, R. Fear appeals and attitude change: Effects of a threat's noxiousness, probability of occurrence, and the efficacy of coping responses. *Journal of Personality and Social Psychology,* 1976, *34,* 54-61.

Rokeach, M. *The open and closed mind.* New York: Basic Books, 1960.

Rokeach, M. *Beliefs, attitudes, and values.* San Francisco: Jossey-Bass, 1968.

Romer, D. Distraction, counterarguing, and the internalization of attitude change. *European Journal of Social Psychology,* 1979, *9,* 1-18.

Ronis, D. L., & Greenwald, A. G. Dissonance theory revised again: Comment on the paper by Fazio, Zanna, and Cooper. *Journal of Experimental Social Psychology,* 1979, *15,* 62-69.

Rosen, N. A., & Wyer, R. S. Some further evidence for the "Socratic effect" using a subjective probability model of cognitive organization. *Journal of Personality and Social Psychology,* 1972, *24,* 420-424.

Rosenbaum, M. E., & Tucker, I. F. The competence of the model and the learning of imitation and nonimitation. *Journal of Experimental Psychology,* 1962, *63,* 183-190.

Rosenberg, M. J. Cognitive structure and attitudinal affect. *Journal of Abnormal and Social Psychology,* 1956, *53,* 367-372.

Rosenberg, M. J. When dissonance fails: On eliminating evaluation apprehension from attitude measurement. *Journal of Personality and Social Psychology,* 1965, *1,* 28-42.

Rosenberg, M. J. Hedonism, inauthenticity, and other goals toward expansion of a consistency theory. In R. Abelson, E. Aronson, W. McGuire, T. Newcomb, M. Rosenberg & P. Tannenbaum (Eds.), *Theories of cognitive consistency: A sourcebook,* Chicago: Rand McNally, 1968.

Rosenberg, M. J. The conditions and consequences of evaluation apprehension. In R. Rosenthal & R. L. Rosnow (Eds.), *Artifact in behavioral research.* New York: Academic Press, 1969.

Rosenberg, M. J., & Abelson, R. P. An analysis of cognitive balancing. In C. I. Hovland & M. J. Rosenberg (Eds.), *Attitude organization and change.* New Haven: Yale University Press, 1960.

Rosenthal, R. *Experimenter effects in behavioral research.* New York: Appleton-Century-Crofts, 1966.

Rosenthal, R., and Rosnow, R. L. *Artifact in behavioral research.* New York: Academic Press, 1969.

Ross, M. Salience of reward and intrinsic motivation. *Journal of Personality and Social Psychology,* 1975, *32,* 245-254.

Rossman, B. B., & Gollob, H. G. Social inference and pleasantness judgment involving people and issues. *Journal of Experimental Social Psychology*, 1976, *12*, 374-391.

Rubin, Z. Measurement of romantic love. *Journal of Personality and Social Psychology*, 1970, *16*, 265-273.

Rushton, J. P. Generosity in children: Immediate and long-term effects of modeling, preaching, and moral judgment. *Journal of Personality and Social Psychology*, 1975, *31*, 459-466.

Sadler, O., & Tesser, A. Some effects of salience and time upon interpersonal hostility and attraction during social isolation. *Sociometry*, 1973, *36*, 99-112.

Salancik, G. R., & Conway, M. Attitude inferences from salient and relevant cognitive content about behavior. *Journal of Personality and Social Psychology*, 1975, *32*, 829-840.

Saltzstein, H. D., & Sandberg, L. Indirect social influence: Change in judgment process or anticipatory conformity. *Journal of Experimental Social Psychology*, 1979, *15*, 209-216.

Sawyers, B. K., & Anderson, N. H. Test of integration theory in attitude change. *Journal of Personality and Social Psychology*, 1971, *18*, 230-233.

Schachter, S. The interaction of cognitive and physiological determinants of emotional state. In L. Berkowitz (Ed.), *Advances in experimental social psychology* (Vol. 1). New York: Academic Press, 1964.

Schachter, S., & Singer, J. E. Cognitive, social, and physiological determinants of emotional state. *Psychological Review*, 1962, *69*, 379-399.

Schachter, S., & Singer, J. E. Comments on the Maslach and Marshall-Zimbardo experiments. *Journal of Personality and Social Psychology*, 1979, *37*, 989-995.

Scheier, M. F. Self-awareness, self-consciousness, and angry aggression. *Journal of Personality*, 1976, *44*, 627-644.

Scheier, M. F., & Carver, C. S. Self-focused attention and the experience of emotion: Attraction, repulsion, elation, and depression. *Journal of Personality and Social Psychology*, 1977, *35*, 625-636.

Scheier, M. F., & Carver, C. S. Individual differences in self-concept and self-processes. In D. M. Wegner & R. R. Vallacher (Eds.), *The self in social psychology*. New York: Oxford, 1980.

Schien, E. H., Schneier, I., & Barker, C. H. *Coercive persuasion*. New York: Norton, 1961.

Schlenker, B. R. Self-presentation: Managing the impression of consistency when reality interferes with self-enhancement. *Journal of Personality and Social Psychology*, 1975, *32*, 1030-1037.

Schlenker, B. R. *Impression management: The self-concept, social identity, and interpersonal relations*. Monterey, Calif.: Brooks/Cole, 1980.

Schneider, W., & Shiffrin, R. M. Controlled and automatic human information processing: I. Detection, search, and attention. *Psychological Review*, 1977, *84*, 1-66.

Schwartz, G. E., Fair, P. L., Salt, P., Mandel, M. R., & Klerman, G. L. Facial muscle patterning to affective imagery in depressed and nondepressed subjects. *Science*, 1976, *192*, 489-491.

Schwartz, S. Temporal instability as a moderator of the attitude-behavior relationship. *Journal of Personality and Social Psychology*, 1978, *36*, 715-724.

Scott, C. A., & Yalch, R. F. A test of the self-perception explanation of the effects of rewards on intrinsic interest. *Journal of Experimental Social Psychology*, 1978, *14*, 180-192.

Scott, W. A. Attitude change through reward of verbal behavior. *Journal of Abnormal and Social Psychology*, 1957, *55*, 72-75.

Scott, W. A. Structure of natural cognitions. *Journal of Personality and Social Psychology*, 1969, *12*, 261-278.

Sentis, K. P., & Burnstein, E. Remembering schema-consistent information: Effects of a balance schema on recognition memory. *Journal of Personality and Social Psychology*, 1979, *37*, 2200-2211.

Shaffer, D. R. Some effects of consonant and dissonant attitudinal advocacy on initial attitude salience and attitude change. *Journal of Personality and Social Psychology*, 1975, *32*, 160-168.

Shaffer, D. R., & Hendrick, C. Dogmatism and tolerance for ambiguity as determinants of differential reactions to cognitive inconsistency. *Journal of Personality and Social Psychology*, 1974, *29*, 601-608.

Shaw, M. A serial position effect in social influence on group decision. *Journal of Social Psychology*, 1961, *54*, 83-91.

Sherif, C. W. *Orientation in social psychology.* New York: Harper & Row, 1976.

Sherif, C. W., Kelly, M., Rodgers, H. L., Sarup, G., & Tittler, B. I. Personal involvement, social judgment, and action. *Journal of Personality and Social Psychology*, 1973, *27*, 311-327.

Sherif, C. W., Sherif, M., & Nebergall, R. E. *Attitude and attitude change: The social judgement-involvement approach.* Philadelphia: W. B. Saunders Company, 1965.

Sherif, M., & Hovland, C. I. Judgemental phenomena and scales of attitude measurement: Placement of items with individual choice of the number of categories. *Journal of Abnormal and Social Psychology*, 1953, *48*, 135-141.

Sherif, M., & Hovland, C. I. *Social judgment: Assimilation and contrast effects in communication and attitude change.* New Haven: Yale University Press, 1961.

Sherif, M., & Sherif, C. W. *Groups in harmony and tension.* New York: Harper & Row, 1953.

Sherif, M., & Sherif, C. W. Attitude as the individual's own categories: The social judgment-involvement approach to attitude and attitude change. In C. W. Sherif & M. Sherif (Eds.), *Attitude, ego-involvement, and change.* New York: Wiley, 1967.

Sherif, M., Taub, D., & Hovland, C. Assimilation and contrast effects of anchoring stimuli on judgments. *Journal of Experimental Psychology*, 1958, *55*, 150-155.

Sherman, S. J. Effects of choice and incentive on attitude change in a discrepant behavior situation. *Journal of Personality and Social Psychology*, 1970, *15*, 245-252.

Sigall, H., & Helmreich, R. Opinion change as a function of stress and communicator credibility. *Journal of Experimental Social Psychology*, 1969, *5*, 70-78.

Sigall, H., & Page, R. Current stereotypes: A little fading, a little faking. *Journal of Personality and Social Psychology*, 1971, *18*, 247-255.

Simms, E. S. Information integration theory and attitude change applied to classroom situations. Unpublished doctoral dissertation, University of Arizona, 1976.

Simpson, D. D., & Ostrom, T. M. Contrast effects in impression formation. *Journal of Personality and Social Psychology*, 1976, *34*, 625-629.

Sistrunk, F., & McDavid, J. W. Sex variable in conforming behavior. *Journal of Personality and Social Psychology*, 1971, *17*, 200-207.

Skinner, B. F. *The behavior of organisms: An experimental analysis.* New York: Appleton-Century-Crofts, 1938.

Skolnick, P., & Heslin, R. Approval dependence and reactions to bad arguments and low credibility sources. *Journal of Experimental Research in Personality*, 1971, *5*, 199-207.

Skolnick, P., & Heslin, R. Quality versus difficulty: Alternative interpretations of the relationship between self-esteem and persuasibility. *Journal of Personality*, 1971, *39*, 242-251.

Slamecka, N. J., & Graf, P. The generation effect: Delineation of a phenomenon. *Journal of Experimental Psychology: Human Learning and Memory*, 1978, *4*, 592-604.

Smith, B. L., Lasswell, H. D., & Casey, R. D. *Propaganda, communication, and public opinion.* Princeton, N.J.: Princeton University Press, 1946.

Smith, F. J. Work attitudes as predictors of attendance on a specific day. *Journal of Applied Psychology,* 1977, *62,* 16-19.

Smith, M. B., Bruner, J. S., & White, R. W. *Opinions and personality.* New York: Wiley, 1956.

Snyder, M. Self-monitoring. In L. Berkowitz (Ed.), *Advances in Experimental Social Psychology* (Vol. 12). New York: Academic Press, 1979.

Snyder, M., & Jones, E. E. Attitude attribution when behavior is constrained. *Journal of Experimental Social Psychology,* 1974, *10,* 585-600.

Snyder, M., & Monson, T. C. Persons, situations, and the control of social behavior. *Journal of Personality and Social Psychology,* 1975, *32,* 637-644.

Snyder, M., & Swann, W. B. When actions reflect attitudes: The politics of impression management. *Journal of Personality and Social Psychology,* 1976, *34,* 1034-1042.

Snyder, M., & Tanke, E. D. Behavior and attitude: Some people are more consistent than others. *Journal of Personality,* 1976, *44,* 501-517.

Sokolov, A. N. *Perception and the conditioned reflex.* Oxford, England: Pergamon Press, 1963.

Spence, K. W. *Behavior theory and conditioning.* New Haven: Yale University Press 1956.

Spence, K. W., & Spence, J. T. Sex and anxiety differences in eyelid conditioning. *Psychological Bulletin,* 1966, *65,* 137-142.

Staats, A. W. *Social behaviorism.* Homewood, Ill.: Dorsey Press, 1975.

Staats, A. W., Minke, K. A., Martin, C. H., & Higa, W. R. Deprivation-satiation and strength of attitude conditioning: A test of attitude-reinforcer discriminative theory. *Journal of Personality and Social Psychology,* 1972, *24,* 178-185.

Staats, A. W., & Staats, C. K. Attitudes established by classical conditioning. *Journal of Abnormal and Social Psychology,* 1958, *57,* 37-40.

Staats, A. W., Staats, C. K., & Crawford, H. L. First-order conditioning of meaning and the parallel conditioning of a GSR. *Journal of General Psychology,* 1962, *67,* 159-167.

Staats, C. K., & Staats, A. W. Meaning established by classical conditioning. *Journal of Experimental Psychology,* 1957, *54,* 74-80.

Stachowiak, J. G., & Moss, C. S. Hypnotic alteration of social attitudes. *Journal of Personality and Social Psychology,* 1965, *2,* 77-83.

Stang, D. J. The effects of mere exposure on learning and affect. *Journal of Personality and Social Psychology,* 1975, *31,* 7-13.

Staw, B. M. Attitudinal and behavioral consequences of changing a major organizational reward: A natural field experiment. *Journal of Personality and Social Psychology,* 1974, *29,* 742-751.

Staw, B. M. Attribution of the "causes" of performance: A general alternative interpretation of cross-sectional research on organizations. *Organizational Behavior & Human Performance,* 1975, *13,* 414-432.

Steele, C. M., & Ostrom, T. M. Perspective mediated attitude change: When is indirect persuasion more effective than direct persuasion. *Journal of Personality and Social Psychology,* 1974, *29,* 737-741.

Steiner, I. D., & Rogers, E. D. Alternative responses to dissonance. *Journal of Abnormal and Social Psychology,* 1963, *66,* 128-136.

Steinitz, V. Cognitive imbalance: A considered response to a complicated situation. *Human Relations,* 1969, *22,* 287-308.

Stern, R. M., Botto, R. W., & Herrick C. D. Behavioral and physiological effects of false heart rate feedback: A replication and extension. *Psychophysiology,* 1972, *9,* 21-29.

Sternglanz, S. H., & Serbin, L. A. Sex-role stereotyping in children's television programs. *Developmental Psychology*, 1974, *10*, 710-715.

Sternthal, B., Dholakia, R., and Leavitt, C. The persuasive effect of source credibility: a test of cognitive response analysis. *Journal of Consumer Research*, 1978, *4*, 252-260.

Stinchcombe, A. L. *Constructing social theories.* New York: Harcourt, Brace, & World, 1968.

Stotland, E., Katz, D., & Patchen, M. The reduction of prejudice through the arousal of self-insight. *Journal of Personality*, 1959, *27*, 507-531.

Stroebe, W., Thompson, V. D., Insko, C. A., & Reisman, S. R. Balance and differentiation in the evaluation of linked attitude objects. *Journal of Personality and Social Psychology*, 1970, *16*, 38-47.

Suedfeld, P., & Borrie, R. A. Sensory deprivation, attitude change, and defense against persuasion. *Canadian Journal of Behavioral Science*, 1978, *10*, 16-27.

Tannenbaum, P. Effect of serial position on recall of radio news stories. *Journalism Quarterly*, 1954, *31*, 319-323.

Tannenbaum, P. H. The congruity principle revisited: Studies in the reduction, induction, and generalization of persuasion. In L. Berkowitz (Ed.), *Advances in experimental social psychology* (Vol. 3). New York: Academic Press, 1967.

Tannenbaum, P. H. The congruity principle: Retrospective reflections and recent research. In R. P. Abelson, E. Aronson, W. J. McGuire, T. M. Newcomb, M. J. Rosenberg, & P. H. Tannenbaum (Eds.), *Theories of cognitive consistency: A sourcebook.* Chicago: Rand McNally, 1968.

Tannenbaum, P. H., & Gengel, R. W. Generalization of attitude change through congruity principle relationships. *Journal of Personality and Social Psychology*, 1966, *3*, 299-304.

Tannenbaum, P. H., Macaulay, J., & Norris, E. L. Principle of congruity and reduction of persuasion. *Journal of Personality and Social Psychology*, 1966, *3*, 233-238.

Tashakkori, A., & Insko, C. A. Interpersonal attraction and the polarity of similar attitudes: A test of three balance models. *Journal of Personality and Social Psychology*, 1979, *37*, 2262-2277.

Tashakkori, A., & Insko, C. A. Interpersonal attraction and person perception: Two tests of three balance models. *Journal of Experimental Social Psychology*, in press.

Taylor, S. E. On inferring one's attitudes from one's behavior: Some delimiting conditions. *Journal of Personality and Social Psychology*, 1975, *31*, 126-131.

Tedeschi, J. T., Schlenker, B. R., & Bonoma, T. V. Cognitive dissonance: Private ratiocination or public spectacle? *American Psychologist*, 1971, *26*, 685-695.

Tesser, A. Thought and reality constraints as determinants of attitude polarization. *Journal of Research in Personality*, 1976, *10*, 183-194.

Tesser, A. Self-generated attitude change. *Advances in Experimental Social Psychology*, 1978, *11*, 289-338.

Tesser, A., & Conlee, M. C. Some effects of time and thought on attitude polarization. *Journal of Personality and Social Psychology*, 1975, *31*, 262-270.

Tesser, A., & Leone, C. Cognitive schemas and thought as determinants of attitude change. *Journal of Experimental Social Psychology*, 1977, *13*, 340-356.

Tesser, A., & Rosen, S. The reluctance to transmit bad news. In L. Berkowitz (Ed.), *Advances in Experimental Social Psychology* (Vol. 8). New York: Academic Press, 1975.

Thistlethwaite, D. L., de Haan, H., & Kamenetzky, J. The effects of 'directive' and 'nondirective' communication procedures on attitudes. *Journal of Abnormal and Social Psychology*, 1955, *51*, 107-113.

Thistlethwaite, D. L., & Kamenetzky, J. Attitude change through refutation and elaboration of audience counterarguments. *Journal of Abnormal and Social Psychology*, 1955, *51*, 3-9.

Thurstone, L. L. Attitudes can be measured. *American Journal of Sociology*, 1928, *33*, 529-544.

Thurstone, L. L., & Chave, E. J. *The measurement of attitude.* Chicago: University of Chicago Press, 1929.

Triandis, H. C. *Attitudes and attitude change.* New York: Wiley, 1971.

Triandis, H. C. *Interpersonal behavior.* Monterey, Calif.: Brooks/Cole, 1977.

Triandis, H. C. Values, attitudes, and interpersonal behavior. In H. Howe & M. Page (Eds.), *Nebraska Symposium on Motivation* (Vol. 27). Lincoln: University of Nebraska Press, 1980.

Troutman, C. M., & Shanteau, J. Do consumers evaluate products by adding or averaging attribute information? *Journal of Consumer Research*, 1976, *3*, 101-106.

Tyler, L. E. *The psychology of human differences* (3rd ed.). New York: Appleton-Century-Crofts, 1965.

Tyler, T. R., & Sears, D. O. Coming to like obnoxious people when we must live with them. *Journal of Personality and Social Psychology*, 1977, *35*, 200-211.

Upshaw, H. S. The personal reference scale: An approach to social judgment. In L. Berkowitz (Ed.), *Advances in experimental social psychology* (Vol. 4). New York: Academic Press, 1969.

Upshaw, H. S. Out of the laboratory and into wonderland: A critique of the Kinder, Smith, and Gerard adventure with perspective theory. *Journal of Personality and Social Psychology*, 1976, *34*, 699-703.

Upshaw, H. S. Social influence on attitudes and on anchoring of cogeneric attitude scales. *Journal of Experimental Social Psychology*, 1978, *14*, 327-339.

Uranowitz, S. Helping and self-attributions: A field experiment. *Journal of Personality and Social Psychology*, 1975, *31*, 852-854.

Valins, S. Cognitive effects of false heart-rate feedback. *Journal of Personality and Social Psychology*, 1966, *4*, 400-408.

Valins, S. Emotionality and information concerning internal reactions. *Journal of Personality and Social Psychology*, 1967, *6*, 458-463.

Vaughan, K. B., & Lanzetta, J. T. Vicarious instigation and conditioning of facial expressive and autonomic responses to a model's expressive display of pain. *Journal of Personality and Social Psychology*, 1980, *38*, 909-923.

Venn, J. R., & Short, J. G. Vicarious classical conditioning of emotional responses in nursery-school children. *Journal of Personality and Social Psychology*, 1973, *28*, 249-255.

Wade, S., & Schramm, W. The mass media as sources of public affairs, science, and health knowledge. *Public Opinion Quarterly*, 1969, *33*, 197-209.

Walster, E., Aronson, E., & Abrahams, D. On increasing the persuasiveness of a low prestige communicator. *Journal of Experimental Social Psychology*, 1966, *2*, 325-342.

Watts, W. A. Relative persistence of opinion change induced by active compared to passive participation. *Journal of Personality and Social Psychology*, 1967, *5*, 4-15.

Watts, W. A., & Holt, L. E. Logical relationships among beliefs and timing as factors in persuasion. *Journal of Personality and Social Psychology*, 1970, *16*, 571-582.

Watts, W. A., & Holt, L. E. Persistence of opinion change induced under conditions of forewarning and distraction. *Journal of Personality and Social Psychology*, 1979, *37*, 778-789.

Watts, W. A., & McGuire, W. J. Persistence of induced opinion change and retention of inducing message content. *Journal of Abnormal and Social Psychology*, 1964, *68*, 233-241.

Webb, E. J., Campbell, D. T., Schwartz, R. D., & Sechrest, L. *Unobtrusive measures: Nonreactive research in the social sciences.* Chicago: Rand McNally, 1966.

Weber, S. J. *Opinion change is a function of the associative learning of content and source factors.* Unpublished doctoral dissertation, Northwestern University, 1972.

Weigel, R. H., & Newman, L. S. Increasing attitude-behavior correspondence by broadening the scope of the behavioral measure. *Journal of Personality and Social Psychology*, 1976, *33*, 793-802.

Weiss, R. F. Persuasion and acquisition of attitudes: Models from conditioning and selective learning. *Psychological Reports*, 1962, *11*, 709-732.

Weiss, R. F., Buchanan, W., & Pasamanick, B. Delay of reinforcement and delay of punishment in persuasive communication. *Psychological Reports*, 1965, *16*, 576.

Weiss, W. Effects of the mass media of communication. In G. Lindzey & E. Aronson (Eds.), *The Handbook of Social Psychology* (2nd ed., Vol. 5). Reading, Mass: Addison-Wesley, 1969.

Wellens, A. R., & Thistlethwaite, D. L. An analysis of two quantitative theories of cognitive balance. *Psychological Review*, 1971, *78*, 141-150.

Wells, G. L., & Petty, R. E. The effects of overt head-movements on persuasion: Compatibility and incompatibility of responses. *Journal of Basic and Applied Social Psychology*, 1980, *1*, 219-230.

Westie, F. R., & DeFleur, M. L. Autonomic responses and their relationship to race attitudes. *Journal of Abnormal and Social Psychology*, 1959, *58*, 340-347.

White, G. M. Contextual determinants of opinion judgments: Field experimental probes of judgmental relativity boundary conditions. *Journal of Personality and Social Psychology*, 1975, *32*, 1047-1054.

White, P. Limitations on verbal reports of internal events: A refutation of Nisbett and Wilson and of Bem. *Psychological Review*, 1980, *87*, 105-112.

Wicker, A. W. Attitudes versus actions: The relationship of verbal and overt behavioral responses to attitude objects. *Journal of Social Issues*, 1969, *25*, 41-78.

Wicker, A. W. An examination of the "other-variables" explanation of attitude-behavior inconsistency. *Journal of Personality and Social Psychology*, 1971, *19*, 18-30.

Wicklund, R. A. *Freedom and reactance*. Hillsdale, N.J.: Erlbaum, 1974.

Wicklund, R. A., & Brehm, J. W. *Perspectives on cognitive dissonance*. Hillsdale, N.J.: Erlbaum, 1976.

Wiest, N. M. A quantitative extension of Heider's theory of cognitive balance applied to interpersonal perception and self-esteem. *Psychological Monographs*, 1965, *79*, (14, Whole No. 607).

Wilson, W., & Miller, H. Repetition, order of presentation, and timing of arguments and measures as determinants of opinion change. *Journal of Personality and Social Psychology*, 1968, *9*, 184-188.

Winer, B. J. *Statistical principles in experimental design*. New York: McGraw-Hill, 1971.

Wolpe, J. *Psychotherapy by reciprocal inhibition*. Stanford, Calif.: Stanford University Press, 1958.

Woodmansee, J. J. The pupil response as a measure of social attitudes. In G. F. Summers (Ed.), *Attitude measurement*. Chicago: Rand McNally, 1970.

Worchel, S., Arnold, S., & Baker, M. The effects of censorship on attitude change: The influence of censor and communication characteristics. *Journal of Applied Social Psychology*, 1975, *5*, 227-239.

Wright, P. Cognitive responses to mass media advocacy. In R. E. Petty, T. M. Ostrom, & T. C. Brock (Eds.), *Cognitive responses in persuasion*. Hillsdale, N.J.: Erlbaum, 1981.

Wyer, R. S. The quantitative prediction of belief and opinion change: A further test of a subjective probability model. *Journal of Personality and Social Psychology*, 1970, *16*, 550-571.

Wyer, R. S. Test of a subjective probability model of social evaluation processes. *Journal of Personality and Social Psychology*, 1972, *22*, 279-286.

Wyer, R. S. Further test of a subjective probability model of social inference processes. *Journal of Research in Personality,* 1973, *7,* 237-253.

Wyer, R. S. *Cognitive organization and change: An information processing approach.* Potomac, Md.: Erlbaum, 1974.

Wyer, R. S. The role of probabilistic and syllogistic reasoning in cognitive organization and social inference. In M. Kaplan & S. Schwartz (Eds.), *Human judgment and decision processes.* New York: Academic Press, 1975.

Wyer, R. S., & Carlston, D. *Social cognition, inference and attribution.* Hillsdale, N.J.: Erlbaum, 1979.

Wyer, R. S., & Goldberg, L. A probabilistic analysis of the relationships between beliefs and attitudes. *Psychological Review,* 1970, *77,* 100-120.

Wyer, R. S., & Hartwick, J. The role of information retrieval and conditional inference processes in belief formation and change. In L. Berkowitz (Ed.), *Advances in Experimental Social Psychology* (Vol. 13). New York: Academic Press, 1980.

Younger, J. C., Walker, L., & Arrowood, A. J. Postdecision dissonance at the fair. *Personality and Social Psychology Bulletin,* 1977, *3,* 284-287.

Zajonc, R. B. Attitudinal effects of mere exposure. *Journal of Personality and Social Psychology Monograph Supplement,* 1968, *9,* 1-27.

Zajonc, R. B. Feeling and thinking: Preferences need no inferences. *American Psychologist,* 1980, *35,* 151-175.

Zajonc, R. B., & Burnstein, E. The learning of balanced and unbalanced social structures. *Journal of Personality,* 1965, *33,* 153-163.

Zanna, M. P. The effect of distraction on resolving cognitive dilemmas. Paper presented at the meeting of the American Psychological Association, Chicago, 1975.

Zanna, M. P., & Cooper, J. Dissonance and the pill: An attribution approach to studying the arousal properties of dissonance. *Journal of Personality and Social Psychology,* 1974, *29,* 703-709.

Zanna, M. P., & Cooper, J. Dissonance and the attribution process. In J. H. Harvey, W. J. Ikes, & R. F. Kidd (Eds.), *New directions in attribution research* (Vol. 1). Hillsdale, N.J.: Erlbaum, 1976.

Zanna, M. P., & Hamilton, D. L. Further evidence for meaning change in impression formation. *Journal of Experimental Social Psychology,* 1977, *13,* 224-238.

Zanna, M. P., Kiesler, C. A., & Pilkonis, P. A. Positive and negative attitudinal affect established by classical conditioning. *Journal of Personality and Social Psychology,* 1970, *14,* 321-328.

Zanna, M. P., Klosson, E. C., & Darley, J. M. How television news viewers deal with facts that contradict their beliefs: A consistency and attribution analysis. *Journal of Applied Social Psychology,* 1976, *6,* 159-176.

Zanna, M. P., Olson, J. M., & Fazio, R. H. Attitude-behavior consistency: An individual difference perspective. *Journal of Personality and Social Psychology,* 1980, *38,* 432-440.

Zellner, M. Self-esteem, reception, and influenceability. *Journal of Personality and Social Psychology,* 1970, *15,* 310-320.

Zillmann, D. Rhetorical elicitation of agreement in persuasion. *Journal of Personality and Social Psychology,* 1972, *21,* 159-165.

Zillmann, D. Attribution and misattribution of excitatory reactions. In J. H. Harvey, W. J. Ickes, & R. F. Kidd (Eds.), *New directions in attribution research* (Vol. 2). Hillsdale, N.J.: Erlbaum, 1978.

Zimbardo, P. G. Involvement and communication discrepancy as determinants of opinion conformity. *Journal of Abnormal and Social Psychology,* 1960, *60,* 86-94.

Zimbardo, P. G., Ebbesen, E. B., & Maslach, C. *Influencing attitudes and changing behavior.* Reading, Mass.: Addison-Wesley, 1977.

Zimbardo, P. G., Weisenberg, M., Firestone, I., & Levy, B. Communicator effectiveness in producing public conformity and private attitude change. *Journal of Personality,* 1965, *33,* 233-255.

Author Index

A

Abelson, R. P., 128, 211, 252, 269
Abrahams, D., 64
Adams, W. C., 253
Adewole, A., 131, 132
Ajzen, I., 24, 25, 26, 28, 37, 181, 183, 193, 198, 201, 202, 203, 204, 210, 211, 212
Albert, R. D., 217, 218, 232
Alessis, C., 92
Allen, V. L., 148
Allport, G. W., 7
Anderson, E. A., 97
Anderson, N. H., 72, 204, 205, 206, 207, 209, 210, 212
Anderson, R., 170
Andreoli, V., 64
Apsler, 107, 109, 269
Arenson, S. J., 51
Argyle, M., 17
Aristotle, 5
Arkin, R. M., 152
Arnold, S., 159
Aronson, E., 34, 64, 105, 137, 139, 145, 146, 203
Arrowood, A. J., 141, 142
Asch, S. E., 93, 223
Atwood, R. H., 19, 20

B

Bagley, G. S., 73
Baier, R., 181
Baker, H., 159
Bandura, A., 53
Barker, C. H., 39
Barlow, J. D., 19
Bartlett, F.C., 252
Bassett, R., 168
Batson, C. D., 140
Bauer, R. A., 82, 86

Baumeister, R. J., 153
Baumgardner, M. H., 92
Beaber, R. J., 251, 252
Bearden, W. O., 212
Beatty, J. J., 253
Becker, L. A., 110
Bem, D. J., 7, 152, 163, 165, 170, 171, 172, 173, 178, 184
Bentler, P. M., 212
Berelson, B., 85
Berger, S. M., 54, 55
Berkowitz, L., 45, 47
Berscheid, E., 67
Biondo, J., 157
Blake, R., 98
Blank, A., 29, 269
Blyth, D. P., 181
Bochner, S., 63, 64, 105, 203
Bock, D., 236
Bonoma, T. V., 127, 153, 155
Borrie, R. A., 253
Bostrom, R. N., 47
Botto, R. W., 176, 182
Bowman, C. H., 196
Bradac, J. J., 86
Braden, M., 139
Brehm, J. W., 127, 137, 139, 141, 145, 146, 149, 155, 156, 157, 159, 171
Brehm, S., 156
Brent, E. E., 100, 101
Brewer, M. D., 34
Brickman, P., 97, 123
Brock, S., 230
Brock, T. C., 34, 67, 218, 225, 230, 238, 240, 252, 265
Brockner, J., 18
Brown, D., 177
Brown, R. W., 47

Bruner, J. S., 8, 93
Bryan, J. H., 52
Buchanan, W., 72
Burnstein, E., 85, 130, 131, 221, 223, 224
Byrne, O., 17, 51, 67, 102, 132

C

Cacioppo, J. T., 18, 21, 42, 63, 65, 71, 79, 84, 89, 109, 123, 132, 133, 157, 168, 181, 204, 210, 227, 228, 232-34, 237, 239-42, 246-49, 251-54, 258-63, 265, 269
Calder, B. J., 70, 71, 84, 146, 242, 263
Campbell, D. T., 18, 30, 31, 78, 249
Cann, A., 168
Carli, L., 83
Carlsmith, J. M., 34, 105, 143, 144, 145, 146, 171, 203
Carlston, D. E., 190
Cartwright, D., 85, 127, 128, 137
Carver, C. S., 27, 224, 225
Carver, M. E., 86
Cascio, W. F., 170
Casey, R. D., 60
Chaiken, S., 67, 83, 86, 87, 92, 123, 179, 180, 259, 261, 263, 265, 268
Chanowitz, B., 29, 269
Chapanis, A., 138
Chapanis, N., 138
Chave, E. J., 10
Choo, T., 64
Cialdini, R. B., 49, 50, 57, 153, 168, 228, 257, 258, 259
Clore, G. L., 51, 132
Coats, D., 97, 123
Cohen, A. R., 137, 139, 146, 171, 172, 264
Cohen, S. J., 97
Coleman, J., 184
Coleman, S. R., 46
Coles, M. G., 182
Collins, B. E., 108, 110, 146, 265
Comer, R., 152, 181
Conlee, M. C., 222
Connolley, E. S., 142
Converse, J., Jr., 145
Conway, G. R., 166
Cook, S. W., 13
Cook, T. D., 31, 91, 92, 94, 236, 237, 263
Coombs, F. S., 196, 198

Cooper, E. E., 178, 179
Cooper, H. M., 83
Cooper, J., 145, 146, 148, 149, 150, 151, 153, 172, 173, 174
Cooper, R. E., 131
Corey, S. M., 23, 24
Cornell, S. D., 102
Cottrell, N. B., 130
Craig, C. S., 64
Craik, F. M., 261, 268
Crano, W. D., 34, 131
Crawford, H. L., 42
Crutchfield, R. S., 252
Czerlinsky, T., 102

D

Dalto, C. A., 181
Darley, J. M., 145, 146, 181, 234
Darwin, C., 20
Davidson, A. R., 24, 25, 27, 196, 198, 212
Davies, R. A., 86
Davis, D., 210
Dawes, R. M., 102
Deci, E., 169, 170
DeFleur, M. L., 18
De Haan, H., 76
De Jong, W., 167, 168
De Paulo, B. M., 122
Dermer, M., 97
DeVries, D. L., 198
Dholakia, R., 210, 236, 237
Dillehay, R. C., 191
DiNubile, M., 96, 120
Dollar, K., 109, 110, 232
Dollard, J., 51
Doob, A. M., 66, 80
Dulany, D. E., Jr., 49
Duryea, R., 98
Duval, S., 224
Dysinger, D. W., 18

E

Eagly, A. H., 70, 72, 81, 83, 86, 87, 92, 105, 106, 107, 109, 179, 180, 232, 251, 262, 265
Ebbesen, E. B., 3, 5
Eckstrang, G., 18
Edwards, A. L., 12
Eiser, J. R., 120, 121
Ekman, P., 20
Elkes, R., 168
Ellsworth, P. C., 34
Ellul, J., 39

Elms, A. C., 50, 144, 216, 219
Epstein, R., 184
Ervin, C. R., 17
Evenbeck, S., 153

F

Fair, P. L., 21
Faison, E. W. J., 75
Fazio, R. H., 27, 28, 149, 150, 151,
  172, 173, 174, 183
Feather, N. T., 134, 136
Feldman, S., 196
Ferris, C. B., 224
Feshback, S., 72, 73
Festinger, L., 125, 127, 137, 138,
  139, 140, 143, 144, 145, 146, 148,
  155, 170, 171, 172, 223
Field, P. B., 80
Firestone, I., 146
Fishbaugh, L., 83
Fishbein, M., 23, 24, 25, 26, 28, 37,
  183, 193, 195, 196, 198, 199, 200,
  201, 202, 203, 204, 209, 210, 211,
  212
Flay, B. R., 91, 92, 94, 263
Folger, R., 169
Frandsen, K. D., 86
Frank, J. D., 39, 188
Fraser, S. C., 167
Freedman, J. L., 123, 149, 167, 227
Freedman, L., 169
Fuller, C. H., 131

G

Gaes, G. G., 149, 153
Gardner, D. M., 70
Gengel, R. W., 135
Gerard, H. B., 117, 142, 149, 184
Gergen, K. J., 82, 155
Gewirtz, J. L., 53
Gibbons, F. X., 27
Gillig, P. M., 91, 94, 237
Gilliland, A. R., 18
Gilmore, J. B., 217, 219
Goethals, G. R., 67, 68, 146, 148, 181
Goffman, E., 152
Goldberg, L., 188
Goldberg, M. E., 79
Goldman, R., 203, 237, 258, 260
Goldwater, B. C., 19
Gollob, H. G., 130
Gordon, A., 82, 83
Gormezano, I., 46
Gorn, G. G., 77
Grabitz-Gniech, G., 156, 157

Grady, K., 65, 227
Graf, P., 218
Granberg, D., 100, 101
Graves, J., 234
Greene, D. 169, 170
Greenspoon, J., 47
Greenwald, A. G., 89, 91, 92, 94, 123,
  144, 145, 172, 217, 218, 225, 232
  237, 248, 249, 250, 252
Griffit, W., 51
Gruder, C. L., 91, 92, 94
Grumet, J. F., 181
Grush, J. E., 56
Gurwitz, S. B., 169
Gutierres, S. E., 95, 123
Gutman, G. M., 131

H

Haaland, G. A., 253
Halamaj, J., 92
Hall, J., 80
Halverson, R., 109
Hamilton, D. L., 193
Hammond, K. R., 16
Harackiewicz, J. M., 170
Harary, F., 127, 128, 137
Hardyck, J. A., 139
Harkins, S. G., 234, 235, 243, 245,
  254, 263
Harris, V. A., 181, 182
Harter, S., 17
Hartwick, J., 193
Harvey, J., 77, 92, 236
Harvey, O. J., 104
Haskins, J., 84
Hass, R. G., 65, 73, 153, 227, 237,
  258
Hawk, G., 176
Hays, R. P., 169
Heesacker, M., 246, 247, 248
Heider, F., 126, 127, 128, 131, 132,
  133, 134, 136, 137, 160
Helmreich, R., 63
Helson, H., 95, 123
Hemsley, G. D., 66, 80
Henderson, J. T., 145, 146
Hendrick, C., 16, 161
Hennigan, K. M., 91, 92, 94
Henninger, M., 190, 192
Herman, C. P., 153, 257, 258, 259
Herrick, C. D., 176, 182
Heslin, R., 83
Hess, E. H., 19
Hess, R. D., 184

Higa, W. R., 43
Higgins, E. T., 146, 148, 151, 152
Hildum, D. C., 47
Himmelfarb, S., 50, 251
Hirschman, R., 176
Holt, L. E., 65, 92, 108, 191
Hood, R., 27
Hovland, C. I., 6, 35, 56, 59, 60, 61,
    62, 63, 64, 68, 69, 70, 74, 76, 80,
    81, 84, 85, 87, 88, 89, 90, 91, 93,
    94, 99, 100, 104, 107, 123, 184, 248
Howell, R. J., 19, 20
Hoyt, M. G., 146, 265
Hunter, E., 39
Husek, T. R., 63, 77, 92

I

Ickes, W. K., 224
Ingham, A. G., 234
Ingraham, L. H., 130
Inkster, J. A., 142
Insko, C. A., 7, 48, 49, 50, 57, 63, 64,
    70, 84, 89, 105, 110, 127, 129, 131,
    132, 136, 146, 160, 191, 203, 242,
    249

J

Jaccard, J. J., 24, 25, 27, 196, 198,
    212
Jacobsen, E., 97
Janis, I. L., 6, 50, 59, 61, 62, 72, 73,
    74, 80, 81, 94, 176, 213, 215, 216,
    217, 219
Janoff-Bulman, R., 97, 123
Jennings, M. K., 184
Johnson, H. H., 105, 138
Jones, E. E., 13, 145, 150, 152, 153,
    170, 178, 181, 184
Jordan, N., 130, 131
Judd, C. M., 122

K

Kagen, J., 242
Kahle, L. R., 43
Kahneman, D., 19
Kalle, R. J., 149, 153
Kamenetzky, J., 76
Kaplan, M. F., 93
Katkin, E. S., 182
Katz, D., 8, 76

Katz, E., 85, 94
Kehoe, E. J., 46
Kelley, H. H., 6, 59, 61, 62, 81, 178,
    252
Kelly, M., 107, 108
Kelman, H. C., 62, 63, 68, 89, 90, 91,
    268
Kenney, K. F. P., 12
Kenrick, D. T., 95, 123
Kerber, K., 182
Kerpelman, J. P., 50
Kerrick, J. S., 136
Kiesler, C. A., 46, 65, 108, 109, 110,
    149, 166, 167, 172, 251
Kiesler, S. B., 65, 251
Kinder, D. R., 117
King, B. T., 213, 215, 217
Kirk, R. E., 31
Klemp, G., 177
Klerman, G. L., 21
Klineberg, O., 184
Klosson, E. C., 181
Knox, R. E., 131, 142
Knurek, K. A., 45, 57
Komorita, S., 184
Konecni, V. J., 222
Konsky, C. W., 86
Koulack, D., 105
Kozlowski, L., 257, 258, 259
Krech, D., 252
Kruglanski, A. W., 169

L

Lacey, B., 19, 242
Lacey, J. I., 19, 242
Laird, J. D., 181
Lambert, J., 23
Lambert, W. E., 184
Lamberth, J., 17
Lammers, H. B., 110
Langer, E. J., 29, 269
Lanzetta, J. T., 54
LaPiere, R., 22, 23
Lasswell, H. D., 60
Latané, B., 234
LaTour, S., 84, 89, 249
Lazarsfeld, P., 85
Leavitt, C., 210, 236, 237
Leibhart, E. H., 182
Leippe, M. R., 92
Lemon, N., 22

Lemons, F., 102
Leone, C., 223
Lepper, M. R., 169, 170, 266
Leventhal, H., 73, 176
Levinger, G., 232
Levings, D. E., 217
Levy, A., 153, 257, 258, 259
Levy, B., 146
Libby, W. L., Jr., 19
Likert, R., 10, 11, 12, 25
Lind, E. A., 80, 84, 89, 249
Linder, D. E., 76, 145, 150
Lingle, J., 252
Liska, J., 63
Lockhart, R. S., 261, 268
Lord, C. G., 266
Lorge, I., 62
Love, R. E., 249
Lumsdaine, A. A., 6, 74, 80, 87, 88, 89, 94

M

McArdle, J. B., 197, 198
McCann, J. M., 64
Maccaulay, J., 135
McCurdy, H. G., 18
McDavid, J. W., 84, 261
MacDonald, A. P., 157
McGinniss, J., 66
McGuire, W. J., 65, 68, 76, 80, 81, 82, 83, 85, 88, 94, 184, 186, 191, 192, 211, 227, 230, 231, 253
Mackay, C. J., 161
McNemar, Q., 12
McPhee, W. N., 85
Mader, S., 52
Maltzman, I., 42
Mandel, M. R., 21
Mandell, W., 64, 76
Manis, M., 97, 102
Mann, L., 17, 176, 215
Mann, R. W., 258
Manoogian, S., 170
March, J. G., 147
Marshall, G. D., 175
Marshall, L. M., 123
Martin, C. H., 43
Maruyama, G., 80, 251, 252
Maslach, C., 3, 5, 175, 177
Maltzman, I., 42
Mazis, M. B., 156, 157, 158
Mehrabian, A., 17

Melson, W. H., 49
Melton, A. W., 18
Mewborn, C. R., 73
Milgram, S. L., 17
Miller, A. G., 181
Miller, C. E., 79, 131
Miller, H., 79
Miller, J. A., 168
Miller, L. W., 102
Miller, N., 78, 79, 80, 108, 110, 249, 250, 251, 252
Miller, N. E., 51
Miller, R. L., 79, 168, 181
Mills, J., 77, 92, 146, 236
Minke, K. A., 43
Minsky, M. A., 252
Monfort, F. W., 130
Monson, T. C., 28, 170, 178
Moore, J. C., 97, 102
Moore, J. W., 47
Morisano, F. A., 51
Moss, C. S., 135
Moss, H. A., 242
Mower-White, C. J., 121, 129, 132
Mueller, M., 109, 110, 232
Munson, P. A., 172
Murashima, F., 105

N

Nebergall, R. E., 99
Nelson, R. E., 67, 68
Newcomb, T., 160
Newman, L. S., 25, 26
Newtson, D., 102
Niemi, R. G., 184
Nisbett, R. E., 82, 83, 166, 167, 169, 170, 178
Norman, R., 28, 70, 77, 92, 237
Norman, R. M. G., 131
Norris, E. L., 135
Nova, M., 181

O

O'Barr, W. M., 80
Olson, J. M., 28
Oman, J. C., 39
O'Neill, P., 217
Orne, M. T., 33
Osgood, C. E., 12, 127, 132, 133, 134, 135, 137, 161
Oskamp, S., 7
Osmon, B. E., 120
Ostrom, T. M., 93, 110, 112, 114, 115, 117, 119, 121, 210, 225, 252

P

Page, M. M., 43, 46
Page, R., 13
Pallak, J., 109, 110, 232
Pallak, M., 109, 110, 149, 232
Papageorgis, D., 65, 227, 230, 231, 253
Parducci, A., 123
Pasamanick, B., 72
Patchen, M., 76, 94
Peak, H., 195
Peckham, V., 232
Pepitone, A., 96, 120
Perloff, R. M., 218
Peterson, P. D., 89, 105
Petty, R. E., 17, 21, 34, 63, 65, 71, 79, 84, 89, 109, 123, 132, 133, 157, 181, 204, 210, 225, 227, 228, 230, 232-35, 237-43, 245-49, 251-54, 257-63, 265, 269
Pilkington, G. W., 12
Pilkonis, P. A., 46
Pittman, T. S., 149, 178, 179
Plato, 69
Poppleton, P. K., 12
Proshansky, J., 16
Pryor, B., 253
Pryor, J. B., 27

Q

Quigley-Fernandez, B., 13

R

Razran, G., 41
Redfield, J., 52
Regan, D. T., 27
Reisman, S. R., 129
Reznick, J., 170
Rhine, R. J., 108, 204, 237
Rhodewalt, F., 145, 148, 149, 151, 152, 181
Riecken, H. W., 125, 139, 140
Riess, M., 146, 148, 155
Rife, D., 80
Robinson, J. R., 12
Rodgers, H. L., 107, 108
Rogers, R. W., 73
Rokeach, M., 67, 183
Romer, D., 253
Ronis, D. L., 144, 145
Rosen, N. A., 190, 192
Rosen, S., 102
Rosenbaum, M., 47, 51, 98

Rosenberg, M. J., 33, 128, 144, 146, 195, 196, 211, 219, 220
Rosenfield, D., 169
Rosenthal, R., 33, 34
Rosnow, R. L., 34
Ross, L., 266
Ross, M., 146, 175, 178
Rossman, B. B., 130
Rubin, Z., 17
Rushton, J. P., 52
Ryan, R. M., 170

S

Sadler, O., 221
Saine, T., 236
Saiyadain, M., 105
Salancik, G. R., 166
Salt, P., 21
Saltzstein, H. D., 117
Sandberg, L., 117
Sandman, C. A., 18, 42, 242
Sarup, G., 107, 108
Sawyers, B. K., 206, 207
Schachter, S., 125, 139, 140, 149, 174, 175, 177, 182
Scheier, M. F., 27, 224, 225
Schien, E. H., 39
Schlenker, B. R., 127, 146, 148, 152, 153, 154, 155
Schneider, W., 268
Schneier, I., 39
Schonberg, P., 181
Schopler, J., 7, 127
Schwartz, G. E., 21
Schwartz, R. D., 18
Schwartz, S., 27
Scott, C. A., 169
Scott, W. A., 47, 144
Sears, D. O., 107, 109, 129, 149, 227, 269
Sechrest, L., 18
Selltiz, C., 13
Sensenig, J., 157
Sentis, K. P., 85, 221
Severance, L. J., 108, 204, 237
Seyfried, B. A., 16
Shaffer, D. R., 152, 161, 173
Shanteau, J., 206
Shaver, P. R., 12
Sheffield, F. D., 6, 74, 80, 87, 88, 89, 94
Sherif, C. W., 67, 99, 106, 107, 108, 109
Sherif, M., 67, 99, 100, 104, 106, 107, 108, 123

Sherman, S. J., 145, 168
Shiffrin, R. M., 268
Short, J. G., 54
Sigall, H., 13, 63
Sigelman, L., 102
Simms, E. S., 206
Simon, H. A., 147
Simpson, D., 121
Singer, D., 102
Singer, J. E., 149, 174, 175, 177, 182
Sistrunk, F., 84, 261
Skib, B., 153
Skinner, B. F., 47
Skolnick, P., 83
Slamecka, N. J., 218
Smith, B. L., 60
Smith, F. J., 29
Smith, M. B., 8, 94, 191
Smith, T., 117
Smith, T. W., 178, 179
Snyder, M., 27, 28, 155, 170, 178
Snyder, M. L., 181
Sokolov, A. N., 19
Speckart, G., 212
Spence, J. T., 149
Spence, K. W., 149
Staats, A. W., 40, 42, 43, 45, 46, 48
Staats, C. K., 40, 42, 43, 45, 46
Stachowiak, J. G., 135
Stanley, J. C., 30
Staw, B. M., 144, 147, 148
Steele, C. M., 115
Steiner, I. D., 129
Steinfatt, T. M., 253
Stern, R. M., 176, 182
Sternthal, B., 210, 236, 237
Stinchcombe, A. L., 34
Stingle, K. C., 53
Stotland, E., 76, 94
Stroebe, W., 120, 129
Suci, G. J., 12
Suedfeld, P., 253
Suls, J., 168
Swann, W. B., 27, 155

T

Tanke, E. D., 28
Tannenbaum, P. H., 12, 127, 133, 134, 135, 137, 161
Tashakkori, A., 132, 136, 160
Taub, D., 99, 100
Taves, P. A., 149, 151

Taylor, S. E., 176, 177
Tedeschi, J. T., 13, 127, 149, 153, 155
Telaak, K., 106, 109
Tesser, A., 102, 176, 220, 221, 222, 223, 228, 266
Thistlethwaite, D. L., 76, 160
Thompson, V. D., 129
Thurber, J. A., 86
Thurstone, L., 9, 10, 11, 12, 89
Tittler, B. I., 107, 108
Topol, B., 169
Torney, J. V., 184
Triandis, H. C., 28, 29, 165, 212
Trope, Y., 223, 224
Troutman, C. M., 206
Tucker, I. F., 51
Turner, J. A., 105, 203
Tyler, L. E., 223
Tyler, T. R., 129

U

Upshaw, H. S., 110, 117, 118, 119
Uranowitz, S., 167, 168

V

Valins, S., 175, 176, 177
Valone, K., 80, 251, 252
Vaughan, K. B., 54
Venkatesan, M., 253
Venn, J. R., 54
Vinokur, A., 85, 223, 224
Vlandis, J. W., 47

W

Walbeck, N. H., 52
Walker, B. B., 242
Walker, L., 141, 142
Walster, E., 64, 67
Warren, R., 81, 82
Watkins, T., 138
Watts, W. A., 65, 88, 92, 108, 191, 216
Webb, E. J., 18
Weber, S. J., 90
Weigel, R. H., 25, 26
Weinraub, M., 156
Weisenberg, M., 146
Weiss, R. F., 62, 72, 85, 86
Weiss, W., 57
Wellens, A. R., 160
Wells, G. L., 17, 238, 240, 265
Westie, F. R., 18
White, G. M., 223, 243

White, P., 165
White, R. W., 8, 94
Wicker, A. W., 23
Wicklund, R. A., 27, 127, 139, 146,
    149, 156, 157, 224
Wiest, N. M., 160
Wilhelmy, R. A., 142
Williams, K. D., 234, 235, 263
Wilson, W., 79
Winer, B. J., 32
Wolpe, J., 57
Wood, W., 83, 179, 180, 262
Woodmansee, J. J., 19
Woodside, A. G., 212
Worchel, S., 64, 76, 146, 159, 181
Wortman, C., 152
Wright, P., 86, 265
Wyer, R. S., 186, 188, 190, 191, 192,
    193, 211

Y
Yalch, R. F., 169
Yandell, B., 70, 84, 242
Young, R. K., 57
Younger, J. C., 141, 142

Z
Zajonc, R. B., 56, 67, 129, 131, 132,
    135
Zanna, M. P., 27, 28, 46, 93, 145,
    148, 149, 150, 151, 152, 166, 167,
    172, 173, 174, 181, 183
Zeevi, G., 169
Zellner, M., 82
Zillmann, D., 175, 246
Zimbardo, P. G., 3, 5, 123, 146, 175

Subject Index

A

Ability to think, 263-66
Accentuation theory, 119-21
Active vs. passive participation,
    213-16
Accentuation theory, 119-21
Adaptation level theory, 95-98
Additive model (of attitudes), 195,
    208-9
Advertising
  audience factors, 102-3
  balance approach, 130
  conditioning approach, 44-45
  informational appeals, 186-87
  message comprehension, 71
  number of sources and arguments,
    244
  perspective modification, 116
  social learning approach, 53
  two-sided appeal, 75
Age, 80
Agreement effect, 131
Anchors, 96, 99, 117
Anticipatory attitude change, 153,
    257-58
Arguments
  memory for, 248-50. *See also*
    Persistence
  number of, 70-71, 242-46
  quality of, 233-48
Arousal
  and bogus feedback, 175-77
  perception of, 170-75
Assertion constant, 161
Assimilation effect, 99-101, 118, 122

Attitude
  change, 200-204. *See also*
    Persuasion
  content vs. rating, 110
  definition of, 7, 20
  functions of, 8
  relation to behavior, 22-29, 198-99
  relation to beliefs, 194-96, 204-6
Attitude measurement
  behavioral techniques, 17-18
  comparison of techniques, 22
  direct verbal reports, 9-13
  discussed self-reports, 16-17
  physiological techniques, 18-21
Attraction effect, 131
Attractiveness (of source), 66-67,
    70-71, 77
Attribution. *See also* Misattribution,
    Self-perception
  augmentation principle, 179
  definition of, 163
  discounting principle, 179
  and perception of communicator's
    attitude, 181
  and perception of communicator's
    intent, 177-80
Augmentation principle, 179
Augmenting cue, 90
Averaging model (of attitudes), 204-5,
    208-9

B

Balance theory
  agreement effect, 131
  attraction effect, 131
  determinants of balance, 131-33
  imbalance, 128-29

p-o-x triad, 129-30
  terminology of, 127
  tetrahedronic balance, 160
Behavior
  definition of, 7
  elements of, 24
  relation to attitude, 20, 22-29,
    198-99
Behavioral intention, 37, 197-98
Beliefs
  change in, 190-93, 200-204
  definition of, 7
  structure of, 185
  types of, 183-84, 200
Biased scanning, 216-17, 219-20,
  223
Bogus physiological feedback,
  175-77
Bogus pipeline, 13
Boomerang, 225

C
Central beliefs, 188-89
Central route (to persuasion), 36,
  255-56, 266-67
Channel factors
  attributes of, 86-87
  face to face vs. media appeals, 85
  and message complexity, 87
Classical conditioning
  of attitudes, 40-46
  definition of, 40
  higher order conditioning, 42
  vicarious, 54-55
Cognitive algebra, 204-10
Cognitive bonding, 126
Cognitive consistency, 126-27. See
  also Balance, Congruity,
  Dissonance
Cognitive dissonance. See
  Dissonance theory
Cognitive effort, 234
Cognitive response approach. See
  Counterarguing
  and attitude change effects,
    238-47
  definition of, 225
  evaluation of, 251-52
  and persistence of persuasion,
    248-50
  and resistance to persuasion,
    226-32
Commitment, 109

Communication. See Message
Communicator. See Source
Compliance, 268. See also Foot-in-
  the-door technique
Comprehension
  and intelligence, 81-82
  of message, 69-70
  and self-esteem, 82-83
  and sex-differences, 84
  in Yale model, 59-61
Conceptual level of research, 30
Conclusion drawing, 76
Conditional probability, 188
Conditioning
  classical, 40-46
  operant, 47-50
Conformity, 223, 243
Confounding, 33
Congruity theory
  assertion constant, 161
  correction for incredulity, 161
  domain of, 34
  incongruity, 134
  mathematics of, 135-36
Consistency
  cognitive. See Balance, Congruity,
    Dissonance
  hedonic vs. logical, 191
Construct validity. See Validity
Contingency awareness, 43
Contrast effect, 4, 96-98, 99-101,
  118, 122, 209
Control group, 30
Correction for incredulity, 161
Counterarguing
  anticipatory, 228
  and distraction, 238-39
  and forewarning, 227-28
  and heart rate, 240-42
  and inoculation, 228-31
  and involvement, 232-33
  and message style, 246-47
  and number of recipients, 233-35
  and number of sources, 242-46
  and persuasive intent, 159
  and repetition, 239-40
  and source expertise, 235-37
Counterattitudinal advocacy. See
  Dissonance, Role playing
Cover story, 33
Credibility, 62-65, 209. See also
  Expertise, Trustworthiness
Crucial experiment, 34
Cults, 39, 139
Cultural truism, 230, 236

D

Decision making. *See* Dissonance
Demand characteristics
  and classical conditioning, 43
  definition of, 33
  and operant conditioning, 49
Descriptive belief, 183
Direct attitude measures, 9-13
Discounting cue, 89-90
Discounting principle, 179
Discrepancy of message, 105-7
Dissociative cue hypothesis, 90
Dissonance theory
  and belief disconfirmation, 139
  conditions for dissonance arousal,
    145-48
  and decision making, 140-42
  and insufficient justification, 142-45
  magnitude of dissonance, 138-39
  phenomenology of dissonance,
    148-52
  and role playing, 219-20
  temporal characteristics of, 148
  versus impression management,
    153-54
  versus self-perception theory,
    170-73
Distraction, 238-39

E

Education, 3
Effort justification, 146
Ego-defensive function, 8
Ego-involvement. *See* Involvement
Elaboration likelihood model, 262-66
Electrodermal response, 18-19
Electromyographic (EMG) response,
    13, 20-21
Emotion
  and bogus feedback, 175-77
  facial expressions of, 20-21, 181
  plasticity of, 174-75
Equal interval scale, 9
Evaluation apprehension, 33
Experimental group, 30
Experimenter bias, 33
Expertise (of source), 63, 70-71, 77,
    105, 235-37
External beliefs, 200
External cues
  and emotion, 174-77
  and peripheral route, 256, 263, 267
External validity. *See* Validity

F

Face-to-face communication, 85
Facial EMG, 20-21
Favorable thoughts, 225. *See also*
    Counterarguing
Fear appeals, 72-73
Foot-in-the-door effect, 167-69
Forewarning
  of message position, 153, 227-28,
    253
  of persuasive intent, 62, 65, 157,
    159
Forgetting. *See* Persistence
Functional measurement, 206
Functional theory, 8

G

Galvanic skin response (GSR), 18-19
Group polarization, 85

H

Habits, 28-29
Heart rate
  bogus feedback, 175-77
  and cognitive response, 240-42
Hecklers, 229-30
Hedonic consistency, 191
Horizontal structure (of beliefs), 185
Humor, 79

I

Identification, 268
Imbalance. *See* Balance theory
Impression management
  and anticipatory changes, 153, 258
  definition of, 152
  and dissonance theory, 153-54
Improvisation, 215. *See also* Role
    playing
Incentive
  and dissonance theory, 143-44
  in observational learning, 53
  and role-playing, 219-20
  within the message, 72
  in the Yale model, 60
Indirect attitude change, 115
Indirect attitude measures, 16-22
Inferential belief, 183
Information error test, 16
Informational belief, 184
Information integration theory, 204-11
Inoculation theory, 75, 228-32
Insufficient justification. *See*
    Dissonance .heory
Intelligence, 80-82

Internal cues, 170-79. *See also* Self-
    perception
Internalization, 268
Internal validity. *See* Validity
Intrinsic motivation, 170
Involvement
    and attributions, 177
    and cognitive responses, 232-33
    definition of, 107, 123
    and persuasive intent, 65
    and social judgment theory, 107-9
    and source expertise, 236, 259

J

Judgmental approach. *See*
    Adaptation, Perspective, Social-
    judgment

K

Knowledge function, 8

L

Latitude of acceptance, 101-4
Latitude of noncommitment, 102-4
Latitude of rejection, 101-14
Learning. *See* Classical conditioning,
    Observational learning, Operant
    conditioning, Persistence, Yale
    model
Likert scale, 11-12
Logical consistency, 191
Lost letter technique, 17

M

Meaning constancy, 205
Meaning shift, 93
Measurement. *See* Attitude
    measurement
Media appeals, 85. *See also*
    Advertising
Mediating variable, 34
Mere thought
    and conformity, 223-24
    and polarization, 220-23
    and self-awareness, 224-25
Message factors
    complexity of message, 81-82, 87
    comprehensibility, 69-70, 83-84
    conclusion drawing, 76-77
    discrepancy, 105-7
    distraction, 238-39
    fear appeals, 72-73
    number of arguments, 70-72,
        242-46

one- vs. two-sided, 74-75
order of arguments, 77-79
quality of arguments, 223-48, 259
repetition of arguments, 79, 239-40
structure of message, 69
style of message, 69, 79-80,
    246-47
Mindlessness, 29, 46
Misattribution, 149, 172-74
Modeling. *See* Observational learning
Moderation, 257
Motivational approaches. *See*
    Balance, Congruity, Dissonance,
    Reactance, Impression
    Management
Motivation to comply, 196. *See also*
    Norms
Motivation to think, 263-66
Multiple operationism, 33
MUM effect, 102

N

Norms, 28, 193, 196

O

Observational learning
    of attitudes, 52-53
    definition of, 51
One- vs. two-sided message, 74-75
Operant conditioning
    of attitudes, 47-50
    definition of, 47
Operational level of research, 30
Overjustification. *See* Self-perception
Own categories procedure, 107
Ownness bias, 218

P

P-O-X triad, 129-30
Parallelism theorem, 205
Perceptual approach. *See* Adaptation,
    Perspective, Social-judgment
Peripheral route (to persuasion), 36,
    256, 267-68
Persistence
    of message learning, 78-79, 87-89
    of persuasion, 248-50
    of role playing, 216
    of source effects, 89-93
Personality. *See* Recipient factors
Personal relevance. *See* Involvement
Perspective theory
    attitude content vs. rating, 110-15
    definition of, 110
    evaluation of, 120-21

indirect influence, 115–17
unresolved issues in, 117–19
Persuasion. *See also* Channel,
    Message, Recipient, and Source
    factors
    approaches to, 35–38
    definition of, 4
    types of, 5–6
Persuasion cues, 256
Persuasive intent, 62, 65, 157
Physiological feedback, 175–77. *See
    also* Heart Rate
Physiological measures. *See* Attitude
    measurement
Polarization
    anticipatory, 228, 257–58
    in groups, 85, 223–24
    with mere thought, 220–34
Positivity bias, 132
Posttest only design, 30
Power (of source), 68–69
Precision (of attitude scale), 22
Pretest-posttest design, 30
Primacy effect, 78
Primary beliefs, 200
Primitive beliefs, 183
Probabilogical approach, 184–93
Projective technique, 16
Propaganda, 3
Psychological warfare, 3–5
Pupillary response, 19

R

Random assignment, 30
Rating scales. *See* Attitude
    measurement
Reactance
    antecedents of, 156–57
    consequences of, 157–60
    and counterarguing, 159, 251
    definition of, 155
Reality search, 222
Recall. *See* Arguments, Persistence
Recency effect, 78
Recipient factors
    age, 80
    heart rate, 240–42
    intelligence, 80–82
    involvement, 107–9, 232–33, 259
    McGuire's model of, 81–83
    number of recipients, 233–35
    self-esteem, 82–83
    sex differences, 83–84, 261–62

Refutational defense, 231
Reliability, 12, 32, 37
Repetition, 79, 239–40
Replication, 32
Research methods, 29–35
Resistance to persuasion. *See*
    Counterarguing, Inoculation
    theory
Retention. *See* Persistence
Reverse psychology. *See* Reactance
Rewards. *See* Incentives
Rhetorical questions, 246–47
Role playing
    active vs. passive participation,
        213–16
    and dissonance theory, 219–20
    persistence of changes, 216–18

S

Schema, 221, 236
Self-awareness
    and attitude-behavior link, 27
    and attitude polarization, 224–25
Self-esteem, 82–83
Self-monitoring, 28
Self-perception theory
    definition of, 165–67
    foot-in-the-door effect, 167–69
    overjustification effect, 169–70
    versus dissonance theory, 170–73
Self-persuasion, 213. *See also*
    Cognitive response, Mere
    thought, Role playing
Semantic differential scale, 12
Sensitivity (of attitude scale), 22
Sentiment relation, 127
Sex differences, 83–84, 261–62
Similarity (of source), 62, 67–68
Sleeper effect, 89–94
Social judgment theory
    and discrepancy, 105–7
    evaluation of, 109–10
    and involvement, 107–9
    latitudes, 101–4
    and physical stimuli, 99
    and social stimuli, 100
Socratic effect, 191
Source factors
    attractiveness, 66–67, 70–71, 77
    credibility, 62–65, 209
    definition of, 61
    and dissonance, 146
    expertise, 63, 70–71, 77, 235–37
    number of sources, 242–46

persistence of, 89–93
persuasive intent, 65, 157
power, 68–69
pre- or postmessage, 77
similarity, 67–68
trustworthiness, 64
Spatial inertia, 192
Speech style, 80
Speed of speech, 80, 251–52
Statistical conclusion validity. *See* Validity
Subjective norm. *See* Norms
Supportive defense, 230
Syllogism, 185

T

Target beliefs, 200
Temporal inertia, 192
Tetrahedron, 160
Theory
    definition of, 29
    evaluation of, 34–35
Theory of reasoned action
    attitude, 194–96
    attitude and belief change, 200–204
    behavior, 198–99
    intention, 197–98
    subjective norm, 196

Thought listing, 252. *See also* Cognitive response, Counterarguing
Thurstone scale, 9–10
Trustworthiness, 62–65
Two-factor theory of emotion, 174–75
Two-factor theory of verbal conditioning, 49–50

U

Unit relation, 127
Utilitarian function, 8

V

Validity
    of attitude change experiments, 34
    of attitude measures, 13
    construct validity, 32
    external validity, 32
    internal validity, 32
    statistical conclusion validity, 31
Value expressive function, 8
Verbal conditioning, 48–50
Vicarious classical conditioning, 54–55